**Thomas Pynchon,
Sex, and Gender**

Thomas Pynchon, Sex, and Gender

EDITED BY
ALI CHETWYND,
JOANNA FREER, AND
GEORGIOS MARAGOS

The University of Georgia Press
ATHENS

© 2018 by the University of Georgia Press
Athens, Georgia 30602
www.ugapress.org
All rights reserved
Set in 10/13 Kepler Std by
Graphic Composition, Inc.
Bogart, Georgia

Most University of Georgia Press titles are
available from popular e-book vendors.

Printed digitally

Library of Congress Cataloging-in-Publication Data

Names: Chetwynd, Ali, 1983– editor. | Freer, Joanna, editor. | Maragos, Georgios, 1981– editor.
Title: Thomas Pynchon, sex, and gender / edited by Ali Chetwynd, Joanna Freer, and Georgios Maragos.
Description: Athens : The University of Georgia Press, [2018] | Includes bibliographical references and index.
Identifiers: LCCN 2018008680| ISBN 9780820354002 (hardback : alk. paper) | ISBN 9780820354019 (pbk. : alk. paper) | ISBN 9780820353999 (ebook)
Subjects: LCSH: Pynchon, Thomas—Criticism and interpretation. | Sex in literature. | Gender identity in literature. | Violence in literature.
Classification: LCC PS3566.Y55 Z946 2018 | DDC 813/.54—dc23
LC record available at https://lccn.loc.gov/2018008680

Contents

Abbreviations   vii

Introduction   ix

A Chronological Bibliography of
Relevant Published Research to 2017   xxxiii

Section 1. Origins

When Pynchon Was a Boys' Club:
V. and Midcentury Mystifications of Gender
MOLLY HITE   3

Section 2. Gender Roles

From Hard Boiled to Over Easy:
Reimagining the Noir Detective in
Inherent Vice and *Bleeding Edge*
JENNIFER BACKMAN   19

Of "Maidens" and Towers:
Oedipa Maas, Maxine Tarnow,
and the Possibility of Resistance
KOSTAS KALTSAS   36

Between *Sangha* and Sex Work:
The Karmic Middle Path of
Vineland's Female Characters
CHRISTOPHER KOCELA   52

Section 3. Sex Writing

"Allons Enfants!" Pynchon's Pornographies
DOUG HAYNES   69

Queer Sex, Queer Text:
S/M in *Gravity's Rainbow*
MARIE FRANCO 88

What Would Charlie Do?
Narrowing the Possibilities of a
Pornographic Redemption in
Thomas Pynchon's Novels
RICHARD MOSS 109

Section 4. Violence: Gendered and Sexualized

"This Set of Holes, Pleasantly Framed":
Pynchon the Competent Pornographer
and the Female Conduit
SIMON COOK 125

Representations of Sexualized Children
and Child Abuse in Thomas Pynchon's Fiction
SIMON DE BOURCIER 145

"Our Women Are Free":
Slavery, Gender, and Representational Bias
in Thomas Pynchon's *Mason & Dixon*
ANGUS MCFADZEAN 162

Section 5. Family/Values

Pynchon and Gender:
A View from the Typescript of *V.*
LUC HERMAN AND JOHN M. KRAFFT 179

"Homer Is My Role Model":
Father-Schlemihls, Sentimental Families,
and Pynchon's Affinities with *The Simpsons*
JEFFREY SEVERS 194

Conservatism as Radicalism:
Family and Antifeminism in *Vineland*
CATHERINE FLAY 209

Choice or Life?
Deliberations on Motherhood
in Late-Period Pynchon
INGER H. DALSGAARD 225

Contributors 241

Index 245

Abbreviations

Pynchon's novels are cited parenthetically in the text using the following abbreviations. See the works cited of each contribution for the editions referenced in them.

V.	*V.* (1963)
CoL49	*The Crying of Lot 49* (1966)
GR	*Gravity's Rainbow* (1973)
SL	*Slow Learner* (1984)
VL	*Vineland* (1990)
M&D	*Mason & Dixon* (1997)
AtD	*Against the Day* (2006)
IV	*Inherent Vice* (2009)
BE	*Bleeding Edge* (2013)

Introduction

ALI CHETWYND, JOANNA FREER,
GEORGIOS MARAGOS

Much media and audience debate about Paul Thomas Anderson's film adaptation of *Inherent Vice* (2009) focused on the sex scene between Shasta Fey Hepworth (played by Katherine Waterston) and her ex-boyfriend Doc Sportello (played by Joaquin Phoenix). The scene sees Shasta provoke the initially reluctant Doc into having sex with her by writhing naked in his lap while detailing her masochistic enjoyment of being dominated and abused by her most recent boyfriend, the real estate mogul Mickey Wolfmann, and his associates. Despite the tenderness Doc shows toward Shasta elsewhere in the film, the ensuing sex is brief, devoid of affection, and aggressive. Immediately afterward Shasta asks Doc, "Does this mean we're back together?" and sheds a tear after he replies, "Of course not." To many viewers, what made the scene comment worthy was its multidimensional violence, the emotional painfulness of the relationship supplementing the more overt acts of physical cruelty. Journalists described it as "brutal, difficult, emotional" and characterized by "a physical aggression" that "makes it feel constantly just on the verge of spinning out of control" (McWeeny par. 9), as potentially "disturbing" (Merry par. 4), as "gratuitous" (Nashawaty, qtd. in Merry par. 3), and, most forthrightly, as "an ugly male fantasy" (Callahan par. 7). Online discussion forums debated justifications for the "anger" Doc shows in response to Shasta's taunting.[1] Interviews with Waterston, by contrast, tended to focus on her experience of appearing nude, the questions implying that she might (or perhaps should) have felt ashamed or afraid to go unclothed on the big screen (see Gorber, Merry, and Zhong). These strands of public interest converged in engaging with the scene's foregrounding of a problematic relationship between sex, gender, and power that plays out not only within the narrative but also extradiegetically, between filmmakers, actors, and audience.

The experience of watching Anderson's film adaptation is, needless to say, not the same as that of reading Pynchon's novel, even if the fact that Anderson's scene was excerpted for hosting on pornographic websites seems a logical end point of Pynchon's early self-description as, among other things, a "pornographer."[2] Any film adaptation has to specify some of what a book leaves to the imagination, but this particular scene makes significant changes to the action even as it preserves dialogue word for word. In the novel Shasta is more submissive (evidenced by her crawling across the floor to kiss Doc's feet) but also in clearer sexual control (using her hands to bring both herself and Doc to orgasm) and more vocally angry (instead of weeping, she shouts out curses that Doc assumes are aimed at another man, probably Mickey). While less overtly violent, Pynchon's version of the scene still, perhaps even more clearly than Anderson's, operates through the highly gendered sexual power dynamic that the film's viewers either found titillating or troubling. The filmic mode may well be more likely to create a voyeuristic relationship between viewer and on-screen subject; as one commentator on Anderson's *Inherent Vice* points out, when you read a sex scene in prose, "you can control the tone" of events, "making it as real or unreal as you want," something that is not possible "when you have an actual naked actress in a long take" (Callahan par. 7). However, Pynchon's novelistic mode also exploits narrative devices and effects that similarly construct (and simultaneously, perhaps, deconstruct) a power dynamic between author, text, and reader. For example, the novel's textual form turns our full sensory attention over to the language of Shasta's monologue: in it she expresses an extreme masochism that fits with the traditional alignment of femininity with powerless objecthood and masculinity with sadistic power. She describes how much she had enjoyed Mickey's "fast, brutal" sexual treatment (of the kind, we assume, she elicits here from Doc) and his ability to make her "feel invisible" (305). She also tells Doc about how she had reveled in Mickey's control of her when they would hang out with his friends in dingy bars: "He might as well have been bringing me in on a leash. He kept me in these little micromindresses, never allowed me to wear anything underneath, just offering me to whoever wanted to stare. Or grab. Or sometimes he'd fix me up with his friends. And I'd have to do whatever they wanted. . . ." (305). She taunts Doc into an aggressive response by adopting his perspective and telling him how to feel: "I know what I'd do. If I had the faithless little bitch over my lap like this—" (305). The scene is thus only the newest in a lineage—there is at least one in each Pynchon novel—in which a female character takes pleasure either from actively adopting a masochistic role in consensual sexual acts or from passively acquiescing in acts whose consensual basis is more dubious.[3] The sadistic "top" role is generally played—with varying degrees of self-consciousness—by a man or group of men: sometimes a villain but just as often a sympathetic character. Such scenes are often formally pornographic, detailing the displayed and subjected female body from a male perspective (as can be seen in the way the *Inherent Vice* scene has been repurposed as internet pornography).

There are notably few sex scenes in Pynchon's writing that operate differently. This pattern has prompted critical objections to its apparent misogyny: criticisms that public responses to the *Inherent Vice* film echoed. However, this scene can be read from other angles. Shasta, for instance, appears quite deliberately to produce her own body as a fetish object, performing a form of female sexual allure that allows her to overcome Doc's sexual apathy, albeit temporarily. Doc's own implied perspective might figure him less as sadistically controlling and more as pathetically enslaved to his sexual impulses or as compelled to live up to a cliché of male sexual impulsivity. This complicates and balances the couple's gendered power dynamic; each body is both empowered and abject, making the indulgence and interrogation of conventional roles simultaneous. Far from simply supplying data for debates about whether to read Pynchon as misogynistic, then, the scene raises questions that engage with the broader ethics and politics of his work. The present collection investigates such questions, making a cumulative case for the previously unarticulated centrality of sex and gender to Pynchon's worldview.

◎ ◎ ◎

Although discussion of sex and gender may never have been central to Pynchon criticism, nor has it ever really gone away. Our bibliography of work on the topic lists seventy-one items: a drop in the "Pyndustry's" ocean, but Pynchon's work has still been the subject of more gender-focused criticism than that of his putative peers—Barth, Gaddis, DeLillo, Wallace—combined. Pynchon's gender thinking is idiosyncratic enough to not simply be equated with either that canon of fellow male "postmodern novelists" or that of the popular figures—Roth, Bellow, Updike, Mailer—that his name recognition might set him beside. Pynchon has never written a novel as narrowly trained on the relationships between individual men and women as those of these big cheeses (Roth's *When She Was Good* [1967], Mailer's *An American Dream* [1965], and Updike's *Couples* [1968] and *The Witches of Eastwick* [1984], for example), but sex and gender have never been extricable from his vision of real-world politics and power either. Amid the current trend toward critical examinations of a "political Pynchon," it would be a mistake either to examine gender in isolation from his broader commitments, or to investigate his politics or worldview without attention to his clearly—sometimes worryingly—gendered sense of values and capacities.

Pynchon's generally skeptical treatment of gender expectations doesn't stop him from offering the occasional essentialist prescription in his fiction, but even these are not often framed in terms of *biology*. Therefore, throughout this volume, discussions of our titular "sex and gender" focus on the pairing less in terms of the competition between biological and cultural identity than on Pynchon's treatment of sex acts and sexuality in terms that connect them to the gendered dimensions of his worldview and literary methods. Consequently, our volume offers an array of approaches to sex and gender in Pynchon's work that examine them not as discrete, peripheral matters for quibble or reservation, but as dynamic determinants of his complex constructive commitments.

In what follows, we first set Pynchon's gender thinking in the context of his peers, his era, his reception, and their covalent evolution over his half century of writing. We then survey the evolution of gender-focused research on his work in order to clarify what major open questions remain before offering a brief summary of how the essays we have assembled make a start on investigating those questions.

Fifty Years of Literary Culture

Outside the confines of Pynchon studies, which retains a not unreasonable reputation as a boys' club, Pynchon's gender politics are still discussed more in terms of limitation than insight.[4] As Sonia Johnson suggests in "Selling the Postmodern Novel," the way Pynchon's early work was marketed, received, and canonized relied on a thoroughly gendered model of genius designed to appeal to a certain kind of male reader, often explicitly at female readers' expense.[5] Pynchon the writer and the figure is certainly a product of his era, but he sits awkwardly among his peers.

Rather than directly comparing Pynchon with those peers, the pieces we compile here aim to stimulate a reconsideration of how gender works within the field of experimental postwar fiction by examining in methodologically varied ways his relation to gender across his writing career. This kind of full-career approach can demonstrate the scope for such revisionary methods and provide a vocabulary or conceptual repertoire with which to examine comparable authors. Pynchon may not seem obviously comparable to fellow experimental authors of his time like Kathy Acker, Joanna Russ, or Rikki Ducornet, whose paratextual writings make clear the extent to which their departures from realist convention followed from gender-focused political projects (equally formally radical authors like Christine Brooke-Rose of course wrote just as eloquently about the separability of their experiments and their identities). Yet if, as our volume aims to show, sex and gender nevertheless prove central to understanding Pynchon, this might cast light on how authors as different as he, Acker, and Mailer organized, and circulated within, the same literary culture, each in their own gendered way.

Unlike many of his putative fellow postmodernists, you won't find him paratextually pushing the well-worn, often gender-conservative equation between formal experiment, sexual transgression, and liberatory politics. Pynchon thus avoids a tendency for equations between formal innovation and masculine writing to lapse into unilluminating machismo. Ronald Sukenick, to take a representative example, turns an interview about how "1968 inspired you artistically" from a brief recital of the "Reichean" equation between sexual, political, and artistic "experiment" into an opportunity to boast about sleeping with his students, courting pubescent girls, and his invincible virility: "Were there any girls you wanted to have sex with and they rejected you?" "No, absolutely not" ("The Sarah Lawrence Orgies"). By contrast, the letters Pynchon sent while writing his formally distinctive, sexually transgressive early novels are, even as they address writing and politics, often almost chaste: literally in lamenting a "long spell of womanlessness" and ethically in his wholehearted approval of friends' monogamy and marriage, under the acronymized heading "I do like t.s.y.p.g.t" (to see young people getting together) (Thomas Pynchon Collection).[6] On the other hand, where the formal innovations of peers like William Gass generate idiosyncratically gender-balanced genealogies—in Gass's case, one in which Gertrude Stein and Colette are as fundamental as Henry James or Rilke—Pynchon's publically acknowledged literary lineage is 100 percent male.[7] Indeed, the letters often express this bivalence directly, pantomiming both crude macho bravado and eggshell sensitivity. For example, in part of a letter addressed directly to Faith Sale, he pretends to seduce her behind her husband's back before apologizing for getting "caught" when the letter shifts back to addressing both; in another letter to his friend Mary Beal, a feminist theorist, he laments his own principled absence from a political rally: "[T]hink of all that great neurotic pussy that always shows up at things like—oh, aww, gee Mary, I'm sorry! I meant 'vagina,' of course!" (qtd. in Rolls).[8] We might see some of the more overtly misogynistic representations in Pynchon's fiction along similar lines: provisionalized with a wink but gleefully indulged.

Contra the unrepentant likes of Mailer and Roth, Pynchon acknowledges his early work's ideological limitations with respect to sex and gender in the introduction to *Slow Learner*.[9] His successive novels are often overt about overwriting earlier attitudes, and even the early stories balance their contemptuous depictions of women with a sense of the absurdity of male pride and peacockery. Where a special issue of *Philip Roth Studies* on Roth and women in 2012, for example, had to set itself the explicit goal of "moving the discussion further away from the Manichean debate over whether Roth is or is not a misogynist" (Gooblar 14), Pynchon's self-consciousness has always given his critics a way out of the "Manichean" mire.[10] In this respect, his nearest analogue may be his English peer, John Fowles, a formally innovative historical novelist likewise subject to much gender-focused criticism. As Bruce Woodcock notes, Fowles like Pynchon was from his first novel onward concerned with the harms of a patriarchal world order but constantly prone to positing solutions that recapitulated the problem one level down.[11] Although neither ever makes sex or gender a whole novel's central concern, its importance to both writers' historical fiction about contemporary questions reveals a shared anxiety about their writerly relations to wider cultural shifts in thinking about gender. Both imagine alternative futures while acknowledging the possibility that their attitudes might reflect those of an earlier time. This leads to conspicuous intracareer revision on Pynchon's part, as with *Against the Day*'s (2006) literal resurrection of Mélanie L'Heuremaudit, the girl dancer fetishized and then violently killed in *V.* (1963), or *Bleeding Edge*'s (2013) suggestion that, in the sexual sphere, romance and connection—"Maybe I see him again? [...] Yeah. That's my fantasy" (180)—might today play the transgressive role that back in *Gravity's Rainbow* was reserved for scenes of rape or coprophagia. To make sense of the imperatives behind such revision, it's worth revisiting the fast-evolving culture within which Pynchon has been writing.

Social attitudes to gender over the course of the period between Pynchon's earliest stories and today are usually understood to have progressed, but recent slippages back toward greater inequality make examinations of the role representational practices play in combatting or reinforcing such inequality particularly relevant and urgent. When Pynchon's literary career was just beginning, the cultural climate in the United States was starting to shift in favor of greater equality between the sexes following an epoch of postwar traditionalist regression. Congress passed legislation that established and protected women's rights, such as the Equal Pay Act (1963) and the Civil Rights Act (1964). The feminist second wave gathered impetus, and Betty Friedan's *The Feminine Mystique* (1963) helped to elucidate the relationship between domestic containment and mental illness in women, while the category of gender as distinct from sex was introduced to public discourse.[12] Despite the widespread acceptance of the new nuclear family social model, the sexual revolution was in its initial phases, and the new availability of the birth control pill had opened the way for the sexual libertinism that publications like *Playboy* magazine had envisaged since the early fifties and that came to fruition in the free love of the counterculture.

Feminism subsequently diversified into a multistranded movement representing a wide spectrum of aims and interests. Writers, theorists, and activists including Kate Millett, Robin Morgan, Germaine Greer, Gloria Steinem, and Andrea Dworkin helped the women's movement achieve a number of successes in the 1970s and 1980s. Gender norms and essentialism were challenged by constructivist arguments, debate raged over the damage done to society by pornography, and further legislative victories were won relating to reproductive rights, domestic violence, education, and employment. Meanwhile, the LGBT rights movement confronted persecution, the first official

Pride march in the United States taking place in June 1970 on the anniversary of the previous year's Stonewall riot.

From the early 1990s third-wave feminism demonstrated a broadening self-awareness within feminist social criticism, placing emphasis on the necessity of an intersectional appreciation of the multiple facets—not only gender, but race, sexuality, age, class, and disability—of each individual's oppression. At the same time, the HIV/AIDS epidemic led to concerted activism from groups like ACT UP, increasing the social acceptance of the LGBTQ community. The 2003 Supreme Court decision in *Lawrence v. Texas* definitively decriminalized consensual sex between same-sex couples. Since the beginning of the new millennium, transgender people have seen significant advances in recognition and rights. The relations between gender and feminism remain complex in the present-day United States, as a fourth-wave feminism supported by campaigns like "He for She" contends with a postfeminism whose cultural products are by and large firmly part of the mainstream. However, at the time of writing statistics show greater gender equality between cisgender men and women in terms of education, pay, and proportionate representation in the labor force, and representation in high-salaried professions ("Facts over Time").

Yet despite such changes in the epistemic frameworks within which the norms of gender and sex operate, there are ongoing problems as well as new issues that must be recognized as limiting or even in some cases reversing to an extent the progress that has been made in these areas. The incidence of violence against transgender people remains well above average, with more transgender people than ever before becoming victims of homicide in 2015 (Human Rights Campaign). Although the general incidence of violence against women has decreased it is still disturbingly high: a study conducted in 2011 suggested that 19.3 percent will be raped at some point in their lives and that 43.9 percent will experience sexual violence of another kind (Breiding et al.). In employment, women still earn only seventy-nine cents on the male dollar, and the situation is barely improving, as the trend of growth in women's earnings relative to men's that was seen over the 1980s and 1990s stalled post-millennium; on the other hand, men have been particularly affected by the economic downturn that began in 2008 (see Costello and Hegewisch). The increased visuality of American culture, involving an ever more intense focus on the airbrushed physicality of male and female celebrities combined with the instant availability of online pornography has had a measurable impact on both male and female self-esteem, while mental health problems are on the rise (see Twenge). Owing to these factors, in 2016 the World Economic Forum placed the United States forty-fifth in national gender equality out of 144 countries, with an equality quotient of 0.722 where 1 represents full equality and 0 represents inequality.[13] Moreover, although the idea that gender is socially formed or "performative" gained significant popular traction in the

1970s, more recent years have witnessed the repopularization of notions of supposedly feminine and masculine characteristics as biologically innate, as genetically or hormonally hard wired (see Walters).

As Pynchon's novels engage with historically as well as culturally specific aspects of the evolving discourse of gender and sex, his treatment of sex and gender has changed over the course of fifty years. Are those changes a direct response to fundamental shifts in the understanding of gender? Are the gendered power dynamics of his sex scenes and valuation of family bonds a 1950s relic or a visionary critique built on parody of older attitudes? All Pynchon makes clear is his increasing self-consciousness about the questions.

This primes critics to read successive novels as "an antidote to his earlier work" or "an attempt to atone for past sins" (Severs 234; Freer 131). Pynchon gender criticism has been driven by a tendency to identify the novel at hand as either a turning point or progress marker. Robert Holton's reading of the early stories frames *V.* as the point where Pynchon "move[s] from accepting the terms of [...] 1950s debates [...] to critiquing them" (49). *Lot 49*'s central female character leads numerous critics to see the novel as Pynchon's first granting of full personhood to women. Critics like Molly Hite who find Oedipa Maas too passive consider Katje in *Gravity's Rainbow* to be a more impressive treatment of feminine experience, in part because Pynchon figures her dilemmas in tight comparative relation to those of the notional male protagonist, Slothrop. Hite sees *Vineland* as the first work in which Pynchon locates the basic "we" and "they" of his political worldview in determinate persons whose relationship is clearly gendered. Severs sees Dally Rideout in *Against the Day* as "a speaking subject" like "no previous female character in Pynchon" and hence her narrative as a new departure in the thoroughness of Pynchon's gendered account of capitalism (223). Simon Cook reads *Inherent Vice* as indicating Pynchon's acceptance of the passing of the era in which pornography could be transgressive and as a narrative that offers a more sympathetic treatment of women required to be constantly available for sex. Finally, the release of *Bleeding Edge* saw numerous favorable comparisons of its representation of female subjectivity in the figure of Maxine with that in *Lot 49* and *Vineland*, and critics also appreciated how it uses her culturally savvy perspective to self-consciously probe the limits of "all-male narratives" and "this Male Gaze she's been hearing about since High-School" (110, 221).[14] Only *Mason & Dixon*, seemingly, didn't move the gender-defensibility needle.

The risk of such an approach is to figure Pynchon's gender writing in terms of a step-by-step purging of impurities rather than as a dynamic part of an evolving worldview. Such readings may reject triumphalist teleology—Severs, for example, sees *Inherent Vice* as a step back from *Against the Day*'s investment in female focalization—but these disjunctive comparisons make it difficult for those who embrace them to develop synthetic accounts of gender's place in the Pynchonian career and cosmos. Our collection cultivates such synthetic thinking by assembling essays that cover the whole of Pynchon's career and advance on prior criticism.

Forty Years of Forerunners

Pynchon gender criticism has evolved essentially separately from the dominant trends in criticism of his work as a whole, despite moments of greater and lesser convergence. A caricature history of Pynchon studies might trace something like the following arc. First, there was source chasing and reference explication. Then, with the academic mainstreaming of postmodernism, he came to be read deconstructively, whether as a doom-mongering harbinger of mere fracture and meaninglessness, a heroic dissolver of order and hierarchy, or a dispassionate theorist of indeterminacies. *Vineland*'s inauguration of his second wave of novels saw increased attention to his worldly commitments. And finally, the end of "postmodernism" sees him examined in historical-contextual terms even as he continues to publish. The gender-focused criticism within that mass has its own broad trajectory: Pynchon as representative part of a male generation scrutinized through changing feminist approaches; a post-*Vineland* examination of the role gender plays in those concrete political commitments; gender treated as one thread of his broader engagement with questions of identity, marginality, power, and violence; and finally a sex- and gender-specific thread of that recent historical and contextualizing work.

Early Pynchon gender criticism is bookended by two very different monographs of feminist criticism—Mary Allen's *The Necessary Blankness* (1976) and Alice Jardine's *Gynesis* (1985)—that make Pynchon part of a transgeneric generational masculine myopia. Allen reads sixties fiction by male novelists in terms of the way it repeatedly figures women as passive canvases across which dynamic male characters play out their philosophically interesting and agentive lives. Finding Pynchon as guilty of this dynamic as anyone, she nevertheless considers his and Barth's allegorical mode more capable of critique than the male-perspective realism of Roth or Updike. Since it foregrounds the conventionality of gendered practices, she argues, "[f]abulation may not help us know the intricate inner side of female characters, but it clearly brings into focus many beliefs about them" (69). Jardine, by contrast, is more interested in "the *process* of (reading and writing) woman than about examining the representation of women in literature" (19). She builds on French feminist theory, using it to treat "woman" as a mode of narrative and textual structuration measured by independence from masculinist formal and psychoanalytic norms. She reads *V.*'s titular figure as a failed effort to imagine such an alternative organizing textuality. Pynchon, she thinks, merely ponders such a principle through conventional male forms: the novel is thus "a perfect example of the thematization rather than constitution of gynesis in contemporary male American writing" (247). Allen and Jardine both focus on *V.*'s well-intentioned limitations: its inability to construct a genuine alternative to the masculinism it diagnoses in its culture.

This first wave was almost all written by female critics, consciously writing as outsiders not only to Pynchon's work but to the whole lineage of American literature of which postmodern fiction framed itself as the culmination.[15] While some are more optimistic about Pynchon's achievements than others, they share Allen's and Jardine's orientation as female outsiders examining Pynchon within a broader tradition.[16] Yet from this external vantage they nevertheless established most of the basic terms within which later criticism would operate: the givenness of misogyny, the credit for insight about a patriarchal world, the imaginative limitations in generating alternatives, and, as Allen and Jardine articulate together, the tension between the feminine as symbolic concept and real women's subjecthood and agency.

Jardine's book represents one of the few 1980s engagements with gender in Pynchon: at the height of the interest in his formal indeterminacies, feminist critics engaged with his work mainly to use it as a foil for their preferred model of engaged literature. By the end of the decade, scholars whose first books had addressed Pynchon or metafiction in general—such as Hite, Patricia Waugh, and Linda Hutcheon—had written second books examining innovative fiction through gendered lenses. While Hutcheon combined feminist theory with Bakhtin to develop an influential account of postmodern historical fiction's antihegemonic politics and Hite mapped the tradition of experimental writing by women over a period canonized as male, Waugh had a different goal: to demonstrate that the antisubjective tendency that 1980s postmodern theory celebrated in fiction like Pynchon's was a distinctly male privilege: women's experimental fiction of the era dwelled less on dissolution, she suggested, which made sense, since "[t]hose excluded from or marginalized by the dominant culture [. . .] may *never* have experienced a sense of full subjectivity in the first place. They may never have identified with that stable presence mediated through the naturalizing conditions of fictional tradition" (2).[17] It took the release of *Vineland* to reinvigorate interest in gender questions internal to Pynchon's fiction.

The first collection of essays on Pynchon's comeback novel contains three that focus on the novel's distinctive gender thinking. N. Katherine Hayles develops an early take on the importance of gendered family commitment to Pynchon's worldview, Stacey Olster reads ninja DL Chastain as a newly concrete embodiment of alternatives to harmful gender roles, contrasting her with betrayer and absent mother Frenesi Gates with respect to Pynchon's career-long concern with the alternatives of worldly work and escapist transcendence, and Hite reads the novel as Pynchon's first properly feminist engagement with the relationship between social power and the contingency of gender roles. For the first time, she says, Pynchon figures the "we" and "they" of his politics in gendered bodies: villain Brock Vond is "unequivocally white and male," as all Pynchon's future villains will be ("Feminist" 135). Hite sees Frenesi's passivity and subservience to Vond's male power, meanwhile, as a diagnosis of the harms of willful acquiescence to gendered roles: Frenesi's eventual realization that she has been thoroughly conditioned into a structural role makes her "the character who most fully exposes the feminine as a necessary construction of the neo-fascist They-system" (140). *Vineland* in Hite's reading offers an antiessentialist feminist argument about the dependence of gender categories on power: "Because oppression—and, correlatively, repression—are the *determinants* of gender in [Pynchon's] world, gender categories prove disconcertingly transposable" (139). It's left to other characters—DL and Zoyd Wheeler, the now single-parent father of Frenesi's daughter—to live ethically viable lives that escape those repressive constructions. Subsequently, critics have both connected this gendered political vision to canonically postmodern categories (as in Patricia Bergh's reading of *Vineland* in terms of the ethical problems that acknowledging the simulacral nature of gender performance can cause for gendered relationships like that between mother and daughter) and reinterpreted Pynchon's earlier texts in light of this vision (as when Wendy Steiner, in a history of U.S. fiction between 1970 and 1990, specifically exempts Pynchon from a narrative that otherwise treats male experimental writing as a disengaged and pessimistic foil to more vitally world-engaged feminist fiction of the era).

The post-*Vineland* decade also saw gender criticism of Pynchon's work by male critics, especially in analyses of his skeptical treatment of masculinity and of the problems with his seeming self-conception within the project of—in Wes Chapman's formulation—"male profeminism." In Chapman's reading of *Gravity's Rainbow*, the key gendered problem is Slothrop's awareness of "how he himself has been written by the codes of dominance and submission" (par. 14). The novel's search for a position outside that coding fails, suggests Chapman, because it "can only gesture to a position outside the problem, a position which it cannot itself imagine, by a kind of masculinist gigantism which reveals its own absurdity" (par. 17); it thus is unable to turn awareness of absurdity into a constructive alternative to it. Articles near the end of the decade offer more optimistic accounts of Pynchon's antimasculinism, particularly a series of articles by Mark Hawthorne about nonhetero sex and homosociality in Pynchon's works.

In the beginning of the 2000s, another edited volume overtly aimed to set an agenda for work on Pynchon, sex, and gender. Almost half the essays in Niran Abbas's *Reading from the Margins* address the theme. The collection explicitly frames its eclectic feminist approaches—from Holton's contextual situation of Pynchon's early stories in relation to 1950s debates about male autonomy to Dana Medoro's psychoanalytic reading of menstrual tropes in *Lot 49*—as part of a broader consideration of the role that marginalized perspectives and margin-center power relations play in Pynchon's vision. Gender, in this collection, is just the predominant example of a wider structural logic in Pynchon's fiction. This approach to gender set the tone for much criticism pertaining to Pynchon and gender over the course of the decade.

Sue J. Kim, for example, builds on *Reading from the Margins*'s interest in the cumulative role of othered identities in Pynchon to substantively rethink the relationship between identity and form that, before *Vineland*, had threatened to strand Pynchon on the side of the politically disengaged fabulists. Kim's book is an attempt to move beyond the simplistic critical politics she calls "Otherness postmodernism," which insists that "experimental texts by minority and/or female writers constitute political resistance by contravening realist narrative forms," while failing to grant that resistance to textually similar work by white men (4). Kim instead aims to develop accounts of the specific formal strategies by which specific nonrealist texts generate constructive new takes on race problems. Reading Pynchon alongside Theresa Hak Kyung Cha and Bessie Head, she argues that his treatment of the Herero in *Gravity's Rainbow* indicates a rejection of the primitivist racial valorizations of his earlier work, explicitly defending his attention to the flaws and limitations of their "variously complex, conflicted, complicit, and confused" worldview (84). This she sees as a preferable alternative to—and "a much more 'respectful' approach to the Other" than—"Otherness Postmodernism's" reductive equation between form, identity, ideology, and effectuality (110). Insofar as gender remains one of these "Othernesses," Kim's work gives Pynchon scholars a means by which to reassess not only the racial but also the gender implications of his work's specifically formal qualities.

Yet while Abbas's collection heralded more research on Pynchon and race, the following years were surprisingly empty in terms of work on Pynchon and gender. The major thread in the first decade of the new millennium might be better traced to a 2000 book by Marilyn Maxwell, who—after a decade in which the bulk of work on Pynchon and gender was published in Pynchon-specific venues—took the Allen/Jardine approach of reading his early work as a symptom of a trend. Focusing particularly on *V.*'s treatment of rape, Maxwell shows how what seem like indictments of male cultural power actually end up reifying a dynamic whereby men are actors and women sufferers. Reading the novel's various scenes of women backed into cultural or literal corners to the point that they can't refuse advances, Maxwell identifies an organizing blindspot: "[W]hat happens when the 'No' really means 'No' and accurately reflects the wishes and intent of the sender? Pynchon does not seem to allow for this possibility" (133). Is not wanting to have sex the final taboo in Pynchon's work? Maxwell makes clear just how worrying this question is: "By portraying women as deliberate senders of inverse messages in sexually charged situations, Pynchon has, in effect, virtually eliminated the concept of rape" (134). Sharon Stockton, later in the decade, elucidates a pattern in *Gravity's Rainbow* whereby repeated representations of women's rape serve no narrative purpose beyond amplifying the violence of the novel's broader pessimism. Women's suffering is thus subordinated to the elaboration of the male ego worry that Waugh had identified as postmodernism's false universal: each female victim of violence "finally disappears from the text, fades into a ghost who adds an audible note of horror to the dissolution of the masculine subject" (143).

This lens of sexualized violence is not the only way that sex and gender converge in recent Pynchon criticism. Herman and Weisenburger's Gravity's Rainbow, *Domination, and Freedom* focuses, for example, on the significance of changes in obscenity law during the process of the novel's composition. Freer's essay on Pynchon and the women's movement in her wider survey of his relationship to the countercultural 1960s shares with Jeffrey Severs's reading of the specifically gendered account of fin-de-siècle capitalism in *Against the Day* both this precise contextualist framing and an awareness of how much of Pynchon's gender thinking is mediated through representations of sex.

This contextualism, then, is where the shorter trajectory of sex-focused Pynchon criticism also ends up, reintegrated with the work on gender. Catharine Stimpson, in an early survey of Pynchon's first three novels, had approached sex and gender together in drawing a parallel between the "simplicities" of Pynchon's early gender thinking and his early fiction's "appal[ed]" treatment of fetishism and lesbianism as violations of women's "normative task of acting out and symbolizing natural fertility" (85). But work on Pynchon's sex writing otherwise begins with the fact that the Pulitzer board refused to award *Gravity's Rainbow* the Pulitzer Prize, despite the jury's unanimous vote in favor, owing to its "obscenity." Early critics concerned with Pynchon's pessimism elaborated on the novel's association of the death-drive with the compulsion toward nonnormative sexual behavior. Such criticism argued in general, gender-neutral terms rather than making its case through analyses of the concrete details of Pynchonian sex, and for all that mainstream reviewers have long characterized Pynchon's sexual imagination in terms of the "polymorphous perversities" of the untamed libido in Marcuse's Freudian counterpolitics, this stress on the value of transgression rarely surfaced in academic criticism even as Pynchon's formal experiments were widely praised in such terms.

Not until the 1990s did critics like Hawthorne and Christopher Kocela start examining Pynchon's treatment of nonnormative, nonprocreative sex on its own terms rather than as part and parcel of the critique of political domination and violated nature. Indeed, these studies are notable for their low-key appreciation of the way many of Pynchon's putative perversities are tied to characters' need for love, acceptance, and other affects that do not feature in standard understandings of pornography. Michael Bérubé in 1992 examined the way that Pynchon's engagement with the genres of pornography conditioned his work's relation to mass culture, but the nonsexual significance of Pynchon's sex writing has only recently received its due in work on Pynchon and genre. Jessica Lawson and Marie Franco, for example, read Pynchon's accounts of sexual and desire dynamics as analogues for writing or narrative structure, restoring the positive association between sex, transgression, and his formal innovations. Examinations of sex in Pynchon have thus, like treatments of gender, migrated from discussion of symbolic universals to something more concretely historical and formal-generic.

Open Questions

What, then, are the questions that remain for studies of Pynchon and his finally inseparable treatments of sex and gender after forty years of criticism on this subject?

One set of questions pertains to gender's role in the way Pynchon the phenomenon—whose paratexts range from self-authored blurbs to reviews and popular coverage—has conditioned understanding of Pynchon the author. Meanwhile, if the standard approach to the gender dimensions of Pynchon's novels has been to set each against its predecessors in a search for turning points, what do we gain or lose by considering Pynchon's gendered thinking in career-spanning terms? These career-structure questions might illuminate Pynchon's relation to the gender thinking of his peers, not to mention offering new accounts, as Steiner and Kim do, of who his peers actually are.

Another set of questions concerns the formal dimensions of Pynchon's work. Following Kim, we can separate Pynchon's authorial identity, his demographic alignment with the male "postmodernists," from the issue of what his particular departures from realist convention accomplish. An investigation of this subject might allow us to ask whether there *is* something distinctly male about Pynchon's particular forms, whether or not that holds for the rest of his generation. Recent work on the relationship of Pynchon's sex writing to larger questions of textuality and narrative structure, meanwhile, can help us explore whether his self-conscious engagement with the conventions and history of pornography, obscenity, and textual transgression yields constructive insights and can perhaps show us where its exaggeration of tropes is indistinguishable from indulgent reveling in them.

Questions about pornographic form naturally lead on to questions about Pynchon's treatment of sex more generally. Does, for example, Severs's association of Dally's sympathetic speaking-subject treatment in *Against the Day* with her exemption from the sexual subordination Pynchon's female characters are usually subjected to suggest that there's an inverse relationship between the humanity and sexual nonnormativity of Pynchon's female characters? Does Pynchon's work ever imagine sexual pleasure independent of a gendered power dynamic? Do nonheterosexual pairings or group sex scenarios also rely on a gendered power structure, or can they subvert such a structure or do without it? More fundamentally, is all sex in Pynchon limited to a model that essentially pits male power against female-pseudovoluntary subservience, or does the fiction posit other formations as plausible or viable?

This opens up questions about gender's relation to the core of Pynchon's vision. Are there elements of Pynchon's worldview—his metaphysics, his politics, his ethics—that don't hinge on gendered categories or from which gender can at least be held a separate concern? Is his reliance on traditional feminine associations with family, procreation, and nature part of a viably anti-status-quo program or just regression disguised as critique? Is romantic/familial love merely a construct that facilitates the biopolitical control of sexual relations? Are all marginalized identities of equal significance in Pynchon, or do they play structurally different roles in his basic worldview? Are there marginalized identity positions that his imaginative limitations bar him from seriously engaging with, despite his career-long commitment to the "preterite"?

Perhaps all of these questions boil down to a basic set. Is Pynchon's fiction fundamentally gender essentialist, and if so, how does this comport with his various antifoundationalisms, and is it necessarily politically reactionary or liberatory? The contributions to this volume investigate such questions and establish groundwork for further elaboration by cumulatively addressing all of Pynchon's novels through a variety of theoretical lenses.

What's in Store

The fourteen essays that comprise this investigation are divided—after Molly Hite's standalone paper brings forty years as a Pynchon critic to bear on her consideration of Pynchon's early misogyny and its influence on his reception—into four sections. The first two address our titular topics—gender roles and the genres of Pynchon's sex writing—at a conceptual level, and the latter two explore the practical gendering and sexualization of violence in Pynchon's work and his career-long interest in the pitfalls and potentials of different models of family.

Hite's "When Pynchon Was a Boys' Club: *V.* and Midcentury Mystifications of Gender" opens the collection with a freshly historicized account of the question of Pynchon's misogyny, allowing the rest of the contributors to proceed without the hedgings that usually characterize criticism on Pynchon and gender. Hite reads the mysterious V. figure as modernity's challenge to the stereotype of the apolitical yet rebellious "real man" by offering a model of "real women" based on nurturance and passivity. The possible ways of representing women are so polarized and so supervenient on male models that they can't be treated in fully human terms. Hite argues that Pynchon was aware of this problem but lacked the tools and terminology to advance beyond it; she identifies the cultural reasons for that, reasons, she suggests, that also partly explain the novel's enthusiastic reception.

Our first group of papers addresses Pynchon's general treatment of gender roles. Jennifer Backman's "From Hard Boiled to Over Easy: Reimagining the Noir Detective in *Inherent Vice* and *Bleeding Edge*" elaborates on Hite's discussion of anxiety about "real" masculinity by showing how later novels treat failures to live up to masculine models in a more productive light than *V.* Backman focuses on the figure of the hard-boiled detective, examining gender and genre in parallel, the etymological connection being more than a happy coincidence. She focuses on Doc Sportello in *Inherent Vice* and Maxine Tarnow in *Bleeding Edge*, a male and female variant, showing how Pynchon both works with and subverts the gender logic of classic crime fiction. Drawing on Christopher Breu's reading of hard-boiled masculinity as a fearful response to cultural change, she demonstrates how Pynchon reworks clichés in order to scrutinize contemporary expectations about masculinity and agency, empathy, and violence.

Kostas Kaltsas also takes a comparative approach in "Of 'Maidens' and Towers: Oedipa Maas, Maxine Tarnow, and the Possibility of Resistance," which treats *Bleeding Edge* as an explicit update of *The Crying of Lot 49* in terms of the heroine's political agency. Maxine in *Bleeding Edge* succeeds, at least partially, where Oedipa failed in resisting the machinations of the faceless powerful: Kaltsas understands Maxine's comparative success in terms of her greater awareness of the conventionality of gender roles, which allows her to deploy feminine performance to advance her pursuits. Between the two novels, the stereotypically feminine thus shifts from a restriction to an appropriable political tool.

Christopher Kocela's "Between *Sangha* and Sex Work: The Karmic Middle Path of *Vineland*'s Female Characters" widens the focus to non-Western traditions. Identifying explicit allusions to the 1980s sex scandals of U.S. Buddhism, Kocela reads the Japanese sections of *Vineland* as an argument against commercial Buddhism's gendered value system, seeing the respective adventures of the novel's major female characters, DL and Frenesi, as articulations of two models of karma: one subject to those capitalist 1980s pitfalls, one able to overcome them and work for the powerless in specifically female terms.

The next group of essays examines Pynchon's treatment of sex, particularly what could be called his "sex writing," moving beyond mere content analysis toward a sexual poetics that includes pornography, sadomasochism, and the redemptive possibilities at the intersection of sex and politics. Doug Haynes's "'Allons Enfants!' Pynchon's Pornographies" moves away from allegorical readings of Pynchon's sex scenes in order to show, through readings of *V.* and *Gravity's Rainbow*, that Pynchon aims at a kind of pornographic indulgence in his sex writing precisely so as to foreground the ethical and political dimensions of sex. Drawing on Sade, Sontag, and Deleuze, Haynes examines the historicizing capacities of desire-driven sex writing and elucidates how Pynchon, across his career, treats sexual economies in relation to historical economic developments.

Along the same lines, Marie Franco links Pynchon's formal idiosyncrasies to his interest in transgressive sexuality. In "Queer Sex, Queer Text: S/M in *Gravity's Rainbow*," she argues that queer sex, in particular sadomasochism, is both a model and a catalyst for Pynchon's narrative nonlinearity. Pynchon's sex writing thus becomes a paradigm case of Brian McHale's account of postmodern narrative instability as an attack on the politics of modernist modes of reading. Transgressive sex thus features in Pynchon's plots not as pathology but as a subversive political agent, undermining hierarchical power structures.

Richard Moss's "What Would Charlie Do? Narrowing the Possibilities of a Pornographic Redemption in Thomas Pynchon's Novels" closes this section by examining the religious figurations that animate Pynchon's sex writing throughout his career. Moss identifies a growing worry from *Gravity's Rainbow* to *Inherent Vice* about how transgression can be harnessed for dubious political ends. The religious terms of transcendence give way to a sense of spirituality's inextricability from political and economic orders. Moss thus provides a new account of Pynchon's changing attitudes to religion and sexuality and to the political and cultural possibilities of their interaction.

With our titular categories of sex and gender thus clarified, the collection turns to investigations of the way they undergird Pynchon's dealing with the practical and ethical matters of violence and family.

Simon Cook's "'This Set of Holes, Pleasantly Framed': Pynchon the Competent Pornographer and the Female Conduit" returns to pornography, examining the connection between two trends in Pynchon's sex writing: his use of tropes associated with the dominant channels through which pornography circulated at the time he was writing each novel and the figuration of female bodies as vectors for communication between men that persists across the evolution of pornographic mediums. Tracing these consistencies across novels from three different periods of Pynchon's career—*Gravity's Rainbow*, *Vineland*, and *Against the Day*—Cook shows how modern views of pornography have been incorporated into the author's historically minded works and illuminates the diagnoses of figurative violence that they make possible.

Simon de Bourcier's "Representations of Sexualized Children and Child Abuse in Thomas Pynchon's Fiction" focuses on Pynchon's parallel sexualization of and sentimentality about child characters throughout this fiction. De Bourcier examines Pynchon's overtly intertextual ways of pursuing this theme through allusions to Nabokov and popular fiction in order to develop a new account of the particularly gendered way Pynchon treats matters of sympathy and innocence through violent events and representations.

In "'Our Women Are Free': Slavery, Gender, and Representational Bias in Thomas Pynchon's *Mason & Dixon*," Angus McFadzean addresses the relationship between representational violence and concrete oppression. *Mason & Dixon*, McFadzean argues, frames three distinct master/slave oppositions: a fixed one between characters and institutions, a fluid one between characters, and an indeterminable one between characters' gender performances and their true selves. Examining gender in light of these oppositions reveals both Pynchon's awareness of the imbrication of gender and exploitation and a bias in moral favor of male heteronormativity throughout the novel. What harms does this bias sustain, and how responsible is Pynchon himself for such harms? McFadzean finally identifies Pynchon's best exculpation as a certain hybridity in his style that mirrors potential hybrid gender identities.

Finally, from the career-long preoccupation with violence, we move to that of family, a subject that Pynchon builds up to addressing, just as our collection does. As this is increasingly the framework within which Pynchon does most of his gendered thinking, we devote more chapters to it than any other topic, investigating two covalent questions: what does the family mean in Pynchon and what values in Pynchon's worldview depend on this gendered family model?

Luc Herman and John M. Krafft's research in the Pynchon archives brings us "Pynchon and Gender: A View from the Typescript of *V*." Examining a short scene from an invented sitcom that Pynchon cut from the novel because it was "ponderous Social Commentary," Herman and Krafft detail the gender dynamics of the scene, connecting the family dynamics in it to concerns in the published version of *V.*, like dehumanization and male disempowerment. Cutting this minor scene, they show, made the novel's investigations of such topics much less "ponderous" but also had the effect of eliminating reference to a concern with nuclear families that would recur much more conspicuously in his later work.

Jeffrey Severs examines sitcoms at the other end of Pynchon's career in "'Homer Is My Role Model': Father-Schlemihls, Sentimental Families, and Pynchon's Affinities with *The Simpsons*." Seeing Pynchon's voice and script work on *The Simpsons* as the source for various plot details in *Bleeding Edge*, Severs argues that the gender politics of Pynchonian families have changed greatly over the course of his career, particularly in the increasing absence or ineffectuality of assertive patriarchs. Homer Simpson, Severs suggests, is a central figure for this tendency in the wider media culture; drawing on these connections between Pynchon and *The Simpsons*, he examines the role family models have played in the wider trend toward greater engagement between literary fiction and popular TV in the years since *The Simpsons* began.

In "Conservatism as Radicalism: Family and Antifeminism in *Vineland*," Catherine Flay explores the importance of family in Pynchon's work through a perspective that connects feminism and economic critique. If, as Flay argues, the family stands against capitalism's individualist ideology, where does that leave women's personal quests for social and sexual liberation? This is a double bind, where women must work both outside the social norms and outside the network of resistance to them. Synthesizing various Pynchonian concerns—transgression, community, freedom from oppression, power—through the nexus of the family model, Flay reveals how much of Pynchon's worldview hinges on his attitudes to this one social formation.

Finally, likewise investigating Pynchon's gender essentialism, Inger H. Dalsgaard's "Choice or Life? Deliberations on Motherhood in Late-Period Pynchon" focuses on Pynchon's treatment of motherhood as not only a valuable social role but a normative criterion by which characters' deserts can be judged. Examining Pynchon's modes of identifying good or bad motherhood in the post-*Vineland* novels, Dalsgaard comes to conclude that Pynchon's worldview is organized by the imperative not just to generate new life but to give children a family to grow up within. Female characters who don't live up to this model, she shows, tend to fare badly in Pynchon's worlds.

As we begin with Hite giving a final word on the oldest question in Pynchon gender criticism with an analysis of his oldest novel, we end with an outward-looking focus on the newer work. That work's preoccupation with family recalls that early letter in which Pynchon described himself as "pornographer [...] maybe; novelist no" while lamenting his incompetence with "traditional realist" material. If the "traditional realist" novel has always been entwined with the representation and ideology of family, then one goal for a writer committed to nonrealist methods might be to use them to advance on realism's understanding of its own turf. Assessing Pynchon's evolution as a novelist may be inseparable from assessing his evolution as a pornographer. He may have more novels to come, and as this collection demonstrates, there is plenty left to investigate about sex and gender's central place in his vision.

NOTES

1. One example is a Reddit thread entitled "Why Is the Sex Scene in *Inherent Vice* So Awful?"
2. In a letter of June 29, 1963, to Faith and Kirkpatrick Sale, Pynchon suggests that he needs to get better at the "traditional realistic" parts of novel writing, framing himself as "surrealist, pornographer, word engineer, maybe; novelist, no" (Thomas Pynchon Collection).
3. Examples include the gang rape of Fina in *V.*, Oedipa's orgasm following Metzger's penetration of her unconscious body in *The Crying of Lot 49*, Slothrop's spanking of Margherita Erdmann in *Gravity's Rainbow*, Frenesi's capitulation to Brock Vond in *Vineland*, the pleasure taken in prostitution by Las Viudas de Cristo in *Mason & Dixon*, Yashmeen's rape in *Against the Day*, and Maxine's sex with Windust in *Bleeding Edge*.
4. Since 2000, the gender balance at International Pynchon Week conferences and in collections of essays has been about six to one.
5. Ali Chetwynd, for example, first came to ponder Pynchon's gender attitudes when as an undergraduate he noticed that every female friend to whom he lent a copy of his then-favorite book *V.* gave it back to him unimpressed without finishing. Finally, one asked, "Don't you think [Pynchon] just hates women?" The usual defense is that the novel itself doesn't endorse the horrible things that happen to its female characters: the more the women suffer the more the male world is indicted! But this perpetuates presumptions about the nature of men's and women's agency and relative narrative interest: that men are dynamic and compelling, that women are passive and significant only as foils. Objection to this pattern motivates many criticisms of Pynchon's gender thinking that don't treat the representation of gendered violence as intrinsically unjustifiable.
6. Pynchon to Faith and Kirkpatrick Sale, March 9, 1963, and Pynchon to Kirkpatrick Sale, May 28, 1962, Thomas Pynchon Collection. Pynchon and Sale co-wrote the crudely misogynistic libretto *Minstrel Island*, which is preserved in the Pynchon archives at the Harry Ransom Center.
7. Pynchon is no doubt innocent of anything as emphatic as John Barth's exclusion of female peers from the fabulatory canon as mere issuers of "secular news reports" (Barth 196). While he has written blurbs for a number of female authors, including Marge Piercy, Mary Beal, Laurel Goodman, Emily Barton, and Lori Baker, none of those blurbs makes matters of sex or gender salient to the recommendation. And while he's on record calling another Marge his "muse" (Marge Simpson), his doing so on the basis of her cooking rather than her writing hardly answers the objection.
8. Beal is, says Wes Chapman, the one feminist theorist Pynchon's early work explicitly references (par. 19).
9. As Joanna Freer has argued elsewhere, however, Pynchon's writing off the early fiction's explicit misogyny as youthful indiscretion may create the impression that he is seeking "to excuse male sexism as merely infantile" when he should instead be "condemning it as something more malicious" (156).

10. The *Cambridge Companion*s to Updike and Roth both also contain chapters that have to start from zero in arguing that there could be anything going on in their authors' depictions of women other than ventriloquized hostility.

11. Woodcock's judgment that even when Fowles "analyses male power most directly, he does so in ways which perpetuate some of masculinity's most tenacious myths" (12) matches that delivered in many readings of Pynchon, and the two authors' career-driving self-consciousness about this fact explains the amount of gender-focused criticism each has received.

12. See Repo for a genealogy of the development of the discourse of "gender" as a "historically specific technology of biopower" (6).

13. See "Global Gender Gap Index 2015: Rankings," http://reports.weforum.org/global-gender-gap-report-2015.

14. Less attention has been paid to the way that Maxine's fluency with feminist culture allows the novel to be self-conscious about the *significance* of female experience. For example, in a scene of dubiously consensual sex Maxine's cultural consciousness saturates the very experience it's supposed to investigate. Although her rational mind is overcome to the extent that it's "impossible for her to know if it's him moving or she's doing it herself," Maxine is able within the moment to judge that this is "not a distinction to be lingered on until much later, of course, if at all, though in some circles it is held to be something of a big deal" (258). Pynchon's work increasingly frames its gendered representations through this self-consciousness about gender theory and gendered culture. Inseparable from her resolution to think about it later, Maxine's claim to momentary mindlessness actually shows her—and Pynchon—more mindful than ever of *context*: of how her gendered actions might signify in "circles" beyond the present moment, the present text.

15. As critics like Elaine Showalter and Judith Fetterly observed soon after Allen, that tradition of writing—in British and American literature, respectively—framed its reader as male, its values as universal, and the obstacles to achieving those values as female.

16. See in particular Cathy Davidson's reading of *Lot 49* as the tale of Oedipa's self-deprogramming from the contingently conditioned role of passive woman, through which she becomes "a woman aware of her own identity, a person more fully human, and thus an androgyne" (49–50).

17. Waugh's work reverberates in Philip Brian Harper's later account of how canonical postmodernism's preoccupation with postsubjective alienation "represents the 'recentering' of the culture's focus on issues that have always concerned marginalized constituencies" (3–4).

WORKS CITED

Allen, Mary. *The Necessary Blankness: Women in Major American Fiction of the Sixties*. Urbana: University of Illinois Press, 1976.

Barth, John. "The Literature of Replenishment." *The Friday Book*. London: Johns Hopkins University Press, 1984. 193–206

Bergh, Patricia A. "(De)constructing the Image: Thomas Pynchon's Postmodern Woman." *Journal of Popular Culture* 30.4 (1997): 1–12.

Bérubé, Michael. *Marginal Forces/Cultural Centers: Tolson, Pynchon, and the Politics of the Canon*. Ithaca: Cornell University Press, 1992.

Breiding, Matthew J., et al. "Prevalence and Characteristics of Sexual Violence,

Stalking, and Intimate Partner Violence Victimization. National Intimate Partner and Sexual Violence Survey, United States, 2011." *Morbidity and Mortality Weekly Report*, 5 Sept. 2014, www.cdc.gov/mmwr/pdf/ss/ss6308.pdf. Accessed 16 Mar. 2015.

Callahan, Dan. "Lots of Sex and Drugs, but Where Are the Believable People?" Review of *Inherent Vice*, by Thomas Pynchon, *The Wrap*, www.thewrap.com/inherent-vice-review-lots-of-sex-and-drugs-but-where-are-the-believable-people. Accessed 10 Mar. 2016.

Chapman, Wes. "Male Pro-Feminism and the Masculinist Gigantism of *Gravity's Rainbow*." *Postmodern Culture* 6.3 (1996). DOI: 10.1353/pmc.1996.0017.

Cook, Simon. "Manson Chicks and Microskirted Cuties: Pornification in Thomas Pynchon's *Inherent Vice*." *Textual Practice* 29.6 (2015): 1143–64.

Costello, Cynthia, and Ariane Hegewisch. "The Gender Wage Gap and Public Policy." *Institute for Women's Policy Research*. Briefing Paper 507, Feb. 2016, https://iwpr.org/wp-content/uploads/wpallimport/files/iwpr-export/publications/C435-The%20Gender%20Wage%20Gap.pdf.

Davidson, Cathy N. "Oedipa as Androgyne in Thomas Pynchon's *The Crying of Lot 49*." *Contemporary Literature* 18.1 (1977): 38–50.

"Facts over Time." United States Department of Labor, www.dol.gov/wb/stats/facts_over_time.htm#labor. Accessed 14 Jul. 2017.

Fetterley, Judith. *The Resisting Reader: A Feminist Approach to American Fiction*. Bloomington: Indiana University Press, 1978.

Freer, Joanna. *Thomas Pynchon and American Counterculture*. New York: Cambridge University Press, 2014.

Gooblar, David. "Roth and Women." *Philip Roth Studies* 8.1 (2012): 7–15.

Gorber, Jason. "Talking to *Inherent Vice*'s Katherine Waterston about Joaquin, PTA, and Nudity." *Cineplex*, 26 Dec. 2014, www.cineplex.com/News/Talking-to-Inherent-Vices-Katherine-Waterston-about-Joaquin-PTA-and-nudity.aspx. Accessed 10 Mar. 2016.

Green, Geoffrey, Donald J. Greiner, and Larry McCaffery, eds. *The* Vineland *Papers: Critical Takes on Pynchon's Novel*. Normal: Dalkey Archive Press, 1994.

Harper, Phillip Brian. *Framing the Margins: The Social Logic of Postmodern Culture*. Oxford: Oxford University Press, 1994.

Hawthorne, Mark D. "'Hi! My Name Is Arnold Snarb!' Homosexuality in *The Crying of Lot 49*." *Pynchon Notes* 44–45 (1999): 65–81.

Hayles, N. Katherine. "'Who Was Saved?' Families, Snitches, and Recuperation in Pynchon's *Vineland*." Green, Greiner, and McCaffery 14–30.

Herman, Luc, and Steven Weisenburger. Gravity's Rainbow, *Domination, and Freedom*. Athens: University of Georgia Press, 2013.

Hite, Molly. "Feminist Theory and the Politics of *Vineland*." Green, Greiner, and McCaffery 135–53.

———. *The Other Side of the Story: Structures and Strategies of Contemporary Feminist Narrative*. Ithaca: Cornell University Press, 1992.

Holton, Robert. "'Closed Circuit': The White Male Predicament in Pynchon's Early Stories." *Thomas Pynchon: Reading from the Margins*. Ed. Niran Abbas. Madison: Fairleigh Dickinson University Press, 2003. 37–50.

Human Rights Campaign. "Addressing Anti-Transgender Violence." Nov. 2015, http://hrc-assets.s3-website-us-east-1.amazonaws.com//files/assets/resources/HRC-AntiTransgenderViolence-0519.pdf. Accessed 16 Nov. 2017.

Hutcheon, Linda. *A Poetics of Postmodernism: History, Theory, Fiction*. London: Routledge, 1989.

Inherent Vice. Dir. Paul Thomas Anderson. Warner Bros., 2014.

Jardine, Alice. *Gynesis: Configurations of Woman and Modernity*. Ithaca: Cornell University Press, 1985.

Johnson, Sonia. "Selling the Postmodern Novel: Marketing and Reception of Literary Masculinities in Postwar American Fiction." PhD diss. University of Iowa, 2014.

Kim, Sue J. *Critiquing Postmodernism in Contemporary Discourses of Race*. New York: Palgrave Macmillan, 2009.

Kocela, Christopher. *Fetishism and Its Discontents in Post-1960 American Fiction*. New York: Springer, 2010.

Lawson, Jessica. "'The Real and Only Fucking Is Done on Paper': Penetrative Readings and Pynchon's Sexual Text." *Against the Grain: Reading Pynchon's Counternarratives*. Ed Sascha Pöhlmann. Amsterdam: Rodopi, 2010. 231–49.

Maxwell, Marilyn. *Male Rage, Female Fury: Gender and Violence in Contemporary American Fiction*. Lanham: University Press of America, 2000.

McWeeny, Drew. "Katherine Waterston on Navigating the Controlled Chaos of *Inherent Vice*." *Hitfix*, 17 Dec. 2014, www.hitfix.com/motion-captured/katherine-waterston-on-navigating-the-controlled-chaos-of-inherent-vice. Accessed 10 Mar. 2016.

Merry, Stephanie. "Katherine Waterston Is Ready for Your Lame Questions about That *Inherent Vice* Sex Scene." *Washington Post*, 8 Jan. 2015, www.washingtonpost.com/news/arts-and-entertainment/wp/2015/01/08/katherine-waterston-is-ready-for-your-lame-questions-about-that-inherent-vice-sex-scene. Accessed 10 Mar. 2016.

Olster, Stacey. "When You're a (Nin)jette, You're a (Nin)jette All the Way—Or Are You?: Female Filmmaking in *Vineland*." Green, Greiner and McCaffery 119–34.

Pynchon, Thomas. *Bleeding Edge*. New York: Penguin, 2013.

———. *Inherent Vice*. London: Vintage, 2010.

———. Thomas Pynchon Collection. Harry Ransom Humanities Research Center, University of Texas at Austin.

Repo, Jemima. *Biopolitics and Gender*. Oxford: Oxford University Press, 2015.

Rolls, Albert. "'A Dual Man [and Oeuvre], Aimed Two Ways at Once': The Two Directions of Pynchon's Life and Thought." *Orbit: A Journal of American Literature* 4.1 (2016). DOI: 10.16995/orbit.188.

Severs, Jeffrey. "'The abstractions she was instructed to embody': Women, Capitalism, and Artistic Representation in *Against the Day*." *Pynchon's Against the Day: A Corrupted Pilgrim's Guide*. Ed. Jeffrey Severs and Christopher Leise. Newark: University of Delaware Press, 2011. 215–38.

Showalter, Elaine. *A Literature of Their Own: British Women Novelists from Brontë to Lessing*. Princeton: Princeton University Press, 1977.

Steiner, Wendy. "Postmodern Fictions, 1970–1990." *The Cambridge History of American Literature*. Vol. 7. Ed. Sacvan Bercovitch. Cambridge: Cambridge University Press, 1999. 425–538.

Stimpson, Catharine. "Pre-Apocalyptic Atavism: Thomas Pynchon's Early Fiction." *Modern Critical Views: Thomas Pynchon*. Ed. Harold Bloom. New York: Chelsea House, 1986. 79–92.

Stockton, Sharon. *The Economics of Fantasy: Rape in Twentieth-Century Literature*. Columbus: Ohio State University Press, 2006.

"The Sarah Lawrence Orgies of 1968: An Interview With Author Ronald Sukenick." *The Write Stuff*, www.altx.com/int2/suk.html. Accessed 15 Apr. 2017.

Twenge, Jean M. "Time Period and Birth Cohort Differences in Depressive Symptoms in the U.S., 1982–2013." *Social Indicators Research* 121.2 (2015): 437–54.

Waugh, Patricia. *Feminine Fictions: Revisiting the Postmodern*. New York: Routledge, 2012.

Walters, Natasha. *Living Dolls: The Return of Sexism*. London: Virago, 2010.

"Why Is the Sex scene in *Inherent Vice* so Awful?" *Reddit*, 20 June 2015, www.reddit.com/r/flicks/comments/3aibe5/why_is_the_sex_scene_in_inherent_vice_so_awful. Accessed 10 Mar. 2016.

Woodcock, Bruce. *Male Mythologies: John Fowles and Masculinity*. Totowa: Barnes & Noble, 1984.

World Economic Forum. "Global Gender Gap Index 2015: Rankings." http://reports.weforum.org/global-gender-gap-report-2015. Accessed 20 Mar. 2016.

Zhong, Fan. "Katherine Waterston's Belated Breakout Role." *W Magazine*, 22 Dec. 2014, www.wmagazine.com/story/katherine-waterstons-belated-breakout-role. Accessed 16 Nov. 2017.

A Chronological Bibliography of Relevant Published Research to 2017

1963
Publication of *V.*

1966
Publication of *The Crying of Lot 49*

1969
Greenberg, Alvin. "The Underground Woman: An Excursion into the V-ness of Thomas Pynchon." *Chelsea* 27 (1969): 58–65.

1973
Publication of *Gravity's Rainbow*

1976
Allen, Mary. "The Fabulators: Barth, Pynchon, Purdy, Kesey." *The Necessary Blankness: Women in Major American Fiction of the Sixties*. Urbana: University of Illinois Press, 1976. 14–69.
Kaufman, Marjorie. "Brunnhilde and the Chemists: Women in *Gravity's Rainbow*." *Mindful Pleasures: Essays on Thomas Pynchon*. Ed. George Levine and David Leverenz. Boston: Little, Brown, 1976. 197–227.
Stimpson, Catharine. "Pre-Apocalyptic Atavism: Thomas Pynchon's Early Fiction." *Mindful Pleasures: Essays on Thomas Pynchon*. Ed. George Levine and David Leverenz. Boston: Little, Brown, 1976. 31–47.

1977
Davidson, Cathy N. "Oedipa as Androgyne in Thomas Pynchon's *The Crying of Lot 49*." *Contemporary Literature* 18.1 (1977): 38–50.
Wolfley, Lawrence C. "Repression's Rainbow: The Presence of Norman O. Brown in Pynchon's Big Novel." *PMLA* 92.5 (1977): 873–89.

1981
Gelfant, Blanche. "Sister to Faust: The City's 'Hungry Woman' as Heroine." *Novel* 15.1 (1981): 23–38.

Pearson, Carol S., and Catherine Pope. *The Female Hero in American and British Literature*. New York: Bowker, 1981. See 155–60.

1983

Slade, Joseph W. "Religion, Psychology, Sex, and Love in *Gravity's Rainbow*." *Approaches to* Gravity's Rainbow. Ed. Charles Clerc. Columbus: Ohio State University Press, 1983. 153–98.

1984

Publication of *Slow Learner*

1985

Baer, Barbara L. "Apart to the End? Women and Men—Different Visions of Nuclear War." *Commonweal*, 22 Mar. 1985: 167–170.
Jardine, Alice. *Gynesis: Configurations of Woman and Modernity*. Ithaca: Cornell University Press, 1985. See 240–51.

1987

McHoul, Alec. "*Gravity's Rainbow*'s Golden Sections." *Pynchon Notes* 20 (1987): 31–38.

1988

Colvile, Georgiana M. M. "Woman's Lot and Cry." *Beyond and Beneath the Mantle: On Thomas Pynchon's* The Crying of Lot 49. Amsterdam: Rodopi, 1988. 77–92.
———. Conclusion. *Beyond and Beneath the Mantle: On Thomas Pynchon's* The Crying of Lot 49. Amsterdam: Rodopi, 1988. 99–102.

1990

Publication of *Vineland*

1991

Duyfhuizen, Bernard. "'A Suspension Forever at the Hinge of Doubt': The Reader-trap of Bianca in *Gravity's Rainbow*." *Postmodern Culture* 2.1 (1991). DOI: 10.1353/pmc.1991.0029.

1992

Bérubé, Michael. *Marginal Forces/Cultural Centers: Tolson, Pynchon, and the Politics of the Canon*. Ithaca: Cornell University Press, 1992. See chapter 4.
Caesar, Terry. "'Take Me Anyplace You Want': Pynchon's Literary Career as a Maternal Construct in *Vineland*." *Novel: A Forum on Fiction* 25.2 (1992): 181–99.

1993

Booker, M. Keith. "Mastery and Sexual Domination: Imperialism as Rape in Pynchon's *V.*" *Literature and Domination: Sex, Knowledge, and Power in Modern Fiction*. Gainesville: University of Florida Press, 1993. 90–116.
Friedman, Ellen G. "Where Are the Missing Contents? (Post)Modernism, Gender, and the Canon." *PMLA* 108.2 (1993): 240–52.
Keesey, Douglas. "The Ideology of Detection in Pynchon and DeLillo." *Pynchon Notes* 32–33 (1993): 44–59.

Sherard, Tracey. "The Birth of the Female Subject in *The Crying of Lot 49*." *Pynchon Notes* 32–33 (1993): 60–74.

1994

Carroll, Jeffrey. "Ninjettes, Nuns, and Lady Asskickers: Thomas Pynchon's Bow to the Mythical Orient." *Gender and Culture in Literature and Film East and West: Issues of Perception and Interpretation*. Ed. George Stimson, Larry E. Smith, and Nitaya Masavisut. Honolulu: University of Hawaii Press, 1994. 253–59.

Hayles, N. Katherine. "'Who Was Saved?' Families, Snitches, and Recuperation in Pynchon's *Vineland*." *The Vineland Papers: Critical Takes on Pynchon's Novel*. Ed. Geoffrey Green, Donald J. Greiner, and Larry McCaffery. Normal: Dalkey Archive Press, 1994. 14–30.

Hite, Molly. "Feminist Theory and the Politics of *Vineland*." *The Vineland Papers: Critical Takes on Pynchon's Novel*. Ed. Geoffrey Green, Donald J. Greiner, and Larry McCaffery. Normal: Dalkey Archive Press, 1994. 135–53.

Kemeny, Annemarie. "The Female Machine in the Postmodern Circuit." *Liminal Postmodernisms: The Postmodern, the (Post-)Colonial, and the (Post-)Feminist*. Ed. Theo D'Haen and Hans Bertels. Rodopi: Amsterdam, 1994. 255–73.

Olster, Stacey. "When You're a (Nin)jette, You're a (Nin)jette All the Way—Or Are You?: Female Filmmaking in *Vineland*." *The Vineland Papers: Critical Takes on Pynchon's Novel*. Ed. Geoffrey Green, Donald J. Greiner, and Larry McCaffery. Normal: Dalkey Archive Press, 1994. 119–34.

Pérez-Llantada Auría, Carmen. "Questing for Social Justice: The Role of Woman in Thomas Pynchon's Narrative." *Estudios de la mujer en el ámbito de los países de habla inglesa*. Vol. 1. Madrid: Universidad Complutense, 1994. 275–87.

Sciolino, Martina. "Objects of the Postmodern 'Masters': Subject-in-Simulation/Woman-in-Effect." *Men Writing the Feminine: Literature, Theory, and the Question of Gender*. Albany: SUNY Press, 1994. 157–71.

1995

Berger, James. "Cultural Trauma and the 'Timeless Burst': Pynchon's Revision of Nostalgia in *Vineland*." *Postmodern Culture* 5.3 (1995). DOI: 10.1353/pmc.1995.0020.

1996

Chapman, Wes. "Male Pro-Feminism and the Masculinist Gigantism of *Gravity's Rainbow*." *Postmodern Culture* 6.3 (1996). DOI: 10.1353/pmc.1996.0017.

1997

Publication of *Mason & Dixon*

Bergh, Patricia A. "(De)constructing the Image: Thomas Pynchon's Postmodern Woman." *Journal of Popular Culture* 30.4 (1997): 1–12.

Hawthorne, Mark D. "A 'Hermaphrodite Sort of Deity': Sexuality, Gender, and Gender Blending in Thomas Pynchon's *V.*" *Studies in the Novel* 29.1 (1997): 74–93.

1998

Burns, Christy L. "Parody and Postmodern Sex: Humor in Thomas Pynchon and Tama Janowitz." *Performing Gender and Comedy: Theories, Texts and Contexts*. Ed. Shannon Hengen. Amsterdam: Gordon and Breach, 1998. 149–66.

Den Tandt, Christophe. "Management and Chaos: Masculinity and the Corporate World From Naturalism to *Gravity's Rainbow*." *Pynchon Notes* 42–43 (1998): 73–90.

Mattessich, Stefan. "Imperium, Misogyny, and Postmodern Parody in Thomas Pynchon's *V.*" *ELH* 65.2 (1998): 503–21.

1999

Hamill, John. "Looking Back on Sodom: Sixties Sadomasochism in *Gravity's Rainbow*." *Critique: Studies in Contemporary Fiction* 41.1 (1999): 53–70.

Hawthorne, Mark D. "'Hi! My Name Is Arnold Snarb!' Homosexuality in *The Crying of Lot 49*." *Pynchon Notes* 44–45 (1999): 65–81.

Maus, Derek. "Kneeling before the Fathers' Wand: Violence, Eroticism and Paternalism in Thomas Pynchon's *V.* and J. M. Coetzee's *Dusklands*." *Journal of Literary Studies* 15.1–2 (1999): 195–217.

Moran, Jay P. "How Is Pynchon Related to the Law?" *Oklahoma City University Law Review* 24.3 (1999): 449–70.

Pérez-Llantada Auría, Carmen. "The Escaping Presence of the Female in the Novels of Thomas Pynchon." *Cuadernos de investigación filológica* 25 (1999): 239–51.

2000

Hawthorne, Mark D. "Homoerotic Bonding as Escape from Heterosexual Responsibility in Pynchon's *Slow Learner*." *Style* 34.3 (2000): 512–28.

Kocela, Christopher. "Re-Stenciling Lesbian Fetishism in Pynchon's *V.*" *Pynchon Notes* 46–49 (2000): 105–30.

Maxwell, Marilyn. "Thomas Pynchon." *Male Rage, Female Fury: Gender and Violence in Contemporary American Fiction*. Lanham: University Press of America, 2000. 115–88.

O'Donnell, Patrick. "Engendering Paranoia." *Latent Destinies: Cultural Paranoia and Contemporary U.S. Narrative*. Durham: Duke University Press, 2000. 77–110.

2001

McHugh, Patrick. "Cultural Politics, Postmodernism, and White Guys: Affect in *Gravity's Rainbow*." *College Literature* 28.2 (2001): 1–28.

2002

Blaine, Diana Y. "Seeing Red: The Female Body and Periodic Renewal." Review of *The Bleeding of America: Menstruation as Symbolic Economy in Pynchon, Faulkner, and Morrison*, by Dana Medoro. *Pynchon Notes* 50–51 (2002): 154–57.

Medoro, Dana. "Thomas Pynchon: Blood, Tears, and War." *The Bleeding of America: Menstruation as Symbolic Economy in Pynchon, Faulkner, and Morrison*. Westport: Greenwood Press, 2002. 15–70.

Parry, Sally. "Catching the War: Jessica Swanlake's Brief Liberation." *Pynchon Notes* 50–51 (2002): 97–107.

2003

Collado-Rodríguez, Francisco. "Tracking the Female Energy of *V.*: Glimpses of the Pynchonian Project." *Nor Shall Diamond Die: American Studies in Honour of Javier Coy*. Ed. Carme Manual and Paul Scott Derrick. Valencia: University of Valencia Press, 2003. 71–77.

Fitzpatrick, Kathleen. "The Clockwork Eye: Technology, Woman, and the Decay of the Modern in Thomas Pynchon's *V.*" *Thomas Pynchon: Reading from the Margins*. Ed. Niran Abbas. Madison: Fairleigh Dickinson University Press, 2003. 91–107.

Hatooka, Keita. "'I Am Not She, but a Representation': Feminism, Gothicism, and the Politics of *Mason & Dixon*." *Geibun-Kenkyu Journal of Arts and Letters* 84.6 (2003): 163–77.

Holton, Robert. "'Closed Circuit': The White Male Predicament in Pynchon's Early Stories." *Thomas Pynchon: Reading from the Margins*. Ed. Niran Abbas. Madison: Fairleigh Dickinson University Press, 2003. 37–50.

Medoro, Dana. "Menstruation and Melancholy: *The Crying of Lot 49*." *Thomas Pynchon: Reading from the Margins*. Ed. Niran Abbas. Madison: Fairleigh Dickinson University Press, 2003. 71–90.

Ostrander, Madeline. "Awakening to the Physical World: Ideological Collapse and Ecofeminist Resistance in *Vineland*." *Thomas Pynchon: Reading from the Margins*. Ed. Niran Abbas. Madison: Fairleigh Dickinson University Press, 2003. 122–38.

Sears, Julie Christine. "Black and White Rainbows and Blurry Lines: Sexual Deviance/Diversity in *Gravity's Rainbow* and *Mason & Dixon*." *Thomas Pynchon: Reading from the Margins*. Ed. Niran Abbas. Madison: Fairleigh Dickinson University Press, 2003. 108–21.

2004

Kinsley, Alexia. "Making Sense of the Obscene and Scatological in Thomas Pynchon's *Gravity's Rainbow*." *Philological Review* 30.1 (2004): 39–57.

Lynd, Margaret. "Science, Narrative, and Agency in *Gravity's Rainbow*." *Critique: Studies in Contemporary Fiction* 46.1 (2004): 63–80.

2006

Publication of *Against the Day*

Stockton, Sharon. "The Disappearing Female Body and the New Worker: John Barth, William Gibson, Neal Stephenson, Nicholson Baker, and Thomas Pynchon." *The Economics of Fantasy: Rape in Twentieth-Century Literature*. Columbus: Ohio State University Press, 2006. 120–48.

2009

Publication of *Inherent Vice*

Collado-Rodríguez, Francisco. "No Either/Or: The Stagnation of Forces in Pynchon's Universe: Ethical and Gender Undecidability in Two Spanish Cases." *Pynchon Notes* 56–57 (2009): 46–56.

Hogue, W. Lawrence. "The Privileged, Sovereign, Euro-American (Male), Post/Modern Subject and Its Construction of the Other: Thomas Pynchon's *V.* and Paul Auster's *The New York Trilogy*." *Postmodern American Literature and Its Other*. Urbana: University of Illinois Press, 2009. 42–93.

2010

Hite, Molly. "'Fun Actually Was Becoming Quite Subversive': Herbert Marcuse, the Yippies, and the Value System of *Gravity's Rainbow*." *Contemporary Literature* 51.4 (2010): 677–702.

Lawson, Jessica. "'The Real and Only Fucking Is Done on Paper': Penetrative Readings and Pynchon's Sexual Text." *Against the Grain: Reading Pynchon's Counternarratives*. Ed. Sascha Pöhlmann. Amsterdam: Rodopi, 2010. 231–49.

2011

Freer, Joanna. "Is Pynchon a Feminist?" *Berfrois*, 9 June 2011, www.berfrois.com/2011/06/thomas-pynchon-relative-feminist-by-joanna-freer. Accessed 16 Nov. 2017.

Severs, Jeffrey. "'The abstractions she was instructed to embody': Women, Capitalism, and Artistic Representation in *Against the Day*." *Pynchon's* Against the Day: *A Corrupted Pilgrim's Guide*. Ed. Jeffrey Severs and Christopher Leise. Newark: University of Delaware Press, 2011. 215–38.

2012

Miller, Emma V. "The Naming of Oedipa Maas: Feminizing the Divine Pursuit of Knowledge in Thomas Pynchon's *The Crying of Lot 49*." *Orbit: A Journal of American Literature* 1.1 (2012). DOI: 10.7766/orbit.v1.1.12.

2013

Publication of *Bleeding Edge*

Hardack, Richard. "Revealing the Bidder: The Forgotten Lesbian in Pynchon's *The Crying of Lot 49*." *Textual Practice* 27.4 (2013): 565–95.

2014

Freer, Joanna. "Feminism Moderate and Radical in *The Crying of Lot 49* and *Vineland*: Pynchon and the Women's Movement." *Thomas Pynchon and American Counterculture*. New York: Cambridge University Press, 2014. 126–56.

Kolbuszewska, Zofia. "'Between Hell and Purgatory': From Baudelaire's Allegory of Commodified Female to Pynchon's Neobaroque in *V*." *Profils americains: Thomas Pynchon*. Ed. Gilles Chamerois and Bénédicte Choirier-Fryd. Montpellier: Presses universitaires de la Méditerranée, 2014. 271–84.

2015

Cook, Simon. "Manson Chicks and Microskirted Cuties: Pornification in Thomas Pynchon's *Inherent Vice*." *Textual Practice* 29.6 (2015): 1143–64.

2016

Rolls, Albert. "'A Dual Man [and Oeuvre], Aimed Two Ways at Once': The Two Directions of Pynchon's Life and Thought." *Orbit: A Journal of American Literature* 4.1 (2016). DOI: 10.16995/orbit.188.

Sweeney, Susan. "Gothic Traces in the Metaphysical Detective Story: The Female Sleuth in Pynchon's *The Crying of Lot 49* and Gibson's *Pattern Recognition*." *Orbit: A Journal of American Literature* 4.2 (2016). DOI: 10.16995/orbit.195.

2017

Franco, Marie. "Queer Postmodern Practices: Sex and Narrative in *Gravity's Rainbow*." *Twentieth-Century Literature* 63.2 (2017): 141–66.

SECTION 1 Origins

When Pynchon Was a Boys' Club
V. and Midcentury Mystifications of Gender

MOLLY HITE

Pynchon in the Academy

In 1982, my first year as a faculty member at Cornell, I taught a course called "The Postwar American Novel." By the middle of the semester I realized I was in trouble, not because I had chosen as many books written by women as by men (such audacity was fairly new in the Cornell English Department, which specialized in radical literary theory coupled with unquestioned adherence to a roster of books called "the canon"), but because the women in the class were furious at the books by men. My choices were quite ordinary—Kerouac, Ellison, Roth, Bellow, and Pynchon's *V.* But the women were enraged by the sexism in these novels, something I had taken as a matter of course.

My initial inclination was to say, "Of course they're sexist, these are the fifties and sixties, what did you expect?" But the overt misogyny of only a few decades earlier was a huge shock to these young women. They did not see gender discrimination, ridicule, and paranoia as historical phenomena to acknowledge and note studiously; they saw the attitudes toward women in these novels as impinging on *them*—and of course they were right. I had to face up to the fact that books I had loved and written about were in many respects impossible for these young women to absorb. And their resistance made the sexism of a whole society more visible to me. I grew up during the period I was teaching, after all, and despite my later participation in the feminist movement, on several different levels I was still used to the discriminatory ideologies that penetrated even the most serious literary fiction during the postwar period. Ironically for me, the novel my female students seemed to hate most was my favorite, *V.* (1963). I had to acknowledge that Pynchon too was a product of his era, an era that in many respects he represented satirically but without seriously questioning norms of gender identity and behavior.[1]

At the same time, I was beginning to contend with the enormous gender imbalance among Pynchon critics. At the science and literature and MLA panels on Pynchon, women were used to being a tiny minority. Usually there would be five or so of us in a packed conference room (Pynchon studies was a hot item from the beginning) and forty or fifty men. The panels were almost entirely made up of men. *Pynchon Notes* was edited by men and might have one contribution by a woman every other issue or so. Collections of critical essays contained mostly articles by men. Women who were writing and publishing about Pynchon also had the experience of being overlooked even after our work was published and had received excellent reviews. I remember having an epistolary argument with a *Pynchon Notes* editor in the 1980s about a list he had drawn up of the best essays on Pynchon to date. None, of course, were by women.

My anecdotes aren't unusual or even particularly outrageous. At that stage in academic history women were always being passed over, not because our male colleagues were working consciously to keep us out of prevailing discourses but because we were underrepresented among literary faculty and they honestly could not see us. Among Pynchon critics the situation was extreme. Pynchon was widely conceded to be a "guys' writer," first because he used scientific metaphors, and science was widely understood to be a "guy thing"; second because his scope was world-historical rather than romantic and/or domestic, which is what most twentieth-century scholars at that point saw as the concerns of the "women's novel"; third because there was a lot of increasingly kinky sex in Pynchon's novels, and it was considered inappropriate for female critics to write or, worse, talk about such matters; and fourth, especially in the case of *V.*, because for all its subtlety and irony Pynchon's writing itself represented without any trace of self-awareness these same trivializing and effacing tendencies—a point to which I return.

The existence of the Pynchon boys' club became especially evident at the 1991 MLA session on *Vineland* (1990), which I had proposed as the first overtly feminist panel on Pynchon, on the premise that *Vineland* was his first feminist book. The three female speakers wore black tops and pants (the pants were still a little radical for the MLA at that time) in emulation of the ninjettes of the novel. I remember sitting on the podium and watching the room fill: 80 percent male, then 90 percent male . . . until it became clear that despite having "feminism" in the title of the session, the room was packed with the usual Pynchon men and maybe two or three other women. Well and good, I thought: we were here to introduce women's issues into Pynchon studies, so we'd bring the guys into the big questions of deceit and betrayal and sexual obsession and family and community in this novel whose main characters were indisputably female. But the logic of the science guys as usual prevailed. Every one of the (exclusively male) questioners ignored all our points about gender and sexuality and instead asked Kate Hayles about a passage in the novel distinguishing between analogue and digital technologies.

While that session did little to disrupt the sense of Pynchon studies as a boys' club, *Vineland* does mark a change in Pynchon's authorial attitude toward women. I have argued in "Feminist Theory and the Politics of *Vineland*" that it is not only a novel centering on three female characters and influenced by certain feminist writings but also a novel that imagines what it would be like to *be* Frenesi or DL and opens up that space of identification to readers, providing a much different kind of access to female characters than in most cases in the previous novels.[2] These *Vineland* characters have a complex interiority and agency. In my experience, female readers especially find them *interesting*—and in class we sometimes air our suspicions that Pynchon himself found them more interesting than most of his previous major female characters. Interiority and agency are attributes that are muted in the depiction of such "feminine" "good" women from the first three novels as Rachel Owlglass, Paola Maijstraal, Oedipa Maas, Jessica Swanlake, and Leni Pökler. Lack of agency is most obviously manifested as a lack of explicable motivation. Despite their often central status as symbols and as functions moving the plot along, these women display cognitive processes and desires that are simple, self-evident, and wholly unlike the reasoning and desires of the male characters, however flawed the latter are (and of course these male flaws are dynamic and central to *V.*). Women, bless their alien little natures, are just like that. My sense is that Pynchon has always done better with women who are not wholly "good" in the novel's own terms, which in these cases seem to be the terms of a particularly midcentury masculine fantasy. Only with *Gravity's Rainbow* (1973), in characters like Katje Borgesius and Greta Erdmann, neither of them nice or good or otherwise idealized in the novel's own terms, do I find more development of and space for reader identification.

Gender at Midcentury

I do not know whether the change in Pynchon's representation of female characters led to more female critics contributing to Pynchon studies. I do know that *Vineland* was the first of Pynchon's novels that I had no trouble teaching to young women, both undergraduates and graduates. I could say that the novels Pynchon published after 1990 had many elements of feminist awareness in them, but it would be more accurate to say that from *Vineland* on there is a dwindling of a *pre*feminist attitude from the postwar period when Pynchon was coming to maturity and, not incidentally, beginning work on *V.* It is important to remember that during that time, and in fact up into the 1970s, there *was* no feminism in general public discourse. I mean not only that very few people, most of us women, read and talked about the theorizations of gender inequality that were coming out of the various second-wave feminist movements but also that we lacked the language for the kinds of subordination, condescension, and violation that we experienced on a daily basis. For instance, widespread use of the word "sexism" to refer to discrimination against women dates to only the late 1960s. In the misogynist culture of the 1950s and 1960s any objection to gender norms was interpreted as personal and pathological. With our current acknowledgment of transsexual rights and gender fluidity it is hard to explain why being told you "wanted a penis" was a stunning putdown, but part of the widespread misogyny, which was also an extreme and dangerous homophobia (another word that did not exist), involved a paranoid policing of gender and sexual boundaries.[3]

In this atmosphere of suspicion and defensiveness about what men and women are, do and want, Thomas Pynchon was writing his extraordinary first novel *V.* The style and structure of *V.* are so sophisticated, authoritative, and daring that as critics we can easily assume that Pynchon emerged into the public gaze fully formed, with exactly the same sensibility that we find in *Vineland* or *Bleeding Edge* (2013), to pick the two most obvious female-centered examples.[4] But in his first book the author inevitably reproduced at least some of the values of his contemporary society.

If *V.* itself seems fully mature, the letters and drafts of this novel now in the Harry Ransom Center reveal a young man shaped by his time and place: sometimes callow, sometimes pretentious, sometimes engaged in projects with frat-boy sensibilities (we see those in his undergraduate story "Mortality and Mercy in Vienna," which features recently graduated partiers who speak and act in ways foreshadowing *V.*'s Whole Sick Crew), often referring reverently to former professors (white, male) and, most endearingly, given to elaborately constructed puns. Because Pynchon's first novel comes out of this frame of mind and historical period—out of the writer's youth and also the strange Cold War culture of the United States—it is a fascinating site for tracking prevailing ideologies of gender.

With its haunting quest theme and satiric evocations of New York bohemian life in the 1950s, *V.* was an instant success in U.S. high culture, reviewed as "a brilliant and turbulent first novel" in the *New York Times Book Review* and predicted to be "one of the very best works of the century" by the *Atlantic Review*.[5] But for all its originality, the novel also reproduced some of the most extreme attitudes of a time in which gender politics were so emotionally fraught and passionately promoted that they seemed to be part of a metaphysics in which qualities attributed to men and women were eternal and innate, if often self-contradictory. Differences between men and women, in high culture fiction in particular, were regarded as both self-evident and mysterious. A similar mysteriousness permeated literary ideas about homosexuality and race.[6]

The central source of mystery was supposed to be women. Cold War literary culture took very seriously Freud's famous observation that "the great question that has never been answered, and which I have not yet been able to answer, despite my thirty years of research into the feminine soul, is 'What does a woman want?'" (421).[7] *V.* of course is a novel about a mysterious woman whose avatars appear at key historical moments in the late nineteenth century and twentieth century. Her association with the archaic, powerful, and enigmatic goddesses chronicled by early twentieth-century popularizers of a new discipline, anthropology, is noted as a scholarly quest in *V.* ("in the tradition of [James Frazer's] *The Golden Bough* or [Robert Graves's] *The White Goddess*" [59]).[8] In *V.*, this mythic woman is more a force than a rational actor, personifying and desiring a historical movement toward decadence, the inanimate, and violence rather than being its cause. She is also identified with femininity. For instance, one character presented as a possible manifestation of V., Victoria Wren, appears to see herself as "embodying a feminine principle, acting as a complement to all this bursting, explosive male energy. Inviolate and calm, she watched the spasms of wounded bodies, the fair of violent death, framed and staged, it seemed, for her alone in that tiny square" (224). This still-familiar representation of the feminine is most important, and most mysterious, because she is conceived as the necessary complement to mysterious masculinity, with its "bursting, explosive male energy." Enigmatically passive, Victoria observes "the fair of violent death" as if it were "framed and staged [. . .] for her alone." A long tradition of gender theorizing mystifies women in this way, treating silence and passivity as the complement of male violence and in many respects its enabler. This V.'s presence is implicitly damaging to men, although by the logic of the plot it is impossible to specify how, exactly, she is the agent of their destruction.

I come back to the mysterious aspect of female gendering and Pynchon's brilliant use of this trope in *V.* I want to look first, however, at one of the ways another celebrated midcentury writer mystified not only femininity but masculinity, and not only in his fiction but in the interest of describing the overwhelming superiority of male writers. In his 1959 collection of short writings *Advertisements for Myself* Norman Mailer announced, "I have a terrible confession to make. I have nothing to say about any of the talented women who write today." He went on—"I can only say that the sniffs I get from the ink of the women are always fey, old-hat, Quaintsy Goysy, tiny, too dykily psychotic, crippled, creepish, fashionable, frigid, outer-Baroque, *maquillé* in mannequin's whimsy, or else bright and stillborn. [. . .] [T]his verdict may be taken fairly as the twisted tongue of a soured taste, at least by those readers who do not share with me the ground of departure—that a good novelist can do without everything but the remnant of his balls" (472).

Mailer's catalogue of the qualities of women's writing is deliberately over the top, with vividly metaphoric descriptions emphasizing infantilism and triviality, sexual dysfunction or aberration, outdatedness or trendiness, psychic disability or perversity ("dykily psychotic"), cosmetic enhancement, and—tucked into a more general disparagement of preciosity—the failure to be Jewish ("Quaintsy Goysy"). Despite the exuberant hyperbole, however, Mailer is in no way parodying himself or a culture of extreme misogyny. In particular, he is not quite offering a metaphor when he concludes that "a good novelist can do without everything but the remnant of his balls." "Remnant" alludes to a truism of midcentury America that women's goal in life is to castrate men. For Mailer, balls—even if badly mutilated by women—are necessary to be a "good novelist."

Pynchon came of age, then, at a time when women were not simply mythologized as constraining, conservative forces pitted against the freedom, adventurousness and irreverence of men (in the long American tradition of Huck Finn escaping Aunt Sally and lighting out for the territories) but were often represented as actively malevolent powers. Further, both male ability and female inconsequence or hostility were conceived in terms of sexual body parts and functions. So in *V.* we find the counterpart to Mailer's male novelist with his necessary testicles in the "authoress" whose own novels are associated by simile with menstrual blood: "His wife was an authoress. Her novels—three to date—ran a thousand pages each and like sanitary napkins had gathered an immense and faithful sisterhood of consumers. There'd even evolved somehow a kind of sodality or fan club that sat around, read from her books and discussed her Theory" (131). The self-evident insignificance of this writer's novels and "Theory" (the capitalization indicates pretentiousness) is gestured at by words like the disparaging "authoress," the ironically elevated "sodality" (religious fellowship) contrasted with the low-culture trivialization "fan club" to characterize her readers, and most of all by the phrase "like sanitary napkins" to characterize the quality of her books. Exclusively female, her readership is further degraded by its association with waste of the female reproductive system.

The "authoress," named, in a characteristic Pynchon flourish, Mafia Winsome, is not only a mediocre practitioner of Pynchon's own craft but embodies the entrapment that in mid-twentieth-century mythology makes even the common woman a menace. In an interchange with Benny Profane she emerges as sexually dangerous to men because she is a constraining and— even more threatening—containing force: "A woman wants to feel like a woman," Mafia says, "is all. She wants to be taken, penetrated, ravished. But more than that she wants to enclose the man." Profane perceives the danger in "enclose" and imagines being caught "[w]ith spiderwebs woven of yo-yo string: a net or trap" (313–14).

In this scene the passivity so central to postwar notions of the feminine is itself a snare, with the woman who demands to be "taken, penetrated, ravished" suddenly reversed in her role, transformed from object of sexual conquest into entrapper and potential castrator. Profane sees her as a spider enticing him from the center of her web.

The Good Woman

Mafia provides a tautological description of her desire—"[a] woman wants to feel like a woman"—in the process suggesting that "woman" is an identity that must be achieved.[9] In her case, feeling like a woman entails using passivity to surround, hold, and perhaps maim. But the female characters defined as (generally) good women are also given to describing how it feels to be a woman and, more generally, what women are, as if it were central to their characterization to embody an essence. In such a deft and generally pitch-perfect novel it is jarring to encounter Rachel Owlglass lecturing to Profane in her characteristic mode of tolerance, maternal solicitousness, and satisfaction with her subordinate role. Toward the end of the novel she closes an argument with him:

> "You have to grow up," she finally said. "That's all: my own unlucky boy, didn't you ever think maybe ours is an act too? We're older than you, we lived inside you once: the fifth rib, closest to the heart. We learned all about it then. After that it had to become our game to nourish a heart you all believe is hollow though we know different. Now you all live inside us, for nine months, and whenever you decide to come back after that."
>
> He was snoring, for real.
>
> "Dear, how pompous I'm getting. Good night..." And she fell asleep to have cheerful, brightly colored, explicit dreams about sexual intercourse. (410–11)

Profane, in the name of schlemihlhood, rejects this offer of superabundant nurture, and the overall values of the novel indicate that he is stupid and childish to do so. Indeed, in terms of midcentury gendered values Rachel is exactly what a good woman should be, the fulfillment of enlightened masculine desire. Her claims about her caretaking nature are in many respects the restrained or "soft" version of enclosing, castrating female potential. Precisely in her essentially good-woman traits, she insinuates a threat that Profane spends most of the novel evading. She is endlessly accommodating, accepting his repeated rejections and playing mother to the boy wanderer who in his own good time ought to become the adult partner. She embraces the Genesis parable of woman as rib, here explained as guarding the man's heart.[10] She explicitly associates her role as lover with maternality ("Now you all live inside us, for nine months, and whenever you decide to come back after that"), a particularly potent combination for an assault on embattled manhood (as the arguments of fiction writer and essayist Philip Wylie, which I take up shortly, suggest). And when Profane falls asleep in the middle of her nurturing she makes fun of herself for offering sage advice ("Dear, how pompous I'm getting") and falls asleep along with him, compliantly having attractive and unthreatening erotic dreams ("cheerful, brightly colored, explicit" and involving mere "sexual intercourse" rather than anything kinkier and/or more damaging).

Although in the novel's terms the good woman carries overt value, in this passage and elsewhere schlemihlhood is represented in a way intended to make it attractive to readers. Most of the present-day sections of the book deal with the roistering of Profane, Pig Bodine, and other young men, who are contrasted to female characters who threaten to confine them or make them grow up. *V.* tries to have it both ways, making schlemihlhood part of the decadent trend toward irresponsibility and inhumanity—"offhand I'd say I haven't learned a goddamn thing" (506)—while also describing the schlemihl's adventures with enthusiasm and humor.[11]

Another good woman who delivers a disquisition on womanhood, or in this case girlhood, is the Maltese Paola Maijstral. In her unexplained disguise as the African American prostitute Ruby, she offers succor to the jazzman McClintic Sphere. When he asks, "Do you ever dig what I'm trying to say," she gives a response that like Rachel's explains her own nature and desire in terms of what the man wants: "'On the horn I don't,' she answered, honest enough, 'a girl doesn't understand. All she does is feel. I feel what you play, like I feel what you need when you're inside me. Maybe they're the same thing. McClintic, I don't know. You're kind to me, what is it you want?'" (306). Like "a woman" in Mafia's and Rachel's disquisitions, in Paola's dictum "a girl" is a somewhat exotic species, incapable of understanding jazz, and perhaps all communication, but able to feel—another kind of relation to reality, perhaps akin to the modes of interaction more often associated with nonhuman domesticated animals. A girl's—or presumably a woman's—capacities, like her desires, are impossible for a man to understand, although he can pronounce on them or, as in this case, write fiction about them.

Paola is a character developed in several contexts, most importantly in the wartime diary of her father, Fausto Maijstral, where she becomes so associated with the mysterious woman V. that she seems to be one of her avatars.[12] In the present-day sections, however, she exists only in the context of men: Profane, the Whole Sick Crew, Sphere, Pig Bodine, Rooney Winsome, and, least appealingly, her violent husband, the very minor, mainly offstage character Pappy Hod, to whom—again without explanation—she returns in the end, offering herself as a faithful Penelope who will sit "home in Norfolk, faithful, and spin. Spin a yarn for your home-coming present" (492).

Rape and Race

Rachel and Paola are both presented as good women—Rachel even sings a blues song to that effect (46–47)—but still, the ways they satisfy male desires also make them threatening as potential constrainers and entrappers, like the negatively coded Mafia Winsome. In the gender lore of postwar America, any woman, however good, could be associated with mind-deadening conformity and conservatism, qualities threatening the freedom and creativity of men—and guaranteeing the mediocrity of female artists, as Mailer's diatribe suggests. One writer most influential in articulating this everyday misogyny was Philip Wylie, whose 1942 best-seller *Generation of Vipers* put the word "Momism" into general usage and placed the word at the center of a theory drawing together various sources of antiwoman resentment, disdain, and fear. According to Wylie, Mom was an object of worship everywhere in the United States, and every American woman, even the youngest (who in her Cinderella aspect lured men to their doom) was Mom, desiring to catch, tame, and castrate men by whatever means she could, most obviously marriage: "Mom had already shaken him out of that notion of being a surveyor in the Andes which had bloomed in him when he was nine years old, so there was nothing left to do, anyway, but to take a stockroom job in the hairpin factory and try to work up to the vice-presidency. Thus the women of America raped the men, not sexually, unfortunately, but morally, since neuters come hard by morals" (188).

The closing pronouncement of this passage, accusing women of metaphorically raping men, is part of a more general mystification of rape during this period, in which women (in various versions) "brought it on themselves" or "liked it," so that rape was always to an extent presumed to be a consensual act in which the woman for some reason (shame at her own sexual desire or more of that hankering to castrate) disavowed her own participation. One of the most disturbing scenes in the present-day sections of *V.* occurs when Josefina, the sister of Profane's Puerto Rican Alligator Patrol buddies, is found after having been raped by a street gang, "having in a way asked for it" (152). "Angel opened a door at the end of the hall and for half a second Profane saw Fina through it lying on an old army cot, naked, hair in disarray, smiling. Her eyes had become hollowed as Lucille's, that night on the pool table. Angel turned and showed all his teeth. 'Can't come in,' he said, 'wait.' The door closed behind him and soon they heard him hitting her. Angel might have been satisfied only with her life. Profane didn't know how deep the code ran" (160).

Fina, hollow-eyed but smiling, embodies the ambiguities of the rape victim in midcentury consciousness. Even more troubling is Angel's reaction: he assaults her rather than the perpetrators, and although we don't know whether he kills her, since Profane leaves, the possibility of an honor killing is real, offered as a requirement of a Puerto Rican "code": "Angel might have been satisfied only with her life." Further, apparently not only Profane (for whom turning away is just another affirmation of his schlemihlhood) but also the text acquiesces: the scene is presented as the tragedy of Fina's undoing, with a dénouement of murder. In this scene not only gender but also ethnicity seems to work according to inscrutably contradictory laws.

The most violent and detailed rape scenes occur in the sections of "Mondaugen's story" about the unnamed young soldier who participates in the extermination of the Herero people in German South West Africa. This piece of writing is a tour de force, the story of a young man's euphoric discovery of his capacity for rape, torture, and murder without any sense of moral violation. Narrated only from the young man's point of view, this story represents both rape and murder as consensual, and here, even more disconcertingly than in the scene of Fina's rape, there is no implied criticism, no tonal cue that might signal a larger context in which the acts and feelings described are understood to be repellant. Instead, the narration presents native Africans who experience not only rape but also murder as sexual: "Later, toward dusk, there was one Herero girl, sixteen or seventeen years old, for the platoon; and Firelily's rider was last. After he'd had her he must have hesitated a moment between sidearm and bayonet. She actually smiled then; pointed to both, and began to shift her hips lazily in the dust. He used both" (287). Pynchon clearly is not presenting such events as authorially sanctioned, acts we can take with the kind of erotic pleasure the point-of-view character does. Within the schema of the novel they can be ticked off as instances of degeneration, decadence, descent into the inanimate, and so on. But it seems important that they also exceed these categories, gaining a kind of pathos and intensity that points ahead to the sadomasochistic games of Blicero, Gottfried, and Katje in *Gravity's Rainbow*. This kind of excessiveness, always associated with the overdetermined female figure V., is what takes the novel far beyond the gender mystifications of its surrounding culture.

Before further exploring this excessiveness, I want first, however, to look briefly at *V.*'s most prominent mystifications of racial difference, which were part of an often well-meaning white intellectual culture at midcentury. We get a passing glimpse of the theme of racial discrimination when the white southerner Rooney Winsome reflects on how his overtly racist wife presumes that he, too, hates black people simply because he uses a deeply disparaging word to describe them. "[S]he was in nearly total ignorance about the Southern feeling toward Negroes. She used 'nigger' as a term of hatred, not apparently being capable herself of anything more demanding than sledgehammer emotions. Winsome was too upset to tell her it was not a matter of love, hate, like or not like so much as an inheritance you lived with. He'd let it slide, like everything else" (132). The mystification here of the traditional relation of southern white people to southern black people amounts to the idea that Rooney views the people he would call "nigger" with something more complicated than "sledgehammer emotions." Instead of these emotions he experiences the relationship, or perhaps black people themselves, as "an inheritance you lived with." The passage explains very little, but it echoes the kinds of bland truism that prominent southern whites often used, especially in opposition to the civil rights movement, to insist that the segregation and subordination of the "Negro" was part of a long, largely benign tradition dating back to slavery, which outsiders couldn't be expected to understand. Although the explanation is focalized entirely by Winsome, the third-person narrator never intervenes with critical commentary or tonal shifts that might nudge readers to acknowledge how self-serving this cozily privileged version of white supremacy is.[13] Even in the North this kind of casual racist statement was not always understood to be racist at all—except of course by black people.

Yet Pynchon also develops the character of the African American jazzman McClintic Sphere to a significant degree, giving him both a prominent place in the present-day sections of *V.* and the status of a point-of-view character who offers thematically important opinions on how values like hipness and coolness exist in tension with a fundamental mandate to care. The research of Luc Herman and John Krafft shows, however, that Sphere initially had a much larger role in the novel and that Pynchon's editor at Lippincott persuaded him to make cuts, which had the effect of reducing the black musician to a secondary character. In this case, Pynchon seems less to have internalized the mores of midcentury literary culture than to have followed advice based on the publisher's ultimate interest in making clear to critics and readers that *V.* belonged in the category of high-culture novel.

Herman and Krafft's research reveals how Pynchon's editor, J. Corlies Smith, prompted Pynchon to play down Sphere because the black musician "strikes something of a false note in that he somehow leads the reader to believe that the Negro problem is going to become at least a side issue" (20). Smith's letter makes clear that from the editorial and marketing point of view in the early 1960s, a major black character who focalizes elements of the text could only exist *as* an emblem of the discrimination against him. According to this logic, to make him important would foreground his blackness and make it the primary point of the story. This attitude shows a peculiar kind of racism, one so wound up with contemporary aesthetic prohibitions that its illogic came off as a species of tact and good taste. It worked to keep black characters on the margins of fiction by members of the dominant culture. They could not appear prominently among white characters as friends, romantic interests, or fellow musicians, even though in the New York that is the setting for *V.*, such relations between black and white people were fairly common.

Gender as Enigma

What is most interesting to me about the conventions for thinking about and representing women during this period is that women are so negligible—and/or so powerful—that they don't and can't exist as human beings. By this I mean that the misogynist discourse on them gives them no interiority, no real point of view, and thus no motivations that make sense. Readers (female as well as male)—and I suspect the male author as well—do not imagine *being* any of the female characters. The young Pynchon followed these conventions, which of course were in the air he breathed as well as on the pages of authors he identified as being most important to him like Jack Kerouac—and Norman Mailer.

But it is precisely this convention of woman's unfathomability that provides the brilliant structural metaphor of *V.* The passage from Sidney Stencil's diary inaugurating his son's search for V. is "There is more behind and inside V. than any of us had suspected. Not who, but what: what is she. God grant that I may never be called upon to write the answer, either here or in any official report" (49). With this intimation that V. is so inscrutable that the figure is a what, rather than a who, V. assumes the incomprehensibility and implicit threat that American high culture imagines women as posing.

Pynchon was bequeathed this construct by his environment and his education, but he went on to enlarge the idea of mysterious, ominous womanhood into an amorphous but never abstract presence associated with violent incidents taking place in the late nineteenth century and first part of the twentieth. I say "associated with," because in her essential passivity V. is never cause or consequence. Indeed, as Stencil's memo suggests, in her fearful quiddity the "more" of her being overflows categories, continually threatening in the way that in *V.* even a good woman threatens, except in the form of radically different avatars and in amorphous, inhuman, apocalyptic ways.

NOTES

1. For discussion of masculinity in Pynchon's short stories see Holton.
2. I don't see Prairie as fully imagined, despite her centrality. Her two-dimensionality coexists with her passivity and her niceness, and to an extent both passivity and niceness are qualities limiting the possibilities for character development in the women Pynchon creates.
3. Of course, there was feminist activism and sophisticated theorizing about gender oppression in the U.S. and in many European countries during the late nine-

teenth and early twentieth centuries, revolving around the movement to give women the right to vote. Most of that history, however, had vanished into archives or had been trivialized away by the 1950s and 1960s: women who protested were silly and narcissistic or deluded about their own natures and capacities or culpably deviant, failing to accept the roles to which biology destined them either because of serious sexual dysfunction or mental illness.

4. Many readers insist that *The Crying of Lot 49* belongs in this list. I don't regard the book as feminist or even female-centric. Oedipa is not a developed character in terms of having an internal presence and a distinctive point of view—Pynchon makes gestures toward both qualities, but he is so devoted to parody and to the schematics of his most formulaic novel that she is barely credible as a human being. She is also in many ways sentimentalized, a figure of succor and even maternity, while also serving as a plot function in her role of questing hero.

5. Blurbs and quotations are from the cover of the 2009 Harper Perennial edition of *V.*

6. I use the phrase "high culture" in the sense it had in the 1950s and 60s, as a term referencing works of art that appealed to the educated tastes of an intellectual (and usually economic) elite. Like the boundary between male and female, the border between high and low culture was passionately and paranoiacally policed.

7. If you were a woman taking this sort of thing seriously, you spent a lot of time considering what you did want and wondering why it didn't seem unfathomable or even terribly different from what men wanted.

8. Pynchon was an undergraduate during a period when one dominant literary-critical method in the United States was the mythic or archetypal approach.

9. A major weapon of gender policing at the time was the notion of the "real woman"—used to denigrate in "You're not a *real* woman." Such a woman failed to live up, or down, to a standard that might be sexual but that also could cover other realms of pleasing, as I discuss in the cases of Rachel Owlglass and Paola Maijstraal.

10. This refers, of course, to the second version of human creation in Genesis. Pynchon seems to have made a rare slip by describing Rachel as being "older than you" but also as having "lived inside you once."

11. Holton is excellent on the predominance of the eternal boy, or man-on-the-run theme, in U.S. fiction after World War II (38–45).

12. She witnessed the dismantling of V. as the Bad Priest and ends up with one of the objects aligned with V., the disconcerting ivory comb (492).

13. Chapters 1 and 2 of my critical study *Woolf's Ambiguities* (2017) deal with the questions raised by tonal cues in free indirect discourse.

WORKS CITED

Freud, Sigmund. Letter to Marie Bonaparte. *Sigmund Freud: Life and Work*. Vol. 2. Ed. Ernest Jones. London: Hogarth, 1953. 421.

Herman, Luc, and John Krafft. "Race in Early Pynchon: Rewriting Sphere in *V.*" *Critique* 52.1 (2011): 17–29.

Hite, Molly. "Feminist Theory and the Politics of *Vineland*." *The* Vineland *Papers: Critical Takes on Pynchon's Novel*. Ed. Geoffrey Green, Donald J. Greiner, and Larry McCaffery. Normal: Dalkey Archive Press, 1993. 134–52.

———. *Woolf's Ambiguities: Tonal Modernism, Narrative Strategy, Feminist Precursors*. Ithaca, NY: Cornell University Press, 2017.

Holton, Robert. "'Closed Circuit': The White Male Predicament in Pynchon's Early
  Stories." *Thomas Pynchon: Reading from the Margins*. Ed. Niran Abbas. Madison:
  Fairleigh Dickinson University Press, 2003. 37–50.
Pynchon, Thomas. *V.* New York: Harper Perennial, 2009.
Mailer, Norman. *Advertisements for Myself*. New York: Signet, 1960.
Wylie, Philip. *A Generation of Vipers*. New York: Farrar and Rinehart, 1942.

SECTION 2 Gender Roles

From Hard Boiled to Over Easy
Reimagining the Noir Detective in *Inherent Vice* and *Bleeding Edge*

JENNIFER BACKMAN

When Michum Huehls states in his review of *Bleeding Edge* that "there is not a major Pynchon and a minor Pynchon, a literary Pynchon and a genre-fiction Pynchon" and that "there's not an early, postmodern Pynchon and a later, postpostmodern Pynchon" but instead "just Pynchon, standing astride the past fifty years of U.S. fiction" (862–63), he captures at the macro level what I hope to illustrate here at the micro: that Pynchon's two most recent novels, though "genre fiction" in the sense that they draw on the long tradition of noir detective stories, depart substantially from that genre and work to refine the same issues and themes Pynchon has addressed throughout his career. In this way, we can see noir as a substantive part of both texts rather than as simply an example of pastiche or spoof or a kind of wrangling device for an otherwise unruly plot.[1] In particular, I argue that *Inherent Vice* and *Bleeding Edge* feature a reworking of noir's central figure—the hard-boiled detective—and that in this reassessment of the noir detective, Pynchon presents a challenge to the rigid, confining masculinity on which the genre rests.

Presenting Doc Sportello and Maxine Tarnow as significant revisions to the hard-boiled identity requires first some agreement on—or at least clarification of—the basic elements of that identity. In his analysis of "the nation's most self-consciously masculine fiction" (2), Leonard Cassuto calls Dashiell Hammett's Sam Spade "the classic exemplar of the hard-boiled attitude" (152), noting that "Sam Spade is famously self interested" and "sexually adventurous, even sleeping with his own partner's wife," and that he "trusts no one fully, and most people not at all" (153). "The detectives of the originary generation of hard-boiled fiction" are, furthermore, "isolated" and "laconic" and characterized by "emotional austerity" (154, 98).[2] According to Sean McCann in *Gumshoe America*, "The heroes of the hard-boiled genre are notoriously far from communally minded" (45); "they are agents with ends in mind, and they pursue those ends by setting out to deceive, beguile, manipulate, and confuse other people," all while maintaining "chaste, professional autonomy" (112, 117).

Stephen F. Soitos describes the hard-boiled detective as "fatalistic, violent, and chauvinistic toward women" and as "a man of the streets, a professional" who speaks and acts "with American vernacular crudeness" (8–9).

To interpret the gendered elements of these broad qualities, I look to Christopher Breu's *Hard-Boiled Masculinities*, which draws on a range of texts from the pulp magazines of the 1920s to the works of Dashiell Hammett, Raymond Chandler, and Chester Himes, among others, to argue that noir fiction was "one of the dominant ways in which masculinity was fantasized in the interwar years" (1). According to Breu, the affectless and violent hard-boiled protagonist at the heart of noir is best viewed as a "resolutely negative cultural fantasy," created in response to fears surrounding corporate capitalism, race, and the growth of the female workforce. The masculinity embodied in the noir detective is then both "a social and a literary phenomenon, one that theorizes the subjective and the socioeconomical with equal attentiveness" (24).[3] In *Inherent Vice* and *Bleeding Edge*, Pynchon takes up these same concerns, using the noir form to comment on the connections between gendered "cultural fantasy" and the socioeconomic conditions of contemporary American culture. In both texts, this critique comes by way of manipulations of generic conventions, specifically through changes to the hard-boiled persona and to the detective's relationships. Pynchon's reassessment of these noir elements ultimately broadens the genre's narrow notion of toughness and provides much needed interiority and agency to female characters.

This is not to say that noir tropes are always used to advance some larger commentary or that Pynchon always makes significant changes to these tropes. Like Scott Macleod, I want to suggest that "Pynchon's narrative strategies [...] strike a delicate balance between instilling readerly familiarity while introducing elements of genre subversion" (117). Noir's secondary plot structures, gritty settings, and laconic narrative voice make appearances in both *Inherent Vice* and *Bleeding Edge*.[4] And while Pynchon ultimately privileges what I call the "over easy" over the "hard boiled" in his detectives, both Doc and Maxine do retain a number of hard-boiled qualities: both characters work primarily alone in a position outside the official police system; they get caught up in the messy muddle of their cases; they work primarily on instinct—though in typically comedic Pynchonian fashion, instead of relying on the gut for these instincts, Doc experiences "Doper's ESP" (215), something called "extrasensory chops" (129), a runny nose (202), and "dick feelings" (313), while Maxine's instincts are dependent on her "antennae" (146), an ability to "scan for spiritual malware" (72), and the "gotta go alarm" of her bladder (84).

The humor with which Pynchon approaches changes to the hard boiled is worth noting; over the course of *Inherent Vice*, Doc Sportello's ability to simultaneously be and not be hard boiled is unmistakably funny, and I think we can read this comedy as one way in which Pynchon challenges the masculinist fantasy surrounding the traditional noir detective persona. Doc's character is a play on the iconic hard-boiled gumshoe, whose "masculinity is embodied as both a physical quantity, one that can be measured in terms of active performance and embodied hardness, and a controlling, affectless personality" (Breu 68).[5]

From early in the novel, it is clear that Doc is frequently in less than total control of his functions. When he is confronted by Bigfoot Bjornsen outside Channel View Estates after being knocked out by an unknown assailant, the narrator tells us, "Doc went through the wearisome chore of getting vertical again, followed by details to be worked out such as remaining that way, trying to walk, so forth" (23). And it is only very rarely that Doc can be said to physically embody "hardness" or "active performance"—for example, "[i]t took only a step or two" of following Xandra into Dr. Blatnoyd's office at Golden Fang Enterprises "for him to dig that she'd logged more dojo hours in the year previous than he'd spent in front of the tube in his whole life" (168). Nor does it take long for the reader to realize that any "affectless" quality Doc possesses is likely a result of his near continuous enjoyment of recreational drugs. In refusing Doc these standard hard-boiled traits, Pynchon is having fun with a typically controlled, famously efficacious character. Making light of the genre's primary indicators of masculine toughness undermines their importance; it takes noir's male detective decisively out of the space of cultural fantasy and pushes him into the tenuous, fragile realities of everyday human life.

Pynchon's interest in playing with the gendered fantasies of noir is particularly visible in Doc's interactions with Shasta, who is immediately recognizable as a variation on the classic femme fatale character. However, contra Eleanor Gold's observation that "Shasta Fay is not a regular femme fatale" (305), I want to suggest that Shasta *is* in many ways the regular femme fatale and that Pynchon's choosing to figure her as such allows him to highlight the theme of cultural loss that runs through a substantial part of the novel as a whole. It is not until the end of the novel that she departs from type; for the most part, Pynchon uses key features of the standard (blatantly misogynistic) hard-boiled detective/femme fatale relationship to produce a cultural critique that is itself an extension of the kind frequently seen in traditional noir.

Doc and Shasta's relationship mirrors that of the traditional detective and femme fatale's in that it is primarily characterized by ambivalence—a constant tension between attraction and rejection; further, "the ambivalence evident in the hard-boiled male's contradictory desires simultaneously to possess and repudiate the femme fatale suggests that his preoccupation with her is structured by melancholia" (Breu 71). It is exactly this kind of melancholic nostalgia that animates Doc's initial interaction with Shasta: the contrast between the past and the present is consistently at the forefront of Doc's descriptions of her. He tells us, "Back when, she could go weeks without anything more complicated than a pout. Now she was laying some heavy combination of face ingredients on him that he couldn't read at all" (3). In Doc's view, the Shasta of the past is simple, almost childlike in her readability; the Shasta of present, by contrast, is unknowable. Doc's tendency to see Shasta through the lens of the past also structures the novel's opening lines: "She came along the alley and up the back steps the way she always used to. Doc hadn't seen her for over a year. Nobody had. Back then it was always sandals, bottom half of a flower-print bikini, faded Country Joe & the Fish T-shirt. Tonight she was all in flatland gear, hair a lot shorter than he remembered, looking just like she swore she'd never look" (1). All of Shasta's actions and choices here are filtered through comparison to the past, and his relaxed tone notwithstanding, Doc cannot conceal the note of anger that concludes his description; her appearance is a broken promise.

Familiarity with noir allows us to understand Doc's reaction to Shasta in this scene as conveying more than personal heartbreak or disappointment in Shasta herself. Because the femme fatale is "the gendered figure through which the hard-boiled male narrates a larger sense of cultural loss and betrayal" (Breu 71), Shasta's movement from the hippie innocence of sandals and beachwear to the "flatland gear" of short skirts and hair stands in for the end of an era. Doc projects his negative emotions about the changing world onto Shasta's changed style; instead of seeing her as a person with agency and a will of her own, he turns her into a repository for the anger, sadness, and worry he feels about the demise of the counterculture—his suspicion that "this dream of prerevolution was in fact doomed to end and the faithless money-driven world to reassert its control" (130). She is, to borrow Doug Haynes's language, one way in which "*Inherent Vice* dramatizes the shift occurring over those years, as the nation, and the world, moves from Fordism to its neoliberal successor" (4). In a time when "the declining California freak scene looks fragile as the habitat of a Pacific island" and "Doc can see the window of dissent is closing" (Haynes 4, 14), Shasta's femme fatale becomes the bearer of that lost innocence.[6]

Images of loss consolidate especially clearly around Shasta's sexuality, particularly in regard to Mickey Wolfmann, which provides further evidence that, as femme fatale, she "allegorizes all the forms of connection—economic, national, sexual, or racial—that the hard-boiled male disavows" (Breu 69). When she details her submissive position in her relationship with Mickey, Shasta articulates all of the authoritarian elements of 1970s America that Doc wishes to renounce. She explains, "He was just so powerful. Sometimes he could almost make you feel invisible. Fast, brutal, not what you'd call a considerate lover, an animal, actually, but Sloane adored that about him, and Luz—you could tell, we all did. It's so nice to be made to feel invisible that way sometimes . . . ," adding, "He might as well have been bringing me in on a leash. He kept me in these little microminidresses, never allowed me to wear anything underneath, just offering me to whoever wanted to stare. Or grab. Or sometimes he'd fix me up with his friend. And I'd have to do whatever they wanted...." (305). Shasta paints a picture here of a sexual availability inspired not by the free love values of the hippie movement but by a kind of misogynistic, controlling coercion. In doing so, Shasta incites Doc's desire by drawing on the exact feelings inspired by the iconic femme fatale—the fraught combination of desire and repudiation that stems from a larger sense of loss. Doc is seduced by a description of the kind of man he abhors, the antithesis of his values. And, again, Shasta is the primary figure of that betrayal.

The invocation of Charles Manson immediately preceding the seduction scene reinforces the connections Pynchon is making between gender, power, and loss, albeit this time from a slightly different angle. Mickey may be associated with the villainy of the economically powerful mainstream "flatland" world that Doc disavows, but Manson is the person Doc blames most explicitly for the breakdown of his most cherished values; Manson is the person who destroyed "a certain kind of innocence" and "fucked that up for everybody" (38). His ghostly appearance in this scene echoes those earlier sentiments. Though I agree with Simon Cook's conclusion that "Charlie is not the libidinal energy behind the novel's sexual narratives," Manson's presence is, I think, more than "just a totem of extremity and control and the source of the thematic materials which grounds them in this 1970" (1146). His presence in this scene underscores the idea of loss—both by association with Shasta and by recalling Doc's earlier statements—and, in being tied together with Mickey, clarifies the role that "extremity and control" play in that loss. Manson might be said to work as a negative image of Mickey, the threat to cultural movements that comes not from the mainstream, but from within—another example of Doc's fears that even innocent gatherings can be infiltrated by "ancient forces of greed and fear" (129).

Pynchon not only deploys the misogynistic elements of the detective/ femme fatale relationship to dramatize cultural change and Doc's most primal, fundamental feelings of loss but also ultimately radically revises the trope by presenting Shasta as having important insight regarding Doc's own subconscious. Of all the myriad characters Doc interacts with over the course of the novel, Shasta has the clearest understanding of his psychology; Shasta identifies Doc's sublimated fantasies of control and makes explicit the fears he projects onto her. During a conversation about her background with Coy Harlingen, Shasta tells Doc, "far as I can see, you and Coy, you're peas in a pod. [...] Both of you, cops who never wanted to be cops. [...] You guys must've thought you'd be chasing criminals, and instead here you're both working for them" (313–14). By calling out Doc's cop identity, Shasta draws attention to his unwitting participation in the workings of the establishment, most clearly represented in the novel by Bigfoot Bjornsen. The savvy reader will recall the narrator's earlier observation that "[t]ime was when Doc used to actually worry about turning into Bigfoot Bjornsen, ending up just one more diligent cop, going only where the leads pointed him, opaque to the light which seemed to be finding everybody else walking around in this regional dream of enlightenment" (207). Of course, Doc's repressed worry about becoming Bigfoot goes beyond "ending up just one more diligent cop," extending into the ways in which he has already been participating in the overarching systems of authority and control that the hippie worldview attempts to resist.

In the typical hard-boiled model, the detective situates himself between the poles of criminal and member of the justice system but sublimates his similarity to the criminal element. Indeed, "the reading of the criminal as a projection of the unacceptable or disavowed parts of the detective's personality is, of course, one of the central tenets of psychoanalytic accounts of the detective story" (Breu 80). In *Inherent Vice*, however—and really throughout Pynchon's novels—the most dangerous criminals are not the "virtual children, driven by undisciplined desires and incapable of adapting themselves to the demands of a routinized world" frequently seen in traditional noir (McCann 126) but rather the representatives of that routinized world. Rob Wilson describes Pynchon's career-long interrogation of privilege and power when he suggests that Pynchon "tracks this centuries-long battle for the soul of America between what he calls the non-flatland Preterite (surfers, dopers, fun seekers, rockers, hippie riffraff, drifters, seekers, Indians, the poor multitudes, restless homemakers in little bars) versus the 'straight world' Elect (land developers, bankers, tax-dodging dentists, big shots, police within police, loan sharks, or worse)" (217–18). Following this logic, the most threatening figures in the novel are not those operating outside of outwardly respectable professions and institutions but those working within them or with their approval—the "little private militia the LAPD uses whenever they don't want to look bad in the papers" (195), Crocker Fenway and the Golden Fang operatives "cleverly disguised [...] as a wholesome blond California family" (349). For Pynchon, then, the most dangerous kind of violence is obscured behind the veneer of respectability. In this world, it is not a kinship with the disruptive force of the outsider criminal that the detective must repress, but the authority of the elect—the mainstream, the powerful and enfranchised. Thus when Shasta identifies Doc's repressed desire to wield the power of the elect, she forces him to reevaluate his most basic sense of self. The modification to noir that Pynchon makes by shifting the detective's repressed identity functions as a critique of powerful social institutions, locating violence within the state apparatus in particular, while the change he makes by giving this insight to the femme fatale augments her autonomy and interiority, making sure that she is not simply a stand-in for the detective's own anxieties.

Shasta's narrative importance is reinforced by Doc's response; instead of lashing out defensively or continuing to repress his fears, Doc immediately wonders, "Could that be true?" (314), and shortly thereafter, he realizes she's right. Pynchon's description of this moment calls attention to its significance: "Doc followed the prints of her bare feet already collapsing into rain and shadow, as if in a fool's attempt to find his way back into a past that despite them both had gone on into the future it did. The surf, only now and then visible, was hammering at his spirit, knocking things loose, some to fall into the dark and be lost forever, some to edge into the fitful light of his attention whether he wanted to see them or not. Shasta had nailed it. Forget who— *what* was he working for anymore?" (314, emphasis in the original). Again, Doc references the past in relation to Shasta as he trails along after her on the beach, trying and failing to step into the footprints she leaves behind. This time, however, he sees the impossibility of recovery. Whether "he wanted to see them or not," Shasta has made visible the parts of his life that have resisted analysis. In forcing Doc to confront his subconscious, Shasta simultaneously frees him from the grip of the past and herself from the role of femme fatale. When she explains him to himself, Shasta is no longer a reflection of Doc's character; she is a character in her own right.

The final image of the novel may seem on its surface to revert back to traditional noir formula, in which the hard-boiled detective ultimately rejects the femme fatale, moving alone into the future; as Doc drives off alone on the fog-covered highway, imagining a "restless blonde in a Stingray" (369), he appears to uphold the "fantasies of autonomy and individualist opposition to the dominant order" that result from "the ritual repudiation of the femme fatale" (Breu 70).[7] However, Pynchon does demonstrate positive movement on Doc's part, past the sense of loss that he maps onto Shasta. Earlier in the novel, Doc confesses his ex-old-lady woes to Hope Harlingen, and she gently admonishes him, saying, "As one who's been down that particular exit ramp [...] you can only cruise the boulevards of regret so far, and then you've got to get back up onto the freeway again" (40). I want to suggest that the novel's ending is, in part, a specific reference to Shasta—if cruising the boulevards of regret stands in for Doc's attachment to Shasta (locating her firmly in the tradition of the femme fatale as a figure of melancholy and nostalgia), then moving finally onto the freeway suggests Doc's movement beyond that limited vision of Shasta as a type rather than as a fully formed person.

Further, the novel's closing scene hinges on an image of community—of people coming together in loose organization, "a temporary commune to help each other home through the fog": "He was in a convoy of unknown size, each car keeping the one ahead in taillight range, like a caravan in a desert of perception, gathered awhile for safety in getting across a patch of blindness. It was one of the few things he'd ever seen anybody in this town, except hippies, do for free" (368). Even Doc's fantasies at the end of the novel are explicitly of community. He thinks: "Maybe then it would stay this way for days, maybe he'd have to just keep driving, down past Long Beach, down through Orange County, and San Diego, and across a border where nobody could tell anymore in the fog who was Mexican, who was Anglo, who was anybody" (369). Doc may be alone, but he does not idealize autonomy. He no longer is subject to the specific fantasies of the hard boiled and imagines instead a kind of openness and assumes a more optimistic view of human connection and possibility. The movement from the closed system of regret and nostalgia to the more open network of the drivers on the freeway is indicative of a growth beyond the hard boiled and is suggestive of a mode of resistance—that in the face of larger systems of control, our best means of navigation is each other.

Ultimately, in *Inherent Vice* Pynchon undoes the noir genre in a way that allows him to use its critical powers while also breaking down some of its more problematic ideas about masculinity and sexuality. By the end of the novel, it is clear that Doc retains only traces of the hard-boiled persona within him, as he confronts his own fraught subconscious as projected onto Shasta, acknowledges fears of his own potential for sadism and the failure of the cultural ideals of the sixties, and turns toward a new openness to human connection. The end result is a different masculine subjectivity—one that is liminal and critical like that of the traditional noir detective but without the latter's misogyny or anxiety.

In many ways, *Bleeding Edge*'s Maxine Tarnow is more recognizably hard boiled than Doc—she has the cynical, knowing tone of a person unsurprised by illegal or immoral behavior; Maxine runs "Tail 'em and Nail 'em" Fraud Investigations (4), observing that "[s]omedays it seems like every lowlife in town has Tail 'em and Nail 'em in their grease-stained Rolodex" (5). As a "defrocked" fraud investigator, she arguably inhabits an even more dubious space than Doc in between the criminal and the officer of the law, with her current status imparting a "halo of faded morality, a reliable readiness to step outside the law and share the trade secrets of auditors and tax men" (17). Indeed, the narrator tells us that "[s]ince going rogue, Maxine has acquired a number of software kits courtesy of certain less reputable clients" (172). And Maxine herself rejects the suggestion that she is a friend of the law when she tells a friend, "I'm not a cop lover Felix, that's Nancy Drew, actually not too flattering a comparison; you need to work on that" (309). She has a hard-boiled love for the gritty environments of New York City as well as a facility with and enjoyment of firearms (51, 275, 473). Her estranged husband and sometimes lover, Horst, suggests that she sees herself in traditionally hard-boiled terms: "You always had me figured for some kind of idiot savant, you were the one with the street smarts, the wised-up practical one, and I was just some stiff with a gift, who didn't deserve to be so lucky" (320). In terms of a general persona, Maxine fits the mold of the directed, capable, and no-nonsense detective. In giving a female protagonist these qualities, Pynchon is asserting that such qualities are not gender specific, breaking down the association between masculinity and physical efficacy and mental toughness.

At the same time, Maxine's brand of self-aware fearlessness is frequently explicitly linked to gender in a way that suggests her experiences as a woman provide important context for her actions. Maxine pursues potentially dangerous leads, but not blindly. We get a sense of her daring during her exploration of Gabriel Ice's "ill-gotten summer retreat" in Montauk, when a "shadowy, almost invisible door over in one corner" catches her attention, and she can't resist looking further (191, 192): "But now as she steps through the door, the interesting question arises, Maxine, are you out of your fucking mind? For centuries they've been trying to indoctrinate girls with stories about Bluebeard's Castle and here she is once more, ignoring all that sound advice. Somewhere ahead lies a confidential space, unaccounted for, resisting analysis, a fatality for wandering into which is what got her kicked out of the profession to begin with and will maybe someday get her dead" (192).

Certainly, in the conflict between her headstrong "fatality for wandering into" and the part of herself that questions her choices, Maxine demonstrates an emotional complexity that sets her apart from the traditional hard-boiled figure. But more interesting still is the satiric filtering of the moment through a folk tale that emphasizes the potentially fatal effects of feminine curiosity. For a female detective, pushing into unknown territory means more than a willingness to confront danger; it also means refusing to be indoctrinated by "centuries" of culture that relied on fear to keep women obedient. Remaining ignorant, "ignoring all that sound advice," may well keep her alive, and Maxine is aware enough to recognize her own pattern of potentially destructive behavior, but she steps through the door regardless.

This fearlessness combined with an awareness of her gendered subject position becomes a useful detection strategy, which we see her deploy, for instance, during her brief foray into exotic dancing at the Joie de Beavre. Kitted out in "platform heels in neon aqua, plus matching sequined thong leotard and thigh-high stocking" (220), Maxine devises a plan "to improvise a MILF-night routine while scanning faces and hoping for a match with Eric's license photo" (221). Maxine uses objectification to suit her own purposes, and Pynchon is careful to highlight her agency and awareness by again drawing on the traditionally sardonic tone associated with hard-boiled fiction: "Maxine's never had what you'd call Big Tits, although the connoisseurs here don't seem to mind as long as they're Bare Tits. The one body part they won't be staring at much is her eyes. This Male Gaze she's been hearing about since high school is not about to intersect its female counterpart anytime soon" (221). Pynchon puts the hard boiled up against the feminist here in typically cheeky style; in simultaneously wielding both tough-guy talk and feminist theory, Maxine might even be said to embody both discourses. And, in the same punny vein, we see emphasis again on the ways in which Maxine's dexterity—now both physical and psychological—is a fundamental part of her work as a detective.

Maxine is not without internal struggle, however. Much like Doc before her, Maxine's subconscious concerns play out in connection with a romantic partner whom she finds simultaneously attractive and repellent. While he may not initially appear to fit the paradigm, I want to suggest that Nicholas Windust functions as *Bleeding Edge*'s version of the femme fatale. He does not saunter into Maxine's office, pulling her into the vagaries of an urban underworld; Windust's connection to the trope lies in the psychologic response he elicits from Maxine. The first indicator of Windust's role is his immediate and peculiar effect on Maxine's psyche; indeed, Pynchon continually comes back to the idea of Maxine's subconscious in relation to Windust, first via dream sequences and later by emphasizing a gap in her ability to reflect on their relationship. After their brief initial meeting, Maxine dreams about Windust twice. In the first instance,

> she has a vivid, all-but-lucid dream about him, in which they are not exactly fucking, but fucking around, definitely. The details ooze away as dawn light and the sounds of garbage trucks and jackhammers grow in the room, till she's left with a single image unwilling to fade, this federal penis, fierce red, predatory, and Maxine alone its prey. She has sought to escape but not sincerely enough for the penis, which is wearing some strange headgear, possibly a Harvard football helmet. It can read her thoughts. "Look at me, Maxine, Don't look away. Look at me." A talking penis. That same jive-ass radio-announcer voice. (106)

And in the second dream, Maxine is caught up in "[a] somehow desperate flight by antiquated bus through jungles to escape a threat, a volcano possibly. At the same time, this is also a tour bus full of Upper West Side Anglos, and the tour director is Windust, lecturing in that wise-ass radio voice, something about the nature of volcanoes. The volcano behind the bus, which hasn't gone away, grows more ominous" (170). Windust's "jive-ass," "wise-ass radio voice" is a telling through line between these separate dream world events; the exaggerated, performative quality of his voice points to an underlying inauthenticity or untrustworthiness that nags at Maxine's subconscious. Reading the images of a "federal" phallus and an "ominous" volcano alongside Maxine's explicit fear that she is "prey," brings Windust together with governmental authority and imminent danger, and the Harvardian helmet serves as a maroon marker of the elect. Yet despite this predominantly negative imagery, the first dream is characterized as an "all-but-lucid" sexual fantasy. Just like the traditional femme fatale, Windust evokes a complex and multilayered psychological response in the detective.

Pynchon elaborates on Maxine's dream logic by extending it into the waking world; consciously, Maxine does recognize Windust to be a primarily destructive force. She observes: "Windust does not after all seem to be FBI. Something worse, if possible. If there is a brother—or God forbid sisterhood of neoliberal terrorists, Windust has been in there from the jump" (108). It is her desire for Windust that remains so uninterrogated as to be almost unacknowledged. Their one brief sexual encounter is positively dripping with such ambivalence. The description preceding what Maxine ends up dismissively calling "a quickie" is overwhelmingly negative, suggestive of her dreamworld intimations of imminent danger: "desolate corridors, unswept and underlit," lead her through a building where "walls glisten unhealthily in creepy yellows and grime-inflected greens, colors of medical waste . . . Open to all sorts of penetration" (258). Yet she finds herself responding to his advances despite herself, thinking, "Shouldn't she be saying, 'You know what, fuck yourself, you'll have more fun,' and walking out? No, instead, instant docility—she slides to her knees. Quickly, without further discussion, not that some bed would have been a better choice, she has joined months of unvacuumed debris on the rug, face on the floor, ass in the air, skirt pushed up" (259). She is unwittingly drawn to Windust even afterward, arguing with herself on the way home:

> What, she is just able to mentally inquire of herself, was I, the fuck, thinking? And the worst, or does she mean the best, part of it is that even right now it will take very little, yes, all pivoting here on FDR's silvery small cheekbone in fact, to lean forward, interrupt the call-in hatefest on the cabbie's radio, and in a voice sure to be trembling ask to be brought back to the homicidal bagman in his dark savage squat, for more of the same. (260–61)

It is no coincidence that Maxine questions her behavior with Windust in the same language she uses when stepping into Gabriel Ice's hidden room in Montauk—the syntactic directness of her earlier query "are you out of your fucking mind?" devolves now into the garbled, disassociative "What, she is just able to mentally inquire of herself, was I, the fuck, thinking?" Maxine's powerful but ultimately ambivalent interest in Windust is thus unmistakably linked to her investigation of Ice's corporate secrets. Just like Bluebeard's Castle in the earlier scene, the decision to sleep with Windust is both a "confidential space, unaccounted for, resisting analysis" and indicative of a "fatality for wandering into" that "will maybe someday get her dead." Maxine's desire for Windust may then be best read as an example of her tendency toward self-destructive behavior, the urge to put herself in dangerous situations despite the potential consequences. In true noir form, desire for the femme fatale is once again rooted in repressed aspects of the detective's subconscious and bound up with the detective's most fervently disavowed forms of economic connection.

Windust is not, however, associated with the kind of nostalgia that typically surrounds the femme fatale, which suggests that his function in the text is not, like Shasta's, to dramatize the detective's sense of loss. Instead, Windust's power over what Maxine sees as her better judgment, his association with the novel's corporate villain, and perhaps most importantly, his position as an agent of "neoliberal terrorism" (108) allow us to read Windust as a stand-in for paternalistic systems as a whole. In this way, Pynchon has transformed the femme fatale from displaced projection to metonym. Where Shasta is (initially) the receptacle for Doc's concerns about negative cultural change—her submission to Mickey and his ilk representative of a broader betrayal—Windust is himself an agent of that change. As such, he poses a direct threat in a way that Shasta does not—a fact that finds expression in Maxine's dream imagery and in the description of Windust's home. The fear and dread conjured in these scenes indicate that Maxine's subconscious is not wrestling with a lost past but rather picking up on the present dangers of millennial New York—especially those associated with the violent and repressive power of the elect.[8] Despite the differences in their construction as femme fatale figures, both Shasta and Windust help reveal the detective's deepest, most uninterrogated fears. For Doc, it is becoming an agent of the law; for Maxine, it is becoming a victim.

Maxine may worry about the simultaneously seductive and destructive qualities of power, but these fears do not ultimately negatively affect her life as a whole or limit her connection to others. Where traditional hard-boiled detectives (and even, to a large degree, Doc) are "solitary figures in the romantic tradition of individual alienation from normal social roles like marriage, religion, and community" (Soitos 12), Maxine is comfortably positioned at the borders of these institutions. Or rather, she's created her own priorities in regard to these traditional forms of social connection. The idea of family is central to Maxine, as she is close with and quite involved in the lives of both her parents and her sons. At the same time, she expresses no particular investment in the idea of traditional marriage, nor does she limit her caretaking to a nuclear family unit; Maxine is separated from, but still occasionally sexually involved with, her "sort of ex"-husband, Horst, and she opens her home to both Driscoll and Eric after they are displaced following the 9/11 terrorist attacks (114, 367). Similarly, Maxine's Judaism is presented as a part of her personal identity, but apart from brief mentions—such as her explanation for why she abstains from pork and a reference to past seders at her parents' house—it is rarely described as practice (103, 250). And while she isn't as zealous when it comes to community action as, say, March Kelleher is, her participation in neighborhood Halloween celebrations, familiarity with local firefighters, and relationships with other parents at the Otto Kugelblitz School demonstrate her ties to the people around her in New York (365, 379, 2). Through these varied social connections, Pynchon suggests that the "hard-boiled" detective no longer need be male or particularly hardened.

Thus, where Doc's detective practice prevents him from participating often in community-related activities and from regularly attending familial gatherings—*Inherent Vice*'s narrative describing only brief meetings and phone calls with friends and relatives, focusing instead on case-related activities—Maxine balances the capable, individual work of the hard-boiled detective with the successful maintenance of her position as a loving and involved parent. For instance, when she goes to investigate hashslingrz's shady internet front, hwgaahwgh.com, Maxine quickly realizes that the visit is going to require a shift in demeanor: "As soon as she catches sight of it, her heart, if it does not sink exactly, at least cringes more tightly into the one-person submarine necessary for cruising the sinister and labyrinthine sewers of greed that run beneath all real-estate dealings in this town" (42). She is able to cruise sinister environments as an isolated individual while a few moments later "[t]oggling [...] immediately into Anxious Mom mode" (48). Similarly, the "working-mom blues" may keep her from switching to Zimartinis with Driscoll as they discuss hashslingrz at Fabian's Bit Bucket, but they do not, as we have seen, keep her from stripping "undercover" at the Joie de Beavre or "blasting away" at the Sensibility gun range (48, 220, 275). Maxine shifts as necessary between the hard-boiled mode and the maternal.

This "toggling" toward community and connection is perhaps Pynchon's most crucial change to the persona of the traditional noir detective in that it renders the detective capable of upholding multiple identities. In contrast, "[t]he hard-boiled male, as relatively positive and stable site of reader identification, becomes celebrated for his rugged individualism and his opposition to all forms of collectivity, whether existing or imaginary. It is this epistemological limit that we encounter again and again in hard-boiled novels" (Breu 176). Maxine's acceptance of and interest in collectivity erases this "epistemological limit," but she still retains an autonomy that allows her to function independently in the world.

This new "stable site of reader identification" provides, then, a broader set of possibilities and ways of being in the world. Francisco Collado-Rodríguez points to the potentially ethical dimensions of this new hard-boiled figure in his analysis of the novel's climactic scene: "It is when his protagonist comes back to meatspace to help March's daughter that Pynchon suggests the way to overcome structural trauma and its trap of commodified victimization. Maxine's resilient reaction at the time results from an ethical recognition of the human other, followed by an explicit confrontation with the face of evil" (239). It is, I would argue, the new hard-boiled detective we see in action here; it is Maxine's particular combination of toughness and humanity that makes her capable of challenging evil in the world.

If *Inherent Vice* confronts, among other things, our collective repressed urge to control, *Bleeding Edge* counters with the ability to resist that urge. When Doc acknowledges the phantasmatic appeal of sadism and his own disavowed interest in exercising power over others, he begins a process of change that effectively frees his literary descendent from repeating the pattern. At the end of *Inherent Vice*, Doc fantasizes about the possibility of a new kind of autonomous community; at the end of *Bleeding Edge*, Maxine puts those values into action. Upon returning home after that frightening final confrontation with Gabriel Ice, Maxine readies herself for the routine of escorting her sons to school, ignoring the suggestion that they are fine on their own. Just as she moves to join them, however, she changes her mind: "But she waits in the door-way as they go on down the hall. Neither looks back. She can watch them into the elevator at least" (477). While Maxine certainly struggles with her own subconscious as it relates to vulnerability in the world, this closing scene serves as evidence that she realizes the vulnerable are not always prey—and that intimate relationships do not have to lead to paternalistic, controlling behavior. In supporting the autonomy of her children as they walk out alone into the rough ideological country of post-9/11 New York, Maxine creates space for the kind of fluid, independent yet connected community that Doc envisioned but did not see realized.

As Christopher Breu notes in his conclusion to *Hard-Boiled Masculinities*, "[T]he legacy of hard-boiled masculinity is still very much with us": "The image of unemotive violent masculinity thus persists, suggesting that if we are to imagine real change in the material and discursive construction of gender in the United States and around the globe, we must imagine ways of producing phantasmatic change as well. [. . .] [S]uch change is possible only by working through the very logic of popular fantasy itself, unmooring its productively critical and libidinally charged negativity from the forms of racial and gendered violence to which it has for too long been bound. Only by working through this logic can a subject's affective relationship to his or her culture be altered" (188). It is this "working through the very logic of popular fantasy itself" that I think we see, broadly, in all of Pynchon's work, but specifically regarding noir in the most recent novels, as taken together, they reformulate the gendered dynamics of the hard-boiled figure. Beyond their functions as variations on the hard boiled, Doc and Maxine embody a new kind of detective hero, one described by *Bleeding Edge*'s March Kelleher. In a post-9/11 blog entry, March describes her fears about a "new enemy, unnamable, locatable on no organization chart or budget line," conceding that they may be "unbeatable" but offering this possibility: "What it may require is a dedicated cadre of warriors willing to sacrifice time, income, personal safety, a brother/sisterhood consecrated to an uncertain struggle that may extend over generations and, despite all, end in total defeat" (399). Doc and Maxine may not a "cadre of warriors" make, but given that they successfully break down the inherently gendered violence of the hard boiled to make such a group possible, there is no better embodiment of March's imagined heroes than the cross-generational "brother/sisterhood" formed by Pynchon's two over-easy detectives.

NOTES

1. These kinds of descriptors have appeared primarily in reviews of the novels: Rob Sheffield declares, "A master of pastiche, Pynchon is working this time in the mode of the hard-boiled detective novel à la Raymond Chandler and Dashiell Hammett" (38). *Inherent Vice* is dubbed "half detective story spoof, half bittersweet love letter to the sixties" (par. 1) and a "slightly spoofy take on hardboiled crime fiction" (par. 2) in reviews by Robert McLaughlin and Louis Menand, respectively. And of *Bleeding Edge*, Tim Martin suggests that "a kind of laconic murder mystery sustains the narrative for a while; but this, as ever, is only there to impart vague direction to the jazzy eddies of dreams, songs and jokey backchat through which Pynchon transmits a large part of his novels" (par. 5).

2. Cassuto's larger argument covers more than this first generation of writers; he suggests, in fact, that the term "hard boiled" can really only be applied to the "originary generation of detectives" and that "postwar crimefighters become passionate and involved defenders of home and hearth" who are better understood as "sentimental action heroes." According to Cassuto, "sentimental action heroes display their active and emotional commitment to the community. This departure from the emotional austerity of the earliest hard-boiled fiction attacks the disinterested profession ideal (which is represented in an almost perfunctory way compared to prewar hard-boiled fiction)" (98).

3. Breu's Marxist, psychoanalytic approach provides a cohesive theory that most clearly elucidates the dynamics at work in Pynchon's reassessment of the hard-boiled detective; for this reason, I draw on other accounts of noir for broad context but almost exclusively rely on Breu's model to orient my close readings of the novels.

4. Stephen F. Soitos provides a comprehensive list of qualities that distinguish hard-boiled fiction from classical detective fiction in *The Blues Detective: A Study of African American Detective Fiction*. The common elements of the genre are an emphasis on "narration/language/character" as opposed to plot, a setting that is largely urban rather than a mix of urban and rural, the representation of murder as a "'dirty' muddle" rather than a "clean puzzle" and the perpetrator as a person who "acts as part of group or gang conspiracy" rather than alone, the pervasiveness of "physical violence in description and act" as opposed to "minimal" physical violence, a tendency to critique society "from below" rather than from above, and closure that is "often morally ambiguous" rather than black and white; common features of the

hard-boiled detective are that he is "democratic/classless" rather than "aristocratic/upper-class," a "paid professional/private eye" rather than an amateur, "inductive/instinctive" rather than "deductive/rational," and "observer involved" rather than "observer detached" and that he relies on "gut reaction" and "coincidence" rather than "scientific investigation" and the "psychology of behavior" (13).

5. This reading departs slightly from Macleod's, which places Doc within the cultural and historical progression of the genre: "Doc represents the counterculture descendant of the 1920s hard-boiled detective hero, which was originally created as an Americanized alternative to the popular 'cozy' English detective story" (129). While I agree with genre theorist Leonard Cassuto that, generally speaking, "the hard-boiled and the sentimental change with the times, and in response to shifting social and historical conditions" (2), I don't see Doc as a natural development of this particular literary tradition so much as a playful experiment with some of its more confounding tropes.

6. Recognizing that Doc's sense of Shasta is based on his public rather than private concerns clarifies the novel's presentation of their dynamic. So while it is true that Doc is "wistfully nostalgic about his time with Shasta" (Cook 1157), this melancholic fascination is not evidence that the novel "succumbs to a pre-feminist sexual nostalgia trip" (Cook 1160) but rather a consistent rendering of the traditional relationship between the detective and the femme fatale. In connecting Shasta with the past, Pynchon does not indulge in nostalgia by way of Doc; instead, he emphasizes the significance of the cultural and economic shifts happening at the end of the 1960s.

7. The space for a possible reunion with Shasta is arguably left open in the novel. While the last time Doc sees her is at Skip's apartment above the surf shop, Shasta is mentioned one more time—in a phone conversation between Doc and his mother, Elmina, who asks if he's seen much of "that pretty Shasta Fay Hepworth" and suggests that he "could do worse." Doc acknowledges that Shasta is living in the neighborhood again and does not entirely foreclose the possibility of reconciliation (352).

8. These fears are only exacerbated in the wake of 9/11, as we see after Maxine's uncanny experience watching local children spontaneously age. Double-checking her surroundings, Maxine notes: "Cars were no more advanced in design, nothing beyond the usual police and military traffic was passing or hovering overhead, the low-rise holdouts hadn't been replaced with anything taller, so it still had to be 'the present,' didn't it? Something, then, must've happened to these kids. But next morning all was back to 'normal.' The kids as usual paying no attention to her. 'What, then, the fuck, is going on?'" (336–37). Maxine's horror here is rooted in a vision of a future dominated by the elect.

WORKS CITED

Breu, Christopher. *Hard-Boiled Masculinities*. Minneapolis: University of Minnesota Press, 2005.

Cassuto, Leonard. *Hard-Boiled Sentimentality: The Secret History of American Crime Stories*. New York: Columbia University Press, 2009.

Collado-Rodríguez, Francisco. "Intratextuality, Trauma, and the Posthuman in Thomas Pynchon's *Bleeding Edge*." *Critique* 57.3 (2016): 229–41.

Cook, S. J. "Manson Chicks and Microskirted Cuties: Pornification in Thomas Pynchon's *Inherent Vice*." *Textual Practice* 29.6 (2014): 1143–64.

Gold, Eleanor. "Beyond the Fog: *Inherent Vice* and Thomas Pynchon's Noir Adjustment." *New Perspectives on Detective Fiction: Mystery Magnified*. Ed. Casey A. Cothran and Mercy Cannon. New York: Routledge, 2016. 209–24.

Haynes, Doug. "Under the Beach, the Paving-Stones! The Fate of Fordism in Pynchon's *Inherent Vice*." *Critique* 55.1 (2014): 1–16.

Huehls, Mitchum. "The Great Flattening." *Contemporary Literature* 54.4 (2013): 861–71.

Macleod, Scott. "Playgrounds of Detection: The Californian Private Eye in Thomas Pynchon's *The Crying of Lot 49* and *Inherent Vice*." *Pynchon's California*. Ed. Scott McClintock and John Miller. Iowa City: University of Iowa Press, 2014. 113–34.

Martin, Tim. Review of *Bleeding Edge*, by Thomas Pynchon. *Telegraph* (UK), 14 Sept. 2013, www.telegraph.co.uk/culture/books/fictionreviews/10304078/Bleeding-Edge-by-Thomas-Pynchon-review.html. Accessed 17 Nov. 2017.

McCann, Sean. *Gumshoe America: Hard-Boiled Crime Fiction and the Rise and Fall of New Deal Liberalism*. Durham: Duke University Press, 2000.

McLaughlin, Robert L. Review of *Inherent Vice*, by Thomas Pynchon. *Review of Contemporary Fiction* 29.3 (2009). www.highbeam.com/doc/1G1-214793689.html.

Menand, Louis. "Soft Boiled." Review of *Inherent Vice*, by Thomas Pynchon. *New Yorker*, 3 Aug. 2009: 74–75, http://www.telegraph.co.uk/culture/books/fictionreviews/10304078/Bleeding-Edge-by-Thomas-Pynchon-review.html. Accessed 16 Nov. 2017.

Pynchon, Thomas. *Bleeding Edge*. New York: Penguin Books, 2013.

———. *Inherent Vice*. New York: Penguin Books, 2009.

Sheffield, Rob. "The Bigger Lebowski." Review of *Inherent Vice*, by Thomas Pynchon. *Rolling Stone*, 3 Aug. 2009: 38–39.

Soitos, Stephen F. *The Blues Detective: A Study of African American Detective Fiction*. Amherst: University of Massachusetts Press, 1996.

Wilson, Rob. "On the Pacific Edge of Catastrophe; or, Redemption: California Dreaming in Thomas Pynchon's *Inherent Vice*." *Boundary 2* 37.2 (2010): 217–25.

Of "Maidens" and Towers
Oedipa Maas, Maxine Tarnow, and the Possibility of Resistance

KOSTAS KALTSAS

    A common observation in appraisals of Thomas Pynchon's eighth novel, *Bleeding Edge*, has been to note its more than passing resemblance to his second novel, *The Crying of Lot 49*, especially in terms of their respective protagonists: Maxine Tarnow and Oedipa Maas (Cha; St. Clair, "Pynchon's Postmodern Legacy"). While most reviews point out this resemblance, they—understandably—do not proceed to discuss it or its implications at any length. Only Keith Miller goes on to note that *Bleeding Edge* "deals with the threat or promise of *The Crying of Lot 49* made flesh: the dream-life of a fully networked world" (50).

What follows is a more focused examination of not only the similarities but also the *dissimilarities* between the two protagonists and what they imply about the possibility of resistance to the threat of the world of *The Crying of Lot 49* and to the fulfillment of that threat in the world of *Bleeding Edge*. Because, despite what a reader might assume based on the aforementioned comparisons, *Bleeding Edge* is not simply retreading familiar ground, especially in the relationship between Oedipa and Maxine, which is not by any means a straightforward equivalence: the two women have very different attitudes toward the roles they are expected to fulfill.

Oedipa and Maxine self-consciously perform a number of roles during their respective quests, roles that are both stereotypically feminine and stereotypically unfeminine. In the case of Oedipa, the feminine roles she assumes initially assist and eventually hinder her in her investigation, while her attempts to move beyond them are met with resistance and rejection by the men she comes into contact with. Maxine, on the other hand, meets far less resistance when performing unfeminine roles. In addition, her negotiation with the conventionality of feminine roles is also, crucially, more complex, and, as a result, she is able to perform them in a different, wider context, treating them ironically *as set roles* while *sincerely* enacting the attributes they have been built around. This allows Maxine to turn the feminine from a restriction into a political tool and to be at least partially successful where Oedipa fails: not in unraveling the conspiracy she suspects is unfolding around her but in her reaction to her inability to do so. In contrast to Oedipa, who is installed "Rapunzel-like [...] in her tower" (12, 29), Maxine acts as an *anti*-Rapunzel; not as "the Princess" but as "the practical elf who comes while the Princess is sleeping [...] and gets the real work of the princessipality done" (25).

It is this "real work" that proves to be the true source of continuity between the two novels and the paradoxical reason why *Bleeding Edge*, despite coming at, and dealing with, a perhaps even more despair-inducing historical moment than *The Crying of Lot 49*, ends on a note of if not optimism, then at least fearful determination to persist, to resist the "indexed world" (476). This hope is linked to themes that have led critics to suggest that Pynchon has "slightly mellowed with late fatherhood" and "taken a domestic turn" (Konstantinou 170), but I argue that it represents a genuine politics rather than a retreat into the personal, a politics that has been present in Pynchon's work since the very beginning and that is brought to the fore in *Bleeding Edge*.

The Crying of Lot 49 Redux?

How similar are *The Crying of Lot 49* and *Bleeding Edge* then? Very, a cursory glance would suggest: they are the only two Pynchon novels to feature a single female protagonist who is in both cases a kind of insider-outsider. Oedipa is a Young Republican housewife who is deeply unhappy with the traditional roles she is expected to fulfill, but she is also in a position to use her insider status as the executrix of real estate tycoon Pierce Inverarity's will to investigate his tangled affairs. Maxine is the Upper West Side mother of two and former certified fraud examiner who can use her know-how and connections to investigate dotcom billionaire Gabriel Ice's affairs with a certain liberty that, were she still a CFE, would perhaps not be available to her. Both women are sort of detectives whose initially seemingly simple investigation brings them into contact with what may or may not be some kind of worldwide conspiracy whose nature will finally remain beyond their understanding. Both abandon their husbands (in the case of Maxine, before the novel opens) and claim a new lover, whom they find irresistible against their better judgment.[1]

So, if the novels' plots are broadly similar and lead to the same conclusion (and if *Bleeding Edge* consistently refers back to *The Crying of Lot 49*), wherein lies the difference? Let us turn to Oedipa and Maxine themselves and the roles they play.

Oedipa's Roles

Famously, at the beginning of *The Crying of Lot 49* we encounter Oedipa as the very image of conventionality; she is in what Theodore Kharpertian has referred to as "a condition of inactive uniformity" that she will gradually exchange for one "of active diversity," as she moves from a state of "unknowledgeable certainty to one of knowledgeable uncertainty" (104).

Despite this, and pace Roger Henkle, Oedipa is not "too slight a little housewife to lead us out of the labyrinths of paranoid California" (106) (a statement that is not only staggeringly condescending but additionally problematic in implying that leading readers "out of the labyrinths" is the goal of *The Crying of Lot 49*). On the one hand, as Georgiana Colvile notes, Oedipa's discourse more often sees her hedging than asserting herself (82): she lets Mucho talk first when he comes home, despite having important news to share (7), decides "not to make a fuss" when Roseman tries to "play footsie with her" (12), and apologizes when Nefastis's portrait of Maxwell doesn't communicate (74). And there are moments when her entrapment within the social roles she is expected to perform is especially evident: in her life in Kinneret, for example, she had "gently conned herself into the curious, Rapunzel-like role of a pensive girl somehow" (12); upon meeting Genghis Cohen, who has "a touch of summer flu," she immediately feels "motherly" (65).

On the other hand, it is also Oedipa's ability as a woman to inhabit such roles in her interactions with the various men she meets while on her quest that enables her to slowly gather information on Pierce's business interests and the conspiracy surrounding the Tristero. With Metzger in Echo Courts, she speaks with "movie-gaiety," later "trying for a brittle voice" (21, 22), by which means she finds out about Pierce's Fangoso Lagoons development. Speaking to Mr. Thoth, she "smiled at him as granddaughterly as she knew how" (63) and finds out about the Tristero's supposed rivalry with the Pony Express. Talking to Stanley Koteks, she "rested her shades on her nose and batted her eyelashes, figuring to coquette her way off this conversational hook" (60) and is told of the existence of the WASTE system. She "put on a sweater, skirt and sneakers, wrapped her hair in a studentlike twist, went easy on the makeup" (102) for her meeting with Emery Bortz and is rewarded with information about the reference to the Tristero in Wharfinger's play *The Courier's Tragedy*. But being in a position to play these roles is a mixed blessing. As a woman, she is not considered a threat, so the men she "interrogates" are willing to give her information, at least up to a point; at the same time, however, she is also easily rebuffed when she insists on digging further: for example, when pressing Metzger to join her to talk to Driblette about the play, he dismisses her as one of "these lib, overeducated broads with soft heads and bleeding hearts" (51), and her visit with Nefastis is cut short when he brushes off her failure as a "sensitive" and invites her to have sex with him (74).

Equally famously, the knowledge Oedipa manages to gain gets her nowhere, finally. The revelation she has been looking for never comes, and we leave her waiting for it in the form of the anonymous bidder for the Tristero lot of stamps perhaps making himself known. Oedipa's feelings of helplessness, her unwillingness and inability to act, are evident throughout the novel: "[C]an't I get somebody to do it for me?" (12); "All she could think of was to [...] wait for somebody to rescue her" (58); "She didn't press the argument. Having begun to feel reluctant about following up anything" (114–15). These feelings indicate the true extent of her trouble, which seems to have as much to do with her internalized assumptions about, and expectations of, her world and her own place in it as it does with the beliefs of men like Metzger (Davidson 43). A telling example is when during her meeting with the old sailor, Oedipa asks, "Can I help?" (86), only to soon conclude that she can't: "'I can't help,' she whispered, rocking him, 'I can't help'" (87). The mechanical, whispered repetition suggests that Oedipa is in reality addressing herself rather than the sailor. As a woman, she believes, she can "mother" him, provide him with temporary comfort, but "nothing she know[s] of would preserve [...] him" (89).

It is this helplessness that comes to dominate by the end of *The Crying of Lot 49*. Oedipa has struggled to move beyond the conventional social roles she is meant to perform and seems to have no patience with them anymore; the "patient, *motherly* look" Mucho gives Oedipa during their final meeting makes her want "to hit him in the mouth" (99, emphasis added). But despite the knowledge she has gained about her world, Oedipa is unable to replace conventional feminine roles with anything else, anything meaningful. Knowledge leads her to isolation and comes at a paradoxical cost: while serving as an imperative to act it offers no effective way to do so alone. (Having failed to confront Tremaine over selling Nazi armbands, she thinks in self-accusation: "This is America, you live in it, you let it happen" [103]). While no longer wanting to be part of Pierce's America, she has also found nothing else to be part of, no "real alternative to the exitlessness" (118), and therefore cannot see a way forward. The Tristero remains her only (menacing) hope because it stands for *organized*, potentially effective resistance to America. If it exists, it has an *active* politics, for better or for worse, whereas Oedipa's politics, if she now has one, is a passive one wrought purely of despair. She wants, as Lois Tyson puts it, to "have a purpose in life yet eschews the responsibility of taking action" (115).

Maxine's Roles

Throughout *Bleeding Edge*, Maxine's response to the roles she is called on to play is markedly different from Oedipa's (as one would expect in light of the vastly different gender politics of the two eras the novels are set in). If, as Cathy Davidson has noted, "the very pervasiveness [of the discouragements that Oedipa encounters] [...] indicates how persistently Oedipa's world conspires to keep her in her 'place'" (41), then Maxine's path in *Bleeding Edge* is much easier, for she meets far less resistance when she acts in ways that are stereotypically unfeminine: talking to Despard, she is "brusque," which has "lost [her] some business. On the other hand, it weeds out the day-trippers" (9). She refuses to "help" Windust with his "self-esteem," telling him to "try the self-help section at Politics & Prose—empathy, we're all out of that today, the truck didn't show up" (106). A taxi driver sees her Beretta and suggests she pay the "special rate for PIs"—which she accepts without correcting him (148). Randy, realizing she's armed, suggests she is not a "cop" or "dealer," then speculates she might be an "insurance adjuster" or "one of these them crime-lab babes, like on TV," and when Maxine tries to puts a stop to his flirting by saying "Randy, if I wasn't so wired into office mode right now?" (187–88) he immediately drops the subject. Her friend Heidi asks Maxine whether she's "expecting trouble" upon the return of Maxine's ex-husband, Horst, to which Maxine replies, "Emotions, maybe" (288).

But it is important to note that the difference with Oedipa is twofold. On the one hand, Maxine is never dismissed simply for being a woman and does not need to assume the stereotypically female roles that Oedipa does when she "interviews" various men while on her quest. On the other, compared to Oedipa, Maxine (in addition to being on the whole assertive rather than hedging) crucially also appears much more self-aware regarding her roles; she is able to accept or reject them, often treating them ironically as set roles *while* performing their essence sincerely. So, for example, immediately after delivering her "Emotions, maybe" quip to Heidi, when Horst and the children return from their trip to the Midwest, she "kneels on the floor and holds the boys till everybody gets too embarrassed" (289). When Despard flirts with her during the AMBOPEDIA cruise, Maxine reacts by considering whether to be offended or not—and not "how much," but "how little" (13). When Despard responds to her genuine attempt to warn him to be careful with a joke about the *Bionic Woman*'s Oscar Goldman, Maxine answers "He was a strong Jewish-mother role model for me" (143–44). With Driscoll she is "immediately [toggled] into Anxious Mom mode" (48). (Note, here, as elsewhere, the ironic capitalization.) Talking to March she refers to herself as the "Insensitive Daughter" (56). With Justin and Lucas, she keeps "finding herself [...] slipping back and forth between Helpful Native and [...] Jewish Mother" (72). Even when meeting Xiomara (Windust's wife), "Jewish-mother defaults switch in" (441).

The key passage in thinking about this self-aware negotiation with feminine roles comes early on, when we are told that in the context of their relationship both Maxine and Heidi consider Maxine as some sort of anti-Rapunzel: "Maxine understood that she was not the Princess here. Heidi [...] *thought she was* the Princess and furthermore has come over the years to believe that Maxine is the Princess's slightly less attractive *wacky sidekick*. Whatever the story of the moment happens to be, Princess Heidrophobia is always the lead babe while Lady Maxipad is [...] the practical elf who comes while the Princess is sleeping [...] and gets the real work of the princessipality done" (25).

This leads to what I suggest is the central question *Bleeding Edge* comes to pose—namely, what is the nature of that "real work"? Because despite being a more willing and experienced investigator than Oedipa, Maxine, by the end of the novel, arrives more or less at the same point: nowhere. In a sense, her final position is even more despair inducing: while Oedipa only sees evidence of the nature of her world indirectly, in its margins, down among the preterites whose very existence and implications are so easy to ignore (which is, in fact, what Oedipa does, for the most part), Maxine is everywhere presented with direct, horrible proof of the nature of her world, in 9/11 itself and its repercussions, in Windust's death (unlike Oedipa with respect to Driblette's disappearance/suicide, Maxine gets to experience the horror of discovering Windust's corpse), in her own terror at the thought that she is unable to protect her children, and finally, in the failure of the promise of DeepArcher and, by extension, the very idea of the Deep Web as a locus of resistance.[2]

DeepArcher, the Tristero, and Resistance

To an extent, DeepArcher functions as the Tristero equivalent in *Bleeding Edge*. Unlike the Tristero, it is unquestionably real, and its origins and goals are not a mystery, but similarly to the Tristero it initially serves as an alternative and antagonist to a commercialized, hypermonitored world, in this case, the world of the internet. It carries the potential for some kind of organized resistance to that world, thanks to a security feature that allows its users to move through the web "without leaving a trail" (37): "DeepArcher [...] forgets where it's been, immediately, forever" (78). The migration of more and more aspects of everyday life to the web is problematic, since, as Maxine's father, Ernie, points out, what seems like freedom on it is "based on control. Everybody connected together, impossible anybody should get lost, ever again. Take the next step, connect it to these cellphones, you've got a total Web of surveillance, inescapable" (420).

This may seem rather too straightforward a rejection by a writer known for far more complex ironies, but it seems indeed to be a departure from Pynchon's tendency to maintain a certain distance from such pronouncements by placing them in the mouths of characters whose views the narrative undercuts, for I read no glaring ironies in the portrayal of Ernie as a caring father and grandfather and perhaps relatively—healthily?—paranoid American leftist (although, as David Cowart has argued, "Ernie's paranoia is ironically mirrored in the very medium he despises" ["Down," par. 39]).[3]

Unfortunately, in line with what has been argued is Pynchon's demonstration from novel to novel of how, historically, the space available for organized resistance becomes ever more limited as They seize ever more absolute control of media and the balance shifts from anonymity that serves the individual to anonymity that serves authority and that "hide[s] the origins of control" (Maragos par. 18), DeepArcher is doomed from the start. The true anonymity necessary for resistance in Pynchon's works eventually proves impossible to maintain on the web, and the kind of anonymity offered in the compromised DeepArcher only increases the chances that anyone a user interacts with may be one of Them, not even alive, not even human, leading to isolation and negating any chance for *organized* resistance. While these interactions take place in a meatspace context, Maxine does in fact ask herself near the novel's end, "Who of all those on her *network* really is trustworthy anymore?" (412, emphasis added).

DeepArcher itself becomes another node in the commercialized web, and though it may seem as if hope remains thanks to those few "going" looking for a new "border country, the edge of the unnavigable, the region of no information" (358), and the creation of spaces like Ziggy and Otis's Zigotisopolis, these ventures are nothing more than temporary respites. Just like DeepArcher, the regions of no information will inevitably be subsumed into the "indexed world", and, as Maxine knows, "the spiders and bots [...] one day too soon will be coming for [Zigotisopolis]" (476).

Pynchon, I contend, signals the falseness of DeepArcher's promise from the start in presenting us with a truer equivalent to the Tristero, namely, Marvin the kozmonaut: mysterious and serving unknown, truly anonymous, potentially malevolent interests, "some kind of otherworldly messenger, an angel even" (111) with "an uncanny history of always showing up with items Maxine knows she didn't order but which prove each time to be exactly what she needs" (107). The religious register here is telling: it directly links Marvin with *The Crying of Lot 49* and Jesús Arrabal's "anarchist miracle"—"another world's intrusion into this one" (83). It should also be juxtaposed with DeepArcher's original conception by Justin and Lucas as "a virtual sanctuary," because the religious register reached for with "sanctuary" is nullified by DeepArcher's being referred to in the very next sentence as a "grand-scale motel for the afflicted" (74). Despite agreeing with Thomas Schaub that Edward Mendelson's reading of *The Crying of Lot 49* is too straightforwardly optimistic (93), I suggest that Mendelson's take on the Tristero as a "manifestation of the sacred" remains a relevant one here (135). In this context, it is clear why

DeepArcher cannot succeed: being a "synthesis" of Justin's desire "to go back in time, to a California that had never existed, safe, sunny all the time," and Lucas's search "for someplace [...] a little darker" (74), DeepArcher is already, as Molly Hite has similarly argued about the effect of Oedipa's efforts to historicize the Tristero, "assimilated to the historical continuum" of the novel's world (79). (Nostalgia for a nonexistent past is very much a feature of this world, and one that distracts from, and limits contemplation of, resistance in the present.) Just like a historicized Tristero, DeepArcher is finally not "the sort of thing that can infuse 'transcendent meaning' into a sterile and banal world" (Hite 79–80), and its ultimate fate can be read as this banal world's intrusion into (what only seemed like) another one.

From Maxine's point of view, the failed promise of DeepArcher is potentially even more devastating than Oedipa's inability to establish the existence of the Tristero. After all, Oedipa has been equally unable to establish its *nonexistence*, and if at least the idea of a Tristero can be maintained, the hope that there exists a "real alternative to the exitlessness" also can be. And yet, even if the realities of *Bleeding Edge* arguably end up being inescapable in a way that the radical uncertainties of *The Crying of Lot 49* are not, Maxine and *Bleeding Edge* do not quite succumb to the politics of despair that haunt the ending of the earlier novel, and this refusal to succumb is intimately related to the way Maxine perceives her roles. It is this that allows her to maintain a sense of purpose in the face of the same exitlessness that overwhelms Oedipa—a sense of purpose that centers (mostly, though not exclusively) on her sons. This is surely why critics such as Konstantinou have spoken of Pynchon "mellow[ing] with late fatherhood" (170), though it is my contention that to do so is to miss the point.

Resistance, Family, Community

Maxine's family does eventually come to play an important role in *Bleeding Edge*, as she gets back together with her ex-husband and finds herself thinking that "the only question it's come down to is, where will Ziggy and Otis be protected from harm?" (412). It is however crucial to note that this does not signal a regression in terms of the novel's gender politics, considering that Maxine is not acting as "wife" and "mother" but as partner and parent—in the face of the horror of 9/11 and its unfolding repercussions there is no room for ironic capitalizations or scare quotes. Indeed, in the post-9/11 part of *Bleeding Edge*, Maxine and Horst walk their sons to school, where Maxine "notices other sets of parents, some who haven't spoken for years, showing up together to escort their children, regardless of age or latchkey status, safely to and from" (321); March and Tallis patch up their relationship (thanks in part to Maxine's intervention), focusing on their common concern for Tallis's son, Gabriel (469–76). Which, it could be argued, does all sound somewhat sentimental and perhaps not particularly political—another case of the "it's Pynchon, Jim, but not as we know him" argument that has to an extent followed Pynchon since *Vineland*.

But this is not some retreat into the bosom of the nuclear family in the face of a terrifying world. For one, to Maxine's "family" are added Driscoll and Eric, who move into the spare room—"It's been happening all over the neighborhood," we are told, "[r]efugees, prevented from entering their apartments in Lower Manhattan [...] have been showing up at the doors of friends farther uptown" (332). We should read this taking in of refugees in conjunction with Horst talking about how on the morning of September 11, he and his friend Jake "notice people out the window, heading for the water, figure it might be a good idea to join them. Tugboats, ferries, private boats, pulling in, taking people out from the yacht basin, all on their own, amazing coordination of effort, 'I don't think anybody was in charge, they just came in and did it'" (320), as well as March's editorializing: "Maybe it's unbeatable, maybe there are ways to fight back. What it may require is a dedicated cadre of warriors willing to sacrifice time, income, personal safety, a brother/sisterhood consecrated to an uncertain struggle that may extend over generations and, despite all, end in total defeat" (399).

What is important to note here is not just the references to neighbors, friends, and refugees, pointing away from isolation and toward community, but the fact that in March's editorial the register shifts to that of family and religion: "sacrifice," "brother/sisterhood," "consecrated." March's politics—the need to "fight back," the possibility of it all ending, as it did for Oedipa, in "defeat"—is extended into an argument for establishing loci of at least persistence, for holding on to the hope that subsequent generations will attempt to stand up against *their* day.

Justin St. Clair notes that "[t]here is little debating conservatism's conceptual claim on the nuclear family, but a narrative effort to rebrand the institution may well be Pynchon's last political stand," although he likewise detects a "sentimentality" in late Pynchon ("Rereading," par. 10). That Pynchon has made a turn is undoubtedly true, but what needs to be stressed is precisely the wide-reaching *politics* of this turn: in rejecting the social determinations that modern conservatives associate with the nuclear family *while* reaffirming its core of altruistic love and sacrifice, Pynchon is able, contra our day's "there's-no-such-thing-as-society" tendencies, to establish family as a viable model for community; this is repeatedly demonstrated by Maxine's tendency to ironize phrases like "Jewish Mother" while simultaneously enacting the very attributes these stock roles have been built around, and *not only* with her actual family.

Joanna Freer has suggested that "Pynchon's early novels express a Beat or 'post-Beat' sensibility in proposing that freedom and spiritual meaningfulness may be gained" by, among other things, "association with communities of exiles" (34). The idea that spiritual meaningfulness can be found in communities is, however, just as present in Pynchon's later work; this is precisely what March's editorial is arguing for and what Maxine demonstrates in choosing the roles she adopts.

Choosing a Politics beyond Anger

Near the end of *Bleeding Edge*, Ernie talks about how he spent Maxine's childhood waiting for her to "turn as cold" as the adults around her and "praying" (that religious register again) that she wouldn't, how she remained so "angry" over "crimes" that Ernie had "hardened [his] heart against years ago," and how all he could tell her in response was "you don't have to be like them, you can be better" (421–22). Maxine responds by acknowledging she is in a similar position with regard to her sons, fearing that if they "start caring too much [...] this world [...] could destroy them" (422).

This is crucial in considering the importance of community-as-family in providing resistance with a purpose. The transition from the child's anger to the adult's hardened heart appears to be an insurmountable problem when it comes to resistance. At best, it seems, what can be hoped for is that the idea of being "better" will be passed on to the members of the next generation, who in turn will grow out of their anger and come to worry about their own children being "better," and so on—the sense of resignation this suggests is not too far off from Oedipa's despair (note how it implies a belief that the world will continue as is, generation after generation). Yet this is not the case with Maxine; while she claims she worries about her sons caring "too much," this arguably proves to be what she, motivated by considerations that prove superior to anger, continues to do: she does not give up on her investigation even when she starts suspecting it may be putting her family in danger (411–16); she does not succumb to despair when her investigation comes to nothing; she does not allow her heart to harden in self-protection.

In his foreword to *Nineteen Eighty-Four*, Pynchon writes that

> Orwell was amused at those of his colleagues on the Left who lived in terror of being termed bourgeois. But somewhere among his own terrors may have lurked the possibility that [...] he might one day *lose his political anger, and end up as one more apologist for Things As They Are*. His anger, let us go so far as to say, was precious to him. He had lived his way into it [...] he had invested blood, pain and hard labor to earn [it], and was as attached to it as any capitalist to his capital. (xix, emphasis added)[4]

Pynchon goes on to mention a photograph of Orwell with his adopted son, Richard, noting that

> Orwell is holding him gently with both hands, smiling too, pleased, but not smugly so—it is more complex than that, as if he has discovered *something that might be worth even more than anger* [...]. [Orwell] was impatient with predictions of the inevitable, he remained confident in the ability of ordinary people to change anything, if they would. It is the boy's smile, in any case, that we return to, direct and radiant, proceeding out of an unhesitating *faith* that the world, at the end of the day, is good and that *human decency, like parental love, can always be taken for granted*—a faith so honourable that we can almost imagine Orwell, and perhaps even ourselves, for a moment anyway, *swearing to do whatever must be done* to keep it from ever being betrayed. (xxv–xxvi, emphasis added)

This passage links the ideas of parental love, community, faith, human decency, and the protection of the weak and innocent into a politics beyond mere anger—and it is this that gives resistance its spiritual meaningfulness in *Bleeding Edge*. It is in fact precisely these elements that combine to bring forth Oedipa's one act of attempted resistance in *The Crying of Lot 49*.

The reason Oedipa is unable to act is suggested near the beginning of the novel, when we learn about her bursting into tears upon seeing Remedio Varo's *Bordando el manto terrestre*, in which the maidens in the tower are embroidering the tapestry that makes the world in which the tower exists: Oedipa is trapped in a "mental prison of binary oppositions" (Tanner 86), demonstrated by the many, many times in which her thoughts about Pierce's estate and the possibility that the Tristero exists assume an either/or shape, despite her having "heard all about excluded middles; they were bad shit, to be avoided" (125). The culmination of this entrapment comes near the end of *The Crying of Lot 49*, when Oedipa lists the famous "symmetrical four" (118) alternative explanations of what is happening to her: "Either you have stumbled indeed [...] onto a real alternative to the exitlessness. [...] Or you are hallucinating it. Or a plot has been mounted against you. [...] Or you are fantasying some such plot" (117–18). Oedipa is stuck in a loop. She can't, or won't, admit that she lives in a world that is in part of her own making and that the only identity she can legitimately lay claim to will necessarily come both from *within* and *in opposition* to that world, a possibility she contemplates but steps back from near the end of the novel: trying to "face towards the sea" (122), which she earlier believed in "as redemption for Southern California (not, of course, for her own section of the state, which seemed to need none)" (37), and having "lost her bearings," she turns around and finds "no mountains either. As if there could be no barriers between herself and the rest of the land" (122).

The significance of the Varo painting and Oedipa's misreading of it has been widely addressed. Cowart argues that Oedipa sees herself as "locked in a tower [...] in which she must embroider or spin out a world she finds uncongenial. [...] [S]he will later hesitate to 'project a world,' because the projectionist, like the embroiderer, produces not reality but illusion" (*Thomas Pynchon* 24, 26). Cowart, however, correctly points out that if all reality is embroidered so is the tower (27) and that "[w]hat Oedipa does not perceive is that embroidering, which we all do, is not necessarily bad. [...] The question is only how freely we do it. Are we forced, unawares, to weave or embroider some approved version of reality?" (28–29). In addition, and in yet another demonstration of her internalized assumptions about her world, Oedipa "does not examine the Varo painting fully, but interprets it in terms of the dominant ideology," in which "women equal frail maidens, trapped by 'outside' forces. [...] She does not see [...] that the women in Varo's portrait do not fit this stereotype. [...] [T]he girls in Varo's portrait create the world. Everything that exists is there because they have, in their godlike capacity, made it" (Miller 50).

And yet despite her "misreading" of the painting, despite her paralyzed vacillation between mutually exclusive explanations, there is one instance when Oedipa overcomes either/ors and briefly acts before succumbing again to despair. While wandering in San Francisco after her meeting with Nefastis, she comes across a

> circle of children [...] who told her they were dreaming the gathering. But that the dream was really no different from being awake, because in the mornings when they got up they felt tired, *as if* they'd been up most of the night. [...] The night was empty of all terror for them, they had inside their circles an *imaginary fire*, and needed nothing but their own unpenetrated *sense of community*. [...] [They] [w]ent on warming their hands at an invisible fire. Oedipa, to retaliate, stopped believing in them. (81–82, emphasis added)

This "as if," this "imaginary fire" around which the "sense of community" is sustained, is the one possible solution that, as Tyson has suggested, Oedipa never considers: to treat the Tristero as the antagonist that must exist even if it is not specifically real, the antagonist that is neither an "organized, underground resistance rooted in the underclass" nor her own hallucination (89). "*Shall I project a world*?" Oedipa asks (60). So are these our only—mutually exclusive—options? Either we solipsistically project a world or are the world's projections? Varo's painting has already exposed the lie in this dichotomy:

we collectively make the world that makes us. The children's "imaginary fire" appears to be Pynchon's way of suggesting that Oedipa should abandon epistemological certainty and act "as if" in order to create the community based on human decency she has been searching for.[5]

Which, despite dismissing the children, is exactly what she does a few pages later, when she comes across the old sailor: she "sat, took the man in her arms, actually held him, gazing out of her smudged eyes down the stairs. [...] She felt wetness against her breasts and saw that he was crying. [...] 'I can't help,' she whispered, rocking him. [...] She let go of him for a moment, reluctant *as if he were her own child*" (87, emphasis added).

The scene "resembles a slum Pietá" according to Catharine Stimpson, who argues that Oedipa "releases a suppressed capacity for maternal tenderness. Psychological motherhood marks her moral growth" (43). Oedipa's "mothering" of the old alcoholic sailor is the closest Oedipa comes to resembling Maxine in *choosing* to adopt a role that may be superficially similar to the socially appropriate roles she is rejecting but that (motivated by the same kind of "parental" love that motivates Maxine) reaches beyond them, into a compassion that is essentially transcendent.

Following this is the one instant in which Oedipa acts *as if* the Tristero is real: she finds a WASTE mailbox and mails the sailor's letter to his wife. Davidson has noted the importance of this moment: if the Tristero is real, then Oedipa has "participated in it"; if not, she has "nevertheless functioned as part of an alternative network" (47), bringing "to an end her encapsulation in her tower" (29).

And yet having acted, Oedipa succumbs again to uncertainty, attempting to follow the carrier who picks up the mail only for him to lead her back to Nefastis's house. She sleeps through the night and has "no dreams to speak of" (91, cf. the children), then returns to Kinneret, thinking that "she had verified a WASTE system. [...] Yet she wanted it all to be a fantasy" (91). For the remainder of the novel she will return to her either/ors and the despair they give rise to. In a sense she will go even further, resisting/rejecting motherhood altogether: told by a doctor that she might be pregnant she gives her name as "Grace Bortz" and doesn't "show up for her next appointment" (118).[6] This rejection is telling in light of George Levine's suggestion that Oedipa is "feeling [...] the possibilities of despair, and the further possibility that despair is a way to avoid the responsibilities of caring" (125) because it is precisely the acceptance of these responsibilities—of motherhood *and* "motherhood"—that saves Maxine from despair at the end of *Bleeding Edge*. A rejection of gendered roles, as Maxine understands but Oedipa seems to fail to, need not lead to the refusal to play *any* role that would resemble them or a refusal to be motivated by the attributes these roles have been built around (in the same way that refusing to "embroider" the "approved version of reality" does not mean one should refrain from attempting to "embroider" a different one). Roles need not only be functions being forced on one; they can also be functions chosen freely, as one participates in a human community; they *are* what create and maintain community. (A small, final point: "motherhood" in this wider sense of accepting the responsibilities of caring is not just a "feminine" quality, at least according to Ernie, who mocks the notion, saying, with "palms raised to heaven"—once again, the shift to a religious register in the guise of Ernie being ironic—"always the mother's heart. [...] [N]obody ever asks about a father, no, fathers don't have hearts" [99].)

This is Oedipa's great lost opportunity—the way she almost comes to see how the children's "imaginary fire" represents a potential solution to her dilemmas and, for a moment only, alas, spontaneously participates in a community that is no less real for having been imagined. It is this rejected attempt at participation that allows us to read Maxine as a version of Oedipa who has moved beyond the mistakes of the past.

NOTES

1. These similarities are reinforced by a number of direct nods to the earlier book in the text of *Bleeding Edge*. To list just a few: Maxine is introduced taking her children to school, in an echo of Tupperware-party-attending Oedipa's conventionality at the beginning of *The Crying of Lot 49*, though, crucially, the reader is immediately told that Maxine does this because "she enjoys it" (1). Pynchon directly references the infamous Tupperware party when Maxine responds to Stu Gotz's suggestion that she audition for a job as stripper the following Tuesday by quipping "Tuesday's my Tupperware party" (219–20). The "philatelic zealotry" of an attendee of the "AMBOPEDIA Frolix '98" cruise means he "must have them all, hunters' and collectors' versions, artist-signed, remarques, varieties, freaks and errors, governors' editions" (14), which is surely a reference to the Tristero forgeries of conventional stamps in *The Crying of Lot 49*. Maxine notices the association seal on her decertification letter and ponders whether it contains any kind of hidden meaning, only to conclude "That's it! Secret anarchist code messages!" (18). Justin and Lucas introduce their creation, the virtual environment DeepArcher, as the evolution of an "anonymous remailer" (78), in a clear echo of the manner in which the Tristero (supposedly) functions as an alternative postal system, while it is also worth noting that the specially marked waste bins used as mailboxes by the Tristero are echoed by the Deep Web's being "mostly obsolete sites and broken links, an endless junkyard," "[a] dump, with structure" (226).

2. When late in the novel Oedipa considers once more the possibility that the Tristero might be real, she realizes that "she might have found [it] anywhere in her Republic [...] if only she'd looked" (136). As Molly Hite suggests, the novel is "not only the story of Oedipa's quest but the story of what Oedipa misses or discounts because she is on a quest" (80).

3. It should also be noted that Ernie is echoing Pynchon himself, who elsewhere deems the web to be "a development that promises social control on a scale those acquainted with twentieth-century tyrants with their goofy moustaches could only dream about," which is as unequivocal a condemnation as could be (foreword xvii).

4. Pynchon has previously referred to both the significance of political anger and the fear that it cannot last using the exact same formulation, when in *Vineland* he has Frenesi's father, Hub, tell his daughter how he eventually made his "shameful peace," "went over" and "sold off [his] only real fortune," his "precious anger" (291).

5. Catharine R. Stimpson has suggested that though "[f]ew children appear in Pynchon's early fiction, [. . .] when they do, their presence signals the possibility of grace" (35). In this context, it is worth considering this "circle of children" next to the attempt at the creation of a "sense of community" by the children of "The Secret Integration," which fails when it is penetrated by the adult world of their parents.

6. Emma Miller has argued that Oedipa's giving her name as Grace indicates "she is pregnant with divine grace." The publication of *Bleeding Edge* adds another layer of potential significance to Oedipa's choice of name: since one of the daughters of the Bortzes, mentioned but never seen in *The Crying of Lot 49*, is also called Maxine (102–3), Oedipa can in a sense be read as Maxine's "mother." Though I hesitate to make too much of this, given the importance that naming has in Pynchon I am equally loath to dismiss it as merely a coincidence.

WORKS CITED

Cha, Steph. "The Man Is Far from Dead: On Thomas Pynchon's *Bleeding Edge*." *Trop*, 15 Oct. 2013, www.tropmag.com/2013/the-man-is-far-from-dead-on-thomas-pynchons-bleeding-edge. Accessed 16 Nov. 2017.

Chabon, Michael. "The Crying of September 11." *New York Review of Books*, 7 Nov. 2013: 68–70.

Colvile, Georgiana M. M. *Beyond and Beneath the Mantle: On Thomas Pynchon's* The Crying of Lot 49. Amsterdam: Rodopi, 1998.

Cowart, David. "'Down on the Barroom Floor of History': Pynchon's *Bleeding Edge*." *Postmodern Culture* 24.1 (2013): DOI: 10.1353/pmc.2013.0060.

———. *Thomas Pynchon: The Art of Allusion*. Carbondale: Southern Illinois University Press, 1980.

Davidson, Cathy N. "Oedipa as Androgyne in Thomas Pynchon's *The Crying of Lot 49*." *Contemporary Literature* 18.1 (1977): 38–50.

Freer, Joanna. *Thomas Pynchon and American Counterculture*. New York: Cambridge University Press, 2014.

Henkle, Roger. "Pynchon's Tapestries on the Western Wall." *Pynchon: A Collection of Critical Essays*. Ed. Edward Mendelson. Englewood Cliffs: Prentice-Hall, 1978. 97–111.

Hite, Molly. *Ideas of Order in the Novels of Thomas Pynchon*. Columbus: Ohio State University Press, 1983.

Kharpertian, Theodore. *A Hand to Turn the Time: The Menippean Satires of Thomas Pynchon*. Rutherford: Fairleigh Dickinson University Press, 1990.

Konstantinou, Lee. "The One Incorruptible Still Point." *Iowa Review* 43.3 (2013): 170–74.

Levine, George. "Risking the Moment: Anarchy and Possibility in Pynchon's Fiction." *Mindful Pleasures: Essays on Thomas Pynchon*. Ed. George Levine and David Leverenz. Boston: Little, Brown, 1976. 113–36.

Maragos, Georgios. "'For every They there ought to be a We': The (Almost) Equivalence of Power and Resistance in *Mason & Dixon* and *Against the Day*." *Orbit: A Journal of American Literature* 2.2 (2014). DOI: https://doi.org/10.7766/orbit.v2.2.71.

Mendelson, Edward. "The Sacred, the Profane, and *The Crying of Lot 49*." *Pynchon: A Collection of Critical Essays*. Ed. Edward Mendelson. Englewood Cliffs: Prentice-Hall, 1978. 112–46.

Miller, Emma. "The Naming of Oedipa Maas." *Orbit: A Journal of American Literature* 1.1 (2012). DOI: https://doi.org/10.7766/orbit.v1.1.12.

Miller, Keith. "Maxine of the Mean Streets." *Literary Review* 413 (2013): 50.

Pynchon, Thomas. *Bleeding Edge*. London: Jonathan Cape, 2013.

———. *The Crying of Lot 49*. London: Vintage, 2000.

———. Foreword. *Nineteen Eighty-Four*. By George Orwell. New York: Harcourt, 2003. vii–xxvi.

———. *Slow Learner*. London: Picador, 1984.

Schaub, Thomas. "Open Letter in Response to Edward Mendelson's 'The Sacred, the Profane, and *The Crying of Lot 49*.'" *Boundary* 2 (1976): 93–102.

St. Clair, Justin. "Pynchon's Postmodern Legacy; or, Why Irony Is Still Relevant." *Los Angeles Review of Books*, 21 Sept. 2013, www.lareviewofbooks.org/review/pynchons-postmodern-legacy-or-why-irony-is-still-relevant. Accessed 16 Nov. 2017.

———. "Rereading Thomas Pynchon: Postmodernism and the Political Real." *Los Angeles Review of Books*, 4 Mar. 2015, www.lareviewofbooks.org/article/rereading-thomas-pynchon-postmodernism-political-real. Accessed 16 Nov. 2017.

Stimpson, Catharine R. "Pre-Apocalyptic Atavism: Thomas Pynchon's Early Fiction." *Mindful Pleasures: Essays on Thomas Pynchon*. Ed. George Levine and David Leverenz. Boston: Little, Brown, 1976. 31–47.

Tanner, Tony. *Thomas Pynchon*. London: Methuen, 1982.

Tyson, Lois. *Psychological Politics of the American Dream: The Commodification of Subjectivity in Twentieth-Century American Literature*. Columbus: Ohio State University Press, 1994.

Between *Sangha* and Sex Work
The Karmic Middle Path of *Vineland*'s Female Characters

CHRISTOPHER KOCELA

Vineland (1990) constitutes a sustained engagement with both feminism and Buddhism, yet scholarship on the novel has only examined these subjects in isolation from one another. On the one hand, although *Vineland* has been read as a "meditation on power and gender" (Hite 136), an ecofeminist narrative that "problematizes all ideologies based on binary thought" (Ostrander 122), and a critique of feminist separatism that "works to destabilize the equation between gender and biological sex" (Freer 149), readings of sex, gender, and power in the novel have largely ignored Pynchon's numerous references to Buddhism. On the other hand, scholars interested in these Buddhist references have interpreted them through their textual association with the martial arts either as the basis for a "preterite spirituality" (McClure 49) divorced from considerations of gender and sex or else as evidence of Pynchon's "Occidental fascination with Oriental folkways" (Carroll 256) or his "Tarantino-esque fetish for 'ass-kicking' women" (Thomas 138). I argue, however, that Pynchon's portrayal of Buddhism, feminism, and sexual and gender politics cannot be fully appreciated without attention to the way that these discourses mutually inflect and reinforce one another. Pynchon's novel contributes to debates in Buddhist feminism that are specific to the novel's setting in the 1980s and yet that assume broader implications over the course of the narrative for his presentation of the relationship between sex, gender, and power.

It is no accident that *Vineland*, set in California in the summer of 1984, portrays feminism and Buddhism as intimately intertwined. The mid-1980s are regarded as a turning point in the history of American Buddhism, owing to a series of sex scandals that received widespread media coverage and severely compromised the reputation of many of the most prominent Buddhist practice centers in the United States. Early in 1984, Richard Baker was forced to step down as abbot of the San Francisco Zen Center when it became known that he had misappropriated funds and carried on secret sexual relationships with his female students. As the most famous Zen institution in the country owing to the influence of its founder, Shunryu Suzuki, whose *Zen Mind, Beginner's Mind* (1970) was already on its way to becoming a Western spiritual classic, the San Francisco Zen Center and its scandal quickly became a symptom of the more general failure of American Buddhism to provide the enlightenment it had promised its first wave of converts in the 1960s. Soon afterward both Taizan Maezumi, head of the Los Angeles Zen Center, and Soen Sa Nim, founder of the Kwan Um Zen School in Rhode Island, were revealed to have had sexual affairs with female students while pretending to lead strictly moral and celibate lives. In 1988 the Vajradhatu community of Tibetan Buddhism in Colorado was shocked to discover that Osel Tendzin, a master well known for his "crazy wisdom" brand of open sexuality, had been sleeping with male and female students for years after being diagnosed with AIDS. By the time Tendzin's activities became public knowledge, America's countercultural honeymoon with Buddhism had already ended. Rather than continue trying to replicate the rigidly hierarchal and patriarchal master/student relationships that characterized Buddhist teaching in the East, American practitioners began calling for more democratic institutional structures capable of providing significant leadership roles for women.[1]

Foremost among those advocating for change were feminist practitioners and academics such as Sandy Boucher, Rita Gross, and Diana Paul, who argued that importing the male-dominated structure of Buddhist institutions into the United States amounted to reinforcing ideas about karma that were denigrating to women. Common to many Brahmanical forms of Indian thought, the notion that birth in a female body was evidence of negative karma accrued in past lives exerted considerable influence on the shape and evolution of Buddhist institutions, where it was repeatedly used to explain why positions of authority were reserved for men. In place of this traditional concept of karma, which establishes a universal, causal relationship between sexual difference, gender identity, and moral activity in past lives, Buddhist feminists advocated attention to more uniquely Buddhist concepts such as "no-self" (in Sanskrit, *anatman*) and emptiness (*sunyata*) that disrupt, through their denial of an essential self, attempts to link identity to sexual difference. They further argued that counteracting the exploitation of women in the Buddhist *sangha* (or community of practitioners) requires reimagining karma as a cause and effect relationship not between past and future lives but between social institutions and individuals in the present (Gross 145).

I argue here that *Vineland* reflects and develops connections between Buddhism, sex, and power circulating in the media and academic discourse at the time of Pynchon's writing. Through its depiction of female monasticism via the Kunoichi Sisterhood, gender role reversal through DL's ninja magic, guru/student sexual relations in Weed Atman's leadership of PR[3], and its revisionist commentary on karma via the Thanatoids, *Vineland* seizes on themes central to Buddhist feminist texts of the period such as Diana Paul's *Women in Buddhism* (1979), Sandy Boucher's *Turning the Wheel* (1988), and Karma Lekshe Tsomo's *Sakyadhita: Daughters of the Buddha* (1988). Yet although I follow precedents set by Molly Hite and Joanna Freer, who use internal evidence from *Vineland* to establish Pynchon's familiarity with a range of feminist writings from the 1970s and 1980s (Hite 136–37, Freer 149), my interpretation does not depend on Pynchon having read any specific work of Buddhist feminism. Rather, my main purpose in contextualizing *Vineland* relative to these arguments is to show how Buddhist thought illuminates Pynchon's seemingly contradictory insistence that there is no essential relationship between sex and gender even as women often appear predestined, in his fiction, to occupy subordinate and objectified positions relative to men. While this tension recurs throughout Pynchon's later work in particular (as Chetwynd, Freer, and Maragos reveal in their introduction to this volume), *Vineland* dramatizes this tension directly through the narrative arcs of its two main female characters, DL Chastain and Frenesi Gates. Where DL's narrative emphasizes the "ultimate truth" of sex and gender in Mahayana Buddhist philosophy, which consists in freedom from fixed forms and characteristics, Frenesi's narrative underscores the "contingent truth" that sexual difference and gender identity are always determined by individual karma. Even in Frenesi's story, however, Pynchon historicizes the workings of karma, opening a middle path between these narratives that encourages the reader to see gender roles as influenced by social institutions and ideologies rather than natural or universal laws.

DL Chastain and the Emptiness of Gender

Darryl Louise (DL) Chastain is the obvious character with which to begin discussion of the relationship between Buddhism, gender, and power in *Vineland*. As revealed in a series of flashbacks that make up much of the core of the novel, DL learns judo and jujitsu as a young girl while growing up on a military base in Japan after the end of World War II. As she quickly discovers, knowledge of the martial arts not only shields her from the beatings which her father regularly inflicts on her mother but also instills a meditative discipline that enables her to overcome the "powerlessness and sooner or later self-poisoning hatred" (121) that children brought up around domestic abuse often experience. This sense of empowerment is amplified when she is recruited to train with Inoshiro Sensei, a ninjitsu master whose martial and magical techniques inspire the "radical conclusion that her body belonged to her" (128). DL's hard-won self-confidence enables her to negotiate the numerous challenges she faces after becoming the de facto security guard for 24fps, a countercultural film collective dedicated to publicizing evidence of government suppression in 1960s California. When her friend and sometime lover Frenesi Gates is imprisoned by Brock Vond in a secret government compound, DL calmly deploys a range of ninja skills, including invisibility and mind manipulation, in order to rescue her (252–57). When DL herself is captured and sold into slavery as a high-priced call girl in Japan, she copes with her situation by "meditating, finding inside herself the way back to shelter she'd wondered more than once if she'd lost for good" (140). Yet after accepting her role as a sex worker in order to avenge herself on Vond, she mistakenly applies the ninja death touch to Takeshi Fumimota, incurring a karmic debt that changes the course of her life. Seeking refuge at the Kunoichi Sisterhood retreat in California, DL is sentenced by the head ninjette to work as Takeshi's sidekick in the "karmic adjustment business" (172) he carries out for the Thanatoids, a ghostly community trapped in the Tibetan Buddhist bardo state between death and rebirth. In the final pages of *Vineland*, DL reflects on her past in light of the three unwholesome motivations or "poisons"—greed, ill will, and delusion—that in a Buddhist understanding of karma must be overcome if one is to escape self-attachment and rebirth in future lives. While DL acknowledges this traditional view of karma, she also suspects that it does not fully explain the trajectory of her life: "Had it only been [...] that many years of what the Buddha calls 'passion, enmity, folly'? Suppose that she'd been meant, all the time, to be paying attention to something else entirely?" (380).

John A. McClure reads *Vineland* as "the story of DL's Progress" (51) in which she uses the martial arts, an inherently impure and "preterite" form of Buddhist spirituality, to survive the collapse of 1960s countercultural idealism. While McClure's reading effectively links Pynchon's presentation of Buddhism to strategies of resistance articulated by Gary Snyder, it oversimplifies the gender politics embedded in DL's story. McClure's answer to DL's final question about the three poisons is that the "something else" to which she should have paid attention is "not 'enlightenment' or even her soul, but Takeshi himself, a partner and friend whom DL learns to love" (55). This heteronormative interpretation makes no reference to DL's lesbian relationship with Frenesi, her experiences as a sex worker, or her use of ninja magic to free her friend from Vond. By ignoring these aspects of DL's story and portraying her most traditional female role—that of partner and lover to a man—as the solution to her concerns about karma, McClure's argument belies the spirit of Pynchon's novel, which goes to great lengths to unsettle traditional representations of karma as a cosmic support for the social status quo. In a world that contains Thanatoids, a thriving karmic adjustment business, and

DL's gender-defying acts of magic, her final question should not be addressed without examining how her story contributes to the novel's critique of karma as a regulatory principle for defining gender roles.

A first step toward answering DL's question is to recognize that her use of magic to challenge heteronormative values aligns her with a long tradition of female *bodhisattvas* exclusive to the Mahayana Buddhist canon. For Buddhist feminists, the significance of this tradition is that it teaches the emptiness of gender identity and sexual difference, often through supernatural transformations of women into men and men into women. One such object lesson occurs in the *Vimalakirti Sutra* when Shariputra, the Buddha's foremost disciple, asks a *bodhisattva* goddess why she does not use her powers to transform herself into a man. Motivated by a traditional understanding of karma, Shariputra assumes that female embodiment is a negative state from which any enlightened being would seek to escape. In response, the goddess changes Shariputra's form into that of a woman, then offers this teaching: "Shariputra, who is not a woman, appears in a woman's body. And the same is true of all women—though they appear in women's bodies, they are not women. Therefore the Buddha teaches that all phenomena are neither male nor female" (91). The point of this lesson is not that sexual and gender difference do not exist but rather that the fact of their existence is only one of two truths—the "conventional" as opposed to "ultimate" truth as defined in Mahayana philosophy. While the unenlightened fixate on the conventional truth of forms and characteristics, the enlightened *bodhisattva* can appreciate this truth while also seeing the ultimate truth of emptiness, the fact that there are no fixed essences or characteristics to be found in any subject or object. Indeed, it is the *bodhisattva*'s task to walk this middle path between the conventional and the ultimate, leading others to awakening. As Rita Gross observes, emptiness is "the only Buddhist concept to have been used in classical Buddhist texts to criticize Buddhist practices of gender discrimination" (174).

In *Vineland*, Pynchon foregrounds connections between Buddhist spirituality and ninjitsu because the latter, by virtue of its Hollywood association with supernatural powers, provides a ready framework for introducing the kinds of magical gender performance found in Mahayana Buddhist sutras. One of the most conspicuous features of DL's magic is that it renders her ambiguous with regard to sex and gender. DL and Frenesi first meet when the latter is threatened by oncoming riot police in Berkeley: "Oh, I need Superman, she prayed, Tarzan on that vine" (116). When DL mysteriously arrives on motorcycle moments later, Frenesi assumes her helmeted rescuer is a man: "With her bare thighs Frenesi gripped the leather hips of her benefactor, finding that she'd also pressed her face against the fragrant leather back—she never thought it might be a woman she hugged this way" (117). Later, in her more elaborate efforts to free Frenesi from Vond's compound, DL again plays the part of a masked male superhero. After using a "nonlethal taste of the Kunoichi Death Kiss" to extract information from a young female prisoner, DL emulates Zorro: "Spanish guitars ringing in her mind, DL slipped the girl's shirt off and with a black-gloved finger traced a big letter Z—above, between, below her breasts" (254). By portraying DL as a protector who comes to the magical aid of Frenesi and others, Pynchon aligns her not only with the goddess of the *Vimalakirti Sutra* but with the most famous sex-changing *bodhisattva* of all, Avalokiteśvara (known as Guanyin in China and Kannon in Japan), whose name means "regarder of the cries of the world." First described in the *Lotus Sutra* as a divine being with the ability to adopt whatever gender and social role best serves those in need, Avalokiteśvara became widely worshipped in Pure Land Buddhism for intervening in the lives of women, mitigating the pain of childbirth, arranged marriages, and sexual assault (Reed 176). The *bodhisattva* ideal represented by Avalokiteśvara provides context both for DL's gender-defying magic and her development as a character who uses magic to help and protect others—especially other women. As her story makes clear, DL does not develop this capacity spontaneously or easily. Her early training in the martial arts endows her with self-confidence but little in the way of compassion. While still living with her parents she displays a "sadistic" habit of inciting her father's violence against her mother—a habit driven by DL's anger at her mother's refusal to seek help for herself (125). Given her age and upbringing it is difficult to fault her for this reaction, but it showcases the later importance of the Kunoichi Sisterhood in steering DL along the *bodhisattva* path. It is not until she enters the ninjette *sangha* led by Sister Rochelle that DL learns to practice more than an instrumental version of her sensei's teachings.

Although the Kunoichi retreat is initially described as a "sort of Esalen Institute for lady asskickers" (107), subsequent details suggest that it conflates features of two of the most famous Zen monasteries in California: Tassajara Zen Mountain Center in the Los Padres National Forest, and Shasta Abbey in Mount Shasta. The torturous dirt road leading up to the retreat (107, 161) and the fact that the sisters sell "cucumber brandy" (107) evoke Tassajara, the monastery established in 1967 by Shunryu Suzuki, who was known to his students and readers as the "crooked cucumber."[2] At the same time, the retreat's white-washed buildings, combined with the fact that it is led by a woman, call to mind Shasta Abbey, established by Jiyu Kennett in 1970 and the only American monastery founded by a woman at the time *Vineland* was published. More important than identifying real-world analogues for the fictional retreat, however, is recognizing that as an all-female practice community, the Kunoichi Sisterhood has no counterpart in American Buddhism and represents an idealized vision of the female *sangha* celebrated by Buddhist feminists. While it may appear strange to speak of idealism in relation to the Kunoichi, whose interests appear at least as mercantile as spiritual, their offering of "fantasy marathons for devotees of the Orient, group rates on Kiddie Ninja Weekends, help for rejected disciples of Zen ('No bamboo sticks—ever!' promised the ads in *Psychology Today*) and other Eastern methods" (107) echoes a strategy that female monasteries in Japan and Korea have adopted in order to survive. Surveying the history of Zen convents in Japan, Grace Schireson notes that because Buddhist nuns have always received fewer donations from the lay population than monks, they have compensated by providing "different services that are not specifically spiritual offerings" such as child and elder care and classes in flower arranging, sewing, and calligraphy (212). Additionally, Pynchon seems to have designed the Kunoichi in response to real-world feminist complaints about the patriarchal and racial constitution of American practice centers. Their promise not to use "bamboo sticks" in retraining Zen students reflects the fact that many American women regarded the traditional *kyosaku* (training stick) as little more than a prop for macho posturing (Boucher 8, 222). Similarly, the racial and ethnic makeup of the ninjettes, "most of them non-Asian, many were actually black, a-and Mexican too!" (108), answers bell hooks's repeated calls for a more racially diverse American Buddhist *sangha* (44).

In the context of DL's development as a character, however, the most important aspect of the Kunoichi Sisterhood is that it demystifies the magic of ninjitsu as a form of attention benefiting others rather than oneself. Sister Rochelle, the head ninjette, manifests this teaching the first time she appears to Prairie and DL, emerging out of the shadows of the coffee lounge. Although Prairie assumes Rochelle's invisibility is a "magical gift," the head nun explains that by memorizing the movement of light on floors and walls, she had "come to know the room so completely that she could impersonate it, in its full transparency and emptiness" (111). In Rochelle's view, attending to the unity of detail and emptiness is the antidote for those who fixate on enlightenment as a "big transcendent moment" (112). This fundamentally Mahayanist teaching on the inseparability of contingent and ultimate truth transforms the self-involved DL into the *bodhisattva*-like protector she becomes in her work for 24fps and, later, the Thanatoids. It is also this teaching with which Rochelle reproaches DL when she returns from her attempt to kill Vond: "Living as always let's say at a certain distance from the reality of others, you descended [...] again into the corrupted world, and instead of paying attention, taking the time, getting prepared, you had to be a reckless bitch and go rushing through the outward forms" (154). DL's fundamental crime consists not in attacking Takeshi but in failing to attend to the details of her "corrupted world" as a sex worker, which might have enabled a compassionate rather than violent response. Such a possibility is explicitly spelled out in the *Vimalakirti Sutra*, which makes clear that a *bodhisattva* can save others even in the form of a prostitute:

> Sometimes he shows himself as a woman of pleasure,
> enticing those prone to lechery.
> First he catches them with the hook of desire,
> then leads them to the Buddha way. (102)

Sister Rochelle's attitude betrays a more general Buddhist ambivalence about prostitution as a transgressive gender role that poses karmic dangers while also providing unique opportunities to educate oneself and others about the folly of sexual attachment (Faure 130–31).

Yet while Sister Rochelle's teaching proves valuable as a framework for gauging DL's moral and spiritual progress, it also reveals the limitations of the *bodhisattva* ideal for purposes of feminist critique. This is because, in her address to DL's experiences as a sex worker, Rochelle offers a neat explanation of her student's failure that amounts to blaming the victim. By holding DL to an otherworldly standard of compassion and focus, Rochelle omits any consideration of the broader cultural and institutional forces at work in her kidnapping and exploitation. Sadly, Pynchon's fictional rendering of the international sex trade appears equally oblivious to these issues. Although the narrative attributes DL's abduction to connections between the yakuza and the mafia (132), its account of the event and her subsequent auctioning into sex slavery does not elaborate on this international network but focuses instead on the remarkably nonchalant attitude DL adopts throughout. Realizing that she has been kidnapped, DL merely wonders whether "being sold into white slavery would turn out to be at all beneficial as a career step" (135); later, preparing for the slave auction, she reminds herself to "*[j]ust relax and have fun*" (137). Yet while these scenes clearly lack cultural and psychological depth, the fact that they perfectly set up DL for Sister Rochelle's criticism raises questions about what is missing more generally in DL's story of magical self-transformation. DL's fear, at the end of the novel, that she should have been paying attention to "something else" suggests that for all her individual efforts to overcome "passion, enmity, folly" (380), her training as a would-be *bodhisattva* has not encouraged her to consider the social, structural, or institutional nature of these karmic poisons. For Buddhist feminists such as Gross and hooks, social change is impossible without a consideration of how prejudice and inequity are perpetuated at the collective as well as individual level. For the reader of *Vineland*, this means that answering DL's final question necessitates juxtaposing her magical narrative with that of her decidedly nonmagical counterpart, Frenesi Gates.

Frenesi Gates and the Three Poisons, Institutionalized

David R. Loy argues that reimagining the three poisons of karmic identity—greed, ill will, and delusion—comprises an urgent task for socially engaged Buddhists and Buddhist feminists (87–88). According to Loy, the problem of the three poisons is not that they determine an individual's birth or social station in a future life but that they collectively shape Western societies in the present. Greed, ill will, and delusion have become institutionalized in the form of corporate capitalism, the military, and the mass media, respectively (89); in these institutional forms they are able to play the role of governing ideologies. If the traditional task of Buddhism is to overcome attachment to the individual ego or *atman*, socially engaged Buddhism must recognize that "[w]e not only have group egos; there are institutionalized egos" (88).

Vineland represents collective karma in the form of the Thanatoid community, whose membership consists of confused, ghostly individuals caught between death and life as defined in the *Tibetan Book of the Dead*. In creating the Thanatoids, Pynchon seems to have been inspired by the therapeutic "conscious dying" movement that developed in the United States and England in the early 1980s, which popularized Tibetan Buddhism among the terminally ill (Sedgwick 173–74). Within the novel, however, their collective existence is attributed to Loy's three institutional poisons. Pynchon repeatedly links the rapid growth of the Thanatoid population to both the Vietnam War (174–75, 320) and systematic financial exploitation (172); it is this combination that Takeshi invokes when he advises Ortho Bob to defer taking revenge against his commanders in Vietnam in favor of "borrowing against karmic futures" (175). The Thanatoids are even more directly shaped by the influence of television, which they watch incessantly after death and which, "with its history of picking away at the topic with doctor shows, war shows, cop shows, murder shows, had trivialized the Big D itself" (218). What is perhaps most interesting about the Thanatoid community, however, is that its boundaries appear to be as permeable as those between life and death in Pynchon's novel. With the exception of DL, every major character in *Vineland* is compared to a Thanatoid or exhibits Thanatoid-like qualities at some point. Takeshi becomes "part Thanatoid" (171) after receiving DL's ninja death touch; Zoyd Wheeler "haunts" his ex-wife Frenesi by projecting himself into her consciousness (40); Prairie sometimes believes she was aborted by her mother and is now condemned to "haunt her like a ghost" (334); and Frenesi herself, after paving the way for Weed Atman's assassination, understands that she is "walking around next to herself, haunting herself, watching a movie of it all" (237). Far from representing a distinct community confined to Shady Creek, the Thanatoids are symptomatic of contemporary American subjectivity and reveal its collective poisoning by militarized ill will, capitalist greed, and media delusion.

Frenesi Gates is the most consistently Thanatoid-like of the major characters in *Vineland*, and her story illustrates how patriarchal gender roles, and the subordination of women to men, are reinforced through the institutionalization of the three karmic poisons. Daughter of politically active parents in the Hollywood film industry, she learns two important truths from her mother, Sasha. The first is that history consists of men "committing these crimes, major and petty, one by one against other living humans" (80). The second is that, regardless of any opposition she might offer to historical power, Frenesi is marked by the "ancestral curse" she has inherited from Sasha, which consists of a "helpless turn toward images of authority, especially uniformed men [...] as if some Cosmic Fascist had spliced in a DNA sequence requiring this form of seduction and initiation into the dark joys of social control" (83). Frenesi's story dramatizes the interdependence of these historical and "cosmic" truths. Although she tries as a documentarian for the film collective 24fps to expose corporate corruption and political injustice, she is drawn into sexual relationships with both Weed Atman, leader of the revolutionary group PR^3, and his enemy, the federal prosecutor Brock Vond. Eventually the domineering Vond gains the firmer hold over Frenesi and convinces her to frame Atman as an FBI plant—an act that leads to his assassination. Later, Frenesi's weakness for Vond also prompts her to abandon her baby daughter, Prairie, while suffering from postpartum depression. Like the Thanatoids, Frenesi spends the majority of her time in the novel's diegetic present ruminating over her past mistakes and lamenting her inability to escape the "clockwork of cause and effect" (90). Estranged from her mother, she takes every opportunity to surveil Sasha's house in hope of catching a glimpse of her (82); she also spies on teenage girls in the belief that she might gain insight into the behavior of the daughter she has not seen in over a decade (68). If Frenesi's regrets about "cause and effect" cast her story as a tale about bad karma, her inability to stop spying also suggests that, as in the case of the Thanatoids, her karmic identity is strongly influenced by the institutionalized poison of the media and television in particular.

Previous scholarship has tended to present Frenesi as a corrupt ideal of passive femininity in contrast to DL's practicality and dynamism. Patricia Bergh portrays Frenesi as the "ultimate Postmodern Woman" (1) whose function is to serve as a screen for the fantasy projections of others. David Cowart likens Frenesi to "sin free" Eve before the Fall: her temptation by the serpent Vond leads to the end of the radical sixties but also to the survival of the women's movement through the resourcefulness of her Lilith-like "sister," DL (106–7). Most recently, Margaret Lynd reads Frenesi as an example of Pynchon's insistence on the "frailty" of woman, a "lapse in Pynchon's otherwise comprehensive and sensitive telling of America's multilayered past" (26). While I agree with these critics that Frenesi's story represents, in part, a fall from grace or innocence, I disagree that this fall highlights the comparative groundedness or practicality of DL's character. As I have suggested, DL's story is itself an idealized rendering of Buddhist feminist arguments about the power of the female *sangha* and the emptiness of gender. In this light, the significance of Frenesi's story is that, pace Lynd, it historicizes karma as a counterpoint to the magical interpretive framework provided by DL's narrative.

Although Frenesi is not a practicing Buddhist like DL, she repeatedly describes her documentary work for 24fps as a search for enlightenment. Like the Kunoichi, Frenesi and her crew place a premium on attending to the minute details of a corrupted world, transforming them into insight about the falsity of political promises. As she tells a TV interviewer, she foresees a future in which her generation will become completely immune to political manipulation "because too many of us are learning how to pay attention" (195). At the same time, Frenesi diverges from Sister Rochelle's teaching by imagining enlightenment as a kind of epiphany or transcendent experience. In searching out scenes of conflict to film, she dreams of encountering "the people in a single presence, the police likewise simple as a moving blade—and individuals who in meetings might only bore or be pains in the ass here suddenly being seen to transcend, almost beyond will to move smoothly between baton and victim to take the blow instead" (117). Frenesi's enthusiasm for mystical oneness reflects the attitude of most American Buddhists in the 1960s, when Beat writers and early Zen popularizers such as Jack Kerouac, D. T. Suzuki, and Philip Kapleau portrayed *satori* as the holy grail of Zen. More specifically, however, Frenesi's fantasy of protestors and police united in a moment of transcendent violence also appears as a sublimated representation of her sexual attraction to uniformed men. That Frenesi should imagine enlightenment as a transformation of this desire makes sense given Pynchon's portrayal of her "ancestral curse" as a kind of karmic burden. But her belief that this transformation can take place through the lens of a camera emphasizes one of *Vineland*'s central themes, which is that karma is socially and culturally conditioned. While Sasha attributes Frenesi's affinity for men in authority to cosmic and genetic influences, Frenesi's interactions with men and their images, like her later spying on her mother and daughter, strongly suggest that her sexual proclivity is learned behavior reinforced by television and film. Early in the novel she is interrupted by a knock on the door while masturbating to an episode of the television program "CHiPs." Upon answering the door she experiences a "Tubefreek miracle" when her televized fantasy of uniformed officers comes to life on her doorstep in the form of a real U.S. marshal, who appears "through the screen, broken up into little dots like pixels of a video image" (84). Frenesi's televisual "framing" of this man reflects her tendency, when behind the camera, to zone male bodies for erotic pleasure in terms that duplicate the workings of the male gaze in feminist film criticism. As Stacey Olster argues, Frenesi's documentary films tend to chop up the bodies of Weed Atman and Brock Vond in a manner similar to that by which, according to Laura Mulvey, female bodies are dismembered and fetishized in classic Hollywood cinema (120–24). That Frenesi also views male bodies in this way when *not* behind the camera suggests that her "uniform fetish" (83) is a product of internalizing the fetishistic gaze of the Hollywood films she watched as a child with her parents. If Frenesi's bad karma, manifested in her recurring subordination to men in power, is the result of her conditioning by visual media, no enlightenment or release from this karma is possible without her fundamentally questioning her relationship to the camera.

While the international sex trade is rendered with little cultural or psychological detail, Frenesi's "sex work" with Vond and Weed Atman is portrayed as a byproduct of her unchecked faith in the protective, transformative power of the camera. After acquiescing to Vond's command that she frame Weed Atman as an FBI spy, she rationalizes her relationships with both men by imagining that she is merely watching a porn film of her own activities: "[S]ex," she concludes, "was mediated for her now" (237). As late as the night before Weed's assassination, Frenesi is still able to convince herself that the imminent violence can be transfigured through careful camera work: "Her impulse was [...] to imagine that with the gun in the house, the 24-frame-per-second truth she still believed in would find some new, more intense level of truth" (241). In light of these fantasies, Weed's murder becomes an ironic parody of Buddhist enlightenment in which the death of the self or *atman* serves to prop up institutionalized delusion, desire, and ill will as personified by Vond.

Weed's undoing as a result of his sexual relationship with Frenesi also alludes to the sex scandals plaguing American Buddhism at the time of Pynchon's writing. Weed's characterization as an impromptu guru who, uncertain of how to lead his flock, winds up having affairs with his female followers resonates with the stories of fallen Zen masters such as Taizan Maetsumi and Soen Sa Nim (Boucher 210–12). His downfall is thus emblematic of the contemporary history of American Buddhism—a history that begins with countercultural enthusiasm for enlightenment and social change in the 1960s and culminates in the 1980s in betrayal, sexual exploitation, and distrust of Buddhist institutions. By calling attention to this history, Pynchon's aim is not to undermine DL's narrative of personal empowerment through self-discipline and compassion. On the contrary, the historical elements of Frenesi's story provide a provisional answer to DL's final question about the three poisons: the "something else" missing in her magical narrative of gender transformation is recognition of the institutionalized nature of ill will, greed, and delusion that work ideologically to limit social and gender roles for women in patriarchal culture.

Where DL's story privileges the ultimate truth of gender emptiness as expressed in Mahayana philosophy, Frenesi's story reminds the reader of the contingent truth of power and gender in American Buddhism, and American culture more generally, at the time of Pynchon's writing. Perhaps the lesbian relationship between DL and Frenesi, which is little more than hinted at over the course of the novel, is best understood as a figurative unity of these ultimate and contingent truths. If so, Pynchon seems to warn against mystifying even this form of "enlightenment" as a transcendent moment of revelation. The few details provided about their relationship suggest that it is both highly idealized and grounded in the same power dynamics that characterize those between men and women in the novel. One of the most poetic passages in *Vineland* depicts DL and Frenesi eating and reminiscing in a Mexican cantina, "their fun-house shadows taken by the village surfaces drenched in sunset, as sage, apricot, adobe and wine colors were infiltrated with night" (258). Two pages later DL recalls that, during sex, "I *made* you do stuff, bitch" (260), while Frenesi takes "mean satisfaction" in having pushed DL into violating her ethical principles and "saintlike control" (260). By simultaneously affirming both DL's empowering traversal of gender roles and Frenesi's karmic predisposition to sexual subordination, this scene crystallizes the tension inherent in Pynchon's depiction of sex and gender throughout *Vineland* and in much of his oeuvre. Where previous scholarship has tended to examine this tension in isolation from Pynchon's interest in Eastern and Buddhist thought, I have attempted to demonstrate how *Vineland*'s sustained engagement with Buddhism and feminism installs a progressive reformulation of karma at the heart of its treatment of sex, gender, and power.

NOTES

1. For more on the significance of these scandals in the history of American Buddhism, see Boucher 210–56 and Seager 218–22.

2. For descriptions of both monasteries, see Boucher 123–28, 133–36; for an account of the road leading to Tassajara, see Chadwick 264–65.

WORKS CITED

Bergh, Patricia A. "(De)constructing the Image: Thomas Pynchon's Postmodern Woman." *Journal of Popular Culture* 30.4 (1997): 1–12.

Boucher, Sandy. *Turning the Wheel: American Women Creating the New Buddhism*. Boston: Beacon, 1988.

Carroll, Jeffrey. "Ninjettes, Nuns, and Lady Asskickers: Thomas Pynchon's Bow to the Mythical Orient." *Gender and Culture in Literature and Film East and West:*

Issues of Perception and Interpretation. Ed. Nitaya Masavisut, George Simson, and Larry E. Smith. Honolulu: University of Hawaii Press, 1994. 253–59.

Chadwick, David. *Crooked Cucumber: The Life and Zen Teaching of Shunryu Suzuki.* New York: Broadway, 1999.

Cowart, David. *Thomas Pynchon and the Dark Passages of History.* Athens: University of Georgia Press, 2011.

Faure, Bernard. *The Red Thread: Buddhist Approaches to Sexuality.* Princeton: Princeton University Press, 1998.

Freer, Joanna. *Thomas Pynchon and American Counterculture.* New York: Cambridge University Press, 2014.

Green, Geoffrey, Donald J. Greiner, and Larry McCaffery, eds. *The* Vineland *Papers: Critical Takes on Pynchon's Novel.* Normal: Dalkey Archive Press, 1994.

Gross, Rita M. *Buddhism after Patriarchy: A Feminist History, Analysis, and Reconstruction of Buddhism.* Albany: SUNY Press, 1993.

Hite, Molly. "Feminist Theory and the Politics of *Vineland*." Green, Greiner, and McCaffery 135–53.

hooks, bell. "Waking Up to Racism: Dharma, Diversity, and Race." *Tricycle: The Buddhist Review,* Fall 1994, www.tricycle.org/magazine/waking-racism. Accessed 2 May 2016.

Loy, David R. *Money Sex War Karma: Notes for a Buddhist Revolution.* Boston: Wisdom, 2008.

Lynd, Margaret. "Situated Fictions: Reading the California Novels against Thomas Pynchon's Narrative World." *Pynchon's California.* Ed. Scott McClintock and John Miller. Iowa City: University of Iowa Press, 2014. 15–33.

McClure, John A. *Partial Faiths: Postsecular Fiction in the Age of Pynchon and Morrison.* Athens: University of Georgia Press, 2007.

Olster, Stacey. "When You're a (Nin)jette, You're a (Nin)jette All the Way—or Are You?: Female Filmmaking in *Vineland*." Green, Greiner, and McCaffery 119–34.

Ostrander, Madeline. "Awakening to the Physical World: Ideological Collapse and Economic Resistance in *Vineland*." *Thomas Pynchon: Reading from the Margins.* Ed. Niran Abbas. Madison: Fairleigh Dickinson University Press, 2003. 122–35.

Paul, Diana Y. *Women in Buddhism: Images of the Feminine in the Mahāyāna Tradition.* Berkeley: University of California Press, 1985.

Pynchon, Thomas. *Vineland.* Boston: Little, Brown, 1990.

Reed, Barbara E. "The Gender Symbolism of Kuan-yin Bodhisattva." *Buddhism, Sexuality, and Gender.* Ed. José Ignacio Cabezón. Albany: SUNY Press, 1992. 159–80.

Schireson, Grace. *Zen Women: Beyond Tea Ladies, Iron Maidens, and Macho Masters.* Boston: Wisdom, 2009.

Seager, Richard Hughes. *Buddhism in America.* Rev. ed. New York: Columbia University Press, 2012.

Sedgwick, Eve Kosofsky. *Touching Feeling: Affect, Pedagogy, Performativity.* Durham: Duke University Press, 2003.

Thomas, Samuel. *Pynchon and the Political.* New York: Routledge, 2007.

Tsomo, Karma Lekshe, ed. *Sakyadhita: Daughters of the Buddha.* Ithaca: Snow Lion, 1988.

The Vimalakirti Sutra. Trans. Burton Watson. New York: Columbia University Press, 1997.

SECTION 3 **Sex Writing**

"Allons Enfants!"
Pynchon's Pornographies

DOUG HAYNES

In a corporate State, a place must be made for innocence, and its many uses. (*GR* 419)

Soft Bodies; Cheap Thrills

In his 1984 essay "Is It O.K. to Be a Luddite?" Thomas Pynchon argues that literatures of sensation are often barred from the canon, due apparently to an official parsimony regarding the sublimation of literary affect. The gothic genre, for example, suffers, Pynchon laments, "because it use[s] images of death and ghostly survival toward *no more responsible end than special effects and cheap thrills*" (par. 20, emphasis added). For the tastemakers of the canon, a more aesthetic purpose should be found for such excessive confections as literary death and haunting. But of course, special effects and cheap thrills are the very stuff of mass entertainment, which often deal in the trades of sex and violence. The gothic, as popular as it is literary, is, in John Bowen's suggestion, filled with such things: "a particularly strange and perverse family of texts which themselves are full of strange families, irrigated with scenes of rape and incest" (par. 1). Pynchon's investment in popular literatures of sensation is of a piece with the impulse to thrill and violate we find in his own work. In the present essay, the notion of the thrill is central, partly as it relates to violence but chiefly as it pertains to sex and, more particularly, to pornography. The Pynchonian thrill opens what I call the affective or "soft" body, both of the reader and the text. And while I argue for the centrality of pornography to Pynchon's work, I also consider the modes of resistance and complicity with power and social institutions this genre enacts, as Pynchon deploys it. Questions of whether pornography can ever be a critical discourse, the identity of the bodies it engages, and the nature of the thrills it provides, also steer what follows.

Commenting on violence in Pynchon's first novel *V.* (1963), Michael Kowalewski makes some observations that could just as easily apply to sex too, noting that violence, "like so much else in Pynchon's work, is less a subject than a theater of operations" (236). Not just thematic or metaphorical, violence is a kind of affective performance, a mode of literary production designed to trouble its own boundaries so that content is not wholly sublimated to the function of narrative. Violent scenes "share the page with parodic excesses"—they often *are* such excesses—and the writer frequently "abdicates any lasting responsibility" for them, as Kowalewski suggests (236). Violence punctuates Pynchon's texts, he adds, to "rupture what Kurt Mondaugen [in *V.*] calls 'the barren touchlessness of the past'" (236). Violent affect, he implies, breaches the text's touchlessness too.

Think of *The Courier's Tragedy* from *The Crying of Lot 49* (1966). The (admittedly, faux-) Jacobean play makes a surprising comic connection with the novel's present owing to the excessive violence it shares with Warner Brothers cartoons: "Every mode of violent death available to Renaissance man, including a lye pit, land mines, a trained falcon with envenom'd talons, is employed. It play[s], as Metzger remark[s] later, like a Road Runner cartoon in blank verse" (58). Both *The Courier's Tragedy* and the Road Runner, that is, attend to the affective body, which is more outside itself than in. The body is either in the "hands" of the tongue-snipping, eye-plucking Renaissance, with Pynchon's anachronistic sixteenth-century landmines tossed in as an "excessive" detail, or it's gripped, like the Coyote, by the repetitious death-driven mechanisms of postindustrial society. One can trace the genealogies of power leading from the authority of the aristocratic family to that of the modern corporate state or private corporation via the modes of violence and control pertinent to them. Indeed, *V.* attempts to do exactly that, coding such a history as an encroaching "inanimacy" that begins with Machiavelli and culminates with the Cold War. In the "V. in Love" chapter of that novel, the writer concentrates not on violence but on representations of sex as control, providing an erotic performance that is critical too, showing a genealogy of pornography linking the decadence of fin-de-siècle France with Cold War–era *Playboy* pornification in America.

◎ ◎ ◎

To exist affectively within any historical formation is, as Gilles Deleuze describes it, to be in "a state of passional suspension in which [the body] exists more outside of itself, more in the abstracted action of the impinging thing and the abstracted context of that action, than within itself" (31). Affect, for Deleuze, is the body's involuntary openness to sensations and forces operating from beyond itself: it is the body "abstracted" or extended outside its own limits—opened, we might say, onto historicity, for where else does sensation occur? Deconstructing the supposed hermeticism of human self and subjecthood, Deleuze's permeable bodies share their substance with the environments and actions that impinge on them. For Pynchon, as Kowalewski indicates, the literary text too might be considered an "impinging thing"—one that contains a surplus that is also a site of sensation. And one that offers us historicity as well. Certainly, an endorsement of acts of writing and reading that serve to excite, encroach on, claim or reject us—as pornography is apt to do—is manifest in "Is It Ok to Be a Luddite and offers a means of reading these tendencies in Pynchon's fiction.

For Pynchon, cheap literary thrills are not confined to any one genre. He imagines them rather as an affective field, or a collective social imaginary, with a residue of religion sometimes appearing as "the miraculous" ("Is It OK?" par. 18), aligning with what Susan Sontag says of pornography in "The Pornographic Imagination" (1967): that it "aims to 'excite' in the same way that books which render an extreme form of religious experience aim to 'convert'" (95). Thrills run from the Great Awakening to the gothic to King Kong and are, in a sense, irrecuperable and nonfungible. They also have a certain relationship to magic, which of course threatens and impinges on us as well. Cheap thrills refer us, Pynchon suggests, to a moment before the consolidation of industrial capital, to an era in which "the laws of nature [have] not been so strictly formulated" ("Is It OK?" par. 18) and in which there are remnants of a folk culture, or precapitalist sociality.

The writer hence dedicates his politics of the literary thrill to the spirit of King Ludd and to working-class resistance to the machines of industrial (re)production: resistance is articulated as a refusal of realism, a prevalence of fantasy, or an investment in what is apparently inutile, momentary, and thrilling. After all, whether as laborer or vandal, the Luddite speaks from outside the capital relationship that determines what counts as real and as serious. Thrills are rooted in an affective economy in which sensations can resist or even criticize codified, bourgeois sentiment and its hegemonic sway.

Pornotopia

Nowhere can such thrills be better experienced than in Pynchon's use of pornography, a genre that, as Andrew Ross has pointed out, is "lower than low" because it refuses the "progressive sublimation" of life into art. Exteriorizing its contents, it provides, rather, "an actualizing, arousing body of inventive impressions" (Ross 200–201). Angela Carter too tells us that pornography "can never be art for art's sake. Honorably enough, it is always art with work to do" (13). And since the eighteenth century, as Gertrude Himmelfarb notes, pornography has been a subcultural medium for the critique of religious and class norms: satire with a bang. In the pages, etchings, and photographs of subversive and political pornography, she says, "the powerless morph into the powerful" (3), although typically it is the bodies of women that do the heavy lifting. Prior to the 1789 revolution in France, for example, widely circulated pornographic texts and engravings depicting Marie Antoinette as an orgiast, lesbian, adulteress, and perpetrator of incest (for which she was tried by the Revolutionary Criminal Tribunal) formed part of the republican propaganda. As Lynn Hunt suggests, these intimate satires attacked the "many bodies" of the queen: regal, maternal, sexual, and others, driving out notions of the feminine in the conception of the new nation (119).

In an American context, Jesse Alemán and Shelley Streeby note the growth throughout the latter half of the nineteenth century of a popular sensational literature that "swerves away from sentimental didacticism" as well as sentimental fiction, turning its attention to women's bodies in particular and exploring "intense emotions rather than regulating, refining, or transcending them" (xviii). Alemán and Streeby claim that these affectively saturated works also translate "political, social, and economic questions" (xviii); even *Uncle Tom's Cabin* (1851) might find a place in such a category, they suggest. But how Alemán and Streeby view the gloopy surplus of feeling is unclear. Surely such texts have a primary affinity with and fashion sensations from the burgeoning pornographic sensibility evident both in racy novels for women in America and the new art of photography.

Pornography is the very paradigm of the cheap thrill; like the term "sensation," a "thrill" can be corporeal or it can be social, slipping between many people. A thriller is a movie, a machine for making thrills, but cheap thrills must come from somewhere lower down the pecking order, somewhere like pornography. And as early as the writing of *V.*, Luc Herman and Steven Weisenburger inform us, Pynchon wrote to his friend and editor Faith Sale that his talents were as a "surrealist, pornographer, word engineer, maybe" (17). Later, in the introduction to his collected early stories, *Slow Learner* (1984), Pynchon considers American pornography of the 1950s in respect of the repressive "excesses of law enforcement" (8) associated with publishing *Howl*, *Lolita*, and *Tropic of Cancer*. The writer considers the chastening, circumlocutory effects these cases had on other authors' descriptions of sex, including his own overly "fancy" efforts in "The Small Rain" (1959) (10).

He uses *Slow Learner* to discuss too what he sees as the "widely shared," masculinized values of *Playboy* magazine, which was founded in 1953 and which brought a big-budget bourgeois respectability to pornography. In fact, as many commentators suggest, *Playboy* takes a central place in American postwar constructions of the good life: a postdomestic fantasy space orienting a lifestyle—itself a new term (see Adler)—of gadgety technomasculinity and imagined "pornotopia," as Beatriz Preciado, borrowing from Steven Marcus (*The Other Victorians* [1974]), describes it. Clearly, the 1950s were a good time for American men; in *Hard Core* (1989), Linda Williams points out that

Marcus's pornotopia refers to nineteenth-century pornography and a period that imagined a limitless economy of male libido and endless jizzing (105); *Playboy* suavely recuperates precisely this patriarchal cultural imaginary but as part of a new image of American men and limitless American power. It's hard then to see this era of pornography as a minor or subaltern cultural product, as its advocates often plead, when the flagship brand consists of a corporate network with global reach and huge social influence. Pynchon, for his part, claims *Playboy* informed his creation of Nerissa in "Low-lands" (1960)—a sexualized child-woman, three and a half feet tall and a bona fide cheap thrill, appearing magically from nowhere and condensing for the main character, Dennis Flange, both paternal and heterosexual-erotic feelings. Dennis wants to father children but is too juvenile for a relationship with an adult woman, Pynchon explains in his introduction.

Dubious as this explanation of Dennis already is, Pynchon makes it even more so with an odd, unnecessary prevarication on the matter of whether this female fantasy figure is personal to him: "It would be easy to say that Dennis's problem was my problem," Pynchon writes, adding gnomically, "[w]hatever's fair—but the problem *could* have been more general" (12). Certainly, the figure of the child-woman had been increasingly prominent in the novels that preceded the publication of *Slow Learner*, and in his 1985 review of the collection, Richard Poirier describes Pynchon's first three major works as "heavily populated with barely pubescent bed partners" (19).

Poirier's right: in *Gravity's Rainbow* there is obviously Bianca, who, like Lolita, is "11 or 12, dark and lovely" (550), but there are also Ilse Pökler and Geli Tripping; maybe the Girl Guides in the park, "bent over, unaware, the saucy darlings, of the fatal strips of white cotton knickers thus displayed," could qualify too. Their "baby-fat buttocks" are, we're told, "a blow to the Genital Brain" (13). There is also Enzian, the mountain gentian plucked by Blicero. In *V.*, there is Mélanie l'Heuremaudit and Esther, whom Kowalewski calls "a cross between a naif and a nymphette [sic]" (244). In *The Crying of Lot 49*, John Nefastis tells Oedipa about his TV habits: "I like to watch young stuff. [...] There's something about a little chick that age," he says; "So does my husband," Oedipa shoots back (72). One might also include the Vroom girls in *Mason & Dixon* (1997) in this category, especially twelve-year-old Els, who sexually taunts Mason, "her nether Orbs upon Mason's Lap, to his involuntary, tho' growing Interest" (64), as well as the assorted pedophilia and semipedophilia in all the works thereafter.

It is perhaps these representations and the representations of nonconsensual sex in *Lot 49* and *Against the Day* (2006), as well as Pynchon's presentation of pornographic images of women on illustrated neckties in both *Vineland* (1990) and *Inherent Vice* (2009), that accounts for critic Joanna Freer's discontent with the *Slow Learner* introduction's performance of contrition, its now-enlightened and sobered perception that grown men can be "small boys inside" (12). Freer challenges claims made by critics like Jeffrey Severs that women are presented in less adolescent fashion—less pornographically—in Pynchon's later works, after the first big three (154–56). These are valid concerns. I hope to show that particularly in his more outré, sexological, and pornographic moments, Pynchon in fact steps outside some of these patriarchal or phallogocentric positions, questioning not just the disciplines of bourgeois sentiment but the nature of sex and sexuality themselves.

Incitements to Intercourse

Before we consider some of Pynchon's particular pornographies, however, we should explore further how the genre functions and some of the politics around it. I've described pornographic writing as a conduit for the cheap thrills Pynchon values so much: a writing that fails or does not wish to sublimate life into art. Sontag argues the other way, seeking to gentrify the "serious" literary end of pornography, although she acknowledges its stimulatory aspects and notes, usefully, its irrecuperable thrill or frisson of *obscenity*. Not simply the secret obedience to the law we find in the deliberate transgression of law, pornography in "the French tradition" from Sade through Lautréamont to Bataille suggests for her that "'the obscene' is a primal notion of human consciousness, something much more profound than the backwash of a sick society's aversion to the body" (103). The obscene has a kind of positive value. And she argues that there is thus *no* healthy, well-adjusted ground of sexuality such as American Freudianism or sexology might lead us to suppose; the essence of pornography is to perform and affirm dirtiness, dissipation, and self-destruction. "What does physical eroticism signify if not a violation of the very being of its practitioners?—a violation bordering on death, bordering on murder?" asks Bataille, in *Death and Sensuality*. "Bodies open out to a state of continuity through secret channels that give us a feeling of obscenity" (17).

Conversely, Rae Langton persuasively presents Catharine MacKinnon's well-known "civil rights" arguments *against* pornography—that it silences and subordinates women and encourages rape in practice—in terms of performativity too. She draws on J. L. Austin's theory of performative speech acts, in which words do more than simply mean. Using Austin's terminology, Langton describes how the "perlocutionary" or persuasive aspects of pornography can encourage an audience to be sexually aroused while, or even through, confirming women's inferiority and readiness to be subordinated. One immediately thinks of the many s&m sequences in Pynchon's work in which dominated women experience sexual pleasure: most famously perhaps, Greta Erdmann's scenes in the making of *Alpdrücken* (*GR* 394). Is the pleasure of the text associated with its violence? Langton writes of pornography's "illocutionary force" (296) too, or the extent to which a speech act, or image, urges, even constitutes a kind of real action, like ranking women as objects in a patriarchal hierarchy or providing a powerful mandate for violent acts. "What is important is whether [pornography] is authoritative in the domain that counts—the domain of speech about sex—and whether it is authoritative for the hearers that count" (312), she argues, pointing out that far from a constituting a subculture, most pornography represents hegemonic, patriarchal perspectives and, citing MacKinnon, that it "sexualizes rape, battery, sexual harassment [...] and child sexual abuse; it [...] celebrates, promotes, authorizes and legitimates them" (307).

Pornography was a subject of heated debate among second-wave feminists starting in the early 1970s, a debate that reached a crisis with the failure of MacKinnon and Andrea Dworkin's ordinances to the U.S. Supreme Court to legislate against pornography in 1986 (see Watson 547; Morgan 169). But Langton's argument offers us another way of looking at the performative nature of pornography, one that belongs to another discourse on sexuality associated primarily with Michel Foucault but also with Judith Butler (whose pioneering *Gender Trouble* [1990] and *Bodies That Matter* [1993] read gender as performative, *producing* sex). One does not have to approach pornography from the "domain of speech about sex" or in terms of a dispute about the direct social effects of pornography and its repertoire of representations; instead, it's possible to "pass behind" this scene to view pornography from another perspective as a type of performativity for which the illocutionary is only supplementary.

A feature of what Foucault in *The History of Sexuality* (1976) calls (after Bataille) a "general economy of discourse on sex" (11) is that all talk on sex, all thinking about, codifying, repressing, and representing of sex, as well as doing it, proves to be not just reactively or managerially "about" or "of" sex and sexuality but constitutive and productive of these phenomena too. In a much-cited passage, Foucault explains how the history of sexuality is not about the repression, management, or liberating of human nature; rather it constitutes the genealogy of a discursive formation:

> Sexuality must not be thought of as a kind of natural given which power tries to hold in check, or as an obscure domain which knowledge tries gradually to uncover. It is the name that can be given to a historical construct: not a furtive reality that is difficult to grasp, but a great surface network in which the stimulation of bodies, the intensification of pleasures, the incitement to discourse, the formation of special knowledges, the strengthening of controls and resistances, are linked to one another, in accordance with a few major strategies of knowledge and power. (105–6)

Expressing doubt that sex has effectively been repressed for the past three hundred years, Foucault suggests that institutional repressiveness should be regarded as just part of "a general economy of discourses on sex in modern societies since the seventeenth century" (11); what really happened, he says, "was a regulated and polymorphous incitement to discourse" (34).

So the kind of repressiveness Pynchon notes regarding the publication of *Howl*, *Lolita*, and *Tropic of Cancer* and that led to his own "fancy" and oblique writing in "The Small Rain" doesn't ignore, repress, or overlook sex or talk about sex; it simply acts as a prompt or incitement to code and discuss it in different ways, the result of which is to shift intensities to other locutions, expressions, and institutions. "The Small Rain," uses no directly sexual terms but instead employs the device of a frog chorus "working itself into a pedal bass" to depict the growing intensity of the act of sex: certainly, this "savage chorus" (*SL* 50) may be considered part of a wider trope that depicts sex as animalistic and fucking as basic nature, but the amphibious musical metaphor here leads us into unfamiliar territory: a little funny; a little unintentionally funny; a little disturbing and alien. The shift into a ranine (froggy) register doesn't intensify sexual discourse exactly; rather, it deterritorializes it by giving it over to the frog army.

Meanwhile, although sex and sexuality are not natural objects, we are, Foucault insists, inextricably bound to them. He closes the first volume of his *History* with a sage reflection on how the many discourses of sex add up to the "austere monarchy of sex" (159). Sex is a discourse, he tells us, that suggests it has a secret to reveal about human nature, just as Freud thought, but its secret is that it has no secret: it is simply an accretion or distribution of points through which power flows, its history a genealogy of that power as exercised by class, church, and, especially in bourgeois modernity, social institutions of administration and education. As society becomes less statist, "softer," more fluid and neoliberal after the early 1970s, searching to innovate markets and invent consumers, so the discourse and apparatus of sex follows similar patterns of derigidification. Thus it is perhaps not surprising that *Deep Throat*, made in 1972, "was one of the first hard-core features to be seen by large numbers of women in theaters" and that "it was also one of the first pornographic films to concentrate on the problem of a woman's pleasure and to suggest that some sexual acts were less than earthshaking" (Williams 25).

Pornography, on this account, is not revelatory or liberatory of sex and sexuality at all. It's simply another institution—Foucault also names "medicine, psychiatry, prostitution, and pornography" (48)—through which pleasure and power are analyzed and multiplied, extending the network, following the contours of a changing capitalist society. Just as homosexuality is codified into a "species" (43), in Foucault's memorable phrase, by nineteenth-century medicine and psychiatry, acting in defense of bourgeois marriage and heteronormativity, so too is pornography, along with other "perversions" that come to be classified by the scientists of sex like Krafft-Ebbing and Wilhelm Reich. Pornography emerges in the twentieth century as a field with its own specialized knowledges and categorizations. In the internet age, we are inducted to the universes of "s&m," "anal," "teen," "European," and so forth. In this sense, Langton's case for MacKinnon—that pornography underwrites rape and violence against women—is correct. Pornography is a key technology in the invention of sex and sex practices and in the co-optation of violent practices for the discourse of sex; violence, however, can never be at its center, because there is no center.

More surely than any of Pynchon's other works, *Gravity's Rainbow* can be seen in this light as itself a pornographic machine, duly developing its own pornographic knowledge and lexicon. The text provides, for example, a sense of how the (particularly masculine) body and discursive field of sex interact: rollicking hero/antihero Pirate Prentice notices that "[l]ike every young man growing up in England, he was conditioned to get a hardon in the presence of certain fetishes" and wonders whether there might be "somewhere, a dossier," and whether "They (They?) somehow have managed to monitor everything he saw and read since puberty" (71–72), a thought conjuring an image of armies of penises erecting together. Meanwhile, the novel has its own porno idiolect: Slothrop is an "ass enthusiast" (469); "subdebs" occupy the role later occupied in American fiction by Bret Easton Ellis's equally pornified "hardbodies" in *American Psycho* (1991); Bianca's breasts are "pre-subdeb" (469); and there's an extended dissertation on women's stockings ("[A]ny underwear fetishist worth his unwholesome giggle can tell you there is much more here—there is a cosmology" [396]), among many more categories and subdivisions of sexual knowledge. Bohdana Kurylo notes that the later Foucault refers to pornography as the modern "sexographic writing" sustaining sex's monarchy and extending its territory, its "Zone." It's pornography—"the queen of sexography," as she says—that makes humans want to "decipher sex as the universal secret" (78), a notion to which we now move.

Pökler in Love

Published in 1992, Michael Bérubé's *Marginal Forces/Cultural Centers* provides perhaps the most sustained excursion into Pynchon's pornographies in the critical field. Inspired by Steven Marcus's comments from *The Other Victorians* that all pornographers are screaming inside for the breast from which they were torn and that pornography aims to satisfy this need endlessly, Bérubé uses a Lacanian model to decipher pornography in Pynchon's work. "*Gravity's Rainbow*," he writes, "gives us something like a poststructuralist version of Marcus's account of (male) deprivation and rage" (245). Working with the notion that the signifier records a desolating maternalized loss as much as it operates symbolically, Bérubé regards Pynchon's pornography as an attempt to reconstruct edenic plenitude in a broken world, citing as evidence the metaphor of the film stills used to reconstruct Ilse as a continuous "daughter" for Franz, who is interpellated as a desiring subject along the plane of these signifiers. His reading recalls Williams's work on Edward Muybridge, whose 1880s stop-frame projections of naked and seminaked women introduced a fetishistic *desire to know* into cinema's infancy. "We see," Williams argues, "how an unprecedented conjunction of pleasure and power 'implants' a cinematic perversion of fetishism in the prototypical cinema's first halting steps toward narrative" (39).

But where Williams already sees the part-body and fetish as the locus of desire and knowledge, for Bérubé, pornography in *Gravity's Rainbow* is "a regressive anamnesia that *recreates illusory, prelapsarian (or prelinguistic) unities* through a complex mechanism of dismemberment and reconfiguration" (248, emphases added). Bérubé, in other words, reads pornography romantically. And there is a cultural-nostalgic sense to this interpretation too: he lists the many yearnings for mother ideas and motherlands in the novel, as Squalidozzi does for Argentina.[1] Perhaps, indeed, it makes the most sense to interpret Bérubé's account of pornography in cultural terms. Bérubé's pornographic anamnesia, that is, wishes exactly to decipher sex as the universal secret, to recall Foucault's comments; he seeks to open sex up, to reveal it as always already tragic and oedipal, even Proustian. Pornography considered thus is a more or less masculinized and unconscious sidestepping of the thwarted desires of infancy, as Marcus suggests: a dreamlike wish fulfillment that confuses adult sexuality with its earlier organization (in fact, for Freud, anal) and adult women with maternal archetypes.[2] Is this really the logic of *Gravity's Rainbow*'s pornographized episodes?

Franz Pökler's desire to fuck "Ilse"—which is as oedipal as the novel gets—is, for example, framed first as indirect confession, as the character imagines Them administrating his happiness, *knowing* about him, opening a dossier on his quirks: the same concern Pirate voices. We hear Them, imagined by Franz, plotting: "Pökler, now, has mentioned a 'daughter.' Yes, yes we know it's disgusting, one can never tell what they have locked up in there [their minds] with those equations" (420). So when Pökler strikes Ilse for wanting to occupy the bed with him, and the precisely worked money shot hits *us*— "before she could cry or speak, he had dragged her up on the bed next to him, her dazed little hands already at the buttons of his trousers, her white frock already pulled up above her waist. She had been wearing nothing at all underneath, nothing all day ... *how I've wanted you*, she whispered as paternal plow found its way into filial furrow" (420)—there is a sense that all this has "already" been written. Notwithstanding the thrill of this passage, which may indeed owe something to oedipal transgression and may too be an example of the soft body, or shared body inhabited by reader and text, it's important that this account of "incest" is already logged in Their account book. This sex crime is already catalogued and ratified; nothing is revealed. Underscoring this is the subsequent speculation that Ilse is a different girl in each of Pökler's furloughs and is hence the fetish of a daughter rather than a real one, which would make this just "play" with incest. Really, then, the episode corresponds to an established example of Foucault's incitement to discourse.

Echoing Adorno and Horkheimer's maxim that in capitalism "something is provided for all so that none may escape" (123), Foucault describes how all and any sexual activities, anarchic and uncategorized, become codified and incorporated into mechanisms or networks of control and surveillance: "The implantation of perversions is an instrument-effect: it is through the isolation, intensification, and consolidation of peripheral sexualities that the relations of power to sex and pleasure branched out and multiplied, measured the body, and penetrated modes of conduct. [...] Pleasure and power do not cancel or turn back against one another; they seek out, overlap, and reinforce one another" (48). The evasion of oedipal injunctions—despite the cultural ascendancy of the oedipal model and despite the incitement to discourse the breaking of the taboo must thus carry—can be no more central to the truth of sexuality or pornography as its sexographer than any other of the "perversions." Far from the tragic encounter with loss Béreubé posits, Pökler's encounter is, rather, the reiteration of a peripheral sexuality in an extant network of possibilities in which all sexualities are, in a sense, peripheral—desire working productively alongside prohibition. If the reader has attached thrills or horrors to the scene, is she not as oedipal as Bérubé, rooted in a Victorian family drama, saturated with the values of the class and epoch that produced it? Are Pökler's (and our) thrills not in fact closer to that of the fetish?

The pleasure of the fetish—let's say, "the incest taboo"—is not its instantiation or recuperation of loss; rather, its pleasure arises from the self-consciousness of itself *as* fetish, as simply an iteration of "sex." If Foucault suggests and Pynchon shows that sex is not a site of truth but a mediation and experience of discourse and power, then sexual desire itself becomes a type of fetish, but one that replaces nothing nor compensates for anything. Sex is part of an apparatus of power, and pornography—as a lever of that power—offers a particularly clear-eyed view of how discourses and species of sex might function socially. Leni Pökler famously unmasks pieties of motherhood in the novel—"Mothers work for Them!" (219)—while Pynchon's pornography in the Franz/Ilse scenes presents oedipalism as really another contingent species. Cognitively and affectively, pornography here is working as critique.

Perhaps this explains why the scene is framed as a fantasy. Herman and Weisenburger note that critics of the parallel Slothrop/Bianca scene in *Grav-*

ity's Rainbow read it as hallucinatory and ambiguous, avoiding a consideration of its "ethical framing" (78) and its representation of pedophilia. For the reader of a text, the purported ontological status of its narrative moments is surely considerably less important than its gestures linking affects with particular contents. The soft body—that of the reader, in this case—is always open for business with the soft body of the text, even if it's not sure what it's getting itself into. In his study of Rat Man, Freud points out that wishes may express themselves as their opposites, but this doesn't diminish their force. He recounts the wisdom that "it was equally punishable to say, 'The Emperor is an ass,' or to disguise the forbidden words by saying 'If any one says, etc., ... then he will have me to reckon with'" (317). The affective charge of the injury to the emperor runs through both phrases, despite their opposite meanings. So it is too with narrative episodes that disavow their own fictional reality or that try to negate what they so palpably seek to realize.

The Self-Induced Orgasm

As I have suggested, Bérubé's figure of regressive anamnesia works far more effectively as a cultural metaphor than a pornographic one. When Pynchon deploys Vanya, one of the Weimar protorevolutionaries in *Gravity's Rainbow*, to denounce culture as pornographic through and through, we see how culture and pornography blur. "[L]ook at the forms of capitalist expression," Vanya says: "[P]ornographies of love, erotic love, Christian love, boy-and-his-dog, pornographies of sunsets, pornographies of killing, and pornographies of deduction. [...] The self-induced orgasm" (155). Stefan Mattessich reads these comments as a parody of the Epic Theatre tradition of Brecht, peeling culture back to investigate its conditions of production (101–2). Arguably, though, Vanya reveals a valuable link between the pornographic and the kitsch: the spectacle or sensation of the sunset, the boy and his dog, killing, can all be consumed with equal self-pleasuring equanimity. As Milan Kundera observes in *The Unbearable Lightness of Being* (1984), "Kitsch causes two tears to flow in quick succession. The first tear says: How nice to see children running on the grass! The second tear says: How nice to be moved, together with all mankind, by children running on the grass! It is the second tear that makes kitsch kitsch" (244). Capitalist culture, he suggests, is overcoded, overdetermined, impossible to experience authentically or nonindustrially. The erotic charge penetrating our experience of the sun, the dog, the murders, the deductions, cathects a structure of feeling prepared in advance, its affective payload carefully freighted for us and its distribution circuit overlapping perilously with the pornographic. Perhaps the soft bodies of discourse are melting together, just as capitalism becomes more fluid.

Such a kitsch experience is the cheapest thrill of all, but not one that Pynchon advocates, of course. As Mattessich astutely notes, the writer's gesture is finally toward the opacity and difficulty of the text itself: "*Gravity's Rainbow* does not want to be merely a good commodity, a prop in the theatre of an autoerotic consumption" (102), he says. Rather, it, along with Pynchon's other works, seeks to generate a different set of affects than those simply reinforcing self-attention or self-congratulation. Can we call this a "good" pornography or a really *special* effect? For Wes Chapman, "the masturbator, physical or emotional, is the ideal [ideologically defunct] citizen [...], unlikely to form the bonds with other people which threaten the effectiveness of the 'structures favoring death' by affirming the value of life. Pornography, then, is for Pynchon a means by which the state wields power over its citizens at the micropolitical level" (par. 10). While it's true, as we have seen, that pornography operates at the micro level, the sense that its forms, tropes, and bodies of knowledge are imposed from the top down, like power nakedly wielded, is precisely what Foucault attempts to dispel by presenting power as productive. Like a kind of Maxwell's demon or a falling rocket, Foucault's idea of power orders and distributes effects, retrospectively instantiating causes. Can such redistributions tip over into the critical? Is a textual machine able to intervene in the field of the pornographic in surprising ways?

Allons Enfants

Turning back to *V.* to gather together the themes of this essay, we might consider how Pynchon solicits from our soft bodies some thrills that go beyond the masturbatory (even if they include the erotic and pornographic). *V.* is, on the face of it, one of the least propitious texts in this regard. As Severs points out, the early Pynchon seems cruel to the point of misogyny: "In 1963, [he] felt compelled to portray a virginal girl being raped and killed by the inanimate as proof that modernity had destroyed cyclic renewal on the eve of war" (235). Oddly, though, it's precisely the pornographic mode *V.* employs in this section that alerts us to the sociosexual production of the figure of the child-woman and its significances.

The chapter in question, "V. in Love," written by Stencil, is set in the Third Republic, belle époque Paris of 1913, a moment on the brink of something terrible and invisible to the characters—a time when the sky is always a nacreous yellow and debauched artists hold black masses. And it does indeed make Severs's point: Mélanie L'Heuremaudit, the fifteen-year-old protagonist, a dancer and naïf of sorts, abandoned by her parents, comes to the city from Normandy to perform *Rape of the Chinese Virgins*, a thinly veiled *Rite of Spring* (1913), replete with characters who proxy for Stravinsky, Diaghilev, and Nijinsky, as David Cowart has detailed (165). Mélanie is rendered a fetishized object in a love affair with the novel's central character V., probably played here by

Victoria Wren. Then, in the riot that accompanies the first performance of the ballet, Mélanie dies bloodily, penetrated by a metal pole that is one of the props. She should have been wearing a chastity belt.

Like Pynchon's writing more generally, though, the chapter is so overdetermined, so laden with potential pretexts and significances, that it would traduce it to isolate one theme so brutally—in this case, the desecration of the White Goddess theme, written about so authoritatively by Judith Chambers. Why not point to the context of the French Empire, made prominent in the orientalism of the chapter and its implied peripheral spaces? Mélanie's father has "fled to the jungles" (399), for example, reminding us of the 1880s scramble for Africa, which links in turn to the new music of Stravinsky—its modernism and incorporation of the "primitive." The rise of Freud is documented here too: Itague, who stands in for Diaghilev, has read "the new science of the mind" (408), as have others, and he knows about fetishism. Transnational Paris and its queer sexual adventurers are also central to the plot. Meanwhile, the writer character Gerfaut, "sat by a window, discoursing on how for some reason the young girl—adolescent or younger—had again become the mode in erotic fiction" (402).

These connecting themes, determining and overdetermining one another—referring anachronistically to the American 1950s and 1960s, to *Lolita* as well as pre–World War I France—seem to produce a complex, self-conscious form of the kind of horizontal, epistemic readings of history for which Foucault is known (see Ligny 174), knotting together empire, art, sex, sexology, and eroticism with encroaching end times. What kind of sexual performativity or incitements to discourse emerge from this web?

◉ ◉ ◉

First, "V. in Love" seems to operate under the sign of the libertine. Decadent Paris and the context of a social circle "inclined toward sadism, sacrilege, endogamy and homosexuality" (407) encourage this view, echoing the writings of Sade, who hovers behind the text and whose intellectual star, as Sontag notes, rose in the postwar years in which Pynchon was writing (95). Indeed, in the chapter, we enter a stock pornographic scenario that could date from any time in the late eighteenth century to the pre–World War I era, in the form of the almost silent heroine, abandoned by her parents, making her way in the city. This is already cognate with the narratives established in Sade's *Justine* (1791) and *Juliette* (1797–1801), the Bildungsromans of the virtuous lost girl and the libertine, respectively, vastly differing sisters cast into the world as orphans: Mélanie as Justine, and Victoria, or V., as Juliette.

The impresario Itaque, for whose company Mélanie dances, wonders of the girl, for example, "Poor, young, pursued, fatherless. What would Gerfaut make of her? A wanton. In body if he could; in the pages of a manuscript most certainly. Writers had no moral sense" (402). Indeed, Gerfaut is writing a book about a girl called, "Doucette, thirteen and struggled within by passions she could not name. / 'A child and yet a woman'" (402). His name means "falcon," and so he joins self-described "peregrine" (or grifter) Max Rowley Bugg, a denizen of the Baedeker Alexandria of chapter 3 on the run from a child sex scandal, and V. too, who, "had found love at last in her *peregrinations*," as morphologically linked predators and libertines in the novel (408, emphasis added). Strangely, Pynchon suppresses Itague's and Satin's—or Diaghilev's and Nijinsky's—historical homosexuality to render them threats to Mélanie as well (although of course the Sadian libertine affirms all sexual identities: "I am polysexual; I love everybody and everything," proclaims Madame de Saint-Ange in *Philosophy in the Boudoir* [10]).

Events are conducted too under the sign of the Apollonian father, also a libertine and Mélanie's lover, in the Sadian style. Traveling through Paris by taxi, "[t]o her left rose the dome of the Opéra, and tiny Appollo, with his golden lyre . . . / 'Papa!' she screamed" (394). She recalls, no doubt, the scenes in the family home in which "while Madeleine combed the hair of Maman in the other room, Mélanie lay on the wide bed beside [Papa], while he touched her in many places, and she squirmed and fought not to make a sound. It was their game" (394). Incest, alongside acts of homosexuality, is not optional for the libertine. Preempting certain kinds of queer theory and inspiring Bataille in his pursuit of the *inutile*, the libertine works directly against all proscriptions: "[W]hat right, I ask, has one man to dare to require of another man, either that he reform his tastes or attempt to model them after the *social order*?," asks one of the predatory monks in *Justine* (188). Later, Stencil's narration, stiff with sexology, reflects on Mélanie's affair with V.: "Lesbianism, we are prone to think in this Freudian period of history," he says, "stems from self-love projected on to some other human object. [. . .] Such may have been the case with Mélanie, though who could say: perhaps the spell of incest at Serre Chaude was an indication that her preferences merely lay outside the usual, exogamous-heterosexual pattern which prevailed in 1913" (407).

◎ ◎ ◎

Much commentary has been generated on Mélanie as fetish; she is directly addressed as "fétiche" by Itague and takes La Jarretière, the garter, as her stage name. I've noted the ecstasies *Gravity's Rainbow* contemplates regarding such lingerie. Really, Mélanie must be the most fetishized figure in Pynchon's oeuvre, a sexual body very much opened to the reader through his prose style. Importantly, though, she is a body who imagines herself as a fetish, a body whose sexuality subsists in imagining herself as a fetish. Fantasizing a Hitchcockian tumble down the steep roof of her family home, for example, Mélanie becomes a classically fetishized part-body, a series of sexual nodes and spaces, as she imagines, in delicate pornographese, how, "[h]er skirt would fly above her hips, her black-stockinged legs would writhe [...], [the] feeling of roof-tiles rapidly sliding beneath the hard curve of her rump, the wind trapped under her blouse teasing the new breasts. [...] [She would] let the dovetailed tiles tease her nipplepoints to an angry red, [...] taste the long hair caught against her teeth and tongue, cry out ..." (395).

But is the voice that objectifies her her voice? Hanjo Berressem regards her as ventriloquized by the father, just as Itague sees her "function as a mirror" for her father's ghost (399): "[I]n taking the perspective of her father's desire in relation to herself, she already inserts herself firmly into a fetish function" (61), Berressem says. But contra such a view, I suggest Mélanie is a character whose mirror constitutes her desiring self: this is where her erotics lie, we are frequently told. Although a naïf, she is not Justine; she is a fetish and a fetishist, as are we all. In fact, she is a profoundly queer figure, fondly recalling her father's desire, desiring herself, entering into nongenital, scopophilic sexual encounters with V., and dressing "transvestite for the street" (407); yet still she is fifteen, poised between childhood and adulthood, one of the first of Pynchon's many child-women, and hence an ethical problem.

Foucault discusses the sexualization of the child in the *History of Sexuality*, noting the convolutions of the bourgeois domestic space and the Victorian family as a provocation for sexualities that work through parents, servants, children: "The power which thus took charge of sexuality set about contacting bodies, caressing them with its eyes, intensifying areas, electrifying surfaces, dramatizing troubled moments. It wrapped the sexual body in its embrace" (44). One might revisit Mélanie's home to see Madeleine combing the hair of Maman in an act both caressive and potentially sexual; the child is sexualized in this act, although not perhaps yet made a fully determined species of sexuality. Certainly, though, we see the circuits of power and sex that gestate such species. And certainly too our soft bodies are implicated in Pynchon's erotic/pornographic prose.

So it might be pleasurable for we readers to troll the landscape of *V.* as a site of unrestrained libertinage, the sexy waif (we've already forgotten her age) flickering before our eyes as willing fetish, Pynchon's textual dismemberments of her body allowing us to participate in the fetish, right up until the shocking moments in the theater. But behind this pornographic vision, something else is at work. "V. in Love," like the Pökler/Ilse narrative in *Gravity's Rainbow*, confronts us with the figure of the child-woman. The chapter's *mise en abyme* featuring Gerfaut and the erotic novel about Doucette, in fact, even enacts a kind of reflexive metapornography, intensifying the troubling figure of the eroticized and erotic child. For Pynchon, this is a problem that, we might recall, in the case of "Low-Lands" "could have been more general." He means surely that the child-woman is less a naturally ready vessel for libertinage than a product of the social-sexual apparatus Foucault writes about: a newly proliferating area of erotic kidultism and a new incitement to discourse. *Playboy* magazine, as he suggests, has its part to play there. In *Pornotopia*, Preciado tells us that the Barbie doll, launched in 1959, was modeled on a German sex toy called Lilli and was Hugh Hefner's vision of ideal femininity. The transformation from Lilli to Mattel's Barbie was "paradigmatic of a double process of the domestication of public sexuality and pornification of the domestic," she says (64). And what both *Playboy* and Mattel achieved was the invention of the "mall-brothel" and the "mall-playground" as simultaneously public and private interiors.

Elsewhere, Simone de Beauvoir was applauding the emergence of a new kind of cinema star in the person of Brigitte Bardot: "She has a kind of spontaneous dignity, something of the gravity of childhood" (32), Beauvoir observes in *Brigitte Bardot and the Lolita Syndrome* (1960), also praising Bardot's Rousseauian naturalness, androgyny, sexual frankness, and appeal. Clearly there is something epistemic here. This sense of Bardot as sexy child—and indeed Beauvoir's reference to Nabokov's pseudoscientific notion of the nymphet—taken together with the new spaces of a more pornified modernity signal a wider codification of the child-woman as a new species. Or, as James Kincaid suggests in his study *Erotic Innocence* (1998), the signs and symptoms of cuteness, attractiveness, and desirability come to be projected onto the guileless, blank faces of children: "[T]he instructions we receive on what to regard as sexually arousing tell us to look for (and often create) this emptiness, to discover the erotic in that which is most susceptible to inscription, the blank page" (16), he writes. His insight suggests a notion of child sexualization as another land grab for neoliberalism: another virgin frontier for desire to conquer, located in new reaches of what Norman Mailer once called "psychic real estate" (106).

Pynchon's repeated representations of child-women across his novels present us, time and again, with the endless manufacture of sexual identities and exposes the edifices of morality built on and around them that take them as the real oedipal thing. In so doing, he plays a double game, intensifying the pornography of the new species—which was in part made *by* pornography—at the same time as he critiques such species and exposes them as the extension of sexology. He also provides a frame for historical pornography—Gerfaut is an example—with which to trace some of its genealogical contours. Such a practice demonstrates both the ineluctable grip sexuality has on us—ruled by the monarchy of sex, we can never not be sexual—and also how hard it is to break the loop of an incitement to discourse once it has been sedimented in culture, no matter how deceptively and apparently transgressive this incitement might seem.

There is a sweetly sour redemptive side to all this: when Mélanie shows up again in *Against the Day* (2006), her grisly demise in "V. in Love" has been commuted, it seems, to rebirth; the viscera wasn't real: "We used the . . . raspberry syrup" (1198), she says, Pynchon's ellipses, as ever, ambiguous, the matter not entirely cleared up. What her death in one novel and rebirth in another have provided her with, however, is something not many child-women in pornography or, indeed, sensational literature get to enjoy: a fulfilled adulthood. Bianca, Ilse, Shirley Temple, even Lolita never get to keep the glamor. They die or they just fade away; the life of this species, as much as it proliferates with such prodigious fecundity in our present culture, is a precarious one indeed.

NOTES

1. The role of Argentina in the novel is explored with remarkable grace and precision by Samuel Thomas in "The Gaucho Sells Out."
2. See Freud, "On the Transformation."

WORKS CITED

Adler, Alfred. *Understanding Human Nature*. London: Allen and Unwin, 1928.
Alemán, Jesse, and Shelley Streeby. *Empire and the Literature of Sensation: An Anthology of Nineteenth-Century Popular Fiction*. New Brunswick: Rutgers University Press, 2007.
Bataille, Georges. *Death and Sensuality: A Study of Eroticism and the Taboo*. Trans. Mary Dalwood. New York: Walker, 1962.
Berressem, Hanjo. *Pynchon's Poetics: Interfacing Theory and Text*. Urbana: University of Illinois Press, 1993.
Bowen, John. "Gothic Motifs." British Library, www.bl.uk/romantics-and-victorians/articles/gothic-motifs. Accessed 15 Nov. 2017.
Carter, Angela. *The Sadeian Woman: An Exercise in Cultural History*. London: Virago, 1979.
Chapman, Wes. "Male Pro-Feminism and the Masculinist Gigantism of *Gravity's Rainbow*." *Postmodern Culture* 6.3 (1996). DOI: 10.1353/pmc.1996.0017.
Cowart, David. "Love and Death: Variations on a Theme in Pynchon's Early Fiction." *Journal of Narrative Technique* 7.3 (1977): 157–69.
de Beauvoir, Simone. *Brigitte Bardot and the Lolita Syndrome*. London: New England Library, 1960.
Deleuze, Gilles. *Francis Bacon: The Logic of Sensation*. Trans. Daniel W. Smith. Minneapolis: University of Minnesota Press, 2004.
de Sade, Donatien Alphonse François. *Philosophy in the Boudoir*. Trans. and ed. Julian Jones. London: Creation, 2000.
———. *Justine; or, The Misfortunes of Virtue*. Trans. Alan Hull Walton. London: Neville Spearman, 1964.
Foucault, Michel. *The History of Sexuality*. Vol. 1: *An Introduction*. Trans. Robert Hurley. New York: Pantheon, 1978.
Freer, Joanna. *Thomas Pynchon and American Counterculture*. New York: Cambridge University Press, 2014.
Freud, Sigmund. "A Case of Obsessional Neurosis." *Collected Papers*. Vol. 3: *Case Histories*. Trans. Alix and James Strachey. London: Hogarth Press, 1933. 296–372.

———. "On the Transformation of Instincts with Special Reference to Anal Erotism." *Collected Papers.* Vol. 2: *Clinical Papers; Papers on Technique.* Ed. Ernst Jones. Trans. Joan Riviere. London: Hogarth Press, 1933. 164–72.

Herman, Luc, and Steven Weisenburger. *Gravity's Rainbow, Domination and Freedom.* Athens: University of Georgia Press, 2013.

Himmelfarb, Gertrude. *The De-Moralization of Society.* New York: Knopf, 1995.

Hunt, Lynn. "The Many Bodies of Marie Antoinette: Political Pornography and the Problem of the Feminine in the French Revolution." *The French Revolution: Recent Debates and New Controversies.* Ed. Gary Kates. New York: Routledge, 2006. 117–38.

Kincaid, James. *Erotic Innocence: The Culture of Child Molesting.* Durham: Duke University Press, 1998.

Kowalewski, Michael. *Deadly Musings: Violence and Verbal Form in American Fiction.* Princeton: Princeton University Press, 1993.

Kundera, Milan. *The Unbearable Lightness of Being.* London: Faber and Faber, 1984.

Kurylo, Bohdana. "Pornography and Power in Michel Foucault's Thought." *Journal of Political Power* 1.10 (2017): 71–84.

Langton, Rae. "Speech Acts and Unspeakable Acts." *Philosophy and Public Affairs* 22.4 (1993): 293–330.

Mailer, Norman. *Advertisements for Myself.* London: Andre Deutsch, 1961.

Mattessich, Stefan. *Lines of Flight: Discursive Time and Countercultural Desire in the Work of Thomas Pynchon.* Durham: Duke University Press, 2002.

Morgan, Robin. *Going Too Far: The Personal Chronicle of a Feminist.* New York: Random House, 1977.

Poirier, Richard. "Humans." Review of *Slow Learner,* by Thomas Pynchon. *London Review of Books* 24 Jan. 1985: 18–20.

Preciado, Beatriz. *Pornotopia: An Essay on Playboy's Architecture and Biopolitics.* New York: Zone Books, 2014.

Pynchon, Thomas. *Against the Day.* London: Vintage, 2007.

———. *Gravity's Rainbow.* 1973. London: Vintage, 1995.

———. "Is It O.K. to Be a Luddite?" *New York Times,* 28 Oct. 1984, www.nytimes.com/books/97/05/18/reviews/pynchon-luddite.html. Accessed 15 Nov. 2017.

———. *Mason & Dixon.* London: Jonathan Cape, 1997.

———. *Slow Learner.* London: Picador, 1984.

———. *V.* Philadelphia: Lippincott, 1963.

Ross, Andrew. *No Respect: Intellectuals and Popular Culture.* Oxford: Routledge, 1989.

Severs, Jeffrey. "'The abstractions she was instructed to embody': Women, Capitalism, and Artistic Representation in *Against the Day*." *Pynchon's* Against the Day: *A Corrupted Pilgrim's Guide.* Ed. Jeffrey Severs and Christopher Leise. Newark: University of Delaware Press, 2011. 215–38.

Singy, Patrick. "*Nous autres, victoriens*: Punctuation, Power and Politics in Foucault's *History of Sexuality*." *Cultural History* 5.2 (2016): 169–78.

Sontag, Susan. "The Pornographic Imagination." *The Story of the Eye,* by Georges Bataille. Trans. Joachim Neugroschel. London: Marion Boyars, 1979. 83–118.

Thomas, Sam. "The Gaucho Sells Out: Thomas Pynchon and Argentina." *Studies in American Fiction* 40.1 (2013): 53–78.

Williams, Linda. *Hard Core: Power, Pleasure, and the Frenzy of the Visible.* Berkeley: University of California Press, 1999.

Queer Sex, Queer Text
S/M in *Gravity's Rainbow*

MARIE FRANCO

In the final episode of *Gravity's Rainbow* (1973), Thanatz tells Ludwig that "a little S and M never hurt anybody." "But why," then, he rhetorically asks, "are we taught to feel reflexive shame whenever the subject comes up?" (751). Thanatz's answer is simple: the state must manage and claim our submission as resources for itself. Although it's a question that Thanatz poses to himself, it's also a question worth turning back on ourselves, since the stigma surrounding s/m might partially account for the scarcity of s/m discussions in Pynchon criticism. Despite frequent and explicit representations of s/m in *Gravity's Rainbow*, few have analyzed s/m's function in the text—either in terms of politics or Pynchon's postmodern aesthetic. Sado-anarchism has been written off, and scholars remain critical of s/m in Pynchon, reading such representations as a pornographic, misogynist fantasy (Bérubé), a regressive representation of homosexuality (Sears), or a commentary on fascism's perverse effects (Herman and Weisenburger). A queer approach to *Gravity's Rainbow* enables a revision of previous Pynchon criticism and illuminates s/m's multiplicity of meanings and functions in Pynchon, complementing and complicating work that primarily sees it in negative terms.

While the state's co-optation of sexuality has been extensively discussed in Pynchon scholarship, the institutional trappings of many s/m scenes have obscured another significant truth. *Gravity's Rainbow* is equally concerned with how state co-optations are complicated by characters who reappropriate their institutionally defined roles. Such instances can even be found in the novel's most fraught s/m scenes: Brigadier General Ernest Pudding's coprophagic masochism, which "may be partly responsible for the advisory board's notorious rejection of *Gravity's Rainbow* for a Pulitzer Prize" (Schlegel 170), and the s/m practices of Nazi captain Blicero, which Luc Herman and Steven Weisenburger describe as "his obsessional and sadomasochistic hetero- and homosexual rape-tortures of Katje and Gottfried" (78).[1] A queer reading of these scenes is problematic given their setting within a wartime state of exception in which individual rights and liberties—and thus the ability to consent to such acts—are suspended. And yet these scenes are not strictly structured in either realist or parodic terms. While certainly part of Pynchon's antitotalitarian screed, they are largely framed as a fantasy scenario Pynchon stages for himself and for us: a pornographic thought experiment, if you will. They operate with their own internal fantasy logic, asking us to suspend our disbelief or moral judgments and inviting us to consider this way of thinking about the world, about love, and about desire. We follow these characters into their fantasy spaces, which are clearly demarcated from the rest of the diegetic world: for Pudding there are the antechambers that ultimately lead him to "his real home" (239), the passing through of which induces an altered state of mind (235); for Blicero, Katje, and Gottfried there is their "game" in "this charmed house in the forest" (99), which becomes the "little Oven-state" (104), "their preserving routine, their shelter, against what outside none of them can bear" (98). In realist terms, there is no question that Katje, Gottfried, and, to a certain extent, Pudding are victims without the power to consent, but in this pornographic fantasy scenario, Pynchon explores the implications of their complicitous pleasures. Like Foucault, Pynchon recognizes that in s/m "a whole new art of sexual practice develops which tries to explore all the internal possibilities of sexual conduct" (*Foucault Live* 330). As in pornography more generally, both the law and the rules of realism can be suspended in the diegetic world, thus bracketing off questions of consent within the fictional context and allowing Pynchon to explore such erotic relations for what they are: a stigmatized but potentially valuable mode of relationality.

Centering on the queerness of s/m allows us to take seriously Thanatz's sado-anarchism—the idea that s/m pleasures might be a threat to power and the political status quo (751). In *Gravity's Rainbow*, s/m's potential destabilization of or resistance to hegemonic narratives and state appropriations of s/m make it a rich site for investigating the relation between queer sexuality and Pynchon's postmodernism, as long as we keep in mind the impracticality of regarding s/m, queerness, and successful resistance to oppression as synonymous. Exploring s/m's ambiguities in *Gravity's Rainbow* reveals that it makes just as much sense to acknowledge the text's queer pleasures as it does to pathologize them. I should note at the outset that my usage of "queer" does not exclusively signify same-sex relations but erotic practices that fall outside the dominant hetero-/homo- binary, like s/m.[2]

This focus on attempted reversals of the state's deployment of sexuality makes the time frame of Pudding's and Blicero's s/m significant: both episodes occur early in the narrative's chronology, prior to VE Day, which is key for understanding the possibilities and limits of s/m's transgressive politics. The s/m in these scenes differs from the more overt liberatory potential of Margherita Erdmann's s/m that occurs in the anarchic Zone, which I have argued for elsewhere. The Zone enables Margherita to refashion and explore s/m on her own terms, distinguishing her s/m from Pudding's and Blicero's, both of which unfold under the sign of fascism despite the fact that their geographical and political situations are different. These characters' differing contexts also account for their different agency conditions: Margherita achieves a level of (narrative) agency unmatched by any other sadomasochist in the text, while Pudding's and Blicero's are more muted.[3] Foucault's claims about the multidirectional nature of power clarify how Pudding and Blicero attempt disruption, despite their imbrication in state power.

Like postmodernism, which actively works to deconstruct the privileged binaries that structure meaning and language, queerness rejects stable identity categories and binary notions of sexuality and gender.[4] This is not to imply that "s/m," "queerness," and "postmodernism" are generally interchangeable terms but rather that s/m is the most illustrative manifestation of queerness in *Gravity's Rainbow*. Queerness invests in sexual practices, communities, and performances of (dis)identity that destabilize hetero-/homonormative notions of bodies, pleasures, and desires as well as the teleological narratives that secure such hegemonic norms. Ironically, these queer revisions draw from canonical work in Pynchon studies and postmodern theory more generally, namely, Brian McHale's notion of the ontological dominant.[5] My intervention's potentially discordant reliance on what might be called a Pynchon orthodoxy should be taken as a queer way of "reconceiv[ing] postmodernism's role in our contemporary critical landscape" (Chetwynd 145) by illuminating the queerness that is embedded in such discourses.

This reading is primarily concerned with how queerness operates within the text itself and thus cannot fully address the history of homosexuality in the Nazi regime or fascism more broadly—though some of Pynchon's historical sources emphasized such connections. Thus, the most relevant history for this reassessment is that which links the s/m practices of the characters in *Gravity's Rainbow* to queer s/m subcultures.[6] According to Susan Sontag, by the mid-1970s, the SS had "become a referent of sexual adventurism": "[M]uch of the imagery of far-out sex" had "been placed under the sign of Nazism" in both pop culture and pornographic literature (101–2). Its 1973 publication situates *Gravity's Rainbow* squarely within a decades-long, transnational proliferation of images, texts, and films that explored the taboo power erotics associated with fascistic imagery like Larry Townsend's erotica, Tom of Finland's art, Liliana Cavani's film *The Night Porter* (1974), and Pier Pasolini's *Salò, or the 120 Days of Sodom* (1975). It is this erotic motif across both high art and low that most usefully historicizes my reading of Pynchon, linking it to queer culture and practice.

By desexualizing sado-anarchism and reading it merely as satire, critique, or allegory, critics have sanitized Pynchon's s/m of its pornographic content and significance within his larger project. These tendencies might be traced back to Lawrence C. Wolfley's insistence that sado-anarchism is "compromised by the humor of Thanatz' motive, and by everything we know about him as a character—his name is an allusion to *Thanatos*, the Freudian term for the death instinct" (877). Wolfley, writing just prior to the AIDS epidemic, could not anticipate the literal ways queerness would be equated with the death instinct, as, for example, in the targeted scapegoating during the 1980s that led New York and San Francisco to permanently close dozens of bathhouses and s/m bars—forever changing the embodied experience of queer sociality. Nationally, this reentrenched the association of s/m, cruising, and queerness with death. However, some queer scholarship has turned this negative association on its head, theorizing the potential of the death drive's stigma for social and political disruption.

In *No Future: Queer Theory and the Death Drive*, Lee Edelman explains how heteronormative society relies on a narrative of futurity and a fetishistic investment in protecting the child at the expense of the queer, whose nonprocreative pleasures are linked to the death drive. Thus, queer *jouissance* becomes the ultimate threat to heteronormativity's narrative telos. The sadomasochistic valences embedded in Edelman's definition of *jouissance*—that which exceeds the boundaries of identity and meaning, of pleasure and pain (25)—are easily identifiable even though Edelman does not explicitly mention s/m. Viewing sado-anarchism through queer negativity reveals what Wolfley couldn't see at the time: the clever pun of Thanatz's name need not compromise the politics of sado-anarchism and might instead reinforce its oppositional potential.

Like Wolfley, Pynchon could not have anticipated the specific ways queerness would be associated with the death drive during the AIDS epidemic. However, it is significant that Pynchon's representations of homoeroticism and s/m reflect the historical ways that nonprocreative pleasures have been viewed as threats to heteronormativity. Pynchon's linking of s/m with antinarrative tendencies and with death prefigures Edelman's antisocial theory; in both, queerness represents the greatest threat to reproducing the dominant social order. I argue that as an antinarrative force, queerness in Pynchon explores ontological questions such as "what happens when different kinds of worlds are placed in confrontation or when boundaries between worlds are violated" (McHale, *Postmodernist* 10), thus challenging interpretations of Pynchon's s/m—like John Hamill's—that distance s/m from queer pleasures and focus instead on its metaphysical aspects and its relation to institutional entrapment. Queerness understood in an ontological light highlights the tension between individual desires and those of the state, placing public and private worlds in confrontation, like when institutional power co-opts s/m—forcing the private (or sexual) into the public sphere—and when individuals use private s/m fantasies to resist the co-optations of sexual pleasure. Queerness's centrality to Pynchon's narrative structure and his construction of queerness as a fraught site of opposition establish the importance of taking seriously Pynchon's representations of sex and gender. Pynchon's s/m can be understood as the point where characters' queer, nonnormative tendencies intersect with the nonnormative narrative tendencies of the text.

Pudding's Coprophagia

From the outset of Pudding's s/m scene, its institutional framework is apparent: Pointsman uses s/m to distract the aging Pudding, render him ineffectual, and prevent his interference with PISCES. "Pudding will not go back on any of his commitments," according to Pointsman; "we have made arrangements with him. The details aren't important" (231); however, the text contradicts that, describing at length Pudding's ritual submission to Katje. Since Pudding's death from an E. coli infection fulfills Pointsman's wish to gain control of PISCES, attributing a queer, disruptive agency to Pudding's masochism might seem questionable. Though I deal at length with this objection, it's worth noting here the narrative emphasis on Pudding's desire for and pleasure in sexual masochism—which establishes at least a degree of sexual agency and makes Pudding's queer negativity more significant than a mere happy accident for Pointsman.

His nightly ritual also reveals s/m as a mode for coping with the interpretive frustrations that define the postmodern era—though it's important to distinguish between Pudding's use of s/m to make sense of postmodern structures, which stands, in McHale's terms, as a metaphor for the modernist reader making sense of Pynchon's postmodernist text, and Pudding's use of s/m as an embrace of queer negativity, which enables him to turn Pointsman's repressive deployment of sexuality back on itself. Unlike the younger enlisted men, Pudding cannot make sense of his social function, his (lack of) access to power, and newer postmodern formations of knowledge—including weaponry advances and the vast amount of (personal) data that intelligence officers have access to, which changes the nature of war and the individual's place within military bureaucracy. Pudding's resistance to these new power structures and PISCES's unorthodox intelligence work inspires Pointsman's deployment of sexuality as a means of control.[7]

Like the modernist reader, Pudding "was brought up to believe in a literal Chain of Command," and like the modernist reader confronting a postmodernist text, Pudding finds that "the newer geometries confuse him" (78). In McHale's account, *Gravity's Rainbow* deconditions the modernist reader's pattern-making behavior (*Constructing* 81) by frustrating modernist interpretive strategies that seek to construct a stable, intelligible whole from fragmented narratives. Such creative anachronism is typically seen in representations of "worldview and ideology," exemplified in *Gravity's Rainbow* by characters like Slothrop or Roger Mexico, whose mentality "seems to flicker back and forth between the 1940s and the 1960s" (McHale, *Postmodernist* 93). But an equally relevant example would be Pudding, whose masochism allows him to momentarily escape and impose order on the polymorphous organization of power in postmodern culture: PISCES's "lush maze of initials" that's for "the New Chaps" (78). Pudding's ritual becomes an illustrative metanarration that reflects the experience of Pynchon's extradiegetic readers and links queerness to Pynchon's postmodern aesthetic. Beyond their metadiscursive significance, Pudding's pleasures are also narratively relevant.

The narrative's internal focalization through Pudding reveals his desire to submit ("please ... please let her accept ..." [236]), his earnest devotion ("he loves to listen to her speak" [237]), and his hope "to stay a while longer with his submissive tongue straining upward into her asshole" [239])—all pleasures that he seems to experience independently of Pointsman's motives. Pudding even expands the fantasy narrative that Pointsman constructs. When consuming Katje's excrement, Pudding thinks "of a Negro's penis, yes he knows it abrogates part of the conditions set, but it will not be denied, the image of a brute African who will make him behave" (238). One could argue that this fantasy isn't any more outside Pudding's socially conditioned desires than the scenario Pointsman orchestrates; however, the repeated interweaving of race, power, and sexuality across a variety of characters of different national origins (manifested, for example, in Margherita's story about "Negro MPs" and Slothrop's sodium amytal vision of the Roseland Ballroom) seems to indicate less about Pudding's conditioning and more about Pynchon and the context in which he wrote *Gravity's Rainbow*—a moment defined by social shifts linked to the civil rights and liberationist movements. More than an indication of any single character's relation to race or further evidence of sexual conditioning in the West, this motif can be taken as a commentary on the West's haunting legacy of colonialism and chattel slavery and its similarity to the racial ideologies of fascism (Herman and Weisenburger 195). In part, the queerness of Pudding's desire distinguishes the black man of his fantasy from more common racist stereotypes like the idea that "black men were uncivilized, unmanly rapists" who "lusted uncontrollably after white women" (Bederman 46). Although Pudding's fantasy portrays the African as savage and sexually virile—in line with racist fantasies and fears of black masculinity and of miscegenation—he also queers this insidious stereotype through his desire to worship, to be penetrated by, and to be made to behave for the man in his fantasy. More significantly, such details reveal how the fantasy operates subversively within the narrative: it "abrogates" the set conditions by inserting homosexual, interracial desire into Pointsman's ritual, further indicating the extent to which Pudding's sexuality is outside the normative. Pudding's homoerotic desires are also mediated by coprophagia, reinforcing the link between Pudding and the pleasures of queer abjection.[8] By using masochism in ways Pointsman doesn't anticipate, Pudding disrupts and counteracts the institutional deployment of sexuality as a means of controlling and regulating individuals: he takes for himself the pleasures of playing with power, pleasures that—according to Thanatz—should be reserved for the state.

Pudding's unanticipated fantasies bear out Foucault's assertion that power is always being exerted from both the top and bottom; here "top/bottom" can be read in terms of its traditional social signification (i.e., hegemonic institutions of power/individuals), as well as in terms of the s/m binary of dominant/submissive or active/passive sexual roles. Like Foucault, Pynchon identifies sexuality as a disciplinary regime that contains within it the potential to disrupt binary meaning-making systems: Katje, once subservient to Blicero, now wields the power of the sadist, subverting both the binary of dominator/dominated and a patriarchal gender binary that assumes female subservience and associates femininity with the passive/receptive role in intercourse. The novel highlights the multivalent functions of sexuality within society by linking this deconstruction of binary power and language to Pudding's masochistic pleasure.

Though Katje occupies the position of the dominant sadist, she remains subservient to PISCES, a larger institution of power. Like Pudding, her erotic pleasure seems unaffected by its institutional uses. We learn of Katje's sexual arousal when she canes Pudding, the "part of her routine she can enjoy" (237), we learn that her initial nervousness has evaporated (238), and we witness the pleasure small agential actions afford her: her smile when Pudding crawls at her command (236), "her toes flexing beneath his tongue" playfully (236), and her desire to moan "at each of his grunts of pain" (237). It might be tempting to assume that her pleasure is even more ancillary to disruption or subversion than Pudding's. And yet the narrative's emphasis on both their pleasures within an institutional context anticipates Foucault's assertion that "pleasure and power do not cancel or turn back against one another; they seek out, overlap, and reinforce one another. They are linked together by complex mechanisms and devices of excitation and incitement" (*History* 48). By exceeding the conditions set, Katje's pleasure, like Pudding's unanticipated fantasies, intervenes in Pointsman's deployment of sexuality, which was only ever meant to distract Pudding.

Additionally, Pudding's queering of history and unanticipated fantasies demonstrate how queer sexual practices "gum up the works of the normative structures we call family and nation, gender, race, class, and sexual identity, by changing tempos, by remixing memory and desire" in order to "jam *whatever* looks like the inevitable" (Freeman 173)—which could just as easily apply to Pynchon's own disruption of narrative inevitability. Pudding's internal fantasies—shifting between his memories of Domina Nocturna on the World War I battlefield and his present interaction with Katje playing Domina Nocturna as a dominatrix—evoke a queer temporality in which the past is not treated as stable. Similarly, Pynchon's encyclopedic novel incorporates the historical fiction genre, revising and "debunking the orthodox version of the past" and "transform[ing] the conventions and norms of historical fiction itself" (McHale, *Postmodernist* 91). This "paranoiac mode of secret history" manifests in apocryphal history, creative anachronism, and historical fantasy (*Postmodernist* 92). When supplementing the historical record, apocryphal history "operates in the 'dark areas' of history, apparently in conformity to the norms of 'classic' historical fiction but in fact *parodying* them" (*Postmodernist* 91). Pudding's ritual of recounting and refiguring World War I history with Katje draws from the official facts and supplements them with personal experience. The narrative context in which Pudding and Katje queer and revise World War I history is itself located in the larger apocryphal history of *Gravity's Rainbow* and its narration of the "dark areas" of history that parodies World War II historical fiction. Like the postmodernist historical revisions from which it is impossible to draw a "final conclusion" (*Postmodernist* 92) and within which Pudding's s/m is situated, Pudding's queer temporality frustrates normativity, "gumming up" institutional power strategies and readers' interpretive strategies.

Pudding's sexual practice might be the most striking example of Pynchon's paranoid account of history, where s/m reveals how the past shapes the present and how queer sexual pleasure facilitates an exploration of the relationship between personal history and dominant cultural narratives. Though Michael Bérubé has already linked Pynchon's pornography to Pynchonian paranoia, there is a fundamental difference between our approaches: most notably, Bérubé's analysis does not limit "the term 'pornography' to sexually explicit representation" (238). His methodology—rooted in Lacan and feminist film theory—redefines "the pornographic" as a practice of "remembering" or, more simply, a desire for (narrative) closure (256). For Bérubé, pornography is "the condition of all language: papering over and denying the lack [...] or reconstituting *différance* into a metaphysics of presence" (264). Privileging s/m's symbolic significance over and above its erotics misses a key point: how sexuality—its representations, its pleasures, its narration—structures Pynchon's postmodern world. The uniquely queer treatment of time and history in Pudding's s/m narrative mirrors the broader postmodernist strategies of *Gravity's Rainbow*. Pudding's s/m accesses queer temporality in terms of its content while also foregrounding the tension between the world according to official historical archives and one "radically dissimilar" to that: "The tension between these two versions induces a form of ontological flicker between the two" (McHale, *Postmodernist* 91), an ontological flicker that will be repeated when Pudding dies.

The episode ends with Pudding's reflection that he has nothing to look forward to except paperwork and "a dose of penicillin that Pointsman has ordered him to take, to combat the effects of *E. coli*. Perhaps, though, tomorrow night ... perhaps then. He can't see how he can hold out much longer. But perhaps, in the hours just before dawn ..." (239). For Pudding, "holding out" becomes synonymous with a passive endorsement of the system's wartime surveillance methods that he vocally opposed; thus, he imagines his own death as a method of opting out of this endorsement and of his daily military routine. We will learn that he "died back in the middle of June of a massive *E. coli* infection, whining, at the end, 'Me little Mary hurts ...' over and over. It was just before dawn, as he had wished" (542). Through this act of resistance—"forgetting" to take his penicillin—Pudding escapes the political structures that attempt to control him through their deployment of sexuality. According to Foucault, "where there is power, there is resistance" (*History* 95); indeed, Pudding subverts and resists institutional power through the very means the system used to exert control.

One could argue that Pudding's fatal s/m allows the institutional deployment of sexuality to succeed by enabling it to interminably protect itself from Pudding's meddling; however, such a claim would go against a great deal of Pynchon scholarship surrounding Tyrone Slothrop's fate, which has been read as a mode of disruption. Indeed, critics have seen the dissolution of Slothrop's subjectivity as a rare moment when the evasion of power at least marginally succeeds. Even more than Slothrop's "minimalist claim of negative freedom, deeply alienated and individuated" (Herman and Weisenburger 212), Pudding's evasion of their system should be taken as a valid mode of resistance because, like other queerness in the novel, it gets consistently linked to communitarian potential: Pudding's pleasures are linked to a broader history of s/m desires and communities by the multiplicity of literary and cultural allusions to s/m's rich history found in the antechambers he passes through.[9] In much the same way, the encyclopedic compendium of sexological "perversions" documented aboard the *Anubis* and the ironically named song "Victim in a Vacuum!" reveal how the text persistently signals s/m's—and, more broadly, queerness's—communitarian potential. Slothrop's fate, unlike Pudding's, is not directly tied to communitarian queer sexual practices that (attempt to) subvert the institutional deployment of sexuality. Furthermore, in Slothrop's case, institutional power actively pursues his sexual nonnormativity, viewing it as a locus of knowledge that might be "harboring a fundamental secret" (Foucault, *History* 69), while Pudding's proclivities are of limited use, benefiting Pointsman alone. After Slothrop's disappearance the narrative offers no "direct discourse telling his whereabouts, actions, thoughts, and reasons" (Herman and Weisenburger 230), limiting our ability to form hypotheses. In contrast, Pudding reappears late in the narrative as a spiritual member of the Counterforce whose "devotion to culinary pranksterism" inspires "the repulsive stratagem" (729) "by which Mexico and Bodine escape the machinations of the VIPs" (Schlegel 174). Thus, we cannot write off the significance of Pudding's fatal s/m practice anymore than we can disregard Slothrop's famed escape.

By choosing to die, Pudding exercises the subversive potential of queer negativity. He refuses to participate in the construction of a social fiction, a refusal that the text's discursive level reflects by emphasizing the "tension between modes of intelligibility and the apparently unintelligible" (McHale, *Constructing* 73). Pudding, like Pynchon's text, frustrates normative narratives and futurity by transgressing the illusory boundary between dominator and dominated, between social subject and unintelligible subjectivity, or more accurately, between social subject and the nonsubjectivity that results from an embrace of queer negativity taken to its logical extreme. Pudding uses sexuality to transgress the boundary between heteronormative and queer, between life and death.

Blicero and Gottfried

Perhaps more than any other part of the text, the Hansel and Gretel episode focalizes the complexities of power's operations and the fraught potential for subversion that inheres in Pynchon's representations of queerness. We see this particularly in the slippage between Blicero's political power and sexual pleasure, between his desire to access and wield power and his masochistic pleasure in abdicating power, the latter achieved by occupying the role of sadist. This slippage is illuminated by José Esteban Muñoz's characterization of disidentification as "a mode of performance whereby a toxic identity is remade and infiltrated by subjects who have been hailed by such identity categories but have not been able to own such a label" (185). Blicero's anxiety about successfully performing the role of a Nazi officer is rooted in the dialectical tension between Aryan masculinism and homosexual and sadomasochistic desires.

Blicero relies on his military power while disrupting the manifestation and uses of that power. Muñoz's theory of disidentification primarily describes how "a subject who has been hailed by injurious speech, a name, or a label, reterritorializes that speech act" (185). Although queer, Blicero has not been interpellated by the state with that "injurious" label, and thus his disidentification is not with an identity deemed toxic to heteronormativity but rather with a majoritarian identity accepted by the state. The strictures of this institutionally defined role elicit a different mode of disidentification for Blicero, whose state-sanctioned identity is toxic to his queerness. It might seem problematic to apply queer of color critique to a sexual scenario involving a Nazi, but Blicero's disidentificatory practice undermines his Nazi identity from within, vis-à-vis what Muñoz calls "an interiorized passing" through which subjects might (performatively) occupy problematic identities (i.e. homophobic, racist, hypermasculine, etc.) and internally undermine them through parody, as Blicero does in his cross-dressing, gender-bending dominatrix performance.[10]

Although Blicero's disruptions occur primarily on the discursive level, they operate materially through drag, which foregrounds gender binaries as social constructs and replaces them with the dominator/dominated binary. By translating the bureaucratic power of his Nazi rank into that of a parodic dominatrix, Blicero's feminized sexual practice works against the Nazi privileging of hetero- and homomasculinity, his campy costume actively mocking the privileged gender binary.

Despite the tacit sanctioning of certain modes of homoeroticism among the Nazi elite, Blicero's drag can be read as a subversive disidentificatory performance, since it was primarily "the masculine homosexual [who] was in complete concordance with the state's anti-Semitic and misogynistic conceptions of masculinity and femininity" (Halberstam 160). Blicero presents himself in "Cuban heels, his penis squashed invisible under a flesh-colored leather jockstrap, over which he wears a false cunt and merkin of sable," and "tiny blades of stainless steel bristle from lifelike pink humidity" (96–97), crushing the symbol of male power beneath artificial—and weaponized—female genitalia. In heteronormative society, the cunt is constructed as a symbol of weakness because of its vulnerability to penetration; *Gravity's Rainbow* inverts this symbol of female difference and disempowerment. Rather than being penetrated, the steel bristles of Blicero's cunt penetrate Katje's "lips and tongue" bloodying them and reinforcing her subjugation (97). Through his aggressively sexualized drag, Blicero disidentifies with the Nazi privileging of hypermasculinity while simultaneously using this disidentificatory performance to sexualize and feminize the power associated with his military rank. Ironically, this Nazi rank is what gives him power to play out the queer desires that should ostensibly exclude him from the Nazi regime, as per the targeted enslavement and genocide of homosexuals in the camps. Any disidentificatory subversion problematically relies on Blicero's interpellation as a Nazi officer and his willingness to exploit that sovereign power for his own queer ends.

As an officer, Blicero can sacrifice his people for the Aryan cause or his own erotic pleasure. Yet despite his military rank, he remains aware of his waning physical and political power as the war nears its end; that he can no longer die a hero's death is greatly frustrating to him (101). Blicero's fraught relationship with a "toxic identity" and his inability to embody the idealized Nazi leads to disidentificatory performances that reject Aryan masculinism and its glorification of youths like Gottfried who represent the future figured in the fetishization of the child in the heteronormative narrative. Gottfried is a symbol of the heteronormative system that by the war's end will condemn the aging Blicero to a slow decline.

Exploiting wartime ontological instability, Blicero redefines Gottfried's sense of subjectivity. His power over Gottfried, who "kneel[s] naked except for a studded dog collar, masturbating metronomic, at shouted commands from Captain Blicero" (97) calls to mind Foucauldian notions of sexuality as discursive constructs through which power operates as opposed to stable and innate drives (*History* 103). The discursive construction of sexuality as a transfer point in power relations renders subjects perpetually open to reconstruction. By removing Gottfried from the army barracks to the cottage, Blicero removes Gottfried from the bureaucratic structure that defined the boy's subjectivity and replaces it with s/m. Through s/m, Blicero strips Gottfried of the privileged subject position that the Aryan glorification of youth has bestowed on him and that is vested in the child by heteronormative ideology.

However, for Gottfried, "the fucking [...], the stinging chastisements, his face reflected in the act of kissing the Captain's boots [...] make specific his captivity, which otherwise would hardly be different from Army stifling, Army repression" (105), the phrase "Army repression" hinting that this scenario allows Gottfried to explore "unplanned pleasures" (*Foucault Live* 189). As Larry Townsend suggests in his influential classic, *The Leatherman's Handbook* (1972), "S & M activities are the most uninhibited behavioral situations in which you are ever likely to find yourself. Carrying this to its next logical degree, I think it's legitimate to ask ... Is this the real you?" (126); indeed, it is in Blicero's game that Gottfried feels "at true ease" (105). In more realist terms, this appears as a choice between two evils, two modes of imprisonment. And yet it's framed far more ambivalently by Pynchon, who uses Gottfried's internal focalization to reveal the pleasure and tenderness he feels and the pride he takes in his new life, which seems preferable to army monotony, hinting at how "S/M is *the use* of a strategic relationship as a source of pleasure (physical pleasure)" (*Foucault Live* 388). In Blicero's hands, Gottfried's stable and state-defined identity disappears, along with his ontological stability (which was already threatened by the war), leaving his body and identity open to penetration and his own innovative exploration. For Foucault, "the deployment of sexuality has its reason for being [...] in proliferating, innovating, annexing, creating and *penetrating* bodies" (*History* 107, emphasis added), an idea highlighted in *Gravity's Rainbow* when Blicero reminds Gottfried of his initial resistance and then acceptance of anal sex: "How tight you were. Until you knew I meant to come inside. Your little rosebud bloomed. You had nothing, not even your mouth's innocence, to lose ..." (106). By linking subjectivity to discursive structures, the narrative initiates a slippage between embodied and discursively constructed subjectivity; destabilizing one necessarily leads to the destabilization of the other, reflecting a tenuous ontology on both the narrative and discursive levels.

This queer ontological disruption on both levels of the text completes its arc in the novel's final episode, when s/m's ritual aspects are interwoven with the ritualized firing of rocket 00000. Nestled into the rocket's tail section, Gottfried recalls his own "eyes pleading, gagged throat trying to say too late what he should have said in the tent last night . . . deep in the throat, the gullet, where Blicero's own cock's head has burst for the last time" (773). Here, queer practice blocks Gottfried's access to futurity, preventing the production of intelligible narrative, echoing Edelman's understanding of queerness as that which blocks signification and heteronormative narrative telos. Pynchon's ellipsis makes visible this absence of signification: the narrator does not indicate what Gottfried should or would have said had his mouth been unoccupied.

The sentence's structure juxtaposes Gottfried's unarticulated thoughts with his penetrated throat; between them, in place of articulation, is only an ellipsis. This queer frustration of language, meaning, and narrative reflects the postmodernist equating of "life with discourse, death with silence" (McHale, *Postmodernist* 228). As a result of fellating Blicero, Gottfried is silenced; unable, or unwilling, to vocally resist Blicero's narrative, he will die. Though a radio speaker was implanted in Gottfried's ear, allowing him to hear Blicero, "there's no return channel from Gottfried to the ground. The exact moment of his death will never be known" (766). These silences are replicated in the text's structure, which stops short of depicting Gottfried's death, further demonstrating how Pynchon uses s/m on both the narrative and discursive levels to destabilize the ultimate ontological boundary between life and death.

During the launch of 00000, Blicero calls out German commands. The narrator indicates how "there ought to be big dramatic pauses here [. . .]. But no, the ritual has its velvet grip on them all. So strong, so warm . . ." (773). Yet the text's structure undercuts its content; in this section, entitled "The Clearing," each call and response is separated by lengthy descriptions of setting and detailed dialogue tags, suspending and slowing narrative progression. After Moritz presses the button that initiates the first stage, there is "a pause of 15 seconds while the oxygen tank comes up to pressure," and then after ignition, "[t]here is a period of four seconds [. . .], four seconds of indeterminacy. The ritual even has a place for that" (773). Here, the narrator emphasizes the importance of these pauses to the sadistic ritual launching of rocket 00000—the terminal, fatal gratification of pleasure toward which Blicero and Gottfried were heading from the beginning. "Sadomasochism plays with and literalizes power *as* time," as Elizabeth Freeman puts it, making "the pause itself corporeal" (153). The discursive structure of the 00000 launch models

Sadean temporality by slowing down narrative time for both the extradiegetic reader and Gottfried, reflecting how the relation between text and reader is, according to McHale, a reenactment of the s/m relationship, particularly in its "*modeling* of erotic relations through foregrounded violations of ontological boundaries" (*Postmodernist* 227). Like Sade, Pynchon draws on philosophical (and scientific) treatises and includes an excessive amount of detail in order to extend and suspend the erotic scene, creating a discursive structure and narrative that produce an endless deferral of gratification. The text's queer, erotic structure—extending beyond individual instances of s/m—is foregrounded by the Sadean pause's reappearance during the novel's conclusion when the rocket is left hovering, its arc incomplete.

Though the launching of 00000 is the climax of Blicero's s/m practice, it is not the conclusion of his narrative arc. Prior to describing 00000's launch, the narrator reads "WEISSMANN'S TAROT": "[L]ook among the successful academics, the Presidential advisers, the token intellectuals who sit on boards of directors. He is almost surely there. Look high, not low. His future card, the card of what will come, is The World" (764). But how can Blicero ultimately be subsumed by the very systems of institutional power his queerness resists and disidentifies with?[11] Does Blicero's fate and his complicity in the horrific violence carried out by Nazis nullify his disidentificatory use of s/m?

Unlike Margherita's s/m experiences, which are largely focalized through her perspective, Blicero's story is generally mediated by the narrator or another character's memory, underscoring Blicero's limited access to all types of control, narrative or otherwise. For Blicero, the power of queer (and feminized) s/m has its limits. Though scattered, he remains bound by the system, precisely because his desire to become part of the elect necessitates a faith in legible subjectivity that both Pudding and Margherita were willing to forgo.

Indeed, the final moments of Blicero and Gottfried's s/m before the rocket launch—when "both are in army clothes. It's been a long time since either of them dressed as women. It is important that they both be men" (736)—are characterized by hypermasculinity and the absence of Blicero's subversive feminization of power. In the place of such a feminization of power, we find a queer sexual performance that aligns with 1920s and 1930s German "'culturalist' notions of male homosexuality that functioned in terms of the erotic connection between two conventionally masculine men" (Halberstam 156). We might read this alignment with Nazi ideology as Blicero's last attempt to reconcile his queer desires with his desire for power by performing a type of homoeroticism tacitly accepted in the Third Reich. Out of all the text's s/m scenes, this one most closely aligns with the hypermasculine s/m styles and militaristic protocol that characterized American gay, male leather cultures after World War II. This fetishization of hypermasculinity—"the leather gear of bike riders with a few paramilitary touches thrown in" (Baldwin 108)—

among American leathermen also represented "a kind of rebellious individualism [...]. Like other black-clad rebels of the 1950s, the gay leather crowd expressed its own disaffection with post–World War II America, although mainly with its antigay attitudes and staid sexual moralities" (Rubin, "Miracle" 254).

Ironically, this queer subculture rebelliously signals its preference for stigmatized sexuality (s/m) vis-à-vis clothing and accouterments like jackboots and peaked caps that are often associated with the aesthetics of fascism—indeed, they are precisely what Blicero deploys in his final pursuit of fascist power. To reiterate, I am referring to the practice of adopting fashion associated with fascistic imagery, a hypermasculine style like that in Tom of Finland's art, and not to specific fascist symbols, which go unmentioned in this scene between Blicero and Gottfried.[12] After their army s/m, Blicero ultimately cathects his erotic embrace of queer negativity onto Gottfried and foregoes s/m's subversive potential and pleasures. His scattering across the American elite means that he will be subsumed by the very culture that leathermen felt disaffected with.

Although Blicero's s/m does not dismantle the system in its entirety, it's important to acknowledge the complexity of his attempts. From the Hansel and Gretel episode through the 00000 launch, Blicero's eroticization of the rockets reveals how his sexual pleasures paradoxically gesture toward both s/m's disruptive potential and its imbrication within systems of control. As a Nazi officer, Blicero should not take pleasure in military failures, such as when the very technology meant to offer protection instead threatens the lives of its creators: "[C]razed, [the rockets] turn at random, whinnying terribly in the sky, turn about and fall according each to its madness so unreachable and, it is feared, incurable" (98). Blicero takes sadistic pleasure in subjugating Katje and Gottfried in the cottage outside of the rocket battery, a location that renders them all equally subjugated to the rockets' erratic nature. In much the same way that Blicero's disidentificatory drag relies on his ranking power over Gottfried, his masochistic pleasure in the rockets' threat is only possible because he's been stationed as captain of the V-2 battery in Holland. Blicero's masochistic desires refigure tools of war as personal tools of pleasure, undermining the rockets' intended political function.[13] Like his drag's disruption of gender roles, Blicero's pleasure in subjugating himself to the rockets resists Nazi masculinist ideals, rendering him both passive and vulnerable to penetration; it also contains the additional risk (or for Blicero, masochistic pleasure in risk) of losing his military rank, since "the effeminate homosexual was persecuted in Nazi Germany both for his rejection of the heterosexual family and for his embrace of the feminine" (Halberstam 161). Perhaps even more than those disruptions that occur on the discursive level, these two material manifestations of Blicero's queer pleasure highlight his paradoxical reliance on and disruption of institutional power.

Taking Sado-Anarchism Seriously

Thanatz explains to Ludwig how the state "needs our submission so that it may remain in power. It needs our lusts after dominance so that it can co-opt us into its own power game. There is no joy in it, only power. I tell you, if S and M could be established universally, at the family level, the State would wither away" (751). The state in *Gravity's Rainbow* does not wither away, and critics have read this as a failure of political rebellion, overlooking how sado-anarchism's political, sexual, and textual functions reveal queerness's centrality to the novel's content and structure. Moreover, reading Pynchon's representations of s/m and sado-anarchism as serious meditations on sex, power, and embodied pleasure situates *Gravity's Rainbow* within a broader proliferation of knowledges on sex and sexuality in the post-Stonewall period. In many ways, the novel narratively prefigures Foucault's theorization of sexuality as a sociohistorical construct. Pynchon's sado-anarchism theorizes sex and power in a way that is strikingly similar to Foucault's theorization of the "deployment of sexuality [that] operates according to mobile, polymorphous, and contingent techniques of power" (106) in volume 1 of *The History of Sexuality*, which was published in France just three years after the U.S. publication of *Gravity's Rainbow*. Though *Gravity's Rainbow* reflects institutions' use of sexuality as a technology for control and regulation, the range of discourses concerning sexuality within the novel also construct sexual practice as a tool of resistance (discourse itself being a tool that "undermines and exposes [power], renders it fragile and makes it possible to thwart" [*History* 101]). Echoing Thanatz's recognition that establishing queer sexuality at the family level would threaten the state, Foucault explains how the family "conveys the law and the juridical dimension in the deployment of sexuality" and how "sexuality has its privileged point of development in the family" (*History* 108); thus, any queering of pleasures that occurs on this level can potentially disrupt the process of founding social order.

The novel's encyclopedic scope models the proliferation of discourses concerning sexuality that Foucault analyzes that forces sexuality "to speak through explicit articulation and endlessly accumulated detail" (*History* 18). The paranoid history depicted in *Gravity's Rainbow*—"a peculiar *structure* that no one admitted to" (196)—aligns with Foucault's theorization of sexuality as "a great surface network in which the stimulation of bodies, the intensification of pleasures, the incitement to discourse, the formation of special knowledges, the strengthening of controls and resistances, are linked to one another, in accordance with a few major strategies of knowledge and power" (*History* 106). *Gravity's Rainbow* is itself a great surface network that links embodied pleasure, sexual practices, and scientific and political knowledge—including knowledge about how queerness might respond to the major strategies of power. Indeed, Foucault investigates the operations of power behind scientific records and official historical facts in much the same way that Pynchon's paranoid history uncovers "layer upon layer of conspiracy behind the official historical facts of the Second World War" (McHale, *Postmodernist* 91) and, we might add, behind the institutional deployment of sexuality.

Insisting on the pleasures of Pynchon's pornographic representations— even those that occur within institutional frames—reveals how Pynchon prefigures Foucault's assertion that "the rallying point for the counterattack against the deployment of sexuality ought not to be sex-desire, but bodies and pleasures" (*History* 157)—that is, that which exceeds the discursive (disciplinary) constraints of sexuality, as defined by official discourses. The possibility of diegetic and extradiegetic queer pleasures challenges Pynchon scholarship that delinks postmodernist narrative subversion from the text's s/m content—such as Herman and Weisenburger's reading in which s/m becomes the basis for their dark conclusion: "[Y]our 'chances for freedom' were never really chances. That too was a useful fantasy" (221).[14] The idea that "the novel imagines no way out from under the dominion of [the] trinity" of technology, capital, and war whose "governing spirits" are Dominus Blicero and Domina Nocturna (Herman and Weisenburger 220) obscures power's multidirectional operations in Pudding's and Blicero's s/m.

Acknowledging the potential queerness of Pynchon's readers further illuminates how postmodernist subversion and s/m reinforce and structure one another. Indeed, Herman and Weisenburger's introduction—which identifies "dominance" "as posing the greatest threat to the 'chances for freedom' in Pynchon's storyworld and, arguably, the readers' as well" (15)—functions as a prophylactic for both critic and reader, protecting us from association with those "salacious but disturbing energies of mock pornographic parodies" (17). By describing "domination" as "freedom's antonym, defining what threatens the supposedly inherent rights upheld in liberal thought and practice" (15), Herman and Weisenburger discount the pleasure that might inhere in Pynchon's s/m—either for extradiegetic readers or characters. Recall Gottfried's enjoyment of "the word *bitch*, spoken now in a certain tone of voice" (105) or Katje's suppressed moans when she canes Pudding (237), not to mention Pynchon's more generalized representation of erotic pain as "the clearest poetry, the endearment of greatest worth" (237). Indeed, previous readings have dismissed the possibility that a reader of *Gravity's Rainbow* might have a sexual life in which—as for some of Pynchon's characters—domination is not experienced as freedom's antonym but rather as a necessary condition of (sexual) freedom. Pain for s/m practitioners is not an end in and of itself but rather that which signals "the ritual, the anticipation, the profound trust" (Drivenwoman 13) that makes s/m practice a valuable exploration of the pleasures of domination and submission.[15]

While Foucault's theories focus on the nineteenth-century creation of sexuality and its relation to power, Pynchon's novel articulates the power/sex dynamics that were contemporary with the publication of *Gravity's Rainbow*, illustrating the lasting and pervasive effects of nineteenth-century sexuality discourses on postwar America. Such lasting effects manifest themselves in Pynchon scholarship, which almost invariably deploys the stigmatizing language of official discourses when reading s/m. This critical strategy attempts to rescue Pynchon's text from its pornographic pleasures by distancing his representations of queer sex from embodied practices and insisting that s/m, or queerness more generally, operates solely as a metaphor or satire in Pynchon. Critics' quest to discover the "true" (i.e., nonsexual) meaning of s/m or to identify its social origins ironically parallels the work of sexology and psychoanalysis, which seek to uncover root causes in order to "cure" patients. By characterizing s/m as a perversion of normalcy, such discourses—critical and medical—fail to see s/m as a significant structuring agent in a text or a patient—neither of which need to be saved. Highlighting the possibility of pleasure in sexual power games—in Pynchon's storyworld and among extradiegetic readers—disrupts s/m's pathologization and challenges the claim that domination invariably forecloses our chances for freedom. Instead, we should see these pleasures as potential vehicles for transgressing institutional power or, at the very least, as overlooked modes of knowledge production; in either case, the queer pleasures of Pynchon's text become fundamental to his paradigmatic postmodernism.

NOTES

1. Pudding, a World War I veteran who "must be pushing 80" (78), reenlisted in 1940 and was assigned, to his dismay, to the political warfare unit. Blicero, a reference to a Germanic folk name for death (from "der bleicher," which means "'The Bleacher,' for what death does to bones" (Weisenburger 37)), is the code name for Nazi lieutenant, and later captain, Weissmann.

2. This counters the anti-s/m feminist claim that s/m is a replication of patriarchal gender dynamics. Despite the nominally heterosexual structure of some of Pynchon's s/m representations, s/m remains fundamentally queer, particularly since "heterosexual S/M is *not* standard heterosexuality. Straight S/M is stigmatized and persecuted. [...] Once someone starts to use whips, ropes, and all the theatre, they are considered to be perverts, not normal" (Rubin, "The Leather Menace" 221).

3. Although there are many ways to reference the distinction between form and content (e.g. "discourse/storyworld," "fabula/sjužet"), I use "discourse" to refer to structure/form, and "narrative" to refer to the story's content.

4. Though not coextensive with "postmodernism," queer theory's rejection of essentialist notions of gender and sexuality are indebted to postmodernism's investment in the dissolution of the subject and destabilization of meaning.

5. For McHale, modernists foreground epistemological questions, whereas post-

modernists foreground ontological questions, which are reflected in the clustering of thematic and formal qualities associated with postmodernist fiction.

6. For example, Edmund White mentions Pynchon's "sado-anarchism" in a 1980 interview published in *Drummer* magazine—America's first gay leather magazine.

7. Despite Pointsman's grasps for power in PISCES, he mustn't be conflated with the newer formations of power; Pointsman is a true Pavlovian and "model of determinist thought and practice serving the ultimate domination of nature and man" (Herman and Weisenburger 7).

8. For an extended discussion of interracial homosexuality and the subversive (queer) potential in embracing the abject, see Scott.

9. This goes against Hamill's assertion that characters' retreats to private fantasies leave them vulnerable to "the tyranny of a wider social agency" (53).

10. Muñoz elaborates on "interiorized passing" through reading a performance by the drag queen Vaginal Davis, who takes on the role of "Clarence," a white supremacist militia man, as "an active disidentification with strictures against cross-racial desire" (104–5) that grafts "aspects of the self that are toxic to the militiaman— blackness, gayness, and transvestitism [. . .] onto this particularly militaristic script of masculinity [. . .], inhabit[ing] and undermin[ing] the militiaman with a fierce sense of parody" (106).

11. This interpretation of Blicero's tarot—that the launching of the rocket points to his having been absorbed by American institutional power rather than an oppressive apotheosis of his power mania—is based on Weisenburger's meticulous research on tarot symbolism that indicates how "Weissmann's tarot points up the end of his romantic desire and its translation into business, into conformity, into the cartelized military industrial sovereignties of the postwar period" (375).

12. We must distinguish between this general aesthetic fetishization of hypermasculinity with fascistic overtones and the much less common practice of adopting "a historically accurate symbol such as the swastika [. . .] in a way that is continuous with the dominant imagery and state-level ideological interests of Third Reich Nazism" or even "choosing a 'plaything' that has been recuperated within the living symbolism of current neo-Nazi subgroups" (Wayne 249).

13. That many of the V-2s were constructed by slave laborers from the Dora concentration camp who were "interned for violating paragraph 175 of the German Penal Code, 'which exacted punishment for certain abnormal sex practices' (Kracauer, *From Caligari to Hitler* 45)" (Weisenburger 182), further demonstrates the paradox of Blicero's queer sadomasochism; his masochistic pleasure in the rockets and sadistic sexual relationship with Gottfried rely on a Nazi regime that both exploited and sought to exterminate homosexuals.

14. One might also consider the utility of fantasy in terms of resistant, queer subjectivities. See Muñoz's *Cruising Utopia* and Judith Butler's *Undoing Gender* (in which she explains how the "critical promise of fantasy" challenges "the contingent limits of what will and will not be called reality" [29]).

15. See also Mains.

WORKS CITED

Baldwin, Guy. "'Old Guard': Its Origins, Traditions, Mystiques and Rules." *Ties That Bind*. Ed. Joseph Bean. Los Angeles: Daedalus, 1993. 107–15.

Bederman, Gail. *Manliness and Civilization: A Cultural History of Gender and Race in the United States, 1880–1917.* Chicago: University of Chicago Press, 1995.

Bérubé, Michael. *Marginal Forces/Cultural Centers: Tolson, Pynchon, and the Politics of the Canon.* Ithaca: Cornell University Press, 1992.

Butler, Judith. *Undoing Gender.* New York: Routledge, 2004.

Chetwynd, Ali. Review of *The Cambridge Companion to Thomas Pynchon*, edited by Inger H. Dalsgaard, Luc Herman, and Brian McHale. *College Literature* 39.4 (2012): 142–45.

Drivenwoman. "Coming Out on S&M." *What Color Is Your Handkerchief: A Lesbian S/M Sexuality Reader.* Berkeley: Samois, 1979. 12–14.

Edelman, Lee. *No Future: Queer Theory and the Death Drive.* Durham: Duke University Press, 2004.

Foucault, Michel. *Foucault Live: Collected Interviews, 1961–1984.* Ed. Sylvère Lotringer. Trans. Lysa Hochroth and John Johnston. New York: Semiotext(e), 1989.

———. *The History of Sexuality.* Vol. 1: *An Introduction.* Trans. Robert Hurley. New York: Vintage, 1990.

Franco, Marie. "Queer Postmodern Practices: Sex and Narrative in *Gravity's Rainbow*." *Twentieth-Century Literature* 63.2 (2017): 141–66.

Freeman, Elizabeth. *Time Binds: Queer Temporalities, Queer Histories.* Durham: Duke University Press, 2010.

Halberstam, Judith. *The Queer Art of Failure.* Durham: Duke University Press, 2011.

Hamill, John. "Looking Back on Sodom: Sixties Sadomasochism in *Gravity's Rainbow*." *Critique: Studies in Contemporary Fiction* 41.1 (1999): 53–70.

Herman, Luc, and Steven Weisenburger. Gravity's Rainbow, *Domination, and Freedom.* Athens: University of Georgia Press, 2013.

Mains, Geoff. *Urban Aboriginals: A Celebration of Leathersexuality.* Los Angeles: Daedelus, 1984.

McHale, Brian. *Constructing Postmodernism.* London: Routledge, 1992.

———. *Postmodernist Fiction.* London: Routledge, 1987.

Muñoz, José Esteban. *Disidentifications: Queers of Color and the Performance of Politics.* Minneapolis: University of Minnesota Press, 1999.

Pynchon, Thomas. *Gravity's Rainbow.* New York: Penguin, 2006.

Rubin, Gayle. "The Leather Menace: Comments on Politics and S/M." *Coming to Power: Writings and Graphics on Lesbian S/M.* Ed. Samois. 3rd ed. Boston: Alyson, 1987. 194–229.

———. "The Miracle Mile: South of Market and Gay Male Leather 1962–1997." *Reclaiming San Francisco: History, Politics, Culture.* Ed. James Brook, Chris Carlsson, and Nancy J. Peters. San Francisco: City Lights, 1998. 247–72.

Schlegel, Keith W. "The Rebellion of the Coprophages." *Pynchon Notes* 46–49 (2000–2001): 170–77.

Scott, Darrieck. *Extravagant Abjection: Blackness, Power, and Sexuality in the African American Literary Imagination.* New York: New York University Press, 2010.

Sears, Julie Christine. "Black and White Rainbows and Blurry Lines: Sexual Deviance/Diversity in *Gravity's Rainbow* and *Mason & Dixon*." *Thomas Pynchon: Reading from the Margins.* Ed. Niran Abbas. Madison: Fairleigh Dickinson University Press, 2003. 108–21.

Sontag, Susan. "Fascinating Fascism." *Under the Sign of Saturn.* New York: Vintage, 1981. 73–105.

Townsend, Larry. *The Leatherman's Handbook*. 1972. Montrouge: Le Salon, 1977.
Wayne, Linda. "S/M Symbols, Fascist Icons, and Systems of Empowerment." *The Second Coming: A Leatherdyke Reader*. Ed. Pat Califia and Robin Sweeney. Los Angeles: Alyson, 1996. 242–51.
Weisenburger, Steven C. *A Gravity's Rainbow Companion: Sources and Contexts for Pynchon's Novel*. 2nd ed. Athens: University of Georgia Press, 2006.
Wolfley, Lawrence C. "Repression's Rainbow: The Presence of Norman O. Brown in Pynchon's Big Novel." *PMLA* 92.5 (1977): 873–89.

What Would Charlie Do?
Narrowing the Possibilities of a Pornographic Redemption in Thomas Pynchon's Novels

RICHARD MOSS

In his 2014 film adaptation of *Inherent Vice*, Paul Thomas Anderson cast Michelle A. Sinclair—otherwise known in the porn industry as "Belladonna"—as Clancy Charlock, in a nod to Sinclair's own extensive pornographic career (giving her lines like "two at a time," showing a glimpse of her buttocks) and his own fascination with the history of the California porn industry, which he had previously explored in *Boogie Nights* (1997). In particular, he is interested in the heyday of the 1970s, what Ben Sachs of the *Chicago Reader* calls "the expansive adult-entertainment industry that would take root in LA not long after the events" the novel depicts (par. 2). By returning to this theme, Anderson is also, more important for us, demonstrating an understanding of the key thematic and structuring motif in Pynchon's novel itself, as well as his wider work. Both the film and the novel demonstrate a sexuality that has been uniformly co-opted by regressive, heteronormative fantasies, often used for nefarious purposes by, as Sauncho Smilax in *Inherent Vice* states, "evildoers known all too well" (238). It is this focus on the sociohistorical aspects of porn, as well as its narrative form, which Pynchon uses, that is the subject of this essay.

I focus on two key ideas surrounding Thomas Pynchon and pornography. The first is how he employs the soft-core pornography of the 1970s in the content of his novel and the second is how this use of mainstream pornography indicates the extent to which he has lost faith in the idea that pornography is powerful, liberating, and often *redemptive*.

Before I begin, it is worth explaining what I mean by the theologically loaded term "redemptive." In simple terms, Pynchon, I maintain, represents a heterodox pornography in his early work (*Gravity's Rainbow*, the most overtly pornographic of his earlier work, serves as my example) as liberating, as capable of establishing territory for a politics of resistance. Luc Herman and Steven Weisenburger argue in Gravity's Rainbow, *Domination and Freedom* that Pynchon's vulgarities don't "just pierce" but "destroy [...] the membrane against vulgarity and obscenity: [they] *profane* [...] the omniscient narrator's imperial position" (174). We can see this intersection with politics when Thanatz theorizes that "if S and M could be established universally, at the *family* level, the State would wither away" (737, emphasis added) and in his attempts to erase the "reflexive shame" (737) associated with it. In her excellent essay "Queer Postmodern Practices: Sex and Narrative in *Gravity's Rainbow*," Marie Franco suggests that Thanatz's remark forms the framework for Pynchon's pornographies, arguing that it "can thus be read as the most illustrative manifestation of queer practice in the novel, an erotic and narrative practice that replicates the text's own discursive structure through embodied sexual pleasure" (143). Here we see Pynchon characterize his pornographies using familiar tropes of family, community, and acceptance of "deviant" or queer practices. Sex in a nonnormative form works as an active counter to the smothering appropriation and control of "Them." A proper Manichean duality is set up in the novel, with the forces of sex (eros) in direct opposition to the forces of death (thanatos). Pynchon's pornographies transcend the need for sanctioning by oppressive or controlling forces; they revel in the raw political power of kink. The resistant power of oppressed or preterite characters, acts of mutual care or community, and the fragility of human connections (Roger and Jessica in *Gravity's Rainbow*, for instance) are often illustrated in Pynchon's writing with sex.

The pornographic content in *Gravity's Rainbow* not only reflects Pynchon's political ideals but also his theology. Pynchon's politics in *Gravity's Rainbow* are heavily inflected by religious ideas, from the control system that is depicted as Calvinist doctrine in motion to the Zone-Hereros who construct an alternative, unorthodox religion of escape for themselves by embracing their own marginalization. John McClure in *Partial Faiths* refers to this political use of theology as "supernatural multiculturalism" (19), a coming together of Pynchon's interest in the religious notion of salvation/redemption, the excitement of reforming religion and politics to create something radically new, and his eagerness to promote a politics of diversity. Indeed, "postsecularism," McClure maintains, "is politics through and through" (20). Pynchon's pornographies, I argue, are an extension of this notion. He is interested in the radical possibilities of pornography, the boundaries it can break and the political power that the erotic can wield. While Pynchon is often critically described as giving voice to a kind of "liberation theology" in his work, I determine that he is also interested in creating what I call "liberation *pornography*," which informs my reading of *Gravity's Rainbow* here and brings to light the underplayed importance of explicit sex therein. As Franco argues, Pynchon's pornographies "might suggest a far more capacious approach to literary categorization in which the importance of sex and sexuality refigures literary history through a pleasure in perversities, linking high and low culture, male and female authors" (142).

Yet while I see *Gravity's Rainbow* as a novel that represents liberation pornography as an expression of positive political ideas, *Inherent Vice* does the opposite. In his essay "Manson Chicks and Microskirted Cuties," Simon Cook points to a narrowing of the otherwise expansive pornographic possibilities in *Inherent Vice*: "Pynchon is a long-time exhibitor of sexual excess and nonnormative sexualities taken to bizarre extremes, to all manners of ends, but in his seventh novel the intimate interactions of his characters are constrained within a kind of *flatness and conventionality*, a shadow of the experimentation of his earlier fictions" (1147, emphasis added). This "conventionality" is key to understanding how Pynchon presents his pornographies in *Inherent Vice* and important for assessing how he now relates porn to notions of spiritual and political redemption. Cook is interested in dissecting the pornographic content of *Inherent Vice*, while I aim to show how the general pornographic tone of the novel is distinct from that of his earlier work and to consider the implications this change in tone has for our understanding of Pynchon's approach to writing pornographically.

My question, then, is why has Pynchon narrowed the scope of the redemptive possibilities of his pornographies? There are two potential answers to this question, answers that could go hand in hand. First, Pynchon sees the 1970s themselves as a period of narrowing, a time of industrialized porn that led to a homogenization of sexual appetites that makes no space for heterodox and liberating approaches to sex and sexual identity. Second, an older Pynchon seems to be rethinking his approach to his pornographic writing, finding problems with his earlier work and seeing in retrospect the exploitation of the industry. In the wake of the hippy era and the sexual revolution, a time that informs much of *Gravity's Rainbow*, Pynchon appears to have become jaded and to have lost hope in the idea of sex as redemptive.

The Aesthetic

Before we delve into a comparative study of the pornographies of the two novels, it is worth looking at the kind of pornography that informs *Inherent Vice*, that of the early days of the California porn industry in the late 1950s and 1960s. The first commercially successful porn films were known as the "nudie cuties," the archetypical film in the genre being Russ Meyer's *The Immoral Mr. Teas* (1959), which was the first American sex film to be booked by art theaters (Briggs 23). The film itself contains no sex at all. Instead, Mr. Teas uses the X-ray vision he has acquired to spy on a variety of women naked. Lewis and Friedman's *The Adventures of Lucky Pierre* (1961) likewise features voyeurism, sans the X-ray vision.[1] Pynchon incorporates this initial focus on voyeurism into the pornographies of *Inherent Vice*. Doc Sportello's adventures in the novel can be read as a series of discrete voyeuristic fantasies. He is the archetypal male within a nudie cutie—hidden, socially awkward, but very horny. He is aroused at the notion of Clancy Charlock's threesome, he is privy to the 1960s sex comedy pastiche of the antics of Rudy Blatnoyd and his secretary, and he is denied interaction with Jade and Bambi at the Chick Planet Massage Parlor but is content to observe ("Doc thought he should keep watching for a while" [21]). Pynchon frequently depicts Doc's hard-ons, erections that are never brought to completion. Like Mr. Teas and Lucky Pierre, Doc becomes the hidden observer and, alongside the reader, the viewer of the porn himself. Pynchon's liberation pornography requires sex between a community of two or more, but Doc is positioned as the isolated outsider, the voyeur, the lonesome masturbator. The pornographies of *Inherent Vice* produce an *internalization* of sex rather than promote the external relations we see in *Gravity's Rainbow*. No power is exercised and there is no redemption, as the eroticism only occurs inside the imaginative fantasies of an isolated individual. There is no space for the community or resistance that Thanatz theorizes. The power of the porn is what withers, not the state.

What's more, voyeurism denies power rather than grants it. The frisson of voyeurism derives from seeing that which you were not meant to see. Consent is not a part of the voyeur's fantasy; in fact those being observed must be unaware that they are being observed: agency is robbed from them and bodies are objectified against their will. The dynamic of the singular onanist is referenced in *Gravity's Rainbow* as an apparatus of control, a counter to the more social and communal pornographies that Pynchon explores: "[A]ll these novels, these films and songs they lull us with, they're approaches, more comfortable and less so, to the Absolute Comfort [. . .], the self-induced orgasm" (155). Russ Meyer himself was less interested in sex and more in the act of illicitly observing vulnerability. His later films such as *Faster Pussycat! Kill! Kill!* (1965), *Mondo Topless* (1966)—which represents the sexual revolution of the 1960s not as a liberating movement but as a vehicle for the voyeur—and the infamous *Supervixens* (1975) all invite the male viewer to enjoy not the sex but the bodies on show. Joe Bob Briggs writes that Meyer "was never concerned with a story arc, and his patented fast cutting was frequently so disorientating as to sap all the eroticism out of his sex scenes [. . .]. [H]e was unconcerned with anything below the waist, with male beauty, or with the sex act itself" (22).

Doc's voyeurism doesn't just emulate the frothy silliness of Meyer's porn and sex comedies. There is a darker side too, represented by the seamy underworlds that Doc descends into, including that of Californian porn. Clancy's sexually provocative relationships are depicted as erotic, but they are also embedded in the narrative of the rise of neo-Nazis in America. The comedy of Blatnoyd fooling around with his secretary is darkened by his pedophilic relationship with Japonica Fenway. In every porn scene Doc finds himself haplessly flung into, there is a dark and deeply historical tale of Californian exploitation, oppression, and violence.

Porn in *Inherent Vice* does not provide avenues of redemption for the preterite or escape from controlling powers but simply serves to cater for Doc's fantasies. One might object, however, that porn in Pynchon's earlier novels never provides an avenue of redemption for women. In *Thomas Pynchon and American Counterculture*, Joanna Freer, for example, points out that "in all of Pynchon's novels, [women] are more often than not [...] objects of desire whose sex appeal is conveyed by (soft) pornographic imagery catering to the male gaze" (151). I am inclined to agree with Freer here, but there is a difference between the pornographic portrayal of women in the earlier work and in *Inherent Vice*: in *Gravity's Rainbow*, porn is intended to provide redemptive avenues that mirror Pynchon's theology and politics, while *Inherent Vice* is a self-critique of the idea that porn is capable of that. Pynchon's pornographies in *Gravity's Rainbow* reflect a time when porn was becoming recognized as an art form. *Deep Throat* came out in 1972; it was the first porn film to achieve critical success and acclaim and went on to become a cinematic milestone. Indeed, Franco believes that Pynchon's postmodernism is deeply invested in a progressive vision of pornography of the day: *Gravity's Rainbow*'s queerness "can destabilize the presumed heteromasculinity of high postmodernism, since we might reconsider postmodernism in relation to the historically and thematically overlapping proliferation of queer pornographies after the 1969 Stonewall Uprising" (142–43). In 2009, Pynchon finds himself in a world where this is no longer the case—porn is homogenized and packaged and has become a huge and exploitative industry in itself. It has been co-opted by the very powers that Pynchon hoped it would act against.

A Genealogy of Objects

As I have argued, and as Cook has before me, *Inherent Vice*'s mosaic of pornographic scenes are playful, imitating a 1970s soft-core model, even as they allude to dark, corrupt, and exploitative worlds. As the novel progresses, the seamy side comes to prevail. This is exemplified in the "return of Shasta" passage, a scene where Doc actually gets to have sex.[2] This transformation of Doc from voyeur to participant comes with a strong and troubling shift in tone.

Shasta's return toward the end of the novel forms a belated climax to discreet pornographic moments that inform Doc's previous adventures—the moment of release of a culmination of hard-ons. However, his sex with Shasta is not merely a discrete event but is also the culmination of his sexual fantasies, and the eroticism of the scene thus derives from the morass of pornographic desires that have infected Doc throughout the novel. The scene is written to be more disturbing than erotic.

Having been corrupted by the darkening California he has immersed himself into, Doc then becomes the cipher for pornographic heteronormative expectations, and in turn Shasta becomes the ideal of the pornified 1970s California girl—not liberated by the sexual revolution but instead transformed by it into erotic persona, a dead-eyed girl lifted straight from *Mondo Topless*. We become privy to the aggressive, exploitative, and violent fantasy laid bare without the frothy artifice that informs the rest of Doc's sexual interactions when Shasta describes how her former boyfriend Mickey used to treat her:

> "[H]e'd bring me to lunch in Beverly Hills, one big hand all the way around my bare arm, steering me blind down out of those bright streets into some space where it was dark and cool and you couldn't smell any food, only alcohol—they'd all be drinking, tables full of them in a room that could've been any size, and they all knew Mickey there, they wanted, some of them, to be Mickey.... He might as well have been bringing me in on a leash. He kept me in these little microminidresses, never allowed me to wear anything underneath, just offering me to whoever wanted to stare. Or grab. Or sometimes he'd fix me up with his friends. And I'd have to do whatever they wanted...." (305)

While deliberately disturbing and full of the menace of an imbalanced power dynamic between male and female, this passage is still constructed pornographically. This isn't the testimony of an abused individual; Shasta knows that Doc finds this erotic, and by extension Pynchon writes this scene using pornographic language. The depiction of abuse (and to be clear—Shasta at this point in the narrative *is* a victim of prolonged sexual abuse) is eroticized. Shasta relates her experiences while beginning to "unhurriedly stroke her nipples" (304); she is "draped across his lap, her hands beneath her playing with her pussy, her ass irresistibly presented" (305). Pynchon seems to be implying that Shasta herself finds her story autoerotic. Pynchon's masterstroke here is to weave in subtle references to pornographic fantasies he has primed us with before. "And I'd have to do whatever they wanted" suggests women's lack of agency in such fantasies, and "offering me to who ever wanted to stare" refers to voyeurism. By making Shasta's abuse a pornographic fantasy for Doc, Pynchon is confronting us with the reality of the pornographic artifices he has presented us with in other novels. By showing this juxtaposition between Shasta's dialogue and her actions, Pynchon shows that sexual exploitation and pornographic language occupy the same disquieting space. Cook notes that it "becomes almost impossible to read the Doc-Shasta play as anything other than explicitly consensual" (1158), but it is precisely this incorporation of consent *into* the fantasy that is troubling.

While this is an isolated scene in *Inherent Vice* and very different in tone from other scenes, Shasta nevertheless represents the zenith of a genealogy of sexualized women across Pynchon's work, and the confrontation of the exploitation and violence that saturates the scene represents the kind of narrowing I have been addressing. Contra Cook's suggestion that Pynchon is a proponent of kink and queerness in his pornographies, this sexual pioneering is still presented—as Freer thinks—from a male perspective, pornified in a fashion that caters for the heterosexual male viewer. Pynchon's representations of sex, while multitudinous, heterodox, and diverse, still either feature or cater to the male. In *Gravity's Rainbow*, the "liberation pornography" that Pynchon embarks on comes at the expense of the novel's many "pleasant-looking female characters" (Freer 12). The character who serves as the prototype of Shasta's problematic "hypersexuality" is Katje Borgesius.

Katje, like Shasta, is treated as a pornographic object in the text. Her sexuality is exploited by various male characters (including Blicero), and, like Shasta, she is depicted taking a certain masochistic enjoyment in her subjugation. Indeed, she takes autoerotic pleasure in her image as a passive sexual object when she looks at herself posing erotically: "At the images she sees in the mirror [she] also feels a cameraman's pleasure" (94). Although, of course, the inclusion of the word "cameraman" grounds the scene in cinematic porn, the pleasure she finds here is not that of external agency; rather, her pleasure derives from a regressive internalized acceptance of her own status as a sexualized object. Vivid and erotic scenes are described in the novel the way stills from a porn film are: "[Katje is] only passive, bound and gagged and false-eyelashed, serving tonight as a human pillow for the Italian's whitening perfumed curls" (94). She is an object for the gratification of powerful controlling males and in turn a proxy for the reader's own gratification. Katje's scenes are pornographic within the context of the story and also pornographic on the page.

A difference between Shasta and Katje, however, emerges from Katje's sex scene with Slothrop. The focus of this scene is again on her body as a sexual object, and it is written in a pornographic style: "[A]s they fuck she quakes, body strobing miles beneath him in cream and night-blue" (196). But while Katje's body is sexual in her orgasm, the mention of the traditional colors of the Holy Mary ("cream and blue") suggest that there are religious allusions encoded within this scene and that it may therefore be oriented toward religious modes of redemption and salvation. Shasta's scene offers no such redemption and can be seen as pointing to a disconnect between sexual fantasy and sexual violence. Doc is depicted as a man whose fantasies damn him to the darkening world he is inhabiting, while Slothrop instead is privy to possibilities of paranoia and potential escape. However, Slothrop's possible redemption still comes at the expense of the objectification of the female body. "She has sunk to the deep bed, pulling him along" (196), suggests a woman playing the role of the sexual agent that caters to the erotic fantasies of men, as further evidenced by Slothrop's hurried and expectant undressing, his childish "oboy oboy" (196), and Katje's own sense of resignation as she "[k]now[s] what is expected of her" (196).

In *Gravity's Rainbow* there is a dichotomy between mutual sex acts and contrived, pornographic ones. The sex scene between Slothrop and Katje is particularly contrived, consciously constructed as a pornographic one. Katje assumes more of an "actor" role than a sex partner role, as Slothrop's paranoia transforms the sex into a manipulative setup at his expense. As his paranoia peaks, Katje appears to transmute into something demonic and threatening: "[A] terrible beastlike change com[es] over muzzle and lower jaw, black pupils growing to cover the entire eye space till whites are gone and there's only the red animal reflection when the light comes to strike" (196). This transformation mirrors Katje's own past relationship with the equally bestial Blicero, so much so that Slothrop imagines her as an extension of him, a sexual construct created entirely by him.[3] The same applies to Shasta. Shasta becomes the vehicle for Wolfmann's own sexual power fantasy, a fantasy that Doc then assumes. Doc's inability to not engage in sex with Shasta could almost be seen as a Pavlovian response to the pornography he has become accustomed to, similar to Slothrop's conditioning.

Slothrop, alert to the possibility that this is all a *constructed* and staged event, a predetermined scene in a film, wonders if Katje is merely playing the part of a willing sexual partner, given that she is "full of careful technique." "[I]s it for her," he asks himself, "or wired into the Slothropian Run-together they briefed her on[?]" (196). As we move toward the end of the passage, cinematic artifice begins to forcibly invade the scene:

> He grabs his own pillow and swings it at her. She ducks, rolls, hits the deck feinting with her pillow, backing toward the sideboard where the booze is. He doesn't see what she has in mind till she throws her pillow and picks up the Seltzer bottle.
>
> The what, *The Seltzer Bottle?* What shit is this, now? What other interesting props have They thought to plant, and what other American reflexes are They after? Where's those *banana cream pies*, eh? (197, emphasis in the original)

The seltzer bottle adds to Slothrop's suspicion that the event is staged, and the narrator joins him in his paranoia. Objects become props, Slothrop's sexual partner an actor, and the scene's tone becomes increasingly focused on the pornography of Katje's body, complete with the implied "money shot" of brandy splashing "around her neck, between her black-tipped breasts, down her flanks" (197). The added comic trope of the seltzer bottle (the "American Reflex") clearly references cinema and turns this scene into a Meyeresque blend of sex and comedy. The "cream pie" also has pornographic connotations, being associated with slang for the act of ejaculating into the vagina.

In *Gravity's Rainbow*, the pornographic content that Pynchon delineates as oppressive is depicted with particularly filmic language. Scenes are consciously constructed as they would be in a pornographic film, similar to *Inherent Vice*, but the intention behind them is different. While both represent certain pornographies as damaging and oppressive, *Gravity's Rainbow* also shows the same pornographies as sexually exciting, explicit, and adventurous. Pynchon depicts the sex in *Gravity's Rainbow* as pornography in order to elicit a sexual reaction from the reader (particularly the heterosexual male reader). *Inherent Vice*'s porn is deliberately flat and conventional and rarely resolves itself satisfactorily. Pynchon's intentional displacement of the raw eroticism of his writing allows for a critique of his prior exuberance regarding exploitative pornographies. Shasta's harrowing seduction of Doc appears pornographic but assumes a more horrific aspect in its emphasis on her exploitation, showing in a stark light the inadequacies and violence of this particular male fantasy, while a younger Pynchon revels in nymphomaniac desire as his female characters are controlled, degraded, and raped. In one scene, a fight between Katje and Slothrop ends in rape, qualified only by the narrator's letting us know that Katje seems to enjoy it: "Katje turns her head and sinks her teeth in his forearm, up near the elbow where the Pentothal needles used to go in. 'Ow, shit—' he lets go the arm he's been twisting, pulls down underwear, takes her by one hip and penetrates her from behind, reaching under to pinch nipples, paw at her clitoris, rake his nails along inside her thighs, Mister Technique here, not that it matters, they're both ready to come—Katje first, screaming into the pillow, Slothrop a second or two later" (222). The image here of the mutual orgasm, a moment of connectivity, could also be considered exploitative, a simulation of female agency that does not present autonomy but instead feeds into a violent category of sexual fantasy. In typical heteronormative fashion, it is Slothrop's orgasm that is the active one here, with Katje's own only there seemingly to justify the rape fantasy. A. W. Eaton in "A Sensible Antiporn Feminism" calls out this kind of pornographic motif for depicting "women deriving sexual pleasure from a range of inegalitarian relations and situations, from being the passive objects of conquest to scenarios of humiliation, degradation, and sexual abuse" and for presenting "these representations of subordination in a manner aimed to sexually arouse" (680).

Indeed, sex in *Gravity's Rainbow* is mostly dedicated to the achievement of the male orgasm. The phallocentric theme of the rocket itself penetrating the earth is even alluded to in the scene described, the violent sexual imagery of Katje's orgasm manifested in her "screaming" reflecting the rocket's own "screaming" as it "comes across the sky" (1), the inevitable and cataclysmic power of the male orgasm referenced in Katje's own realization of the world as "over its peak and down, plunging, burning, towards a terminal orgasm" (223). Katje's agency never amounts to more than realizing certain truths about the domination of male power in the world that Pynchon creates, and her only option is to accept it. As Yves-Marie Léonet observes in "A Tale Reversed: Thomas Pynchon's Rewriting of Grimm's 'Hansel and Gretel,'" "[Katje] plays her part perfectly, but one is never allowed to affirm that she is doing more than carrying out orders" (45). While Léonet claims this is indicative of the novel's "ontological uncertainty" (45), it also reflects Pynchon's own attitudes to pornography. He allows his pornographic writing to cater to the male perspective (be it in the liberating or the oppressive mode), and he thus allows the female players within it only to acquiesce to it. The trajectory from Katje to Shasta is clear: these women are young, pretty, and often silent and resigned to their position as sexual objects. This is precisely what Andrea Dworkin refers to as "sexual colonialization," in which "scenarios of dominance and submission are internalized" (Wilson 25). The clear difference between Katje and Shasta is that in Shasta's case Pynchon wants us to be horrified, not titillated, by this notion. The idea of the pornified woman is now the subject rather than the object of his narrative.

Pynchon performs this subtle shift by allowing Shasta to narrate her own pornography instead of presenting it through the third-person narration:

> "If my girlfriend had run away to be the bought-and-sold whore of some scumbag developer? I'd just be so angry I don't know what I'd do. Well, no, I'm even lying about that, I know what I'd do. If I had the faithless little bitch over my lap like this—" Which was about as far as she got. Doc managed to get in no more than a half dozen sincere smacks before her busy hands had them both coming all over the place. "You fucker!" she cried—not, Doc guessed, at him—"You bastard..." (305)

Shasta is therefore given agency, which she underscores by conjuring up erotic imagery that feels more like a series of accusations leveled at Doc's onanism than an attempt to cater to it. Of course it is not that Doc is the "fucker" in question because of Wolfmann, but simply because he is not a fucker, he is a fantasizer. She teases Doc with his own dark sexual fantasies: "I hope they're not planning to sell me to some horrible Chinese Communist gang of perverts who'll do all kinds of horrible Chinese stuff to me..." (307). A younger Pynchon may have provided us with a comic version of this scene once upon a time, featuring deliberately stereotyped Chinese gang members, Shasta struggling coyly in chains like Fay Wray in King Kong's grip, but instead there is no artifice, no possibility of softening the reality of what happened to her under Wolfmann, and we are left with a bare accusation of this fantasy, Shasta implying that Doc can be turned on by sex slavery, exploitation, and rape (the bread and butter of the 1970s soft- and hard-core scene). Indeed, it seems to work, and much like Slothrop, whose relationship with the rocket is predestined, Doc inevitably succumbs to an act of violent sex (albeit much more explicitly in Anderson's adaptation).

So to conclude, we see Pynchon's growing awareness of the exploitation he is engaging in when he writes women into his pornographic scenes. In Katje's sex scenes, we are invited to ogle the otherworldly beauty of her body, enjoy the erotic possibilities of her acquiescence to control. Slothrop is depicted as the fool, a hapless agent caught up in a pornographic scene and brought to ontological instability by it. Shasta on the other hand allows no such innocence for Doc—we are not invited to find her arousing despite the pornographic overlay the scene has. Instead, like Doc, we are invited to take on the perspective of the controlling power structure, given a stark choice to revel in her trauma or find discomfort in her accusations of what we/Doc find erotic.

While Pynchon is therefore not offering any liberation via *Gravity's Rainbow*'s sex scenes to the female characters—and this in itself is deeply problematic as Freer states—these pornographies offer up spiritual possibilities to male participants. Katje's sex scene with Slothrop grants him escape via anonymity when his identification is stolen midcoitus and enables him to free himself to a degree from his paranoia. The gross but incredibly pornographic section with Pudding and Katje follows a gnostic ritual that provides him some catharsis despite being part of Pointsman's plan to bully and control him. Greta Erdmann becomes the kabbalist image of the Shekhinah, the feminized aspect of God, as she is presented as literal pornographic object fathering children across the Zone via her porn films. Tchitcherine's sex with Geli Tripping allows him to escape a predestined meeting with Enzian, Geli expressing her sexual agency in the form of a prayer: "May this, my own darkness, shelter him" (734). Female sexuality and the pornographic representations of it are given transcendent power, and this is universally expressed in the novel as male transcendence via, or at the cost of, female sexual agency. In fact, representations of female sexuality usually give way to the exposition of wider religious themes—often apocalyptical—at the expense of an authentic portrayal, and as Catharine Stimpson has argued, this "provokes a mixture of contempt for contemporary sexuality and reverence for an atavistic mode" (77). In *Inherent Vice* the pornography is never permitted these connotations. Male characters are not "protected" or given routes out of their oppression but spiral further into controlling fetishism, damaging pornographic fantasy, and exploitative actions.

A Narrowing

Pynchon's approach to porn in his later works does then both suggest a narrowing of the redemptive possibility of the medium and also a more pessimistic take on the movements and ideas that birthed his positive take on it in the first place. I have described how Pynchon saw porn as potentially liberating, an idea that came to him during a period of the avant-garde acceptance of porn as an art form, and how this mentality grew out of sexual liberation. However, in *Inherent Vice*, Pynchon points to the shadowy side of the sexual revolution with one very telling line: "Anybody with any claim to hipness 'loved' everybody, not to mention other useful applications, like hustling people into sex activities they might not, given the choice, much care to engage in" (5). I believe that this single line goes a long way to expressing this narrowing of the redemptive possibilities of sex and porn in his later work and in fact goes so far as to remove it from the narrative of liberation that Pynchon engages with entirely. However, an easy mistake to make here would be to conclude that an older Pynchon is becoming more *conservative* about sex, about the sexual revolution and the positive forces that it spawned. This is not the case; this narrowing is not a condemnation of the free love movement but more of a lament over the realities of what it became. Pynchon's liberating spaces, at least in his earlier novels (the Zone being the prime example of this), are always transitory and usually collapse in on themselves. Pynchon seldom critiques these spaces or the ideologies that inform them, but he does often *lament* their inevitable co-option into control systems. This is true of free love and pornography. In *Inherent Vice* he is wrestling with the tawdry end result of pornography and also voicing a disquiet about his own depictions of it in his past novels.[4]

Cook claims that the material in *Inherent Vice* on Charles Manson stands as a sort of avatar for the end of the hippie dream, "a tokenistic piece of horrorshow: paranoids writing on the wall about the end of the hippie era and implosion into violence," and sees Manson as a "totem of extremity and control" (1145). Cook is correct that Manson's ghostly presence in the novel represents some sort of epochal shift in Pynchon's view of hippies, but I would argue that he is less totemic and more symptomatic of the deep problems I have laid out in this chapter. The Mansonoid fantasies of Doc, the pornified notion of the "submissive hippie chick," are part of Pynchon's own much more critical view of pornography as a literary device. Porn no longer presents us with the political resonance of Thanatz's s/m treatise or the spiritual resonance afforded by Slothrop or Pudding's catharsis through a "divine female," but instead reflects a darker, more embedded, social malady, what Sauncho calls "an *obsessive death wish*" (119) and what Denis refers to as "darker type activities" (136).

Pynchon's porn is still written, I would say, to arouse. He uses pornographic language that reflects the sensibilities of the mainstream porn industry. He does not shy away from the erotic in his old age but instead demands that we share in his unease, his disquiet, and his reformation of his sense of the history of pornography. *Inherent Vice* is an immolation of his previous pornographic ideas, an erasure of his previous desire to synthesize religion, politics, and sex. The novel offers very little in the way of answers as to how porn can be a positive within his literary worlds, offering instead a critical and self-aware look backward into the corpus.

NOTES

1. *The Adventures of Lucky Pierre* crops up more often that you would imagine in postmodern American fiction. Robert Coover's 2002 novel *The Adventures of Lucky Pierre* references the film, and even more tellingly, Pig Bodine (Pynchon's resident smutty boor) broadcasts "LUCKY PIERRE RUNS AMOK" (*V.* 219) from the USS *Scaffold*.

2. Discounting his sex with Penny—we are not privy to this, and this is not depicted pornographically. In fact, it is Penny who points out the pornographic fantasies of Doc that are realized later.

3. While I am tracing a lineage between Katje and Shasta, it does seem apparent that Pynchon is aligning Blicero and Wolfmann here. The use of the wolf as an image of an aggressive, animalistic trait of male power fantasy is employed in both texts. Shasta describes Wolfmann as "fast, brutal, not what you'd call a considerate lover, an animal, actually" (305), and Blicero is described at times as a werewolf: "Blicero had grown on, into another animal . . . a werewolf . . . but with no humanity left in its eyes" (485). This connecting idea of "wolf-hood" is an interesting one, and this congruence of Blicero and Wolfmann does suggest a perennial notion of masculinity running across Pynchon's work, as well as aligning the women that fall under male power.

4. We can see this disquiet forming in *Vineland*. The Kunoichi Sisterhood are presented as a stone-cold military outfit, a sustainable and ethical community. However, Pynchon plays around with its pornographic potential. Customers arrive "with ogling in mind, expecting some chorus line of Asian dewdrops" (107). Instead they are given the opposite—a pannational and deeply serious group. The Kunoichi transcend the smut of being pornified, which they use to gain political capital. As Samuel Thomas in *Pynchon and the Political* writes, "[T]he Kunoichi want to sell 'fantasy' experiences to dubious men with military haircuts and large credit limits" (145). The exploiters become the exploited.

WORKS CITED

Briggs, Joe Bob. "Big Bosoms and Square Jaws: Russ Meyer, King of Sex Films." *Cineaste* 31.1 (2005): 20–26.
Cook, Simon. "Manson Chicks and Microskirted Cuties: Pornification in Thomas Pynchon's *Inherent Vice*." *Textual Practice* 29.6 (2015): 1143–64.
Eaton, A. W. "A Sensible Antiporn Feminism." *Symposium on Education and Equality* 117.4 (2007): 674–715.
Franco, Marie. "Queer Postmodern Practices: Sex and Narrative in *Gravity's Rainbow*." *Twentieth-Century Literature* 63.2 (2017): 141–66.

Freer, Joanna. *Thomas Pynchon and American Counterculture*. New York: Cambridge University Press, 2014.
Herman, Luc, and Steven Weisenburger. *Gravity's Rainbow, Domination, and Freedom*. Athens: University of Georgia Press, 2013.
Hume, Kathryn. "Attenuated Realities: Pynchon's Trajectory from *V.* to *Inherent Vice*." *Orbit: A Journal of American Literature* 2.1 (2013). DOI: 10.7766/orbit.v2.1.50.
Léonet, Yves-Marie. "A Tale Reversed: Thomas Pynchon's Rewriting of Grimm's 'Hansel and Gretel.'" *Merveilles & Contes* 4.2 (1990): 43–47.
Lewis, Gordon H., dir., and David F. Friedman, prod. *The Adventures of Lucky Pierre*. Lucky Pierre Enterprises, 1961.
McClure, John. *Partial Faiths: Postsecular Fiction in the Age of Pynchon and Morrison*. Athens: University of Georgia Press, 2007.
Meyer, Russ, dir. *Faster Pussycat! Kill! Kill!* Eve Productions, 1965.
———, dir. *The Immoral Mr. Teas*. Pad-Ram Enterprises, 1959.
———, dir. *Mondo Topless*. Eve Productions, 1966.
———, dir. *Supervixens*. RM Films International, 1975.
Pynchon, Thomas. *Gravity's Rainbow*. New York: Penguin, 1973.
———. *Inherent Vice*. New York: Vintage, 2010.
———. *V.* New York: Vintage, 1963.
———. *Vineland*. Boston: Little, Brown, 1990.
Sachs, Ben. "Pornography Remains a Major Influence on Paul Thomas Anderson." Chicagoreader.com, 19 Jan. 2015, www.chicagoreader.com/Bleader/archives/2015/01/19/pornography-remains-a-major-influence-on-paul-thomas-anderson. Accessed 19 Nov. 2017.
Schaefer, Eric. "Gauging a Revolution: 16mm Film and the Rise of the Pornographic Feature." *Cinema Journal* 41.3 (2002): 3–26.
Stimpson, Catharine R. "Pre-Apocalyptic Atavism: Thomas Pynchon's Early Fiction." *Thomas Pynchon*. Ed. Harold Bloom. Philadelphia: Chelsea House, 2003. 77–92.
Thomas, Samuel. *Pynchon and the Political*. New York: Routledge. 2007.
Weisenburger, Steven. *A* Gravity's Rainbow *Companion*. Athens: University of Georgia Press, 1988.
Wilson, Elizabeth. Interview with Andrea Dworkin. *Feminist Review* 11 (1982): 23–29.

SECTION 4 **Violence: Gendered and Sexualized**

"This Set of Holes, Pleasantly Framed"
Pynchon the Competent Pornographer and the Female Conduit

SIMON COOK

1973-1990-2006

A woman poses amid masturbating tunnel drillers in the Austrian Alps. In this pre-gangbang warm-up, gazing at "provocative and voracious" siren Ruperta Chirpingdon-Groin (*AtD* 367) has these men standing around "stroking themselves without shame" (656). This desultory facsimile of male sexual camaraderie is reminiscent of much twenty-first-century gonzo porno: the school that turned away from feature-film narrative structures and diegetic segues. A spot-lit single female professional is positioned at the crux of desire for a shadowy convocation of invited amateur male fans: all that is missing is the fluffer tasked with maintaining their hard-ons. Gonzo has reached back a century, and Ruperta has assumed the porn star position, with all the engaged hobbyism of touring English nobility, in a daytime rehearsal for her nocturnal pastime of "being penetrated by a small queue of tunnel hands, often two at a time, who cursed her in unknown tongues" (657). She recounts her submissive encounter to arouse Reef Traverse, and he has rough sex with her without delay.[1]

Perhaps surprisingly for a novelist resolutely aligned with the counterculture, sexual extremity in his work can be mapped onto contemporary pornographies, after they crossed over from underground stag and loop to mainstream features in the early 1970s up to the 2000s. I have argued elsewhere that Pynchon's seventh novel, *Inherent Vice* (2009), uses a 1960s nostalgia trip to normalize, render uncontroversial, the insidious influence of a sexualized mainstream colonized by hard core. *Against the Day*, however, brazenly exhibits motifs like double penetration and misogynist verbal humiliation, which have become staples of a twenty-first-century internet-streamed hard core, whose on-screen transgressions exceed both the porno-chic era concurrent with *Gravity's Rainbow* (1973) and the subsequent antiporn backlash that dissipated around the time *Vineland* was published (1990). Brian McNair uses the term "porno-chic," taking it from a 1973 *New York Times* article (Blumenthal), to denote two periods in which pornography was fashionable. The first was the early 1970s: "For a brief time between the flowering of the sexual revolution and the emergence of the antipornography lobbies later in the 1970s the consumption of pornography was not viewed as the shameful obsession of emotionally stunted perverts, nor the sadistic pastime of patriarchal predators, but the valid entertainment choice for mature, sexually liberated, 'swinging' society" (*Striptease* 62). The second began in the early 1990s, "in a radically altered political context informed by feminist and gay liberation ideals" (64). It saw serious porn studies scholarship led by Linda Williams and became the subject of "pastiche, parody and aesthetic appropriation" (64). These are Pynchon's techniques, as he anachronistically superimposes modern porno tropes on historical storyworlds, scripting power relations far beyond the narrowly sexual.

Pynchon described himself in a 1963 letter as a competent "surrealist, pornographer, word engineer, maybe" (qtd. in Herman and Weisenburger 17). *Gravity's Rainbow*'s sexual deviance polarized debate over the 1974 Pulitzer Prize for fiction: the committee's recommendation was unanimous in favor of Pynchon's novel, but a squeamish Pulitzer board vetoed it on the grounds that it was "obscene" and "unreadable" (Kihss), a combination familiar from the *Ulysses* prosecutions and burnings. However, where obscurity had once mitigated obscenity in the eyes of the judiciary, the two charges now apparently compounded one another in the eyes of the commentariat. In a new world of publishers who had helped graphic sexual description in Lawrence Miller, Updike, and Vidal to brave censorial interference, mainstream representations of "vanilla" sexualities had been disarmed, neutered, mainstreamed. As the stag and loop era ebbed and porno-chic features began to appear in mainstream theaters, *Gravity's Rainbow*'s much-cited "polymorphous perversity" seemed infinite, attaining "onscenity," to use Linda Williams's term. Rekindling cherished period fetishes for complex underwear, cantilevering, and nylon hosiery, the novel superimposes transgressive 1970s BDSM on sepia-tinted stag interludes. Simulacra derived from interbellum film stimulate dark imaginings of domination/submission, long before mainstream cinema countenanced BDSM. Episodes express power through sadomasochistic sex, the adornment and fetishizing of bodies, and myriad variation. Sexual prosthesis binds characters to rockets, plastics, and sex toys, as "technology supersedes humans" (Sears 112), and troilism plugs Tyrone Slothrop, through his conquests, into other male players in the Zone. Bérubé's reading of pornography in *Gravity's Rainbow* as "the enactment and exposure of strategies of power, domination, and control" (266) expresses the critical consensus.[2]

If *Gravity's Rainbow* appeared during the "golden age of porn" (Paasonen and Saarenmaa 23), everything changed in the seventeen-year interval before *Vineland*, an era of what Brian McNair terms "a then still-hegemonic strand of radical feminism" (*Porno* x) that condemned pornography as inherently wrong. The time lapse between publication date and the primary time frame of the novel is relatively short, and this pre-internet 1990 take on still-analogue 1984 contains only passing references to the dominant sexual media of those years: print magazines and VHS. Frequent focalization through sardonic fourteen-year-old Prairie Gates (whose most sexual experience is watching friends "playing centerfold" in lingerie [332]) means there is much less action than usual in Pynchon. Occupied with family ties and domestic consumption in a television era, *Vineland* retreats from *Gravity's Rainbow*'s deviations but nevertheless depicts men making walkie-talkies of Frenesi Gates's and DL Chastain's bodies. The mafioso, the nark, and the hippie do not relish conversation in plain sight, but through these mobile, malleable, corruptible women, criminal and federal elects breach walls that hide them from one another and the countercultural preterite. In applying Eve Kosofsky Sedgwick's concept of homosociality to *Vineland*, Molly Hite observes that "[i]n the masculinist upper echelon where relations between men structure ideologies and institutions, sexuality and power are so interwoven that neither can be isolated as the 'real' ground of motivation" (137). *Vineland* is a crucial intermission between porno-chic eras. Though women are still conduits, sexual extremity is reined in dramatically because the dominant medium is prime-time television scrubbed clean of sexual content at a time when Reaganite neoconservativism united under a flag of convenience with antiporn feminism.

Brian McHale calls *Against the Day* "a virtual library of early twentieth-century entertainment fiction" (20), arguing that throughout his oeuvre Pynchon remediates and appropriates popular genres from the time frame in which his novels are set. These notably include 1940s cinema and stag in *Gravity's Rainbow* and the 1980s tube in *Vineland*, which "imitates the form of a television programme" (Madsen 130). *Against the Day* was published in the digital porn era, as streaming superseded the sixty- to ninety-minute DVD, bringing unprefaced beginnings and accelerating the drive toward extremity. As Jonathan Meades has pointed out, "The principle of pornography is incremental—there must always be more participants, more contortions" (281).[3] The novel leaps a century back in time but incorporates multiple troilisms, the most graphic of which instantly morphs Frenesi's great-aunt Lake Traverse from virgin bride into objectified package and "fuckmouth whore" (268) at the apex of "homosocial desire" between "pardners" Deuce Kindred and Sloat Fresno. *Against the Day* speaks of sex in a vernacular hardened by the new schizoid harshness of twenty-first-century gonzo.

My concern here is to show that Pynchon has not been immune to the pornographic zeitgeist. In *Vineland*, narcotizing dysfunction spread by the tube means sex is nostalgia driven: the Brock-Frenesi-Weed triangle dates from the end of the 1960s, and though the DL-Takeshi mistaken-identity coitus takes place a few years later, DL's seductive disguise is a "high-sixties outfit" (152). Conversely, *Gravity's Rainbow* and *Against the Day*, despite homages to sexual representations from their historical settings, are infused with the porno that was chic when they appeared. Male-to-male communication via the female conduit consistently drives sex in both clashing chronologies. Such networks of control reduce to the agentic state of both female vectors and the male vertices to which they lead. I argue that these architectures within Pynchon's fictions since *Gravity's Rainbow* are blueprinted from patterns of mediated sex prevailing outside them. Hite foregrounds the conduit logic in incorporating feminist theory in *Vineland*'s retrospective analysis of the 1960s (136–37), writing before internet access logarithmically multiplied and rescripted supply. Those alarmed at this explosion posit spiraling harm to both human medium and consumer, as both female consent and penis ownership are rendered moot. Sometimes obscuring its historical setting, gonzo sex in *Against the Day* updates the female vector for the age of streaming.

Organizing Principles

The serpent holding its own tail: it is tempting to interpret the circular orgy aboard the decadent vessel *Anubis* in *Gravity's Rainbow* (467) as an heuristic for the novel's sexual (dis)organizing principle, given critical accounts of its structure as topological rather than linear, cyclical rather than narrative, almanacic rather than novelistic. In addition to voyeurs who watch from the periphery, there are an even dozen enthusiasts (including two pairs of waiters and schoolgirls) who engage in activities with those most adjacent to them in the ring, including but not limited to "vaginal and anal penetration, fellatio, cunnilingus, and anilingus linking various hetero- and homosexual pairs" (Herman and Weisenburger 51). "[A] wide array of paraphilias" also feature, including "voyeurism, frotteurism (rubbing), sadomasochism, pedophilia, and fetishism" (51). This catalogue, as Herman and Weisenburger note, "could have been lifted straight from Richard von Krafft-Ebing's 1886 classic *Psychopathia Sexualis*, mentioned earlier in the novel" (51).[4]

Pynchon concisely narrates this paraphilic ring cycle in a single 250-word sentence sustained by punctuation no stronger than a comma. The infinite variety of this action is often attributed to "polymorphous perversity" (440). Pynchon uses this term once, applying it to the music of Bach, but he derived it from Norman O. Brown's *Life against Death*, which foresaw, according to Weisenburger, "the disappearance of history: this would mean simply, the disappearance of repression, the rebirth of a 'polymorphously perverse' erotic being that stands beyond guilt and even consciousness and that would embody the childish, 'mindless pleasures' Pynchon represents" (249) (the phrase "mindless pleasures" refers to the embryonic title Pynchon used while he was circulating the novel among publishers). This may be construed as a return to innocence: "According to the term Brown takes from Freud, children are polymorphously perverse: nothing is unnatural to them" (Wolfley 12). Countercultural thinking in the 1960s encouraged escape from guilt and consciousness, and hippie ideologies of permissiveness, often speaking in terms of rediscovered childhood, sought to return "that much-abused word 'pornography' to its true antiestablishmentarian standing" (Thompson 207), positing boundless erotic utopias devoid of consequences. The Zone is a place of boundlessness: its topography is unstable; it is characterized by lawlessness and a barter economy that invites the commodification of sex; sexual and social codes there have been rescinded or at least suspended. If it were not for all the deprivation, danger, and paranoia, it would be something of a hippie paradise.

It is not the orgy or bacchanal, however, that writes the Zone's topography. The tighter logic to these sexual chains in the Zone is based on a smaller number: three. Men communicate through female proxies: a distanced troilism. Very frequently when man and woman conjoin there is another male consciousness intruding, albeit not in the room. From the Trystero to Lamont Replevin's secret sect communicating through coal gas with "*secret interconnections*" (*AtD* 607), esoteric media extend tentacles throughout Pynchon's storyworlds. Women, until Yashmeen Halfcourt breaks the pattern, become such a medium, as heteronormative patriarchy eschews intimate confrontation between men, instead routing interconnection through female bodies and consciousnesses. Analogously, most moving and still-image porno propagates a male-female-male dynamic, as male photographers, filmmakers, and distributors frame images of women for the male gaze.

Out in the Zone, Tyrone Slothrop is the primary vertex of *Gravity's Rainbow*'s conduits through sex with the novel's female leads Katje Borgesius, Geli Tripping, Margherita (Greta) Erdmann and Leni Pökler/Solange (Clerc 14). The only fully developed and recurring female character he does not have sex with is romantic heroine and girl next door Jessica Swanlake. These couplings with a Dutch triple agent, an apprentice witch, a horror film actress (and her young daughter Bianca) and a German Marxist open channels through which Slothrop posts and receives messages to and from physically remote male powers, including Blicero/Weissmann, the White Visitation, Soviet officer Vaslav Tchitcherine, film director Gerhardt von Göll/Der Springer, imposter film producer Karel Miklos Thanatz, Peter Sascha (deceased), and rocket scientist Franz Pökler.[5] They put him in indirect touch with German, British, and Russian military and intelligence services, with capitalism, fascism, communism, the rocket, and the beyond. The American lieutenant is the locus of a sexual conference further reaching than Yalta, seeing across the unseeable

Zone through a third eye. These mediated conversations instill sex panic in a number of ways: through the conviction that a woman has sought him out to have sex at the behest of an invisible male pimp or director, which is after all the essence of much pornography and/or prostitution, the sense that every utterance requires decoding and that every sexual favor comes at a price, and the consciousness of undetectable connections between people. However, this switchboard of glamorous women (dominatrix-submissive-switch, besotted girlfriend, submissive performer turned showbiz mother to a corrupted teenage daughter, wife compelled by harsh circumstance to turn whore) offers a panoply of excuses for rampant, unleashed female desire and sudden availability. Perversity and duplicity, submissiveness and pandering, a supernaturally induced trance, and dire economic straits set them off.

The awareness at a remove of an uninvolved other during the sexual act (masturbation, intercourse, or other) is the essence of porn-fueled fantasy and therefore of remote-controlled sex. In Pynchon, this phenomenon is most explicitly articulated in *Vineland* when Brock Vond, the federal manipulator with the weakness for what his colleagues call "radical snatch" (279), addresses co-opted observer-participant Frenesi Gates before she returns to countercultural rallying point Weed Atman: "You're the medium Weed and I use to communicate, that's all, this set of holes, pleasantly framed, this little femme scampering back and forth with scented messages tucked in her little secret places" (214). The female body is reduced to a capsule of transmission in this fluid-exchange fantasy from the 1960s, when consciousness of HIV was yet to dawn. In complementary sexualized plotlines, controlling men engineer the downfall of male threats to their hegemony through female emissaries. Brock (socks on like a porn star [215]) colonizes Frenesi's submissiveness and dispatches her to destroy Weed. The Mob first abducts DL Chastain, then buys her out of prostitution and white slavery (the erotic trope of white slavery returns in *Against the Day* in the form of Dahlia Rideout's early performances) to force her into an assassination attempt on Vond, which degenerates into an abortive farce. *Vineland*'s triangles interpose women between forces federal, criminal, and countercultural. DL Chastain's critique of Brock Vond's homosociality establishes Frenesi as a conduit between not only the prosecutor and the counterculture but also between him and his superiors: "Maybe your mom's only in there to make it look normal and human so the boys can go on discreetly porkin' each other" (265–66). Homosociality is dysfunctional here because Brock and Weed and the forces they represent can only speak the same language through this woman.[6] *Against the Day*'s Traverse-Gates genealogy implies it has long, if not always, been so.

Warring clans may broker peace by tendering marriageable princesses to one another, but the opposed Manichean families of anarchy and plutocracy in *Against the Day* do not make it official. Their submissive daughters neither need nor heed patriarchal instruction; instead, they covertly surrender to the other. Scarsdale Vibe's niece Dittany gamely pursues Kit, youngest son of Web Traverse, down to the stables when he is a guest at Vibe's house, shows him a wide range of whips and crops, and settles for a bare hand spanking as a prelude to sex (162). Conversely, Kit's sister Lake not only marries her father's plute-sponsored assassin Deuce Kindred but seeks self-erasure in a hard-core threesome with him and his equally thuggish "runninmate" (265) Sloat Fresno. Conversations between the pardners are reminiscent of the kind that take place in the smoker, "the place where men talk about sex without having to worry about what women think" (Williams 162). When Deuce focalizes for a moment, we hear an outlaw's arrogance: "Women could protest from now till piss flowed uphill, but the truth was, there wasn't one that didn't secretly love a killer" (262). This villainous voiceover is one of the crasser expressions of an endlessly recurring Pynchon dynamic.[7] Submissive Traverse-Gates women lose agency in the face of male dominance. Lake becomes a "badwoman" who relishes being chained to the bed, harnessed like an animal, derided and double teamed. In their homosocial union the two "badmen" use her so they can have sex in the same room without being homosexual, a dynamic she is not expected to breach: "Only once had she been incautious enough to suggest, 'Why don't you boys just leave me out of it and do each other for a change?' And the shock and outrage in the place, why you could feel it for days" (269). This willing chattel has designed a submissive fantasy with her father's murderers and is further objectified as her body becomes a compass and melts into American topography and cartography: "They took her down to the Four Corners and put her so one of her knees was in Utah, one in Colorado, one elbow in Arizona and the other in New Mexico—with the point of insertion exactly above the mythical crosshairs itself. Then rotated her all four different ways" (269). Lake's liminalities include being a geographical intersection point between states, a conduit for inexpressible love between men, and a valve between forces of anarchy and oppression. Much like Humbert's Lolita, she is transported across borders and loses her bearings. She can fulfill her desires if they have been recorded in the masculine playbook, if they register on the masculine map.

Sadomasochism, Fetishism, Prosthesis

"As for sadomasochism, it is extremely rare in the classic stag film," Di Lauro and Rabkin confidently assert (97). They concur with critics from porn studies and film studies (Williams, Thompson) that the stag era ended in the early 1970s. Men no longer needed to gather covertly in fraternal societies if they could simply run a finger down the newspaper listings and buy a ticket to see *Deep Throat* in a mainstream movie theater. Despite their detailed accounts of recurring sexual "perversions" in stag, their viewing suggests the relative dearth of activities later categorized under the umbrella of BDSM, which conflates bondage, discipline, domination, submission sadism, and masochism. Di Lauro and Rabkin attribute the 1970s paradigm change to porn's compulsion to preserve its own shock impact from the threat of porno-chic: "Why then the mid-70s proliferation of S-M material on all levels—hetero and homo, porno and peep? Sadomasochism's increasing command of the mainstream pornography market undoubtedly represents an attempt (for commercial rather than aesthetic reasons) to restore a sense of transgression and guilt to a genre weakened by toleration. When pornography was infused with the frisson of illegality, sadomasochism had a more specialised appeal" (97–98).

Against this zeitgeist, Herman and Weisenburger, examining scenes of coprophagia and pedophilia, assert *Gravity's Rainbow*'s unrivaled transgressiveness: "In 1973, the text outdid anything then available in the twentieth-century literary canon" (77). However, beyond their shock value, these scenes map power structures in wider military, political, and social macrocosms onto expressions of, or rehearsals for, those relations conducted in private sexual microcosms. Julie Christine Sears makes a strong case that Pynchon equates deviant sexuality with death in *Gravity's Rainbow*, but the deviance with which she is concerned is primarily homosexuality/bisexuality. She sees difficulties in Pynchon's presentation of "the stereotypes of the Cold War period that equated Nazism with homosexuality" (112) and problematizes "deviant sexuality [...] as regimented as lockstep marching in military uniforms" (111). Pynchon's database of perversities is drawn from the source that also inspired contemporary Nazisploitation films including *Love Camp 7* (1969), *Ilsa: She-Wolf of the SS* (1974) and *The Night Porter* (1974).[8] Film in this shameless low-brow genre achieved notoriety in the 1970s by fetishistically associating "fascism with non-normative sexuality" and showing willingness "to consider Nazism's erotic dimensions" (Magilow, Vander Lugt, and Bridges 13). If a sexual act threatens to be absorbed into the pale, having it performed by a Nazi will send it back beyond.

Similarly, pedophilia is another measure of offensiveness in *Gravity's Rainbow*'s theaters of sexual power. A sliding moral scale yields doubt about the age of Margherita's daughter Bianca. When he sees her on the *Anubis*, Slothrop forges a hebephiliac fantasy in which he casts her in the role of an eleven- or twelve-year-old (463), a construction many commentators, including Herman and Weisenburger, follow. Bernard Duyfhuizen, however, suggests she is between sixteen and seventeen, having been conceived during the filming of *Alpdrücken* in 1928. Either way, though her youthful age may be designed to rekindle the extinguished guilt Di Lauro and Rabkin posit, it is not salient here. During her punishment ritual performance with her mother, it is accoutrements and accessories that the fetishist Slothrop hears and sees. The engineering encasing her body speaks to him like working machinery: "[S]uspender straps shift and stretch as Bianca kicks her legs, silk stockings squeak together, erotic and audible" (466). Greta's ruler inscribes the delineated geometries of her body mathematically: "[W]hite centimetre markings and numerals are being left in mirror image against the red stripes with each blow, criss-crossing, building up the skew matrix of pain on Bianca's flesh" (466–67). Slothrop had earlier patterned Greta's flesh with a whip at her behest, but she recasts herself for this show, instantly switching all we have previously known about her sexuality and rendering her unrecognizable: "[W]here is the old masochist and monument Slothrop knew back in Berlin?" (466). Slothrop is mentally assembling a database of stimuli for later use, just as Pirate Prentice does in another act of inscription, in an "interpretative gesture" noted by Jessica Lawson (234). Asked to mimic porn performer/consumer and ejaculate on demand so that he can rub seminal fluid into chemically coated paper to unveil a hidden message, Pirate is supplied with the archaic stimulus of an erotic line drawing. As he retrieves a fantasy, not a memory, the eyes, face, and body of the adulterous wife of a past affair are occluded on his mental screen by more dependable stimuli. All he can think about is what she is wearing: "Scorpia sprawled among fat pillows wearing exactly the corselette of Belgian lace, the dark stockings and shoes he daydreamed about often enough but never—'No, of course he never told her. He never told anyone. Like every young man growing up in England, he was conditioned to get a hardon in the presence of certain fetishes, and then conditioned to feel shame about his new reflexes'" (71–72). It is precisely this nostalgic fantasy of complex underwear and hosiery that entered the contemporary public consciousness in Bob Fosse's *Cabaret* (1972) with its burlesque fetishism and "aura of carefree decadence for which post–Great War, pre-Hitler Germany is now renowned" (Thompson 60). Posters featured star Liza Minnelli in corset, stockings, suspenders, and bowler hat. Pynchon's legophilia, a partialist paraphilia, is historiographic: stockings and stays in *Against the Day* (on the persons of an anthropologist, an actress, and a mathematician) and *Gravity's Rainbow* yield chronologically to bare legs and miniskirts in the late 1960s California of *Vineland* and *Inherent Vice*. Here, real past erotic experience is accessed through a performance of femininity Scorpia never gave, adorned by period accoutrements she never wore, which precedes the woman herself.

The women of *Gravity's Rainbow* are subsumed in cyborg fantasy enactments: their bodies have no natural state in which to exist and are never unaccommodated. The adored part-objects are no longer components of their human body but rather fetishes that adorn it or, as in the coprophagic encounter between Brigadier Earnest Pudding and Katje Borgesius (Domina

Nocturna) that so appalled the Pulitzer board, are expelled from it. The body is remade and regendered by prosthesis when Captain Blicero appears in high drag, "his penis squashed invisible under a flesh-coloured leather jockstrap over which he wears a false cunt and merkin of sable" (95). Blicero procures his accoutrements on a covert and highly specialized illegal market, but Pynchon was writing in an era in which such objects emerged from backstreet darkness into public visibility. The over-the-counter sale and marketing of sex toys got under way after former World War II pilot Beate Uhse opened the world's first sex shop in Germany in 1962, which subsequently grew to become Germany's largest sex industry concern. The Ann Summers chain of sex shops appeared on UK high streets in 1970, initially designed "to create a sex supermarket based on the German Beate Uhse stores" (Kent and Brown 201). However, even after successive 1960s Supreme Court decisions effectively decriminalized the sex shop, strict zoning regulations limited the spread of this female-friendly, sex-positive model to the United States. The taboo objects still came from nefarious backstreet establishments.

In sex-toy-free *Vineland*, Frenesi effectively repurposes hypodermics and suppositories, using them as dildos. Masochism causes her to frame her suffering as sexual during her stint as a political prisoner when she is subdued with antipsychotics Stelazine and Thorazine at Brock Vond's PREP gulag: "I got to like it—I wanted them to come and hold me down, stick needles in me, push things up my ass. Wanted that ritual...." (261). Sex and death are both matters of insertion in her 1960s hippie chick riposte to Brock's semen-medium fantasy (213–14), a cliché of phallocentricism in left-political and feminist vernacular. Equating homicide and sodomy, she tells the prosecutor that men "prefer to do it by forcing things into each other's bodies" (214). Accoutrements also expose a chink in Brock's emotional armor: "[H]e loved Frenesi but did not possess her, and was driven to fetishism in faraway countries as his only outlet" (141). Would-be assassin DL must impersonate Frenesi and requires Aryan prostheses to approach close enough to apply the ninja death touch: lurid makeup, blonde wig and, crucially, tinted contact lenses to reproduce those "fluorescent blue eyes" (141). This eye color is an essential component of mythologized Californian womanhood, which recurs in *Inherent Vice*, and the key element of disguise. Vond may carry a torch for the novel's antiheroine, but she is a clonable commodity.

Between 1973 and 2006, mediated sex evolved, incrementally but almost beyond recognition. The internet united dispersed schools of specialized fetishists in image-sharing communities, pandering to every niche micromarket. However, outside all these pockets of perversity, a mainstream (if such a constantly self-erasing concept can ever be applicable to pornography) took shape in the form of a harsh, male-dominant, misogynistic gonzo, often shot as ultra-low-budget male POV by performers doubling as cameramen/

directors. Gagging, choking, slapping, insults, facials, and obsessions with large-scale gangbangs and heterosexual anal infested a mainstream more edgy, more transgressive than a BDSM environment predicated on informed consent and prenegotiation.[9] This new normative paradigm is encoded in *Against the Day*, its viciousness most memorably rendered in the way Lake Traverse's body becomes a battleground between anarchism and corporatism.

Lake's three brothers each bind themselves to other worlds by gazing on three beautiful women in fetishistic encounters. The youngest, Kit, marries street actress and singer Dahlia, daughter of photographer Merle Rideout with Erlys, yet another traitorous Pynchon woman, who had abandoned her family to run away with if not the circus, then at least a magician. Dally is persuaded to move out of the "white-slave simulation industry" (339) into compromising positions as a sculptor's model mock-sodomizing a "Well Set-Up Young Man" (897), wearing only infantry boots, distributing her own freshly worn "intimate apparel" to the aristocracy, suffering her toes to be adored by them (899), and masturbating while Clive Crouchmas "sat at his safe distance, watching" (900). Her 1910 career encompasses many tropes common to the sex industry a century later, including the use of prostheses (purely soft core: she is not provided with a dildo), diverse foot fetishisms, the (postal) tendering of preworn underthings, and a purely performative sexuality: girl solo. Jeffrey Severs sees Dally as a working-girl heroine defending her virginity in a predatory world and argues that Pynchon, "while putting threats in her path, wants to keep the story relatively pornography-free as long as possible" (223). Dally's activities, which maintain her libidinal economic worth by sparing her penetration, are anachronistically aligned with internet-age mediated sex acts targeting niche fetish markets (prosthesis, feet, and used lingerie) or solo performance as low-resistance gateway to later girl-on-girl, boy-girl, threesome, and so on. He rescues the damsel from prostitution then, by a fine line, but not from self-pornography.

No sooner has middle son Frank become entwined with plucky girl anthropologist Wren Provenance than the pair visit a brothel forcing costume changes and subtle mockery of the damsel-in-distress plot. Once ensconced in Jennie Rogers's House of Mirrors, Wren dons stays and stockings, adopts "one of those looks of insincere dismay you saw in erotic illustrations from time to time," and assumes an anachronistic voice, lamenting, as she bats her eyelashes, that "you have simply ruined me for everyday bourgeois sexuality. Whatever am I to do?" (276, 277). In this world women must confront the commodification of the body: "*Gravity's Rainbow* reads sadomasochism as the model for all state policies. *Against the Day* reads the sex market as the model for markets in general" (Severs 230). Where Dally defends her virginity and resists abduction into white slavery by lover boy Crouchmas and pimping by Ruperta or the Principessa Spongiatosta, Wren revels in the brothel as a burlesque dress-up playground, a type of dress-up that is not unakin to the porno-chic appropriations of Madonna or Gaga discussed by McNair (*Porno*). She (or Ruperta or Yashmeen) would not be out of place among the "young women [who] choose, as sexual subjects with free will, to be sex objects, from time to time and in certain circumstances; to play the game of sociosexual interaction using the language and symbols provided to them in the surrounding culture" (McNair, *Porno* 98). Wren's burlesque is an instance of Pynchonoid fetish nostalgia, a knowing twenty-first-century postfeminist time traveler reveling in the trappings of a bygone era.

Firstborn Reef, entranced by the sleeping partially clad form of his brother Kit's bisexual mathematician ally Yashmeen Halfcourt, is masturbating as she awakes: "'Are you committed to this disgusting activity,' she inquired [...], 'or might the vagina hold interest for you, beyond the merely notional?'" (858). After upgrading him from voyeur/onanist to sexual partner, she later resorts to display and feeds the prevailing fetish by revealing her "much commented-upon legs in black silk hosiery, which she now pretended to inspect and adjust" (882). Assertive adventuress Yashmeen creates a playful threesome between herself, ultramasculine Reef, and *fellatrice* Cyprian Lakewood. Her power arises from her verbal dexterity in guiding the narrations that steer this troilism. These games are the only prenegotiated sex in the novel, and although "[p]roceedings had been limited to the two heterosexual legs of the triangle" (881), one day when she is absent these two male polar opposites engage in surprisingly tender sex. Speaking sex opens channels between them unexplored by Sloat and Deuce, Brock and Weed or Tyrone, and all those other men.

The stylized interactions featuring prenegotiated consensual whipping of Brigadier Pudding by Katje Borgesius and of Margherita Erdmann by Tyrone Slothrop may be conceived of as scenes or play, as delineated by this useful definition: "Stressing its performative qualities, the term 'scene' is frequently used for the engagement in actual BDSM acts; others choose the term 'play', which as well as stressing its separation from the real has the advantage of indicating it is governed by predetermined rules" (Allen 199n). Pudding's and Erdmann's whippings dramatize the explicit permission that has been granted to inflict pain: Pudding's ritual request is an added humiliation, and Margherita ascribes her predilection to her appearances in the films of Gerhardt von Göll. Margherita's ultimate arousal is being encased in Imipolex and rubbing her face against the gigantic Imipolex penis Dröhne (a robotically named plastics connoisseur) wears over his own (488): a fetish that helps her more closely aspire to becoming the "machine which no one will be able to tell from a human being," in the words of Rotwang, the inventor in Fritz Lang's *Metropolis*.

Conversely, in *Against the Day*, excepting the Yashmeen-Reef-Cyprian triangle, domination is posited as coercive and consent as at best implicit, with all the implied risk and potential abuse. At no point do we hear Lake Traverse importune her badmen to humiliate her or Ruperta enjoin her tunnel drillers to penetrate her. This sex occurs outside the boundaries of the game, acquiring an edge associated with the possibility of assault, which has not been diffused in speech or in thought.

Pornoscapes: Film, Tube, Internet

Horst Achtfaden is trapped in loops both personal and literal aboard the toilet ship in *Gravity's Rainbow*: "He has watched voluptuous Gerda and her Fur Boa go through the same number 178 times since they put him in here, and the thrill is gone" (451). That this hand-cranked peep show stag loop retained its cachet approaching the 177th view is a joke about the efficacy of unvaried repetition in sexual stimulation. Pirate's mental movie of Scorpia shares stag narrative conventions: it commences in medias res without elaborately plotted foreplay; it is shot in a single setting; it lasts precisely long enough to transport the male beholder from arousal to orgasm, upon which it both culminates and immediately terminates. This microscopic episode in Pynchon's text can be mapped onto a single-reel blue movie like Gerda's. Lawrence Wolfley is among many to have mapped the diegetic macrocosm onto the cinematic feature: "For the content of the novel *Gravity's Rainbow* is a hypothetical movie" (873).

In a truly stag scene, secretary Maud Chilkes is magnetized by Pavlovian physiologist Ned Pointsman and his control complex. Maud provides an attractive visage and skillful fellatio, her sudden enthusiasm validated by semen swallowing. The visible orgasm trope was certainly not unknown in stag, and according to Di Lauro and Rabkin it "traditionally consists of the man ejaculating on the female's belly (for the viewer's benefit)" (89). Nevertheless, Linda Williams has shown that it becomes much more prominent in porno features after 1970, which require external penile ejaculation or the "money shot" as a demonstration of male pleasure: "to prove that not only penetration, but also satisfaction has taken place" (73). The brisk, unprompted routine between Maud and Pointsman is consummate ("bold Maud, this is incredible, taking the pink Pavlovian cock in as far as it will go, chin to collarbone vertical as a sword-swallower, releasing him each time with some small ladylike choking sound" [168]), and its soundtrack does not include the gagging and slurping noises endemic in later porno. Her conscientious neatness, "swallowing, wastes not a drop" (*GR* 169), is stag, not the sloppy external money shot of later features. The written text, of course, need not suffer the accusation of fakery (essentially that hard core has been replaced by a less valuable currency: soft core) with which the cinematic text contends. Her covert task accomplished, Maud abruptly disappears from view. This abrupt ending, this absence of narrative closure, is another feature that Williams associates with stag (72), a genre that, if not entirely prenarrative, dispensed with much dramatic content and relied on primitive, linear single-scene plots conceived to fill a ten-minute film reel. Maud appears subsequently only as a view from behind and a brief smile, and there is no attempt to ascribe rationale to her seduction of Pointsman. This "utterand" with a single, sexual purpose in the narrative leads a life otherwise unilluminated by Pynchon, but we might imagine a defense of Maud proceeding along the same lines as Di Lauro and Rabkin's of the stag: "If women are 'degraded' as sex objects in these films it is rarely because they are actively humiliated, but rather because they engage in sex without their larger reality as individuals being acknowledged" (26).[10] Gerda and Scorpia's stag interludes as burlesque stripper and adulteress are mediated through the loop and the line drawing, but Maud the secretary steps suddenly into storyworld reality. These vignettes may evince nostalgia for a time before the explicit escaped the underground to encroach on the mainstream, but we must look to Margherita Erdmann to find a woman asserting sexual agency, if such can be said of her submission.

As film orchestrates sexual response in Pynchon, characters in search of sexual stimulus edit and extract unstimulating or distracting context. Film stimulates only two senses of the five and enhancing the stimulus it provides entails zooming in on partial, cropped sections of images or bites of sound, lopping, looping, and repeating them. Paranoid consciousness recognizes these stimuli as preprogrammed and nonunique, and paranoid tumescence is triggered by repetition of previously studied images and narratives: it is a drilled, conditioned, Pavlovian response. In the daring days of the early sound era, pre–Production Code Hollywood made salacious but euphemistic horror and crime genre flicks, and Weimar cinema was never bound by the code.[11] The first feature Gerhardt von Göll (alias Der Springer) makes with the pseudonymous Max Schlepzig and Margherita Erdmann (their pseudonyms are not porn names but are rather adopted to conceal Jewishness) is *Alpdrücken* (the title means "nightmare dread"). Men leave the film engorged by images of Erdmann and father children, Franz Pökler among them (397). Von Göll is the mendacious manipulator of this icon of passivity, in movies screened under the cover of the horror genre but aspiring to soft core: "I never seemed to move. Not even my face. Ach, those long, long gauze close-ups . . . it could have been the same frame, over and over. Even running away—I always had to be chased, by monsters, madmen, criminals—still I was so [. . .] stolid, so . . . monumental. When I wasn't running I was usually strapped or chained to something" (394). This is not hard core.[12] It derives eroticism from repetition, motionlessness, immobility, restraints, and the moment of pause. The movie camera as still camera objectifies. However, the suggestive techniques are those of mainstream cinema: there is neither simulation of sex nor hardcore penetration or ejaculation. Objectification, a commonplace charge of antiporn rhetoric, here paradoxically keeps the film on the right side of the law. The damsel-in-distress plot, familiar from many early twentieth-century detective magazines and designed to circumvent censorship but nevertheless appeal to perverse specialist taste, counts confinement and helplessness, escape and flight among its recurring tropes. An antiporn reading of *Alpdrücken* might claim that Greta's performance in it exacerbates damage caused during a prior traumatic experience, that it galvanizes submissive/masochistic proclivities on which her later liaison with reluctant sadist Slothrop is predicated. However, how are we to discern that it is not the experience Margherita undergoes on "footage [...] cut out for the release prints" when "jackal men come in to ravish and dismember the captive baroness" (*GR* 461) that produces this effect?[13] Furthermore, is it not Stefania Procalowska's disparaging assessment ("Margherita's problem was she enjoyed it too much, chained up in those torture rooms. She couldn't enjoy it any other way" [461]) that robs her of agency, denies her the right to assert submissiveness? *Alpdrücken*, both not-stag and director's cut stag/slasher flic, gives Erdmann both agency and no agency. For Maxwell, she is culpable for embracing the politics of her own oppression in "adopting strategies of survival in a culture that denies female empowerment" (187). This is a convincing defense of Pynchon's exhibition of rape against the charge of complicity: "While *Gravity's Rainbow* is not an overtly feminist tract, it does in general, indict the masculinist culture for promoting the principles of phallic violence against all of its citizens, especially women and children" (Maxwell 187).

There is neither stag nor porno in *Vineland* because other media are subsumed by the hegemonic tube. Both Zoyd Wheeler and Frenesi separately masturbate to ostensibly nonsexual tube programs with which they invest a frisson. Frenesi has understandable trouble with the tubal/real distinction since, just as she is settling down to *CHiPs*, cute real-life law enforcement officers arrive.[14] Frenesi's uniform fetishism accords with the paranoid theory of the television as the political instrument of the cryptofascist right. She fantasizes about a U.S. marshal because "they" have aired *CHiPs* and countless other cop shows to induce her so to do. Near-universal disapproval kept 1980s mediated sex predominantly obscene/invisible, so Zoyd and Frenesi repurpose the tubal blandness for their own DIY porno.

Ruperta and Lake live within the narrative confines of fin-de-siècle genres but have sex in a twenty-first-century vernacular. McHale treats *Against the Day* as revisionist reading of the Old West that approaches authenticity by including a gamut of tropes banned by Hollywood, including sexuality, and sees the flagrant homosexuality of Cyprian Latewood as the intentional queering of the British spy novel (23). This overlay of a later sexual landscape, or set of sexual conventions, onto metafictions reinventing historiographic time periods has far-reaching consequences. Pynchon sexualizes or, more specifically, pornifies three of the four plot clusters John Clute distinguishes—the "Western Revenge," "the Geek Eccentric Scientist," and "The Flaneur Spy Adventuress"—respecting the chastity of only one (the adolescent Chums of Chance) (287–88).

A wave of twenty-first-century antiporn commentators (Dines, Paul, and Walter among them) have vilified the growth of the San Fernando porn industry powered successively by VHS, DVD, and streaming technologies, accusing it of hijacking and corporatizing sexualities. Individual preferences are preprogrammed into a male-dominant mode that unquestioningly incorporates industry-standard rough sex. David Foster Wallace in "Big Red Son" and Martin Amis in "A Rough Trade" were among the investigative journalists and essayists to catalogue these tendencies around the turn of the millennium, and their voices are appalled. Colonization of the female body by aggressive henchmen acting in a ruthlessly stylized manner both coded by machismo and fostered by mechanisms of corporate control is apparent in work by many directors, among them Gregory Dark and Rob Black (Wallace 27n) and John Stagliano (Amis par. 1). Deuce and Sloat's double teaming of Lake is a scene from the dirtiest of their movies.

A Competent Pornographer

In *Between Men*, Sedgwick sets out "to hypothesize the potential unbrokenness of a continuum between homosocial and homosexual—a continuum whose visibility, for men, in our society, is radically disrupted" (1–2), an idea that Hite draws on in her interpretation of *Vineland*. Tyrone Slothrop exchanges messages with distant men through female conduits, a practice articulated by Brock Vond. But it is only in *Against the Day*'s passage from West to East that this continuum fully emerges into the light. Unreconstructed masculinity in Pynchon's genre-poached, dime-novel Wild West (McHale 17) follows gonzo hard-core rules, so Sloat and Deuce have to be content with Lake as a pipeline between them. Back East, with assertive Yashmeen at its female apex, the homosocial liaison between Reef, another cowpoke (who is disinclined to consider the passive role), and Cyprian can find genital expression, as "Pynchon takes the 'shocker' out of the closet in his version of the spy novel" (McHale 24).

Looking backward from the vantage point of 1973, Pynchon could exceed the bounds stag set itself, because, as Di Lauro and Rabkin suggest, "in literary pornography [...] it is possible for the imagination to savour the idea of transgression without having to assimilate the actual images of its realization"; this is why, they point out, pedophilia and sadomasochism are more common in literary pornography than in stag films (96). However, McNair, among others, recognizes that "pornography has to be *outside* and *beyond* the mainstream [...] to perform its function and retain its value as a commodity" (*Striptease*, emphasis in the original). Excising informed consent from the diegesis is one way to stay outside and beyond. Katje and Greta enact BDSM rituals with semblances of prenegotiation, though these rituals always map wider power relations, but Lake and Ruperta's humiliations are not BDSM, just gonzo.

The three novels treated here, respectively, pushed the limits of transgression in a new era of rolled-back literary censorship, retreated from it during the antiporn backlash, and threw around liberal doses of extreme sex after gonzo colonized the mainstream. This countercultural, historiographic novelist has written against a pornoscape first cleared by regulatory retreat and then driven by successive format innovations. Control has always been his subject, and he has used contemporaneous stag, chic, and BDSM tropes to enact hierarchies extending down from Them through women to men. He has traced conditioning back to Them through science and technology, lawmaking and enforcement, and cinema and the tube, but the gonzo, fetish, and *amateur* porn in *Against the Day* comes from the internet, with its pretension of being not just Them but also Us. Either Pynchon reads internet gonzo to distill in *Against the Day* a model of sexual relations between people or he sources the model from a twenty-first-century mainstream in turn sexualized by that porno. The disturbing point is that this distinction is at best fine. There is no normative dimension. It is also no coincidence that an overused metaphor for unbridled online license is the Wild West.

NOTES

1. A woman's erotic account of coupling with another man to stimulate her lover is a recurring cuckolding fetish in Pynchon. See, for example, the story Shasta Fay Hepworth, one among legion microskirted women in *Inherent Vice* I have catalogued elsewhere, tells Larry "Doc" Sportello (304).

2. See Herman and Weisenburger, who see *Gravity's Rainbow*'s pornography as a "withering satire of control"; see also Sears.

3. For Meades, pornography and genealogy are the two chief generators of internet traffic. Pynchon traces the Traverse family line, along with genetic female submissiveness, back four generations from *Vineland* to *Against the Day*. David Cowart describes Pynchon's first "feminist genealogy" in *Vineland* as "a generational unfolding that proceeds matriarchically from Eula to Sasha to Frenesi to Prairie" (187). Eula Becker married Jess Traverse, son of Reef and Stray, and so Lake is Frenesi's great-aunt.

4. J. G. Ballard appropriates this sexology pioneer's surname as a metonym for sexual panoply in *The Atrocity Exhibition* (1970).

5. Slothrop also eventually meets Von Göll, Pökler, Thanatz, and Tchitcherine in person.

6. A counterexample of male-to-male miscommunication is Weed's cluelessness as to the why or wherefore of repeated summonses to Dr. Larry Elasmo's dental clinic (228). Ralph Wayvone pursues DL to send a lethal message to Brock (130–32).

7. In Pynchon, not "every woman loves a fascist," as in Sylvia Plath's "Daddy," but those who do are legion, even unto *Bleeding Edge*'s Jewish protagonist Maxine Tarnow and her "instant docility" (258) in the face of Nicholas Windust's obtuse sexual advance.

8. See Sontag on the allure of Nazi chic.

9. See Allen for an extended discussion of "informed consent" and the changing representations of BDSM in mainstream cinema: "Whereas explicit BDSM prior to the 1990s was depicted almost universally as deviant and dangerous through being linked to oppressive regimes and the underbelly of society, alternative mainstream formulations became available, with these taking account of its normalcy and the role of willed consent" (196).

10. John Clute coined the term "utterand" to describe the archaic multitude from which Ruperta emerges in *Against the Day*: "They are utterands: people-shaped utterances who illuminate the stories of the old world that their Author has placed before us in funeral array; they are codes to spell his book with" (289). This is equally applicable to *Gravity's Rainbow*.

11. The Hays Code in popular parlance, enforced after 1934.

12. I would quarrel with Bérubé's application of the term "hard core" (245) to *Alpdrücken*, a horror film shown in theaters with no fictional sex, his casual assignment of the position of "snuff" film director to Pynchon (264) and his speculation regarding the author's sexual proclivities (264n). Hard core entails visible erections and penetration, or in Williams's terms "genital display" and "genital action." Evidence of "snuff" as a commercial film genre, other than in urban myth, is unforthcoming, and Pynchon's tastes are neither apparent nor germane.

13. Furthermore, though the ravishing, or imputed gang rape, is apparently hard core and understood as the moment of Bianca's conception, the dismembering evidently cannot be seen as hard core.

14. This series about the California Highway Patrol, which originally aired from 1977 to 1983, features motorcycle cops in tight breeches and big boots.

WORKS CITED

Allen, Steven. *Cinema, Pain and Pleasure: Consent and the Controlled Body*. Basingstoke: Palgrave Macmillan, 2013.

Amis, Martin. "A Rough Trade." *Guardian*, 17 Mar. 2001, www.guardian.co.uk/books/2001/mar/17/society.martinamis1. Accessed 22 Nov. 2017.

Ballard, James Graham. *The Atrocity Exhibition*. London: Cape, 1970.

Bérubé, Michael. *Marginal Forces/Cultural Centers: Tolson, Pynchon, and the Politics of the Canon*. Ithaca: Cornell University Press, 1992.

Blumenthal, Ralph. "Pornochic; 'Hard-Core' Grows Fashionable—and Very Profitable." *New York Times*, 21 Jan. 1973: 28.

Clerc, Charles. *Approaches to* Gravity's Rainbow. Columbus: Ohio State University Press, 1983.

Clute, John. "Aubade, Poor Dad." *Canary Fever: Reviews*. Harold Wood: Beccon, 2009. 284–89.

Cook, Simon. "Manson Chicks and Microskirted Cuties: Pornification in Thomas Pynchon's *Inherent Vice*." *Textual Practice* 29.6 (2015): 1143–64.

Cowart, David. "Continuity and Growth." *Kenyon Review* 12.4 (1990): 176, 177–90.

Di Lauro, Al, and Gerald Rabkin. *Dirty Movies: An Illustrated History of the Stag Film, 1915–1970*. New York: Chelsea House, 1976.

Dines, Gail. *Pornland: How Porn Has Hijacked Our Sexuality*. Boston: Beacon Press, 2010.

Duyfhuizen, Bernard. "'A Suspension Forever at the Hinge of Doubt': The Reader-Trap of Bianca in *Gravity's Rainbow*." *Postmodern Culture* 2.1 (1991). DOI: 10.1353/pmc.1991.0029.

Herman, Luc, and Steven Weisenburger. *Gravity's Rainbow, Domination, and Freedom*. Athens: University of Georgia Press, 2013.

Hite, Molly. "Feminist Theory and the Politics of *Vineland*." *The* Vineland *Papers: Critical Takes on Pynchon's Novel*. Ed. Geoffrey Green, Donald J. Greiner, and Larry McCaffery. Normal: Dalkey Archive Press, 1994. 135–53.

Kent, Tony, and Reva Berman Brown. "Erotic Retailing in the UK (1963–2003): The View from the Marketing Mix." *Journal of Management History* 12.2 (2006): 199–211.

Kihss, Peter. "Pulitzer Jurors Dismayed on Pynchon." *New York Times*, 8 May 1974: 38.

Lawson, Jessica. "'The Real and Only Fucking Is Done on Paper': Penetrative Readings and Pynchon's Sexual Text." *Against the Grain: Reading Pynchon's Counternarratives*. Ed. Sascha Pöhlmann. Amsterdam: Rodopi, 2010.

Maddison, Stephen. "'Choke on it, Bitch!' Porn Studies, Extreme Gonzo and the Mainstreaming of Hardcore." *Mainstreaming Sex: The Sexualization of Western Culture*. Ed. Feona Attwood. London: I. B. Taurus, 2009. 37–53.

Madsen, Deborah L. *The Postmodernist Allegories of Thomas Pynchon*. Leicester: Leicester University Press, 1991.

Magilow, Daniel H., Elizabeth Bridges, and Kristin T. Vander Lugt. *Nazisploitation! The Nazi Image in Low-Brow Cinema and Culture*. London: Continuum, 2012.

Maxwell, Marilyn. *Male Rage, Female Fury: Gender and Violence in Contemporary American Fiction*. Lanham: University Press of America, 2000.

McHale, Brian. "Genre as History: Pynchon's Genre-Poaching." *Pynchon's* Against the Day: *A Corrupted Pilgrim's Guide*. Ed. Jeffrey Severs and Christopher Leise. Newark: University of Delaware Press, 2011. 15–28.

McNair, Brian. *Striptease Culture: Sex, Media, and the Democratization of Desire*. London: Routledge, 2002.

———. *Porno? Chic! How Pornography Changed the World and Made It a Better Place*. New York: Routledge, 2013.

Meades, Jonathan. *Museum without Walls*. London: Random House, 2012.

Paasonen, Susanna, and Laura Saarenmaa. "The Golden Age of Porn: Nostalgia and History in Cinema." *Pornification: Sex and Sexuality in Media Culture*. Ed. Susanna Paasonen, Kaarina Nikunen, and Laura Saarenmaa. New York: Berg, 2007. 23–32.

Paul, Pamela. *Pornified: How Pornography Is Damaging Our Lives, Our Relationships, and Our Families*. New York: Times Books, 2005.

Pynchon, Thomas. *Against the Day*. London: Jonathan Cape, 2006.

———. *Bleeding Edge*. Random House, 2013.

———. *Gravity's Rainbow*. London: Picador, 1975.

———. *Inherent Vice*. London: Jonathan Cape, 2009.

———. *Mason & Dixon*. London: Jonathan Cape, 1997.
———. *Vineland*. London: Seeker & Warburg, 1990.
Sears, Julie Christine. "Black and White Rainbows and Blurry Lines: Sexual Deviance/Diversity in *Gravity's Rainbow* and *Mason & Dixon*." *Thomas Pynchon: Reading from the Margins*. Ed. Niran Abbas. Madison: Fairleigh Dickinson University Press, 2003. 108–21.
Sedgwick, Eve Kosofsky. *Between Men: English Literature and Male Homosocial Desire*. New York: Columbia University Press, 1985.
Severs, Jeffrey. "'The abstractions she was instructed to embody': Women, Capitalism, and Artistic Representation in *Against the Day*." *Pynchon's* Against the Day: *A Corrupted Pilgrim's Guide*. Ed. Jeffrey Severs and Christopher Leise. Newark: University of Delaware Press, 2011.
Sontag, Susan. "Fascinating Fascism." *New York Review of Books*, 6 Feb. 1975: 23–30.
Thompson, Dave. *Black and White and Blue: Adult Cinema from the Victorian Age to the VCR*. Toronto: Ecw Press, 2007.
Wallace, David Foster. "Big Red Son." *Consider the Lobster and Other Essays*. New York: Little, Brown, 2005.
Walter, Natasha. *Living Dolls: The Return of Sexism*. London: Virago, 2010.
Williams, Linda. *Hard Core: Power, Pleasure, and the "Frenzy of the Visible."* Berkeley: University of California Press, 1999.
Wolfley, Lawrence C. "Repression's Rainbow: The Presence of Norman O. Brown in Pynchon's Big Novel." *Publications of the Modern Language Association of America* 92 (1977): 873–89.

Representations of Sexualized Children and Child Abuse in Thomas Pynchon's Fiction

SIMON DE BOURCIER

Thomas Pynchon frames the sexual abuse of children in *Gravity's Rainbow*, *Against the Day*, and *Bleeding Edge* in terms of the desirability, exploitation, and commodification of innocence. In *Gravity's Rainbow* Shirley Temple, who achieved fame as a child star in the 1930s and thus belongs to the cultural milieu of the novel's setting, is invoked as the personification of innocence as a desirable commodity. In *Gravity's Rainbow*, *Mason & Dixon*, and *Against the Day* children are depicted as precociously sexual and seductive. To critically frame such depictions it is necessary to look at the social and cultural context of the novels' production. In this essay I draw on Judith Herman's account of three distinct "discoveries" of child sexual abuse in the nineteenth and twentieth centuries and from there move to the cultural representation of such abuse in postwar U.S. culture, paying particular attention to Vladimir Nabokov's 1955 novel *Lolita*. Seeing Pynchon's writing against the background of the contested representation of adult-child sexual activity in European and North American culture—repeated attempts to expose the reality of survivors' experiences of abuse versus efforts to suppress or normalize those experiences—enables us to understand why *Gravity Rainbow*'s representations of sexually abused children struggle to break out of a limited vocabulary consisting of, on the one hand, the spectacle of desirable innocence personified by Shirley Temple, and on the other, the projection of adult male desire in the figure of the seductive daughter, exemplified by Nabokov's Lolita.

Censorship was an important factor in the construction of Temple as an image of eroticized innocence, and I further argue here that episodes of child abuse and incest in Pynchon's fiction often depict sexual desire displaced as if in response to censorship.

Finally, I show that in his later fiction Pynchon adopts a new strategy for the representation of child sexual abuse that moves beyond these two images of girlhood defined by male desire. I argue that the story of the time-traveling Trespassers who menace the Chums of Chance in *Against the Day* is a coded representation of the sexual abuse of children by adults, a reading strengthened by understanding that the time-travel plot in *Bleeding Edge* is a return to the same story from a different perspective. This new strategy focuses more on the experience of the abused child than on the desires of the abuser, but in presenting the experience of abused boys rather than girls it still fails to break out of the male point of view.

Bianca and Shirley Temple

Childlike innocence is highly prized in *Gravity's Rainbow*, and often linked to sexual desire. Jessica Swanlake "looks only 9 or 10" to Roger Mexico as they make love, her face as she orgasms like that of a child about to cry (122). She, in turn, loves "the back of his bumpy head like a boy of ten's" (123). They both incite people's protectiveness because they "look so innocent" (121). Tantivy Mucker-Maffick's French girlfriend Ghislaine has a "six-year-old face" when she smiles (194); when Geli Tripping smiles at Slothrop "four-year-old happy and not holding a thing back" he decides he can trust her (294).

Zofia Kolbuszewska's analysis of the way children are used in *Gravity's Rainbow* turns out to be, primarily, a study of the uses of innocence. She cites Philippe Ariès's argument that "the child's helplessness and fragility, construed as purity, have become an essential part of the modern notion of innocence" (112). For Kolbuszewska, it is innocence consisting of "weakness and purity" that is so erotically arousing for Ned Pointsman (112). The key passage she cites is this: "How Pointsman lusts after them, pretty children. Those drab undershorts of his are full to bursting with need humorlessly, worldly to use their innocence, to write on them new words of himself, his own brown Realpolitik dreams, some psychic prostate ever in aching love promised ah hinted but till now ... how seductively they lie ranked in their iron bedsteads, their virginal sheets, the darlings so artlessly erotic...." (50).

As Kolbuszewska acknowledges, this passage refers to men Pointsman wishes to use as experimental subjects, who are only metaphorically children (119). One might add that his desire to make use of them is only metaphorically sexual. However, in a novel premised on the literalization of the metaphorical connection between rocket and penis, it is not surprising that Pynchon's narrative modulates seamlessly into a description of Pointsman's literal pedophilia: he attempts to pick up children at a bus station, occasionally succeeding in taking one back to his "spermy bed" (51). The narrative emphasizes the smallness of the children's bodies, mentioning their "little heels" (50). Pointsman's literal pedophilia is the source of the metaphor that the narrator employs to describe his desire to exploit Spectro's patients. Moreover, the passage quoted is partly a representation of Pointsman's own perceptions of the men: "pretty children" and "darlings" are his terms, rendered in free indirect discourse. His sexual desires for children provide the language in which he thinks about the men he wishes to experiment on; conversely, his scientific ambitions provide a channel for his pedophilic desires.

The most frankly sexualized child in *Gravity's Rainbow* is Margherita's daughter, Bianca.[1] On board the riverboat *Anubis*, the protagonist Slothrop first sees Bianca when Margherita, playing the role of "stage mother" (465), prompts her to perform a musical number for the boat's passengers. Slothrop is expecting—or hoping for—"something sophisticated, bigcity, and wicked" (465), but what Bianca sings is "On the Good Ship Lollipop," performed "in perfect mimickry of young Shirley Temple" (466). This is not *Gravity's Rainbow*'s first reference to Temple. Early in the novel Slothrop receives a "Shirley Temple smile" (24) from a child rescued from a rocket strike: a little girl's open-hearted beam reminds childless Slothrop of Temple's cinematic caricature of childhood. Subsequent references grow progressively less innocent: Slothrop has a drink called a Shirley Temple at Raoul de la Perlimpinpin's party (246), and garlands of "aluminum shavings as curly-bouncy 'n' bright as Shirley Temple's head" are draped onto him as prelude to the "fabulous orgy" that he (presumably) daydreams in the Mittelwerke (304).

As Bianca sings, it appears to Slothrop that "her delicate bare arms have begun to grow fatter, her frock shorter," but despite the "billowings of asexual child-fat" he perceives that her eyes "remain as they were, mocking, dark, her own...." (466). This physical metamorphosis lends the episode the quality of nightmare or hallucination. Slothrop feels himself drawn into a scenario in which he feels sexual desire for not just a very young child but the mawkish caricature of childhood presented in Temple's films. More disturbing for the reader, however, is the fact that the reason the transformed Bianca still excites his desire is that, in Slothrop's view, Bianca's "own" gaze is knowing and consciously sexual, even though she is a child.

The Shirley Temple routine does turn out to be part of a "wicked" performance in keeping with the orgiastic atmosphere aboard the *Anubis*: Margherita tells Bianca to follow up "On the Good Ship Lollipop" with "Animal Crackers in My Soup"; Bianca refuses, and the obviously staged row that ensues—"It's an act" (466)—culminates in Margherita physically chastising her daughter with a steel ruler, provoking renewed sexual activity among the adult onlookers. The point of view remains Slothrop's throughout: there is no space for Bianca's consciousness in the description of her "[b]eautiful little-girl buttocks," the "tender crevice," the "erotic and audible" squeak of her stockings rubbing together (466). Pynchon's parody of the erotic invites more complicity than critique.

According to Ara Osterweil,

> In the seventy years since Shirley Temple was America's sweetheart, the fundamentally pedophilic appeal of her star persona has become

increasingly apparent. [...] Temple's body was [...] constructed as an intensely erotic spectacle [...]. In an era of motion picture history that explicitly forbade the on-screen representation of adult sexuality, the adorable toddler supplanted Mae West as the largest box office draw in the nation. Whereas West's excessive, undisciplined body had been the bane of censors and was one of the motivating factors of the [Motion Picture] Production Code, the erotic appeal of the body of the child star was inextricable from its supposed innocence. (1)

In Osterweil's reading, Temple's childhood innocence is exploited for erotic and commercial purposes by the film industry: "It is clear that Temple's innocence—and those signature shots of her underpants—were crucial to her erotic appeal" (2). In this Osterweil follows Graham Greene, who was sued by Temple's parents and 20th Century Fox for his "ribald reviews [...] insinuating that the studio had procured Temple for 'immoral purposes'" (5). Moreover, although the presentation of her image in films served the function of circumventing censorship, appearing as a substitute for the highly eroticized images of adult actresses in pre-Code cinema, the substitution ends up pandering to and gratifying far more troubling desires: "In her own infantile way, Temple was no less irresistible to men than West had been. This displacement of adult sexuality onto the body of a child involved an industrywide fetishization in which Temple's infantile sexuality was both deliberately manufactured and scrupulously preserved" (2).

The metamorphosis of Bianca into Shirley Temple is part of *Gravity's Rainbow*'s wider treatment of innocence as erotic commodity. The dreamlike substitution is ambiguous: on the one hand, it can be read as a scathing critique of the culture of which Temple's films are a product; on the other, it can be seen as legitimizing Slothrop's desire for Bianca, whose normal appearance and persona are contrasted with her grotesque appearance as a simulacrum of Temple.

Pynchon's "Sexy Little Girls" and the "Seductive Daughter" in Postwar U.S. Culture

In his 1976 account of reading *Gravity's Rainbow*, David Leverenz confesses to having "idled over the sexy little girls" (229). Few twenty-first-century critics would countenance the phrase "sexy little girls," let alone hint at deriving personal erotic pleasure from reading about them. What has changed? In the 1970s, new discourses, communities, and identities were forged by the survivors of childhood sexual abuse. Roger Luckhurst draws attention to "the extraordinary achievement of second-wave feminism in forcing the acknowledgement of incest and familial sexual abuse, in the face of professional and general cultural denial" (74). For an insight into both the feminist rewriting of the discourse of sexual abuse and the culture of 1970s America from which it emerged—and which, I suggest, is the context in which we must understand both Leverenz's remark and *Gravity's Rainbow* itself—I turn to Judith Herman's 1981 study *Father-Daughter Incest*, written with Lisa Hirschman. Herman approaches the subject from an avowedly feminist perspective, arguing that the "growing awareness" of sexual abuse within families "is largely a result of the women's liberation movement" (vii).

Herman documents two previous discoveries of widespread sexual abuse within families. In 1896 Sigmund Freud "announced that he had solved the mystery of the female neurosis. At the origin of every case of hysteria, Freud asserted, was a childhood sexual trauma" (9). All his women patients disclosed sexual abuse in childhood, usually committed by their fathers, and this, Freud believed, was the cause of their hysteria. This came to be known as the "seduction theory." However, Freud "remained so distressed by his seduction theory that within a year he repudiated it entirely" (10). Instead, he formulated the alternative theory of the ubiquity of childhood sexual *fantasy* about parents, which became the cornerstone of psychoanalysis as we know it.

After the Second World War, Herman explains, incest was "discovered" again by sociologists like Alfred Kinsey (11–12), but the discovery had little impact on public awareness. Kinsey "did as much as he could to minimise its importance" (16). However, the sexual abuse of girls within families was "rediscovered for a third time in the 1970s by the women's liberation movement," and "this time, the information could not be suppressed once it was uncovered, for it began to reach the awareness of those who stood in the greatest need of knowledge, namely, the victims themselves" (18).

Herman's study focuses on the abuse of girls by fathers or other men in a paternal role, but the key characteristics she emphasizes apply to all forms of child sexual abuse. First, "incest is a crime, one for which the adult is fully responsible" (4): "the final choice in the matter of sexual relations between adults and children rests with the adult" (27). Second, "it is always, inevitably, destructive to the child" (4). Long-term effects include guilt, shame, depression, and low self-esteem (30–31). Such "residual psychological damage can be observed lasting into adult life" (31).

Herman cites a range of texts that, despite these facts, promote the idea of the seductive daughter, that is, which place the responsibility for father-daughter incest on the daughter rather than the father, ranging from "professional clinical literature" to men's magazines (38–39). It is in this context that she introduces *Lolita*, the 1955 novel about a sexual relationship between a man and his pubescent stepdaughter, into her discussion: "Vladimir Nabokov's immensely successful novel has been understood on many levels, but on perhaps the simplest level, *Lolita* is a brilliant apologia for an incestuous father. Humbert Humbert is charming, intelligent, and maddeningly witty in defence of his passion. Since he has expiated his sin by transforming it into art, the reader is permitted to enjoy it, indeed, to revel in it, as he does. And this in no small measure may account for the novel's enormous popular appeal" (37). Herman concedes that this is the "simplest level" on which *Lolita* can be read, and it will become clear that her reading does the novel a disservice. Nevertheless, the passage she cites undeniably portrays a consciousness that perceives the victim of abuse as a knowing seductress: "Frigid gentlewomen of the jury! I had thought that months, perhaps years, would elapse before I dared to reveal myself to Dolores Haze; but by six she was wide awake, and by six fifteen we were technically lovers. I am going to tell you something very strange: it was she who seduced me" (Nabokov 149–50; qtd. in Herman 36). Herman highlights the similarities between this passage and a pornographic story published in *Chic* magazine in 1978 in which the first-person narrator describes a sexual encounter with, and initiated by, his thirteen-year-old daughter (38).

Pynchon's depiction of Bianca fits the pattern of these narratives of the seductive daughter. When Slothrop first sees Bianca, whose mother is already his lover, he desires her sexually, despite her age:

> He gets a glimpse of Margherita and her daughter, but there is a density of orgy-goers around them that keeps him at a distance. He knows he's vulnerable, more than he should be, to pretty little girls, so he reckons it's just as well, because that Bianca's a knockout, all right: 11 or 12, dark and lovely, wearing a red chiffon gown, silk stockings and high-heeled slippers, her hair swept up elaborate and flawless and interwoven with a string of pearls to show pendant earrings of crystal twinkling from her tiny lobes ... help, help. Why do these things have to keep coming down on him? He can see the obit now in *Time* magazine—Died, Rocketman, pushing 30, in the Zone, of lust. (463)

Bianca is a pubescent girl, but in this passage, focalized through Slothrop, he in danger from her, not the other way around. The minimal acknowledgment that his desire for her is wrong—"more than he should be"—is subsumed within a narrative in which he, not she, is "vulnerable" and must cry for "help." Just as Humbert insists that it is Lolita who seduces him, Pynchon presents us with an abuser's abnegation of responsibility and attempt to blame the victim.

Both Leverenz's remark about "sexy little girls" and the writing that occasioned it, such as Pynchon's graphic account of the sexual encounter between Slothrop and Bianca, can be understood, then, as representative of the wider, and deeply problematic, cultural trend in late twentieth-century America that Herman documents.

Pynchon and *Lolita*

As Herman's critique makes clear, the publication and reception of Nabokov's *Lolita* are important events in the history of the cultural understanding of child abuse in postwar America. In this section I describe in more detail two ways in which Pynchon's writing about sexualized children evokes *Lolita*, using examples from *V.*, *Gravity's Rainbow*, *Mason & Dixon*, and *Against the Day*. First, I show that Pynchon narrates sexual encounters between men and young girls primarily from the male point of view, conjuring up images of seductive and desirable children. Second, I discuss ways in which these episodes take up motifs pertaining to hell, damnation, and the demonic that run through Nabokov's novel.

John Dugdale reads *V.*'s account of the relationship between the "nympholeptic novelist" Porcepic and Mélanie L'Heuremaudit as, primarily, an allusive nod to Nabokov, "Pynchon's former teacher at Cornell" (96). Dugdale's argument and—if he is correct—Pynchon's allusion both depend on an implicit conflation of Nabokov with Humbert. Dugdale's argument that the Tristero in *The Crying of Lot 49* represents a "literary tradition of unpublishable desires [...] from incest in Ford [...] to nympholepsy in Nabokov" (181) similarly assumes that *Lolita* is a book about Humbert's "desires" rather than his stepdaughter's experience of abuse.

Humbert admits that Lolita—the imaginary object of those desires—is his "own creation," having "no will, no consciousness—indeed, no life of her own" (Nabokov 68). As Jessica Lawson points out, the victims of Pointsman's predatory sexual behavior in *Gravity's Rainbow* are similarly drained of subjectivity, "blank entities": "The only access that either the reader or Pointsman have to the sexual object is mediated, always passing first through the filtering circuit of how it affects Pointsman" (242–43). Pynchon is perhaps, like Nabokov, expertly depicting a pedophile's failure to grant personhood to his victim. However, as Joanna Freer observes, many of the women in *Gravity's Rainbow* are also presented as "voiceless objects of male desire" (140). There might seem to be a contradiction between this characterization of the victims of abuse as deprived of subjectivity and, on the other hand, the figure of the seductive daughter, who is represented as possessing agency and responsibility. The point, however, is that her agency and responsibility are phantasmal, fictions in the service of male desire, and the projection of these fictions onto a child is the mechanism by which she is stripped of authentic subjectivity and agency.

Some readers assume that Nabokov—like Humbert—denies Dolores Haze any "life of her own." Ellen Pifer contends that both those early readers of the novel who argued that "the novel's design encourages readers to sympathize with the protagonist and artist-figure, Humbert Humbert, to the detriment of the child" as well as more recent critics who claim that "Nabokov's art encourages the reader's participation in Humbert's sexual exploitation of a little girl in order to disguise the author's own complicity" fail to appreciate "the ways in which Nabokov deploys the devices of artifice to break the reader's identification with *Lolita*'s narrator" (186). Humbert is, she maintains, the "most *unreliable* of narrators," but the narrative is "designed to *reveal* what the narrator attempts to *conceal*, or blindly ignores" (187, emphasis in the original). Specifically, in "*Lolita*'s first person narrator Nabokov created a character whose voice and vision prove sufficiently complex to reflect, within the frame of the fiction, the identity of the child eclipsed by his desire" (195). Especially significant in the present context is Pifer's argument that Humbert's "efforts to attribute his actions to the 'demonic' power of the nymphet grow increasingly lame"; in fact, "it is Humbert's obsessed imagination that is demonic, transforming the helpless child into a figment of his fantasy" (194, 191).

Humbert describes himself as being in "a paradise whose skies [are] the color of hell-flames" (188). This image is richly ambiguous: is Humbert in a blissful place that has only the *appearance* ("color") of hell? Does the hellish hue of the "skies" indicate a damnation that is *about* to fall upon him? Is it Lolita who is in hell? Perhaps the most important implication is that *Lolita* is, in Humbert's mind at least, a Fall narrative in which Lolita figures as temptress.

Pynchon, picking up this motif, repeatedly sets episodes of sexualized childhood in locations associated with hell or the underworld. The "Lollipop Lounge" in *Against the Day*, a "child bordello" where the services of "pre-pubescent houris" are offered to Darby Suckling and Chick Counterfly (398–400), is originally located by the narrator in the Tenderloin district of Manhattan, but a song sung by Angela Grace, a "plump and energetic chanteuse of some ten summers" (399), places it more specifically in "Hell's Kitchen" (400). The term "houris" likens the child prostitutes to the companions promised to Muslims in the afterlife. When the two Chums leave the bordello accompanied by Angela Grace and her pimp Plug Loafsley, they pass through an arch bearing a quotation from Dante's *Inferno*: "I AM THE WAY INTO THE DOLEFUL CITY" (401). This episode differs from others discussed in this essay because the Chums themselves are not adults. Neither are they exactly children; they are rather of a strange indeterminate age reflecting their status as storybook characters. The Lollipop Lounge episode is in part a parody of films such as *Glad Rags to Riches* and *Kid in Hollywood* produced by Jack Hays in the 1930s under the title "Baby Burlesks" in which all-child casts (including a three-year-old Temple) act out adult scenarios parodying Hollywood movies. The name "Lollipop Lounge" alludes to the song "On the Good Ship Lollipop," made famous by Temple and featured—as I have noted—in the Slothrop/Bianca episode in *Gravity's Rainbow*.[2] Pynchon perhaps has the 1976 film *Bugsy Malone*, in which child actors play Prohibition-era gangsters and showgirls, in his sights too. The queasiness created by a young girl playing a highly sexualized adult role such as a nightclub singer (whether Temple in *Glad Rags to Riches* or Jodie Foster in *Bugsy Malone*) may be partly mitigated by the fact that the male roles are played by boys of the same age, but not completely. The young actors are still presented to the gaze of adult male viewers in a way that has come to seem less acceptable since the third and decisive "discovery" of sexual abuse described by Herman.

An episode of sexualized childhood in *Mason & Dixon* also follows the Nabokovian template of seductive daughter and infernal setting. Charles Mason finds himself billeted in the Vroom household, where the lady of the house encourages her daughters to work Mason into a state of sexual excitement so that he will impregnate her slave Austra (65). As part of this intrigue twelve-year-old Els Vroom, who "began long ago the active Pursuit of Lads twice her age" (62), contrives to "reposition her nether Orbs upon Mason's Lap, to his involuntary, tho' growing Interest" (64). The agency here is represented as lying entirely with the seductive child rather than the adult male. Mason regards the Cape, where this episode occurs, as "one of the colonies of Hell" (71).

In *Gravity's Rainbow* Slothrop has sex with Bianca aboard the *Anubis*, a boat named after the Egyptian god of the underworld. In *Lolita*, the question implicitly posed is, is the desiring male engineering his own damnation, or is he inflicting hell on his victim? A close reading of *Gravity's Rainbow* shows that while it is Bianca who is trapped in the underworld, the text is ultimately more interested in Slothrop's fate. When they have sex, the initiative comes from her, but the narrative point of view remains his, and his point of view may be as unreliable as Humbert's. The tone of the passage is more appropriate to erotica than to testimony about traumatic abuse. It focuses on Slothrop's sensory impressions: "She smells like soap, flowers, sweat, cunt" (469). There are frequent reminders of her age and size: she is "little Bianca," a "little girl"; she has "baby rodent hands," "little feet," and "pre-subdeb breasts"; her face is "round with baby-fat" (469). The interweaving of this emphasis on Bianca's immaturity, in particular the repeated word "little," with a pornographically explicit narrative in which agency is consistently attributed to Bianca rather than to Slothrop—"the little girl takes the head of Slothrop's cock into her rouged mouth" (469)—makes for uncomfortable reading. The trouble is that Pynchon aims no further than drawing the reader into complicity with Slothrop's desires. The underworld motif gestures toward a Nabokovian complexity in which the "identity of the child" is visible through the desiring male's "demonic" imagination (to borrow Pifer's terms), but in practice any attempt to venture beyond Slothrop's point of view is half-hearted if not absent. The brief paragraph that describes Bianca's feelings as Slothrop leaves her, rather than conveying any sense of personhood, layers on tropes that erase her individuality: her feelings are the same as her mother's, her dreams resemble film, and she is likened, bafflingly, to an abandoned monastery. There is a fleeting reference to an unnamed trauma in her past, but this inconsequential foray into her mind dovetails quickly into Slothrop's own recollections of leaving behind another girl, back in the United States (471). Indeed, it is for *leaving* Bianca that, the narrator informs us, Slothrop is "to be counted, after all, among the Zone's lost" (470) rather than for having sex with a girl of only eleven or twelve. Indeed, despite the text affirming that Slothrop is "lost," it is Bianca's voice that is lost in *Gravity's Rainbow*. It is she, and not Slothrop, who has "no will, no consciousness—indeed, no life of her own."

Not only is Slothrop "lost," but his penis is "unflowering," like the "barren" staff of the pope in the Tannhäuser legend (470). The sexual act between the adult Slothrop and the child Bianca is problematic, it is implied, less for any emotional or psychological damage it might inflict on her than because it incurs the "hostility" which, as Catharine R. Stimpson notes, Pynchon exhibits towards sexual behaviors (such as homosexuality and cross-dressing) that "sever libido from conception" and are "barren in terms of the future of the race" (80). Slothrop's behavior toward Bianca does not exemplify "[h]ealthy male sexuality" primarily because it does not "promise fertility" (80).

"Amazing Incest"

The episode in which Franz Pökler's incestuous desires for his daughter are revealed in a fantasy in which she plays the role of the seductive daughter, instigating "hours of amazing incest" (420–21), is focalized through the adult male point of view even more consistently than the encounter between Slothrop and Bianca. Pökler suspects that it is not really his daughter who is being brought to visit him, but a succession of girls impersonating her. If "Ilse" (421) is not his daughter, then his desire for her does not violate the taboo against "real incest" (418). When she climbs into his bed, Ilse addresses Pökler as "Papi" (420): Pynchon sets up an echo between their relationship and the "surrogate daughter/father relationship" (Stimpson 87) of Paola and Pappy Hod in *V.*, which, according to Stimpson, delivers "the mysterious plenitude of sex" but "avoids incest" (87).

In considering the substitution of Ilse for Pökler's "lost" and "forgotten" wife Leni (418), Osterweil's reading of Temple is again relevant. She writes that "by continuously featuring her as the child 'love interest' or de facto 'wife' of a perennially single or widowed adult male, Fox (and later Paramount) constructed Temple as a significantly less problematic romantic partner than her adult female counterparts. Shunning the 'predatory' desire of adult women in favor of the devoted adulation of this perennial Daddy's girl, the manufacture of pedophilic desire disavowed the perceived threat of mature female sexuality" (2). An example of this positioning of Temple as "love interest" for an adult male is found in the 1935 film *Curly Top*. Edwin Morgan, played by John Boles, is so charmed by Elizabeth, an orphan played by Temple, that he courts and marries her sister Mary in order to bring the child into his home. Throughout the film Temple's character speaks about Morgan marrying "us" (meaning her and her sister). The conventions of romantic drama are arranged around Morgan and Elizabeth rather than Morgan and Mary. This confusion of familial and romantic roles means that the desires encoded in the film are not only pedophilic but also, more specifically, incestuous.

Pökler imagines a sexual relationship with a young girl who may or may not be his daughter after the breakdown of his relationship with his wife; Slothrop has sex with Bianca after becoming her mother's lover, just as Nabokov's Humbert embarks on a sexual relationship with Lolita after marrying *her* mother. Pynchon's fiction is full of sexual relationships and desires mapped onto familial relationships, either literally or figuratively: in *Against the Day*, Chick Counterfly's stepmother Treacle is "unusually attentive" (1034), Yashmeen Halfcourt insists to herself, in the paternal embrace of her lover Reef, "I am not his child" (962), and Scarsdale Vibe looks at Kit Traverse in a way that is not "fatherly or even foster-fatherly" but full of "desire" (158).

All these relationships participate in an economy of censorship and displacement. Both literal censorship (as in the case of the Motion Picture Production Code that helped create the Shirley Temple phenomenon) and repression in the Freudian sense are circumvented by substituting alternative figures for either the desiring subject or the object of desire or both. Freud himself writes that "the phenomena of censorship and dream-distortion," that is, the way in which forbidden desires are disguised in dreams, "correspond down to their smallest details" (225). Ilse's supposed substitution by an imposter who is not really his daughter mitigates, in Pökler's mind, the wrongness of his desire, but from a child's point of view such a confusion of roles exacerbates the harm caused by abuse. It is Humbert's attempt to occupy both the role of father and the role forbidden to a father—that of a lover—that is so toxic for Lolita. As Osterweil shows, a substitution intended to circumvent one form of censorship can open a channel for another, far more dangerous, set of desires to be expressed.

Incest and Innocence in *Against the Day*

The confusion of familial and sexual roles is the defining characteristic of the relationship between Yashmeen Halfcourt and her adoptive father Auberon Halfcourt in *Against the Day*. Yashmeen explains to Kit Traverse that after she and her family were sold into slavery, "Major Halfcourt found me in a bazaar in Waziristan and became my second father" (595). She describes their meeting in decidedly erotic language: "To the world here, I enjoy a reputation as 'my own person' ... yet I am also, ever ... *his*. [...] My true memories do not begin until the moment *he* first saw me in the market—I was a soul impaled, exactly upon the cusp between girl and young woman, a cusp I could literally feel as it penetrated me, as if to bisect me" (596, emphasis in the original). The emphatic "*his*" is ambiguous: does Yashmeen belong to Halfcourt because he has purchased her, because he adopts her, or because he possesses her sexually? The image of impaling—which alludes to the death of Mélanie in *V.*—explicitly eroticizes Yashmeen's immaturity. The same episode is narrated from Halfcourt's point of view later in the novel. He recalls her "contours" and "her form, already womanly": "His intent toward the child, he would protest, had never been to dishonor but to rescue. Rescue, however, had many names, and the rope up which a maiden climbed to safety might then be used to bind her most cruelly" (759). The blurring of a benign liberation from slavery with a new possession that is unmistakably erotic, indeed—as Yashmeen's adult sexual encounters often are—sadomasochistic, is the most striking note of both accounts. As Halfcourt continues to meditate on his feelings for Yashmeen, the narrator stresses their sexual element: Halfcourt recalls "her naked limbs" and "her odors" (760). His use of the word "child" in his description of his feelings to himself as a "passionate attachment to a child" (760) is ambiguous, meaning either a young person or one's own offspring. In another conversation with Kit, Yashmeen is unable to find the right term to describe her relationship to Halfcourt: "'My—' She allowed a dotted quarter-rest. 'Colonel Halfcourt is involved'" (628). She cannot bring herself to designate him as either her "father" or her "lover" and so refers to him by name and rank instead.

Yashmeen, sold in the slave market, is simultaneously eroticized and, literally, commodified. As Osterweil points out, what is eroticized and commodified in Temple's films is, specifically, her innocence (1). In *Against the Day* innocence as a commodity that can be lost, stolen, or traded is associated especially with the Chums of Chance. When the Chums discuss the motivations of the time-traveling Trespassers they have encountered for the first time in the person of "Mr. Ace," Randolph St. Cosmo suggests that they may be "not pilgrims but raiders," raising the question of what "particular resource" they seek (416). Lindsay Noseworth is in no doubt: "It's our innocence [...]. They have descended on our shores to hunt us down, capture our innocence, and take it away with them to futurity" (416). I want to suggest that this plotline in *Against the Day* can be read as, among other things, an extended metaphor for the sexual abuse of children by adults. Rather than remaining in their own time, that is, seeking sexual relationships among their peers, the Trespassers metaphorically travel back in time by turning their attention to children. What attracts them is children's "innocence," that is, their inability to genuinely reciprocate sexual feelings, to grant or withhold consent with adult understanding.

Clues to this meaning of the time-travel plot are subtle but abundant. Led by Alonzo Meatman to the house in which he encounters Mr. Ace, Chick Counterfly is unable "to rid himself of an impression, lying deeper than he cared, or was able, to go, of having been psychically interfered with" (414). The phrase "interfered with" does *not*, despite the opinions of some contributors to the *Against the Day* wiki, literally mean "sexually abused." The narrative makes clear exactly what form this psychic interference takes: "*[P]ositive expressions* of silence and absence [are] being deployed against him," and "his optic sensorium [is] being locally addressed and systematically deluded" (414, emphasis in the original). However, being "interfered with" *is* a common euphemism for being sexually abused, and the imposition of silence and of what is understood in retrospect to be delusion are common elements of the experience of abuse. This passage hints, then, at themes of childhood sexual abuse behind its ostensible narrative of time travel and psychic manipulation. Chick later recalls his intuition that the offer made by Mr. Ace "was nothing but a cruel confidence game" (555). This fits the same pattern: the fantastical plot about time travel is narrated in language that would be equally appropriate to describing the experience of sexual abuse.

It starts to look as if Pynchon is more open to examining the experience of abuse from the perspective of the victim when the victim is male. Although Kolbuszewska's essay "The Use of the Child" is only passingly interested in the ways in which Pynchon depicts, or fails to depict, the trauma of childhood sexual abuse, she does highlight the stark difference in readers' responses to the sexual exploitation of Bianca and that of Ludwig, a young boy who has "seen a lot of foreign cock" in the Zone (*GR* 729). She notes that "discussion of Bianca's age on [. . .] an Internet discussion group [. . .] shows that a deep concern about child molesting makes readers worry about whether child characters are represented as sexually abused" (111) but that "the molesting of Ludwig has not become a topic of heated discussion" (120). This difference reflects both the contrast between the pornographically detailed account Pynchon gives of Bianca's sexual experiences and the matter-of-fact mention of Ludwig's and the underlying fact that they are different sexes.

In *Against the Day* Pynchon also suggests that the raped male is rendered shamefully feminine: "To all appearance resolute, adventurous, manly, the city could not shake the terrible all-night rape, when 'he' was forced to submit, surrendering, inadmissibly, blindly feminine, into the Hellfire embrace of 'her' beloved. He spent the years afterward forgetting and fabulating and trying to get back some self-respect. But inwardly, deep inside, 'he' remained the catamite of Hell, the punk at the disposal of the denizens thereof, the bitch in men's clothing" (154). This passage represents the effects of sexual abuse in terms familiar from Herman's account—shame, guilt, low self-esteem—rather than the pornographic narratives she critiques. Readers might find it ethically preferable to Pynchon's "sexy little girls." However, in describing the shame of the male victim in terms of his been having been made a "bitch," that is, shamefully female, it is arguably symptomatic of the sexism that Freer finds undiminished in the later novels (154–56).

Bleeding Edge

Bleeding Edge, like *Against the Day*, abounds in references to sexualized or sexually abused children. The Deep Web, where some of its action takes place, offers "forbidden expressions of desire, beginning with kiddie porn and growing even more toxic from there" (240). On Halloween, Maxine Tarnow, the novel's protagonist, encounters a group of youngsters, "none of them in junior high yet," dressed as "French maids, street hookers, and baby dominatrices" (371). March Kelleher's ex-husband is living with "some 12-year-old named Sequin" (129). Sequin may be, like the objects of Pointsman's lust, only figuratively a child (expressing March's distaste for her ex having taken up with a younger partner), but it all adds up to a portrait of a culture in which children are not protected from adult sexuality. Tallis, March's daughter, performs an eroticized caricature of childishness: she has "one of these small, sub-Chipmunk voices fatally charming to certain kinds of men" (125), sticks out her lower lip, and pronounces "problem" as "pwobwem" (127).[3] Further, she is compared explicitly to Shirley Temple (127).

Moreover, *Bleeding Edge* revisits *Against the Day*'s use of time travel as a metaphor for the sexual abuse of children. Maxine learns about time travel on the Deep Web. She enters a virtual representation of a military bunker where she encounters a colonel with a voice "synthesized several generations back" and "lip movements [that] don't match the words" (242). His face on Maxine's screen is "broken up sporadically, smeared, pixelated, blown through by winds of noise and forgetfulness, failing links, lost servers" (242). A similar technological glitchiness characterizes Mr. Ace in *Against the Day*: "A strange electrical drone overtook and blurred Mr. Ace's voice for an instant. 'The *nzzt* Chums of Chance?'" (415). Mr. Ace is apparently a visitor from the future; the colonel is speaking out of the past about a military time-travel program:

> "Given the lengthy schooling, the program prefers to recruit children by kidnapping them. Boys, typically. They are taken without consent and systematically rewired. Assigned to secret cadres to be sent on missions back and forth in Time, under orders to create alternative histories which will benefit the higher levels of command who have sent them out.

"They need to be prepared for the extreme rigors of the job. They are starved, beaten, sodomized, operated on without anaesthetic. They will never see their families or friends again." (*BE* 243)

This is, explicitly, an account of sexual abuse, boys taken "without consent" and "sodomized." Sodomy is not depicted erotically or pornographically but purely as violence, as when Scarsdale Vibe in *Against the Day* boasts that the plutocracy "harness and sodomize" the children of the working class (1000). It is noteworthy that the abuse of *boys* is described thus, as opposed to sexual acts involving girls, which, as we have seen, Pynchon tends to write about in pornographic language, from the adult male point of view. One might tentatively offer the explanation that while Pynchon has, along with the wider culture, moved beyond a discursive framework in which it is normal to depict victims of sexual abuse as seductive, he finds it easier to depict abuse *as* abuse, to summon the empathy and indignation which that requires, if the victims are male.

The strongest hint that the Montauk time-travel program in *Bleeding Edge* is the origin of the visitors from the future encountered by the Chums of Chance in *Against the Day* is the way they are connected by the theme of innocence. The Montauk time travelers are men abused in their own boyhoods who travel back in time to exploit and steal the innocence of other boys. "Those poor innocents," says Miles Blundell, one of the Chums. "Back at the beginning of this . . . they must have been boys, so much like us. . . ." (*AtD* 1023). Maxine imagines her lover Windust as one of the travelers, "an innocent kid, abducted by earth-born aliens" (*BE* 243). It is clear from these consonances not only that both novels are relating different aspects of the same story but also that Pynchon is more concerned here with the emotional and psychological reality of stolen innocence than with time travel as science fictional *novum*.

Limited Progress

Bianca, the most graphically sexualized of Pynchon's "sexy little girls" is, above all, a product of her time, an avatar of twentieth-century culture's icons of erotic girlhood: Shirley Temple, Lolita, the seductive daughter. Although some readers have heard Lolita's voice behind Humbert's, Pynchon grants Bianca scant subjectivity behind these reflected identities. All of Pynchon's abused and sexualized children are enmeshed in an economy of censorship and displacement that blocks one forbidden desire but enables another: Els Vroom becomes a fluff girl for the breeding of slaves; "Ilse" becomes Pökler's daughter at the price of becoming a substitute for his wife. In the time-travel plot of *Against the Day* and *Bleeding Edge* Pynchon begins to write, indirectly, about sexual abuse in language less erotic and more attuned to the discourse of trauma. The fact that the victims are boys rather than girls, however, suggests that, while it has absorbed some of the changed cultural awareness of sexual abuse achieved by the women's movement, Pynchon's fiction has yet to fully engage with the experience of women and girls.

NOTES

1. An argument attributed on pynchonwiki.com to John M. Krafft and Bernard Duyfhuizen suggests that although Slothrop estimates her age as eleven or twelve (*GR* 463), Bianca must be sixteen or seventeen years old (see http://gravitys-rainbow.pynchonwiki.com/wiki/index.php?title=Bianca). However, the *Anubis* episode, during which the two have sex, presents a hallucinatory reality seen almost entirely through Slothrop's eyes, in a setting almost mythical in its separation from quotidian space and time. It is legitimate to read it on its own terms rather than demanding consistency with the wider chronology of the novel, and on those terms Bianca is very emphatically a "little girl" rather than an adolescent.

2. The Pynchon wiki suggests that "lollipop" is a slang term for an underage girl, but I have found no corroboration for this.

3. The reference is to characters in the cartoon and feature film franchise *Alvin and the Chipmunks* (who have high-pitched, sped-up voices) rather than to rodents of the genus *tamias*.

WORKS CITED

Bugsy Malone. Dir. Alan Parker. Rank, 1976.
Curly Top. Dir. Irving Cummings. 20th Century Fox, 1935.
Dugdale, John. *Thomas Pynchon: Allusive Parables of Power*. Basingstoke: Macmillan, 1990.
Freer, Joanna. *Thomas Pynchon and American Counterculture*. New York: Cambridge University Press, 2014.
Freud, Sigmund. *The Interpretation of Dreams*. Ed. Angela Richards. Trans. James Strachey. Harmondsworth: Penguin, 1976.
Glad Rags to Riches. Dir. Charles Lamont. Jack Hays Productions, 1933.
Herman, Judith, with Lisa Hirschman. *Father-Daughter Incest*. Cambridge: Harvard University Press, 1981.
Kid in Hollywood. Dir. Charles Lamont. Jack Hays Productions, 1933.
Kolbuszewska, Zofia. "'It Has to Be More Than the Simple Conditioning of a Child, Once Upon a Time': The Use of the Child in *Gravity's Rainbow*." *Pynchon Notes* 42–3 (1998): 111–20.
Lawson, Jessica. "'The Real and Only Fucking Is Done on Paper': Penetrative Readings and Pynchon's Sexual Text." *Against the Grain: Reading Pynchon's Counternarratives*. Ed. Sascha Pöhlmann. Amsterdam: Rodopi, 2010.
Leverenz, David. "On Trying to Read *Gravity's Rainbow*." *Mindful Pleasures: Essays on Thomas Pynchon*. Ed. George Levine and David Leverenz. Boston: Little, Brown, 1976.
Luckhurst, Roger. *The Trauma Question*. London: Routledge, 2008.
Nabokov, Vladimir. *Lolita*. London: Penguin, 2011.

Osterweil, Ara. "Reconstructing Shirley: Pedophilia and Interracial Romance in Hollywood's Age of Innocence." *Camera Obscura* 24.3 (2009): 1–39.
Pifer, Ellen. "The *Lolita* Phenomenon from Paris to Tehran." *The Cambridge Companion to Nabokov*. Ed. Julian W. Connolly. Cambridge: Cambridge University Press, 2005. 185–99.
Pynchon, Thomas. *Against the Day*. London: Jonathan Cape, 2006.
——. *Bleeding Edge*. London: Jonathan Cape, 2013.
——. *Gravity's Rainbow*. London: Vintage, 1995.
——. *Mason & Dixon*. London: Jonathan Cape, 1997.
Stimpson, Catharine. "Pre-Apocalyptic Atavism: Thomas Pynchon's Early Fiction." *Thomas Pynchon*. Ed. Harold Bloom. New York: Chelsea House, 1986. 79–91.

"Our Women Are Free"
Slavery, Gender, and Representational Bias in Thomas Pynchon's *Mason & Dixon*

ANGUS MCFADZEAN

The representation of the characters in Thomas Pynchon's *Mason & Dixon* (1997) is predetermined by a gendered master-slave relation that is clearly expressed in the frame narrative. During a conversation between Wicks Cherrycoke and his sister's family about the appropriate way of retelling history, Ethelmer, Wicks's nephew, figures "History" (350) as a woman whose fate is in the hands of two implicitly male groups, each of whom has a different way of treating her. History can be treated as a female slave by those who represent "Power," "Government," or "Facts": "She is too innocent, to be left within the reach of anyone in Power" (350). Or History can be treated as a beloved by those less concerned with hard facts who compel her to dress up in some indeterminate way (perhaps by neutralizing or swapping her gender) that hides her from such rational, factual "Power": "She needs rather to be tended lovingly and honorably by fabulists and counterfeiters, Ballad-Mongers and Cranks of ev'ry Radius, Masters of Disguise to provide her the Costume, Toilette, and Bearing, and Speech nimble enough to keep her beyond the Desires, or even the Curiosity, of Government" (350). Ethelmer's figure of History suggests that both "factual" and "fictional" genres violently entrap women within a cultural imaginary defined by men. Although Ethelmer appears to privilege his "lover's approach" to history, this preference should not be taken as Pynchon's own. The representation of history in *Mason & Dixon* combines both approaches, blending a fidelity to the historical Mason and Dixon and the period they lived in (the "Facts") with a kind of camp theatrical role-playing, a "fabulist" invention with musical interludes and all the characters in costume ("Jolly Theatrickals about the Past" [350]). This combination of both approaches to history suggests that the point in common, the gendered master-slave relation in which history is a passive, subordinate female dominated by an active, heteronormative, and implicitly male master, is more important for Pynchon's own fictional representation of history than either one of the approaches by itself. Yet the idea that such a gendered master-slave relation could underpin Pynchon's representational strategy contravenes readers' hopes of finding in Pynchon's writing positive representations of progressive gender identities and sexualities.[1]

This chapter traces the effect of this gendered master-slave relation on *Mason & Dixon*'s representational strategies. Throughout, Pynchon uses a real social relation appropriate to the time of the novel, that of slaves and slaveholders, to thematize the relations of husbands and wives, friends, sexual partners, and the relation of the individual to power generally.[2] This thematization means that relations between characters, whether of the same or different sex, tend to manifest a gendered master-slave relation that shows both genders to be fixed in a subservient position with regards to powerful and opaque institutions, identifiable with patriarchy, even though the identities of master and slave are fluidly swapped between them. Furthermore, the history of Mason and Dixon in which we meet these characters is ostensibly delivered by a narrator, Wicks Cherrycoke, who is both adhering to the facts and dressing them up with fantasy.[3] Cherrycoke correlates with Ethelmer's figure of History in his control of the story, and the implication is that even the frame narrative featuring Cherrycoke is subordinated to a greater masculine power that blends "fact and fancy" (351) and lies beyond representation entirely. Indeed, the effect of this masculine power on *Mason & Dixon* is evident in the way it promotes representations of patriarchally sanctioned masculinity while depictions of nonpatriarchally sanctioned femininity and nonnormative genders and sexualities are sidelined.

Whether this male power that controls the representation of history can be identified with Pynchon himself remains an open question, but critics have commented on the scarcity of characters with marginalized identities in Pynchon's writing. As Kyle Smith writes: "It is one of Pynchon's major purposes [. . .] to uncompromisingly represent the fact that so many remain unrepresented, but, at times, it seems he stands perilously close to merely not representing the Other at all. This is both a very dangerous and a very brave strategy, which may need some space and time to prove its worth or, perhaps, its failure" (198n29). Stefan Mattessich claims that Pynchon has no choice but to embrace a form of writing that risks such failure: "For Pynchon [. . .] one's options do not extend to refusing discourse. One must take a stand on or within discourses in order to see how they subjugate, inscribe, and define bodies as subjects" (514). It is clear that scholars are not yet certain about the effects and consequences of this representational strategy. The danger for Pynchon's writing is that, by framing the field of representation as entirely dominated by a power that lies outside of it, it cedes the ground to patriarchal power and marginalizes alternatives. This chapter suggests that *Mason*

& Dixon knowingly underscores the limitations of representation under patriarchy but shows that patriarchy can be escaped through nonbinary gender identities that exist beyond representation.

In the story of Mason and Dixon as related by Wicks Cherrycoke, we find that all the characters are trapped in a master-slave relation with a higher, abstract, disembodied power. For example, both Mason and Dixon are subservient to the masters of the Royal Society, who Mason calls "the Elevated, the Chosen" (746). However, by drawing the boundary line between Pennsylvania and Maryland, Mason and Dixon begin to realize they are actively, if quasi-unconsciously, extending an even greater power, "some Engine whose higher Assembly and indeed Purpose they are never, except from infrequent Glimpses, quite able to make out" (683). They only become fully conscious of their own subjugation to this "Engine" when their boundary line between Pennsylvania and Maryland is as good as completed, but even then, its nature remains a mystery. The Royal Society is only one of a number of institutions (along with the East India Company, the Jesuits, the Dutch Company, and Lepton Castle) through which this higher power is distributed, and none of them fully align with its ultimate identity.

Although little can be known for certain about this power, it instantiates and promotes *gendered* master-slave relations, and this is clear from the fact that the institutions that represent it are united in perpetuating the subjugation of women—a subjugation that is both directly and indirectly violent. Subjugated male characters are limited to the group of slaves Dixon frees toward the end of the story and to the figure of Gershom, George Washington's manservant, whose identity as a Jewish minstrel telling "Slave-and-Master Joaks" (284) complicates his other identity as an "African servant" (278).[4] Indeed, although the novel is preoccupied with slavery, actual African slaves are largely absent as characters.[5] Rather, it is *women* who are represented most prominently in slavery and servitude. The Company Brothel in Capetown, the Widows of Christ convent in Quebec, and the Ridotto in Lepton Castle are parts of a network of exploitation of female slaves, a violent exploitation that in many cases seems to spring from "hopeless desire for, revenge on, escape from some Woman" (151). There is a room in the Company Brothel where "Slave Women" (151) are locked in with a madman who often kills them. Women in the Widows of Christ have been abducted and forced into prostitution, murder, cannibalism, and religious sacrilege. At the Lepton Iron Plantation, Wade LeSpark sees women working silently and obediently and thinks that "this was how the world might be" (411). It is clear that the higher power that subjugates all the characters affects female characters disproportionately and so can be understood as a form of patriarchy.[6]

This does not imply that all male characters are masters, however, nor that all women are slaves ("Masters and Mistresses resume the abuse of their

Slaves" [101]). As we have just seen, even Mason and Dixon are trapped by a fixed master-slave relation with an elusive patriarchal power, and any male character who tries to embody this power finds that he is still an expendable subordinate. For example, Mason's failure to become astronomer royal reveals the extent to which he remains a servant of the Royal Society and not its master. Maskelyne comes closer to this power when he obtains the position of astronomer royal, but he is forced to test Harrison's watch and potentially render his life's work on the longitude tables useless. Higher-positioned male characters also fail to fully and consistently embody the power they represent. Lord Clive of the East India Company suffers from an opium addiction, and Lord Lepton, master of the Lepton Ironworks, was once indentured to an ironmaster. Even Zarpazo struggles to control his students and prevent them from exploring the forbidden feng shui. The masculinity of these characters seems to depend on obtaining positions of apparent power, and they largely believe themselves to be beneficiaries of the patriarchal order. Yet these characters remain subservient to power and suffer from their inability to fulfill the male role that patriarchy expects of them. Furthermore, the relative freedom of all male characters is shown to be under threat. The victorious Prussian cavalry at the Battle of Leuthen in 1757, which achieved new levels of military regimentation, its soldiers seeming like "rank'd Automata, executing perfect manoeuvres upon the unending German Plain" (659), is presented as heralding a future in which men will be enslaved to a degree comparable to that of women in the eighteenth century. *Mason & Dixon* takes place before such violent regimentation is imposed more broadly, but this postulated future reminds us that the current freedom of the male characters is relative.

Both genders are *fixed* in a subordinate position with regards to this elusive patriarchal power. However, Pynchon's characters interact in ways that manifest fluid master-slave relations in which power flows between the characters, preventing any fixed hierarchy from establishing itself. Such fluidity occurs with both mixed-sex and same-sex relations. For men in heterosexual partnerships, giving up mastery appears to be a necessary prelude to reimagining masculine-feminine bonds. Tom Hynes, who beats his fiancée and kidnaps their baby, apologizes in a fashion ("Maybe I was young then,—maybe even, even foolish" [580]), is forgiven and ends up marrying happily. Peter Redzinger abandons his wife Luise to follow Christ but returns "chasten'd, even at times dejected" (480), and is accepted back. Rhodie Beck supports her husband through his affliction of turning into a were-beaver because he has reciprocated for her: "[Y]ou've seen ev'ry-thing I can turn into" (620). The narrative highlights penitent and broken men submitting to their female partners and implies that giving up mastery allows for a fluid exchange of power between them. These examples suggest that heterosexual partnership and marriage is not the scene of male mastery and female submission but a magical space in which "Love" (541) and unconditional female forgiveness rebalance the relationship between the sexes by challenging associations between mastery and masculinity and slavery and femininity.

The importance of renouncing mastery is highlighted by the focus on Charles Mason, a character who refuses fluid master-slave relations with the people closest to him. For example, Mason assumes the role of master with respect to Rebekah, insisting that they leave the town of Stroud and travel over the world, without considering whether this way of life is something that she desires. Rebekah suddenly dies in childbirth, and Mason's responsibility for this is exposed when Austra, a slave, compares English wives to slaves that sell their babies. Mason protests that "in England, no one has the right to bid another to bear a *child* [...]. Our Women are free" (65, emphasis in the original). Austra, however, insists on a correlation between slavery and English marriage: "White Wives are much alike [...]. Many have there been, oblig'd to go on bearing children,—for no reason but the man's pride. [...] How is English Marriage any different from the Service I'm already in?" (65). Most wives, Austra argues, no matter how free in other respects, are enslaved to a system of reproduction that is imposed by a "man's pride" without due concern for women's well-being. She implies that Mason's desire to have a child killed Rebekah. Later, Mason has gained enough perspective to realize that he may have enslaved Rebekah to his own sense of entitled mastery: "How could he allow that she [Rebekah] might have her own story?" (207–8).[7] Although Mason's ultimate return to England, his reconciliation with his son Doc Isaac ("the Boy he had gone to the other side of the Globe to avoid" [768]), and the disappearance of Rebekah's ghost, suggest that Mason has gone some way toward accepting his complicity in her death and relinquishing his mastery, his dragging his family along unwillingly for his final trip to America indicates that old habits die hard.

Mason & Dixon, then, seems to value the renunciation of male mastery in favor of fluid relations between couples. However, it also exposes the limitations of this renunciation when it portrays the difficulties of escaping from subjugation experienced by female characters in mixed-sex relations. Wives, mothers, sisters, and homemakers, that is, women defined according to a determining male figure (husband, brother, father, partner), constitute a large number of the women in the novel. All of these women's trajectories are predetermined by their status as the subsidiary figure in a partnership; for example, as the "White Wives" (65) that Austra likens to slaves. Mrs. Martha Washington, a "cheerful rather than happy" (280) wife, appears as a servant to her husband. Ma Oafery is stuck looking after her werewolf son Lud. Mrs. Price is trapped in an unhappy marriage to her husband and separates from him when they end up on different sides of the Mason-Dixon line. Mrs. Edgewise, a master cardsharp and hustler, experiences marriage as a "prolonged chastisement" (366). Thus even as *Mason & Dixon* trades in traditional gender stereotypes (the power of female forgiveness and the magical ability of female love to tame wild masculinity) as a way of sharing power between the genders, it is clear that women continue to be subjugated and disempowered. Mastery (particularly the decision to claim or dispense with it) often remains with the male, and female characters are not enfranchised into mastery themselves.

Out of all the male characters, Dixon, as the subservient partner to Mason, is most capable of establishing more equal mixed-sex relations. Where Mason courts the elusive power of the Royal Society, Dixon seeks "routes of Escape, pockets of Safety,—Markets that never answer to the Company" (69). He finds one such space in the Malay Quarter in Capetown to which he makes frequent nighttime visits, pursuing an "unconceal'd attraction to the Malays and the Black slaves,—their Food, their Appearance, their Music, and so, it must be obvious, their desires to be deliver'd out of oppression" (61). Dixon's activities in such spaces lead him away from master-slave relations (such as he might find himself embroiled with if he engaged the Vroom daughters or Austra) and toward multiple relations with women that we might presume are based on mutual desire rather than love. However, it is unclear whether Dixon avoids subjugating the women he patronizes. It is not directly stated whether his nightly visits "up in the Malay quarter, inspecting some harem of his own" (147), "rollicking with your Malays and Pygmies" (67) in "Lustful Adventure" (70), actually involve sex, although the language implies that they do. Although "it must be obvious" that Dixon wants to help the Malays out of their oppression, he appears to be a "john" visiting prostitutes, and so his attempt to escape from master-slave relations is perhaps no more successful than Mason's. However, the displacement of any direct representation of Dixon's encounters onto his passion for spicy Malay cuisine, which allegedly encourages "Lust that crosses racial barriers" (62), suggests that there might be something between Dixon and the Malays that genuinely escapes the master-slave relations of direct representation.

Mason & Dixon also represents gendered master-slave relations in same-sex relations. One might assume that same-sex relations would counteract the association between masculinity and mastery and femininity and slavery that underpins representation in *Mason & Dixon*. Certainly, there are same-sex relations in the novel that go further than mixed-sex relations in equalizing master-slave relations and even offer the possibility of nonheteronormative sexualities. However, the representation of these possibilities is limited. The most prominent male same-sex pairing is, of course, Mason and Dixon themselves. They agree that between them, Mason is the "Master" (72) and Dixon is the "Second" (72), but their relationship is characterized by tensions about this hierarchy. Dixon's visiting Lancaster Jail disguised as Mason makes it clear that subordinate members of a same-sex pair can switch positions and start performing as masters. Furthermore, Mason gradually renounces his mastery over Dixon, and they develop an affection and respect for each other, which goes further than the qualified equality available in mixed-sex relations but still has its limits. As Wicks comments, "Love is simply not in the cards. So must they pursue other projects [...]. Mason and Dixon could not cross the perilous Boundaries between themselves" (689). Wicks raises the possibility that their supersession of master-slave relations is incomplete due to patriarchal limits on homosocial affection.[8] Indeed, the persistently jokey tone of references to homosexuality between them—Mason's affection for Dixon being "comparable to that occurring between Public-School students in England" (697) and Dixon's comment, after an argument, about "[c]alling off the Wedding, again" (70)—indicates the characters', and perhaps the novel's, anxiety about transgressing those patriarchal limits.

Nevertheless, Mason and Dixon's friendship is the most intimate male same-sex relation represented in *Mason & Dixon*. Other relations of this kind fail to vex the master-slave dynamic. Indeed, they accentuate it. For example, in the group relations of the all-male crew of the *Seahorse* and the largely male crew participating in the drawing of the boundary line, Pynchon represents a rowdy male camaraderie characterized by fluid master-slave hierarchies between its members. Because most of the male characters identify with a patriarchy that subjugates them, men compete in their relations with other men for status and power through the assertion of a hypermasculinity and the promotion of heteronormative ideas of the body, gender, and sexual desire. Among the drunken antics and lascivious cavorting of the crew of the *Seahorse* is the playing of a trick that makes sailors "bend down [...], becoming thereupon subject to Posterior Assault" (53). And Moses Barnes, part of the line crew, advises Mr. McNutley to "[g]row Titts [...] and learn to talk for an Hour without taking a Breath," so that maybe as McNutley's wife "grows more daz'd with her Pregnancy, she'll mistake ye for another Woman, taking from it what comfort she may" (455). The ribald tone of these comments suggests the anxiety of male-only communities over other genders and sexualities. Although these fluid male heterosexual groupings are clearly preferable to the regimented organization of the Prussian cavalry, they neutralize any political force male same-sex relations could have in upsetting the overarching master-slave logic and instead reflect the internalization of the patriarchal desire to coerce and co-opt other sexual and gender identities that turns those other identities into objects of male heterosexual mockery.[9]

When we turn to female same-sex relations, we find that groups of women, equivalent to the bawdy line crew, are entirely controlled and silenced by organizations like the East India Company and Lepton Castle. Meanwhile, female couples appear infrequently, and although these relationships go further toward equality and even love than Mason and Dixon's does, none of them present a serious challenge to the general predominance of master-slave relations. Conversations between female characters revolve around boys, sexuality, marriage, and their own bodies, as if women have no other identity to perform to each other than that which is enmeshed with patriarchy. The Vroom sisters are defined by their blond hair and their obsession with local boys. Dixon's mother, Mary Hunter, and her daughter Elizabeth talk about how to handle husbands (namely, by playing tricks on them) and how Elizabeth should negotiate her attachment to "the Raylton lad" (240). Rebekah and Miss Bradley talk only of boys and weddings. Mitzi Redzinger's only point of discussion with her mother concerns how she wants to wear her hair in such a way that boys can see it. It is clear that these female characters have internalized patriarchal values as their own and so continue within same-sex relations to perform identities that have been shaped by them (heteronormativity, an identification between the female body and female identity, an emphasis on beauty and finding a husband). Even though master-slave relations are barely present between these female characters, they are still subordinated to an external master whose presence is felt in their interactions.

Only in a few cases are female same-sex relations able to escape from patriarchal power, and when they do love and nonheteronormative sexualities become possible. The lesbian relationship between Eliza Fields and Zsuzsa Szabó involves a kind of affection that precludes any master-slave dynamic between them: "Zsuzsa striding in and embracing her co-adventuress-to-be from behind. They smile and stretch, glowing" (540). Furthermore, Eliza and Zsuzsa's joint rejection of heteronormativity permits alterations in gender performance. Zsuzsa is a masculine woman who rides on an Arab horse and dresses in a Hussar uniform (a "Lady in breeches" [552]). Eliza at one time dresses as an Indian boy with a shaved head. However, whether Eliza and Zsuzsa's loving relationship genuinely represents an escape from the master-slave logic remains in doubt. They have both had traumatizing experiences with patriarchy—Eliza through her time as one of Father Zarpazo's Viudas de Cristo, Zsuzsa in witnessing the Battle of Leuthen—and these experiences seem to define them. Zsuzsa's unorthodox gender and sexual identity has emerged in reaction to patriarchal control, and Eliza dresses as an Indian boy to escape from the convent in Quebec. Furthermore, lesbian relations in themselves are not a sign that characters have escaped from the influence of patriarchal mastery. Johanna Vroom's sapphically forcing female slaves to lick pomegranate juice off her hand and Lady Lepton's seduction of the chambermaid show same-sex desires reinstituting a sadistic master-slave binary that mimics the power fantasies of patriarchy. In the absence of any comparable representation of male homosexuality, the use of lesbianism to portray a positive space that is not shaped by master-slave relations hints at the continuing presence of a male gaze that finds lesbianism titillating.

Mixed- and same-sex relations, then, offer the possibility of an affection that allows for greater equality, but in practice, such relations do not fundamentally alter the reigning association between masculinity and mastery and between femininity and slavery. This is because mixed- and same-sex relations in this novel are biased by a patriarchal power that emphasizes masculinity and heteronormativity and deprioritizes nonpatriarchally sanctioned femininity and nonnormative genders and sexualities. Although the friendship of Mason and Dixon exhibits a kind of equality, male same-sex relations are generally patriarchal and heteronormative and represented noncritically. Mixed-sex relations in which the man renounces mastery and the woman forgives him escape patriarchy, but this escape is undermined by the other aspects of the female experience of mixed-sex relations (Austra's comment that all wives are slaves). In the absence of direct narratorial comment, it is unclear whether the positive effects of male renunciation are sufficient in light of the presentation of unhappy wives. In any case, no mixed- or same-sex couple is shown to have escaped fully from patriarchy. And other potential spaces of escape—Dixon's acquaintances in the Malay Quarter, female group relations, lesbianism—have been compromised by a patriarchal representative power, and at times, even co-opted into supporting it.

To understand how this happens, we can turn to the comments made by Patsy, a member of the Sons of Liberty, who claims that political "Representation must extend beyond simple Agentry [...] unto at least Mr. Garrick, who in 'representing' a rôle, becomes the character, as by some transfer of Soul" (405). According to Patsy, performance isn't merely the adoption of a contingent, arbitrary, or circumstantial identity but a kind of transformation that produces a new identity. So, from the point of view of representing fact and fiction, the "essential" femininity of Ethelmer's female History is a kind of aggregate mass of historical potentiality, which disappears when it is presented as being factual under "Power" or fictive under a "fabulist."[10] Femininity, meaning a freedom from all master-slave relations, may be "essential," but it genuinely disappears under the disguise imposed by a "fabulist" or, at most, occasionally "peeps out" from behind that disguise.

We can see this disappearance of underlying identities in the gender representations of female and male characters. Under the pressure of patriarchal power, women are forced into patriarchally sanctioned roles. For example, practically all the women in the novel not portrayed as wives and homemakers are "wenches" (330), "doxies" (273), "Milk-maids" (459), and the like, women whose identities are dependent on their bodies and men's attraction to them. However, these identities are depicted as being merely performances. The "lasses" are playing at being milkmaids, "'Coy Milk-maids' being a Game courtly as any back in the Metropolis" (464). The courtesan Florinda has "Experience upon the Stage" (114): rather than expressing her real desires, "she has decided to get in a bit of exercise, in that endless Refining which the Crafts of Coquetry demand, using Mason as a sort of Practice-Dummy" (114). Performances in which the female body is synonymous with female identity play into patriarchally sanctioned roles for women and clearly fail to reflect women's underlying self-conceptions. Although the actual identities of many of these women, as well as their reasons for adopting "disguises," are not always apparent, smart, capable women appear to be hiding under at least some of these facades. Molly and Dolly are revealed to be Ben Franklin's assistants, and Molly has surveyor skills. Dark Hepsie's aged appearance turns out to be a laborious pretense: "[B]eneath her layers of careful Decrepitude," there was "a shockingly young Woman hard at work" (26). Their lack of choice in assuming their "disguises" may be suggested by the fact that women performing identities that violate patriarchal codes (for example, Zsuzsa Szabó) are conspicuous by their rarity.

Furthermore, in the rare moments when the minds of female characters are represented through free indirect discourse, it is revealed that they have assumed patriarchally sanctioned female roles. Mitzi's thoughts in an interior monologue, for instance, are entirely focused on her body's changes: "Breasts, hips, Fluxes, odd Swoons" (387). Female interiority (at least, as it is related by the narrator Wicks Cherrycoke) offers little sanctuary from the patriarchal control of desire, gender performance, and the association of body and self. The performance of a patriarchally sanctioned femininity, rather than reserving and protecting an underlying identity, produces the desires that are expected of such "wenches" (330) and "doxies" (273); it even produces the desire to submit to the worst excesses of masterful masculinity. Austra, a veteran of the Capetown Company Brothel, the Widows of Christ in Quebec, and the Lepton Ridotto asks, "Who says Slavery's so terrible, hey?" (427). Eliza Fields feels a strong pull toward the torture she would receive in the dark dungeon of the Widows of Christ: "a mysterious Space she has more than curiously long'd to enter..." (534). The Vroom girls dream of their own confinement by the "unchallengeable Love of a Tyrant" (155).

When we turn to the men in *Mason & Dixon*, we find that male characters also perform their genders under the influence of a subordinating patriarchy. For example, we first meet Captain Zhang when he is a servant of his nemesis, the Jesuit priest Father Zarpazo. Even after Zhang has escaped from him, he remains haunted by his prior subjugation by Zarpazo and finds Zarpazo's face appearing when he experiences heterosexual desire: "Tho' any sight of [Eliza], even at a distance, begin in Delight, soon enough shall *his* evil features emerge from, and replace, those belov'd ones... yet do I desire... not him, never him ... yet ... given such Terms, to desire *her*, clearly, I must transcend all Shame" (631, emphasis in the original). Zhang's heterosexual desire for Eliza is thwarted by a homosexual desire to again submit to Zarpazo; when he thinks that Zarpazo has come to the camp, Zhang goes "half insane" (545) and to protect himself dresses up as his enemy in a costume that is notably feminine (a "man in skirts" [552]). Zhang's experience with Zarpazo has affected his desire and his gender performance. His adoption of Zarpazo's guise is a desperate attempt to control the patriarchal force ("*Sha* [...], Bad Energy" [542]) enslaving him.

Another male character who comes close to abandoning a patriarchally sanctioned masculinity is Philip Dimdown. Dimdown is a printer of broadsides against the British authorities but dresses as a "macaroni" (a form of eighteenth-century dandy, described during the period as "a kind of animal, neither male nor female, a thing of the neuter gender") to disguise his political activities.[11] Dimdown's macaronism expresses something of his true self ("I was probably indulging Fop Sentiments long kept under, unknown even to myself" [567]), but unlike Zsuzsa, his political activities do not lead to a more lasting gender alteration. Dimdown later abandons the disguise of his own volition for a normative gender performance that communicates his heterosexuality, suggesting that his "Fop Sentiments" are only allowed brief and strategic indulgence and that his political identity is not dependent on any nonnormative gender identity.

Indeed, Zhang and Dimdown are practically the only male characters who register that gender performance is the naturalized product of patriarchy. This sense is absent in the performances of most of the male characters, even Dixon's. Male characters are generally represented as possessing an essential masculinity, a stable "natural" identity, that cannot be altered and that is not troubled by alternative identity performances. Although male characters are continually enacting forms of behavior and adopting costumes and disguises that misrepresent their underlying identities, they do so strategically, consciously, and voluntarily in particular moments. Dixon is identified by his military redcoat, which he wears "upon the theory that a Representation of Authority, whose extent no one is quite sure of, may act as a deterrent to Personal Assault" (49). Captain Grant of the *Seahorse* has developed a technique of "*pretending to be insane*, thus deriving an Advantage over any unsure as to which side of Reason he may actually stand upon" (51, emphasis in the original). Wicks Cherrycoke is advised by Captain Grant that being a cleric in Capetown is dangerous, and Dixon suggests "[t]ha could pretend to be an Astronomer" (85). The masculinity of these characters is not interrupted by these performances of false identity. Even when Mason and Dixon are represented through free indirect discourse, there is no obvious distinction between their internal masculinity and that of their performances. If it is the case that "in 'representing' a rôle, [one] becomes the character, as by some transfer of Soul" (405), then it is clear that men in this novel have naturalized their patriarchally sanctioned performances to a greater extent than women and that male political radicals like Zhang and Dimdown are unable to synchronize their political radicalism with nonnormative genders and sexualities to the same degree as Zsuzsa and Eliza.

That Pynchon does equate political radicalism with nonnormative genders and sexualities is evident in his gestures toward a more complete escape from patriarchy and master-slave relations in a space that is figured as being beyond representation, a retreating magical world referred to as the "subjunctive" (345).[12] It is glimpsed from a distance throughout the novel, as when the narrator refers with approval to "Sylphs of mixed race, mixed gender" (81) in Capetown, the "independents, brave girls and boys who are young enough to enjoy the danger of going up against the Compagnie" (81). These young people disappear into spaces where they seem to transgress the romantic and erotic divisions between white and black, slave and free, male and female, divisions instituted by the "sex industry in Cape Town" and the Dutch Company "seeking as ever total control" (81). The subjunctive, then, appears to be a space in which nonnormative genders and sexualities, hinted at by Zsuzsa Szabó, Eliza Fields and Captain Zhang, find fuller expression. The subjunctive even holds out the possibility of nonbinary gender identities, including a third gender aligned with inanimate life ("of Genders they have three,—Male, Female, and the Third Sex no one talks about,—Dead" [195]), one instance being Vaucanson's "mechanickal Duck," an automaton that comes to life through the addition of female sex organs and "the kiss of . . . *l'Amour*" (373, emphasis in the original) and that desires another ungendered automaton duck as its partner: "The other, being yet sexually unmodified, is neither,—or, if you like, both" (377).[13]

However, by conceiving of alternative and nonbinary genders and sexualities as belonging to a "subjunctive" realm beyond representation, the narrative cedes the ground to patriarchal discourse and assigns alternative gender identities a marginal status. The nonbinary and nonnormative genders and sexualities of the subjunctive are never fully explored in the novel. Nor are clichés pertaining to the renunciation of male mastery and the magical powers of unconditional female forgiveness sufficiently challenged. Yet the very presence of the subjunctive argues that Pynchon's text is well aware of its own representational bias. Indeed, how can we explain the expressions of discontent from the wives concerning married life, Austra's comment that "White Wives" are "slaves," the gendered representation of the female slavery of the East India Company, Lepton Castle, and so on, and the smart women visible under patriarchally sanctioned gender performances, except as criticisms of a patriarchal force that does violence both to the characters and, as implied through Ethelmer's figure of History, the text itself? History's underlying "essential" femininity is aligned with the "subjunctive"; it is full of possibility but is corralled through a relationship with an external patriarchal force that reduces gender to a binary of "the Feminine and the Masculine" (551), naturalizes gender performance, identifies the female body with female identity, represses nonnormative genders and sexualities, and produces a desire for slavery and self-destruction. Rather than fantasizing a miraculous escape into a world of nonnormative gender and sexual identities, Pynchon creates a space of "fluid Identity" (469) in which the various effects of this patriarchal bias on the gender presentations of women and men are depicted and in which spaces of emancipation and escape are receding and only glimpsed briefly. History may be shaped by the fabulist to protect it from "Power," but it can never quite be safe, since its femininity, its subjunctivity, continues to peep out from under the disguise.

NOTES

1. On Ethelmer's figure of History, see Schaub 192–93, and McHale 48. On the contemporary construction of gender as performance in the context of power relations, see Foucault and Butler. For an account of the modern biopolitics of gender, see Repo.

2. Other conceptualizations of master-slave relations are possible. Hegelian-inspired criticism offers a theory of master-slave relations, and Harris mentions the "Colonizer/Colonized, Screwer/Screwee, Tyrant/Slave binary" (211).

3. For Cherrycoke's role as narrator, see Dewey.

4. For more on Gershom's hybrid ethnic identity and his comic manipulation of master-slave roles, see Heon.

5. Cherrycoke himself upbraids LeSpark for omitting mention of African slaves in his account of the work done at Lepton Castle. Smith briefly comments on this (191–92).

6. On slavery, see Hill 127, 137–39, and Baker 172–73, and for specifically sexualized female slavery, see Hill 142–44, Sears 114–16, and Harris 203.

7. On the relationship between Rebekah's ghost and slavery, see Punday 271–72.

8. On their failure to become real friends, see Wallhead. On the homosexuality of their relationship, see Sears.

9. For the representation of communities in *Mason & Dixon*, see Hill 135–37.

10. On issues of Pynchonian realism and representation see Hill 127–33, 154; for a different approach to representation involving cartography, see McLaughlin.

11. *Oxford Magazine* June 1770, as quoted under the second definition of "macaroni" in the *OED*.

12. On the subjunctive, see McHale. Note, however, that McHale does not consider how gender might appear in the subjunctive. For how slavery is abolished in the subjunctive, see Thill 73–74.

13. For more on Vaucanson's Duck, see Collingnon, Berressem, and Saar and Skirke. Fitzpatrick discusses the representation of mechanical life and gender with regard to the character of V. For hybrid identities and composite beings, see Hinds.

WORKS CITED

Abbas, Niran, ed. *Thomas Pynchon: Reading from the Margins*. Madison: Fairleigh Dickinson University Press, 2003.

Baker, Jeff. "Plucking the American Albatross: Pynchon's Irrealism in *Mason & Dixon*." Horvath and Malin 167–88.

Berressem, Hanjo. "'Of Metal Ducks, Embodied Idorus, and Autopoietic Bridges': Tales of an Intelligent Materialism in the Age of Artificial Life." *The Holodeck in the Garden: Science and Technology in Contemporary American Fiction*. Ed. Peter Freese and Charles B. Harris. Normal: Dalkey Archive Press, 2004. 72–99.

Butler, Judith. *Gender Trouble*. New York: Routledge. 1990.

Collingnon, Fabienne. "The Ballistic Flight of an Automatic Duck." *Orbit: A Journal of American Literature* 1.2 (2012). DOI: 10.7766/orbit.v1.2.23.

Copestake, Ian D., ed. *American Postmodernity: Essays on the Recent Fiction of Thomas Pynchon*. Bern: Peter Lang, 2003.

Dewey, Joseph. "The Sound of One Man Mapping: Wicks Cherrycoke and the Eastern (Re)solution." Horvath and Malin 112–31.

Fitzpatrick, Kathleen. "The Clockwork Eye: Technology Woman, and the Decay of the Modern in Thomas Pynchon's *V.*" Abbas 91–107.

Foucault, Michel. *The History of Sexuality*. Vol. 2.: *The Use of Pleasure*. London: Penguin, 1992.

Giles, Paul. "Virtual Englands: Pynchon's Transatlantic Heresies." *Virtual Americas: Transnational Fictions and the Transatlantic Imaginary*. Durham: Duke University Press, 2002. 225–53.

Harris, Michael. "Pynchon's Postcoloniality." Abbas 199–214.

Heon, John. "Surveying the Punch Line: Jokes and Their Relation to the American Racial Unconscious/Conscience in *Mason & Dixon* and the Liner Notes to *Spiked!*" Copestake 193–216.

Hill, Robert R. "Rationalizing Community: Victims, Institutions and Analogies for America in *Mason & Dixon*." *Pynchon Notes* 52–53 (2003): 124–65.

Hinds, Elizabeth Jane Wall. "'Animal, Vegetable, Mineral': The Play of Species in Pynchon's *Mason & Dixon*." *Humans and Other Animals in Eighteenth-Century British Culture: Representation, Hybridity, Ethics*. Ed. Frank Palmeri. Burlington: Ashgate, 2006. 179–99.

Horvath, Brooke, and Irving Malin, eds. *Pynchon and* Mason & Dixon. Newark: University of Delaware Press, 2000.

Mattessich, Stefan. "Imperium, Misogyny, and Postmodern Parody in Thomas Pynchon's *V.*" *ELH* 65.2 (1998): 503–21.

McHale, Brian. "*Mason & Dixon* in the Zone; or, A Brief Poetics of Pynchon-Space." Horvath and Malin 43–62.

McLaughlin, Robert L. "Surveying, Mapmaking and Representation in *Mason & Dixon*." Copestake 173–91.

Olster, Stacey M. "A 'Patch of England, at a Three-Thousand-Mile Off-Set?' Representing America in *Mason & Dixon*." *Modern Fiction Studies* 50.2 (2004): 283–302.

Repo, Jemima. *The Biopolitics of Gender*. New York: Oxford University Press, 2016.

Pöhlmann, Sascha. "(Un)Making America: The Postnational Spaces of *Mason & Dixon*." *Pynchon's Postnational Imagination*. Heidelberg: Universitätsverlag, 2010. 177–276.

Punday, Daniel. "Pynchon's Ghosts." *Contemporary Literature* 44.2 (2003): 250–74.

Pynchon, Thomas. *Mason & Dixon*. London: Vintage, 1997.
Saar, Martin, and Christian Skirke. "The Realm of Velocity and Spleen: Reading Hybrid Life in *Mason & Dixon*." Copestake 129–46.
Schaub, Thomas H. "Plot, Ideology, and Compassion in *Mason & Dixon*." Horvath and Malin 189–202.
Sears, Julie Christine. "Black and White Rainbows and Blurry Lines: Sexual Deviance/Diversity in *Gravity's Rainbow* and *Mason & Dixon*." Abbas 108–21.
Smith, Kyle. "Serving Interests Invisible: *Mason & Dixon*, British Spy Fiction, and the Specters of Imperialism." Abbas 183–98.
Thill, Brian. "The Sweetness of Immorality: *Mason & Dixon* and the American Sins of Consumption." *The Multiple Worlds of Pynchon's* Mason & Dixon: *Eighteenth-Century Contexts, Postmodern Observations*. Ed. Elizabeth Jane Wall Hinds. New York: Camden House, 2005. 49–76.
Wallhead, Celia M. "Mason & Dixon: Pynchon's Bickering Heroes." *Pynchon Notes* 46–49 (2000): 178–99.

SECTION 5 Family/Values

Pynchon and Gender
A View from the Typescript of *V.*

LUC HERMAN AND JOHN M. KRAFFT

Judging by the many cuts and alterations to the typescript version of his first novel, *V.* (1963), held in the Thomas Pynchon Collection at the Harry Ransom Humanities Research Center in Austin, Texas, it is clear not only that Pynchon struggled with the structure of his book but also that he was trying to work through daunting issues of race and gender.[1] Elsewhere (Herman and Krafft, "Race"), we have suggested that the published novel's version of the African American character McClintic Sphere is still inhibited by the set of liberal clichés marring the typescript original. Here, we consider a typescript episode, one of several deleted from the published novel, that is steeped in sexual politics. It delineates an installment of an imaginary family situation comedy in which various constructions of sexual identity vie for dominance and in which women come out on top. We find the overall effect satirical, but we also acknowledge that many readers may find the novel's depictions of both men and women and its representations of their roles to be sexist if not downright misogynistic. As Richard Hardack observes in a different context, "[I]t is sometimes hard to differentiate what Pynchon is critiquing from what he perpetuates" (592n31). In any case, if the episode had been kept in, it might well have been interpreted as an extrapolation of the role of the V. figure in the published novel. Indeed, as they wield power and take a certain pleasure in conspiring to hold down their men, the mother and daughter in the sitcom look like two contemporary versions of the elusive female protagonist in the novel's historical chapters, which provide Stencil's perspective on events related to his father's life. Perhaps, then, Pynchon cut the sitcom to prevent the narrator of the 1956 plot from duplicating what he may have expressly conceived as Stencil's sexist projection of an almost mythological femininity. As we show toward the end of this essay, a late addition to the novel at the beginning of the historical chapters connects this problematic idolatry with the figure of the White Goddess as described by Robert Graves, which at least seems to indicate Pynchon's awareness of Stencil's fixation on overbearing female strength.

Critics have debated possible sexism in *V.* at least since the mid-1970s, when Catharine R. Stimpson described what she saw as "Pynchon's sexual conservatism," a conventional idealization of stereotypical female fecundity and nurturance (32). Kathleen Fitzpatrick, like Molly Hite (in this volume), sees *V.* as misogynistic—"though," she suggests, "it also shows signs of beginning to question" that attitude (106n8)—and sees the V. figure as a projection (both Stencil's and Pynchon's) of threatening, decadent machinic female otherness. Joanna Freer laments that *V.*'s "female protagonist is never fully present as a real woman, instead remaining splintered, distanced, disturbingly inhuman, and primarily symbolic" (130). On the other hand, Dana Medoro argues that this figure, a figure of women's solidarity and power, representing "resistance to systems of domination" (25), is one in whom "the promise of cyclical regeneration for a fallen world lies latent" (31). Medoro thus denies that *V.* connives in the sexism it depicts. Perhaps most relevant to our purpose here is Mark D. Hawthorne's argument that *V.* ultimately succeeds in blurring and blending gender roles in a critique of the binary sexual and gender differentiations so troublesomely characteristic of the 1950s culture the novel depicts. Aptly, Hawthorne locates Pynchon's parodic and humorous treatment of immature male characters in the 1950s storyline "in the masculine identity confusion of the 1950s when the two essential masculine roles of sexual partner and breadwinner were being 'domesticated' and, at the same time, emasculated *by popular media*" (82, emphasis added), popular media like the family sitcom. The sitcom Pynchon cut from the final version of the novel illustrates and satirizes exactly such confusion over gender binarism: the male characters neither quite figure out what it means to *be* a man nor manage to do whatever it would be to *act* like a man. Furthermore, two tropes prominent in the sitcom, varieties of inanimacy/dehumanization and the allure/threat of the road, are obviously central to the gender thematics of the novel as a whole and so appear to help integrate the episode neatly. But Pynchon may have cut it because its treatment of such important issues was at once too heavy handed and not probing enough, and he wanted his novel to address more complicated gender concerns, as our discussion of the White Goddess suggests.

As we have detailed in our 2007 overview essay on the typescript, Pynchon submitted a first version of his first novel to J. B. Lippincott in June 1961. At the beginning of August, he received a very nice acceptance letter from Cork Smith, who promised he would go "over the script in detail" so as to provide some "specific suggestions" for improvement. Still, Smith didn't hesitate to issue an early warning: "I do think some very careful cutting would help, and I confess I am at times bothered by your fiddling with the time sequence" (Stephen Tomaske Collection). While Smith promised a more substantial letter "within a couple of weeks," it wasn't until the end of February 1962 that Pynchon received his editor's comments. So there was a lot of time for Pynchon to think not just about potential cuts and the time sequence of the novel but about other matters relating to the book as well. And indeed, while Smith offered three substantial comments in his letter of February 23, Pynchon in his reply of March 13 listed no fewer than fourteen changes. Number 4 on the list reads as follows: "The TV show in chapter 27 is ponderous Social Commentary which I am no more fond of than Social Protest, so out it should go, also" (Stephen Tomaske Collection).[2] "Social Protest" alludes to a comment Smith made about Sphere in his letter of February 23: "There is something about him which gives the reader a certain feeling that the book is, at least in part[,] a Protest Novel" (Stephen Tomaske Collection).[3] While Pynchon doesn't reply in detail to this remark until later in the letter of March 13, he alludes to it in the third change he notes (the deletion of speeches by irredentist Sgherraccio and by an African American patriarch) and then swiftly links evidently undesirable "Social Protest" with "Social Commentary," his pejorative label for what he has apparently come to see as objectionable about the TV show.

Chapter 12 of the typescript, "In Which Profane Returns to Street Level" (187–202), provides most of the material for section 2 of chapter 6 in the published novel—the section in which Benny Profane realizes that his job with the Alligator Patrol is nearing its inevitable end, and Fina Mendoza, who has rescued Profane from yo-yoing on the subway and taken him to live in her family's apartment, urges him to start looking for a new job. At first reluctant, he eventually obliges her but then backs out of the interview she has arranged for him. A few days later, coming off the job, Profane and his friends Angel and Geronimo go to a bar on upper Broadway. Afterward, the three of them take part in a long search for the missing Fina.[4] She has been "out with the Playboys" (150), the street gang she "mothers," and the searchers find her "lying on an old army cot, naked, hair in disarray" (151). The seven-page sitcom parody Pynchon cut from the typescript (192–99) is part of the scene in the bar, where the three friends "sat and drank beers and watched a family situation comedy on television" (TS 192). One practical reason for getting rid of the sitcom might have been that it slows down the action relating to Fina, but as we have already suggested, Pynchon may have had more thematic reasons for deciding to leave it out.

The plot of the sitcom will sound familiar. Its stereotypical prosperous suburban nuclear family, the Marshalls, living the "safe and happy" consumerist "good life" (TS 196), actually consists of an ambitious but ultimately clueless white-collar father, an indulgent but quite controlling wife and mother, an egotistical teenage daughter (notably if implausibly buxom for her supposed fifteen years) with an adventure-seeking but still more clueless boyfriend, a "small obnoxious son" (TS 192), and even a hapless family dog. The mother firmly resists her husband's plan to move to the West Coast in pursuit of a promotion, and the daughter vehemently objects to her boyfriend's plan to go to South America in search of adventure and fortune. Despite the father's advice to the boyfriend to "[g]o home ... and stand up to [opposition] like a man" (TS 195), neither the father himself nor the boyfriend shows much backbone, and both their plans come to naught. The son, afflicted by the same "Wanderlust" (TS 194) as the older men, runs away from home but doesn't get far "out on the road" (TS 196) and is happy enough to be rescued and brought home by, of course, the boyfriend.[5]

Most of the New York storyline in *V.* is set in 1956, when family sitcoms were still relatively new, just as television itself was. This may explain why, a page or so into the episode, Pynchon's narrator feels the need to expound on the artificial merriment, in the form of canned laughter, added to the program: "The laughter was dubbed into the sound track, either from a real tape-recorded audience or from a machine Profane had read about in the Daily News a few days back. This was an all-electronic device which could duplicate various kinds of audience reaction, from applause to snickers to mob scenes to loud hysteria" (TS 193). Then a network executive is quoted explaining why all of this is so useful: "[T]he dramatic or comic impact of a production cannot be lessened by any improper audience reaction," and "the viewers at home will now get the full benefit of knowing what a large scale response is supposed to be," which will "aid ... their own appreciation" (TS 193). With its disdain for the dehumanization this technology implies, this passage and the allusions to it later in the episode are oddly moralistic, something Pynchon may also have realized while waiting for his editor's comments. Needless to say, if the passage had stayed in, *V.* would have looked more dated, perhaps already by the time it was published. The same is true of the description of the family's material luxury that opens the typescript episode: "A marvelous family it was. They lived in the suburbs and were at peace with their two cars, washing machine, clothes dryer, refrigerator, dishwasher, disposal unit, electric stove and television set. The things worked all the time. ... Every comic situation in this family arose from the actions of human beings, in accord with classical principles, and the appliances and objects were there only as willing and amiable servants to facilitate the plot's movement; no gods ever emerged from the machines" (TS 192). This is all very knowledgeable and nicely observed, but who needs to know? Talk about "ponderous," as Pynchon puts it in the March 13 letter to his editor. The sitcom parody as a whole may not fail as an instance of "Social Commentary," and it does manage to convey the silliness of this relatively new form of popular art, the television sitcom. But perhaps it is both too heavy handed and not silly enough to belong in a book that tries hard to avoid didacticism.

Pynchon's capitals in "Social Commentary" suggest a misplaced grandiosity, and, indeed, the sitcom story is presented by a narrator who holds himself above the lowly entertainment, not only by lampooning the show but also by explaining some of the unimaginative reactions of the watchers in the bar and by providing insights into the composition of the audience at large. Some of the narrator's comments are simple displays of knowledge, for instance, about prime time: "[Y]ou could be sure that kids watching coast to coast (it was prime listening time—before the hour, established by numerous surveys, when the normative American child is sent off to bed) were laughing as uproariously as the dubbed-in audience" (TS 193–94).[6] Other comments, however, suggest something more than innocent and wholesome entertainment. When the father dictates a letter at the office, his secretary's skirt is described as "tight and [riding] up a blond, healthy-looking pair of crossed thighs" (TS 194). The narrator is keen on parenthetically lifting the veil on the show: "This was a 'family' program, but surveys had pointed out that paperback books with erotically conceived covers and dealing exclusively with eccentric-sadistic sexual behavior sold best among men with wives and children. So to please the male segment of the families who watched families in comic situations, the net was opened wide enough to include the closed thighs of Bob's secretary, with the implication that what can be crossed can also be spread" (TS 194).[7] Earlier in the episode, when Sharon, the teenage daughter, stamps her foot "so hard it made her well-developed breasts shimmer alluringly" (TS 192), the expert narrator readily comments on Angel's admiration: "The usual shifting scale applied here: any girl character over the age of thirteen is played by an 18 year old actress. If the character is 18 or over, however, she can be played by anybody up to 40 plus. Sharon was supposed to be around 15" (TS 192–93). The narrator's connoisseurship reveals a commodifying interest in women Pynchon may have wanted to eliminate from the final version of his first novel in an attempt to distinguish between a more neutral narrative voice and the sexism of some of his male characters. However, further evidence from the sitcom episode complicates this suggestion.

If the narrator's desire to explain is over the top (and if it was perceived that way by Pynchon), the parody of the sitcom's story and its characters does reveal certain aspects of the genre that average viewers may not readily have recognized, especially if those viewers were eager to imitate the role models displayed on the screen. The parental roles are typical of those in family sitcoms of the fifties. Father works outside the home and is good at his job. He is the provider who knows it all (as in the series *Father Knows Best*). He solves the household's problems (albeit sometimes, as here in the typescript, after creating them himself) and amounts to the sympathetic manager of his little family unit. Mother is really a glorified servant who prepares food, does the cleaning, educates the children, and obeys her husband (although, again as here, she can be uppity, sarcastic, and the real brains of the family). Her role is perhaps best summarized in the opening sequence of *The Donna Reed Show*, in which the heroine answers the telephone and passes it on to her husband, hands the children their sweaters and lunches on their way to school, and then kisses her husband goodbye while helping him to his doctor's bag. Already in the 1950s, there are exceptions to this pattern: for instance, in *I Love Lucy*, Lucille Ball is always trying to convince her old-school husband that she needs a job in show business, and in *Ozzie and Harriet*, Ozzie often appears to be a wimp, while his wife, Harriet, occupies the power position. The parody in the *V.* typescript echoes these exceptions in that it questions the compatibility of the stereotypical roles, the tensions between which almost result in a crisis; but in the end, the dominant ideology prevails, and order of sorts returns.

The narrator seems to lament this outcome, even expressing a degree of frustration at the conclusion: "And the last dissolve left you looking in on a kind of collective love-feast, in which sexual identity wasn't really as important as Togetherness" (TS 199).[8] The narrator's problem with this outcome is not necessarily that "sexual identity" as such *should be* "important" but that the stereotypical sex roles and responsibilities that confuse the men in the episode are ultimately reaffirmed rather than undermined. This reaffirmation might not be sophisticated enough for the intellectual commentator the narrator clearly wants to be, and it might also hurt his own male gaze because the men lose in the episode's rivalry between the sexes. Or perhaps, on the other hand, the sitcom on the whole is not sexual enough for the narrator, and he does his best to compensate for the lack by commenting (albeit sophomorically) on the teenage daughter's breasts and the secretary's thighs. In the latter case the episode's conclusion would let the narrator down because it could have been much less mellow: it could have become the climax of a story that relates to the novel's V. figure at large through the erotically charged power the women in the family are seen to wield over their men, who are by no means sure of their own masculinity and might therefore need or desire women's control to negotiate their sexual attraction. Of course, this possible reading might be an overly dramatic interpretation of the effect of history as imagined by Stencil; roleplay in the family sitcom may hark back to a version of the past, but the genre's primary function of providing entertainment prevents it from having any meaningful impact on the present. If so, Pynchon may have cut the sitcom episode not because he wanted a neutral narrator for the 1956 plot but rather because he didn't want to trivialize Stencil's historiographical work. Then again, sitcoms may not be as banal as that interpretation makes them seem (cf., e.g., Olson and Douglas). If Pynchon had become more concerned with sitcoms' potential to indoctrinate (not merely to entertain, much less to subvert), his 1956 versions of V. would then be role models he might have decided not to feature because they were too cartoonish.

There is yet more evidence to consider. When Schuyler, the would-be adventurous boyfriend, replies to Sharon's angry "How can we ever get married if you'll be off for years and years wandering around in the jungle?" (TS 192) with a "morose ... 'Gee, ... I figured you'd wait for me'" (TS 193), Geronimo, the bartender, and even the canned audience laugh, presumably to underline the young man's naïveté about the power women hold over men. Everybody knows better, and nothing in the entire episode really challenges this conventional wisdom, which is, after all, as much of a cliché as the servant role of mothers in the average 1950s sitcom. Sharon "throw[s] a temper tantrum," and the narrator doesn't hesitate to spell things out: "It was Punch and Judy in reverse" (TS 193).[9] Sure enough, after the dictation scene in Bob's office, the family's "two females ... [discuss] the situation" (TS 194) by putting down the men: "The conversation was filled with all manner of wit ... : 'The best cure for an itchy foot is to cut it off,' and 'You'd think he was a cross-country bus, to hear him snore,' and 'About the only rooting your father does is when he's acting like a pig'" (TS 194–95).

The men's impotence is exposed during a scene in which they meet in town. Schuyler has been shopping for jungle clothes but "reveal[s] an all-embracing incompetency for dealing with the opposite sex in a fumbling speech about how confused he [is]" (TS 195) as a result of Sharon's reaction to his ambitious plans. "Bob admit[s] he [does]n't know much about women either" (TS 195), and when Schuyler learns that Bob hasn't yet gotten Betty (his wife) to agree to their making his career-related move, the two men find some comfort in each other: "'I didn't [persuade her],' said Bob, putting his arm around the lad's shoulders," and, mustering some courage, says they should "[g]o home ... and stand up to it like a man" (TS 195).

When Bob arrives home, he "find[s] his small son Chip with a duffel bag about to run away from home" (TS 196). He immediately acts the part of the wise suburban father, explaining to Chip "how in order to live the good life you had to stick around to enjoy it, and how the road"—"where bums lived" and "inanimate automobiles ... [ran] you down and kill[ed] you"—"was not like the street," which "was safe and happy," just like their home (TS 196). Having thought and dreamt about the street earlier in the typescript, Profane, watching television in the bar, finds this distinction "interesting" (TS 196), if not (we might assume) spurious, but the narrator stays with the sitcom story. Bob is apparently unaware of two things: the glaring contradiction between his own travel plans and the supposed wisdom he imparts to his son and the fact that, in true vaudeville fashion, the women of the family have hidden themselves behind the TV set (where else!) in order to overhear the conversation between Bob and Chip. Taking advantage of Bob's proclaimed values, Betty tries immediately to foreclose the matter of a move, and Sharon "ask[s] him to talk some sense into Schuyler too" (TS 197). Here is the chance for Bob to assert himself "like a man," but he only "blurt[s]" confusedly "that he was supposed to be going, the deal had gone through, that is if anybody didn't mind," and at that exact moment Schuyler enters "in a mountain-climbing costume" and asks confidently, "Did you give them the word yet, Mr. Marshall?" (TS 197).

Now "infuriated," the women "harangue their respective menfolk" and assert their own power, sending the men for that night literally to the doghouse, albeit an "air-conditioned" one (TS 197), much to the distress of the family's Irish setter, Clancy. When the men wake up, their conversation quickly turns to identity politics. Bob expresses a marked insecurity. "It's hard to figure out what a man is, these days," he says, and women make life difficult because "they ke[ep] changing their minds about what they [a]re" (TS 197). Since men, in Bob's mind, are supposed to be the opposite sex, they have to wait patiently for women to decide what they themselves are and then just "be the opposite" (TS 197). "Be the opposite" as a solution is so obviously shallow and rings so hollow coming from a wise father that it sounds like an admission of defeat. Is *that* all it turns out to mean to act "like a man" (to "be the opposite" of a woman, a strong, determined one at that)? Pynchon's calculated refusal to take this question more seriously suggests that he had already come to see its precisely gendered terms themselves as suspect. No peculiarly manlike and notably laudable behavior, whether as husband, lover, brother, friend, or even ordinary human being, is illustrated seemingly anywhere else in the novel. Instead, Profane kills alligators, Angel Mendoza beats his sister, Pig Bodine attempts to rape Paola, the Gaucho leads a mob of rioters, and Foppl murders Bondels.

Undeterred as well as unenlightened, Schuyler, however, doesn't give up immediately; he calls Sharon to say he is leaving for South America. But then both men quickly revert to type in connection with Chip, who had left the house with his duffel bag while everyone else was having the vehement and violent argument. Bob promises Betty he will turn down his new job because he has "realized it was better to stay here in Laurel Acres and live the good life than go out on the treacherous road, which may have done in his only son" (TS 198). It is only then, of course, that Schuyler and Chip can bring each other home, Schuyler having found Chip "sleeping by the side of the road," and Chip having convinced his sister's boyfriend not to go to South America by telling him "about the mosquitoes" (TS 198). So much for masculine bravery on the road. The women and Chip (who may or may not be too young to understand) have made sure stereotypical male behavior can be exercised only within the supposedly safe confines of the home and street. It is no coincidence that the episode has a scene or two in the doghouse, because the men's leash is very short indeed. If it does reach from the "safe and happy" home to the street at all, it most certainly does not stretch as far as the dangerous road, with its apparently excessive demands on masculinity.

In a letter of March 22, 1962, Cork Smith replies point by point to the changes Pynchon proposes in his letter of March 13. Here is what he says about the family sitcom: "I found the TV show in Chapter 12 (not Chapter 27) very entertaining. I did not read it as Social Commentary. I kind of wish you'd leave it in" (Stephen Tomaske Collection). A mere two days later, Pynchon acknowledges the chapter-number mistake but doesn't give in: "I will think again about retaining the TV program, which I don't find entertaining. If I decide to keep it, though, I'll act on your general guideline of keeping what is (in this case marginally) 'fresh and funny'" (Stephen Tomaske Collection).[10] The sarcasm here prefigures the reaffirmation of Pynchon's decision to cut the sitcom. His further thinking, however, may also have involved another change to the typescript he must already have been in the process of making. The image of woman in Pynchon's novel is controversial because the historical chapters in particular may seem to reduce women to manipulative temptresses bent on creating havoc, but the published version of *V.* contains an allusion to a female archetype that is not in the typescript and that prompts some more speculation about the deletion of the sitcom episode.

In his letter of February 23, Smith asks Pynchon to "give some indication (without insulting the reader's intelligence) that you are making a radical shift in time when you launch into 'Under the Roses [sic]'" (Stephen Tomaske Collection). Chapter 13 of the typescript, "Under the Rose," is the already revised version of the Pynchon short story with that title published in 1961. In response to Smith's remark, Pynchon writes on March 13 that he wants to put the chapter "someplace else." It became chapter 3 of the published novel. In addition, Pynchon created a transition within the chapter by writing a two-and-a-half-page introduction to the Egypt episode.[11] These pages have determined the direction of much *V.* criticism because of their appeal to famous examples of nonfiction that aspires to grand historical synthesis. In the new introduction to the chapter, the narrator describes Stencil's predicament as follows: "He would dream perhaps once a week that it had all been a dream, and that now he'd awakened to discover the pursuit of V. was merely a scholarly quest after all, an adventure of the mind, in the tradition of *The Golden Bough* or *The White Goddess*. But soon enough he'd wake up the second, real time, to make again the tiresome discovery that it hadn't ever stopped being the same simple-minded, literal pursuit" (61). Since Stencil awakes in "real time" to find that his pursuit is not even the kind of mere "scholarly quest" or "adventure of the mind" for which James G. Frazer and Robert Graves stand, it seems that these authors have been relegated to a state of being that is less real and therefore perhaps less relevant for an understanding of Stencil's historiographical enterprise than many readers have assumed. Indeed, the scholarly quests of Frazer and Graves seem to constitute a foil against which

Stencil's real quest or "simple-minded, literal pursuit" must be judged, and therefore they also relativize Stencil's image of woman as it may seem to derive from Frazer and especially from Graves.[12]

Both *The Golden Bough* and *The White Goddess* establish a basic pattern with respect to human history. In fact Graves built on Frazer, suggesting he was only rendering explicit Frazer's implication that the Christian tradition boils down to "the refinement of a great body of primitive and even barbarous beliefs" (242). Frazer had submitted that ancient religions were in fact fertility cults of a sacred king incarnating a solar deity who had engaged in a mystic marriage with a goddess of the earth. Graves considered this goddess the more basic of the two earthly figures and described her as a matrix for the many goddesses in various European mythologies. This led early Pynchon critic Joseph Slade to suggest that Pynchon borrowed the female V. from Graves, regarding her as "the principal archetype of our culture" (35), in order to show its specific perversion in the twentieth century. Graves included the element of degeneration in his analysis by suggesting that the language of poetic myth lost its magic when the early Greek philosophers turned their "back on the Moon-goddess who inspired [myths] and who demanded that man should pay woman spiritual and sexual homage" (11). Graves went on to suggest that major aspects of Western civilization had nevertheless been influenced by this figure, noticing, however, that "true poetry" (9) had been replaced early on by a "synthetic substitute" (10).

V. projects this essential disenchantment onto the goddess figure herself. The title character not only is an agent of inanimation but also becomes more and more inanimate herself, until finally being literally disassembled in 1943, or so the reader is led to presume on the basis of Fausto Maijstral's confessional letter (*V.* 342–45).[13] In the novel's contemporary culture, men are far less likely to prostrate themselves before woman or women than to objectify and try to dominate or otherwise exploit them. If Stencil's projection of V. is in part based on an outdated notion, he may cling to it in deference to his father, who wrote that "There is more behind and inside V. than any of us had suspected" (53). So he creates a "grand Gothic pile of inferences" (226) and a suitably monstrous, possibly mythical or possibly historical V. figure to inhabit it. He admits that V. is not necessarily a woman, a human being, or anything concretely real at all (226), but "even as a symptom" (386), his V. figure serves as a powerful metaphor (if still, to be sure, a tendentiously female one) for the dehumanized and dehumanizing culture of the novel's present. The various love (or at least erotic) interests in the New York chapters paint such a diverse picture of male attitudes that it becomes implausible to suppose Pynchon gives priority to the survival of the Western worship of woman or, for that matter, offers it as an answer to the sexual woes of Americans in the 1950s. If the White Goddess is Stencil's problem, she is not Pynchon's solution.

Eliminating the family sitcom reduced the number of powerful—read: domineering—women in the published novel. Maybe Pynchon wanted to limit their presence outside of Stencil's mind, or maybe he wanted simply to eliminate some obvious stereotypes. Either way, there is still room for female strength in Pynchon's fictional world. Indeed, before concluding that the published version of *V.* is misogynistic because it features an antiquated archetype of woman and/or many contemporary sexist stereotypes, we should remember that there is a very different kind of relatively strong woman character in the novel—relatively in the context of the novel's present—namely, Rachel Owlglass. Rachel is inclined, up to a point, to romanticize the rolling stone Profane, for whom she appears to have a genuine affection. She wants him as a friend before she takes him as a lover. The daughter of sheltering wealth and privilege, she longs to hear about "[y]our boy's road that I'll never see" (27), assuming he must know much about "the world" (26) she cannot know.[14] Paradoxically, she is also ready to take charge of him when given the opportunity, although Profane's sense of being subject to her "umbilical tug" on his yo-yo string (29) reveals more about him than about her. As much as Profane dreads encroachments of the inanimate, he wallows in his self-image as a schlemihl, "somebody who lies back and takes it from objects, like any passive woman" (288). In fact, he also takes it like a sponge. Rather than cultivate complicated human relationships, he prefers to be "an object of mercy" (137), and he does not necessarily appreciate a responsive sexual partner. He believes "[i]nanimate money was to get animate warmth" (214), but in the typescript he loses his desire for a prostitute when she responds energetically instead of remaining passive like his idea(l) of a virtual rape victim (see TS 169, and Herman and Krafft, "Monkey Business" 28). At one point Profane even fantasizes, "Someday, please God, there would be an all-electronic woman. Maybe her name would be Violet. Any problems with her, you could look it up in the maintenance manual" (385).

Profane might be content for Rachel only to feed him, to become the same kind of stereotypically indulgent, selfless, there-to-serve Jewish mother as his actual mother apparently is (see 222). We see his real mother only in the abundant evidence of her "compulsion to feed" (men's) literal appetite (379). After Profane loses his job, he refuses to take responsibility for "two dependents" (380), even though one of them is himself. But while Rachel does utter a few cringe-inducing lines, not all of which may be explainable as self-ironizing, she eventually refuses merely to serve, to sacrifice her dignity, her integrity, or her independence to try to hold on to Profane.[15] Thus the nuanced behavior of this real character contrasts notably with the enigmatic fantasies Stencil develops in the historical chapters.

We are sensitive to Hite's assertion that Pynchon in *V.* necessarily shares in the pervasive sexism of mid-twentieth-century U.S. culture and so is more apt to perpetuate the gender stereotypes of his time than to challenge them. But we do not assume Pynchon must subscribe to all the clichés his characters utter or enact, and we see him as (nearly) an equal-opportunity satirist: Paola Maijstral is no more Pynchon's "real woman" than Stencil's V. construct is, any more than the Randolph Scott Profane admires but cannot emulate (136–37) is Pynchon's "real man." We recognize the justice of Mary Allen's observations that weak male characters in U.S. fiction of the period rarely seem as vapid or unsympathetic as weak female characters and that men may even "project a kind of horrible blankness of the age onto the image of women, an idea epitomized in Pynchon's V." (7). Yet we note that Allen herself goes on to acknowledge that "the women of V. are as corrupted but at least as interesting as their male counterparts" (40). Likewise, Hawthorne observes on the one hand that "although [Pynchon] satirizes [extreme stereotypes of masculine domination], his satire itself is grounded in phallocentric attitudes" (81) and observes on the other hand that "few Second Wave Feminists drew a picture so demeaning of men in general" (83). Thus we argue for a certain undecidability or ambivalence in Pynchon's representations of men and women. In the case of the deleted sitcom, if we assume Pynchon understood that sitcoms were intended primarily for women, as Muriel G. Cantor says they were, we may infer either that his satire comes down at least a little more heavily on the men characters than on the women or that he skewers this form of popular entertainment as harshly, perhaps indeed as misogynistically, as he does Mafia Winsome's novels about "Heroic Love" (V. 125–26).[16]

If the sitcom parody had remained part of the novel, it might have provided an additional signal that the White Goddess was an antiquated, no longer viable notion. But its presence in the 1956 plot might also have complicated the issue, since there Pynchon seems intent on exhibiting a somewhat greater variety of gender roles. In any case, there was other "Social Commentary" in the sitcom that made him want to delete it, and the correspondence between Pynchon and Smith indicates that Pynchon did not regard the sitcom characters as particularly significant to the rest of the novel. In fact, his remark in the letter to Smith of March 24 (see n. 13) about the stuffed monkey in the "Millennium" chapter might imply that he was oblivious of any connection between the women of the sitcom and the V. figure in the historical chapters. But obviously, Pynchon's statements to Smith do not have to be taken as his only or definitive thoughts on the subject.

NOTES

1. Genetic criticism of Pynchon's fiction was once quite rare, consisting of studies of how the early short story "Under the Rose" (1961) was transformed into chapter 3 of V. (see Fowler, Martínez, Patteson, Seed); this changed when the complete typescript of V. in the Thomas Pynchon Collection became available in 2001. Especially

when analyzed alongside the correspondence between Pynchon and Corlies "Cork" Smith, his editor for *V.* at J. B. Lippincott, the typescript offers new insights into Pynchon's development as a young novelist. For more details, see Herman and Krafft, "Fast Learner."

2. The reference to the TV show as part of chapter 27 is a simple slip, as Pynchon himself acknowledges on March 24 in a letter we turn to near the end of this essay. All the other chapter numbers mentioned in the March 13 letter correspond to those of the typescript, where the TV show is part of chapter 12. Pynchon's "also" refers to the fact that in the first three points of his letter, he has announced other cuts, specifically of the chapters "Millennium" (10) and "No Man's Land" (16) and two long speeches (one by the Italian irredentist Sgherraccio and one by an African American patriarch) in chapter 23 of the typescript. For our discussion of "Millennium," see Herman and Krafft, "Monkey Business." The speech by the patriarch is considered in Herman and Krafft, "Race." The patriarch does not appear in the published novel, and only two references to Sgherraccio remain there (see Herman and Krafft, "Fast Learner" 8–9).

3. When we asked Smith in 2001 which protest novels or authors he might have meant here, he was quick to suggest James Baldwin, implying that Pynchon would have thought so as well. See also Herman and Krafft, "Race."

4. The time references in this sequence in the published novel, unlike those in the typescript, are confused, a fact Pynchon himself deplores in a March 9, 1963, letter to Faith and Kirkpatrick Sale (Thomas Pynchon Collection).

5. The son's name is Chip, which is also the name of the youngest character in the TV series *My Three Sons*; however, the episode "Chip Leaves Home," in which he runs away, first aired in January 1962, months after Pynchon had submitted the typescript to Lippincott. Still, the runaway motif was a familiar one: for instance, the *Leave It to Beaver* episode "Beaver Runs Away" aired in June 1958.

6. The reference to "prime listening time" rather than "prime viewing time" may be the slip of an author (born in 1937) who grew up during the so-called golden age of radio.

7. Later on, a commercial reinforces this psychological theory, and it also brings up an all too familiar motif: "The commercial had to do with something called a living brassiere. Profane had no idea what this might be. Animate/inanimate? Wha. The models looked all right, and the commercial was well received by those in the bar" (TS 195–96).

8. "Togetherness" is the title not only of the short article Pynchon wrote for *Aerospace Safety* in December 1960 but also of an episode of *Father Knows Best* that aired in January of the same year. This doesn't mean that Pynchon was inspired by *Father Knows Best*: he satirizes the concept of togetherness in passing in "The Small Rain" (1959) and in "Entropy" (1960) as well (*Slow Learner* 50, 91).

9. Sharon throws "stuffed animals" (TS 193) too, inanimate objects that connect with the stuffed monkeys owned by both Profane and an enigmatic young woman in the typescript chapter "Millennium," also removed from the published novel (see Herman and Krafft, "Monkey Business").

10. "Fresh and funny" is in quotation marks because Smith had used this phrase in his March 22 letter.

11. For a more detailed discussion of this revision, see Herman, "Pynchon's Appeal."

12. Another grand synthetic female figure is, of course, Henry Adams's Virgin. But while Graves's White Goddess informs the V. figure itself, the reference to Adams

also included in these new pages seems to connect with the form rather than with the content of Stencil's historiographical undertaking. In the typescript, Stencil's self-references are still in the first person. In the final version, all of them have been converted to third person, just like Adams's in *The Education*—a practice of self-reference the narrator likens in the new pages to that of "small children" and "assorted autocrats" (*V.* 62; see Herman, "Pynchon's Appeal" 293, 300).

13. In the typescript, as elucidated by Pynchon's March 24 letter to Smith, an avatar of V. has survived into the contemporary storyline: "It had been my fuzzy and half-assed intention to hint in the 'Millennium' chapter that V. had indeed progressed so far into the inanimate as to have become in 1955 (or whenever it was) a toy ape. However since Stencil never finds out about Profane's adventure with this ape, the point is not worth a whole chapter to make" (Stephen Tomaske Collection). See Herman and Krafft, "Monkey Business."

14. She overestimates him. Near the end of the novel, when Brenda Wigglesworth similarly assumes that "[b]oys do" "so much more" than girls do and asks almost enviously if he hasn't learned from "all these fabulous experiences," Profane answers, "No, ... offhand I'd say I haven't learned a goddamn thing" (454).

15. Profane realizes too late that he has lost New York's "one unconnable (therefore hi-valu) girl" (453).

16. The latter reading would seem to be supported by the distancing effect of the largely or exclusively male bar-audience's reactions.

WORKS CITED

Allen, Mary. *The Necessary Blankness: Women in Major American Fiction of the Sixties.* Urbana: University of Illinois Press, 1976.

Cantor, Muriel G. "Prime-Time Fathers: A Study in Continuity and Change." *Critical Studies in Mass Communication* 7.3 (1990): 275–85.

Fitzpatrick, Kathleen. "The Clockwork Eye: Technology, Woman, and the Decay of the Modern in Thomas Pynchon's *V.*" *Thomas Pynchon: Reading from the Margins.* Ed. Niran Abbas. Madison: Fairleigh Dickinson University Press, 2003. 91–107.

Fowler, Douglas. "Story into Chapter: Thomas Pynchon's Transformation of 'Under the Rose.'" *Journal of Narrative Technique* 14.1 (1984): 33–43.

Freer, Joanna. *Thomas Pynchon and American Counterculture.* New York: Cambridge University Press, 2014.

Graves, Robert. *The White Goddess: A Historical Grammar of Poetic Myth.* Rev. ed. New York: Farrar, 1966.

Hardack, Richard. "Revealing the Bidder: The Forgotten Lesbian in Pynchon's *The Crying of Lot 49.*" *Textual Practice* 27.4 (2013): 565–95.

Hawthorne, Mark D. "A 'Hermaphrodite Sort of Deity': Sexuality, Gender, and Gender Blending in Thomas Pynchon's *V.*" *Studies in the Novel* 29.1 (1997): 74–93.

Herman, Luc. "Pynchon's Appeal to the Canon in the Final Version of *V.*" *Reading without Maps? Cultural Landmarks in a Post-Canonical Age: A Tribute to Gilbert De Busscher.* Ed. Christophe Den Tandt. Brussels: Peter Lang, 2005. 291–303.

Herman, Luc, and John M. Krafft. "Fast Learner: The Typescript of Pynchon's *V.* at the Harry Ransom Center in Austin." *Texas Studies in Literature and Language* 49.1 (2007): 1–20.

———. "Monkey Business: The Chapter 'Millennium' Removed from an Early Version of *V.*" *Dream Tonight of Peacock Tails: Essays on the Fiftieth Anniversary of Thomas*

Pynchon's V. Ed. Paolo Simonetti and Umberto Rossi. Newcastle upon Tyne: Cambridge Scholars, 2015. 13–30.

———. "Race in Early Pynchon: Rewriting Sphere in *V.*" *Critique* 52.1 (2011): 17–29.

Hite, Molly. "When Pynchon Was a Boys' Club: *V.* and Midcentury Mystifications of Gender." *Thomas Pynchon, Sex, and Gender*. Ed. Ali Chetwynd, Joanna Freer, and Georgios Maragos. Athens: University of Georgia Press. 2018. 3–18.

Martínez, M. Angeles. "From 'Under the Rose' to *V.*: A Linguistic Approach to Human Agency in Pynchon's Fiction." *Poetics Today* 23.4 (2002): 633–56.

Medoro, Dana. "Traces of Blood and the Matter of a Paraclete's Coming: The Menstrual Economy of Pynchon's *V.*" *Pynchon Notes* 44–45 (1999): 14–34.

Olson, Beth, and William Douglas. "The Family on Television: Evaluation of Gender Roles in Situation Comedy." *Sex Roles* 36.5 (1997): 409–27.

Patteson, Richard F. "How True a Text? Chapter Three of *V.* and 'Under the Rose.'" *Southern Humanities Review* 18.4 (1984): 299–308.

Pynchon, Thomas. *Slow Learner*. Boston: Little, Brown, 1984.

———. Thomas Pynchon Collection. Harry Ransom Humanities Research Center, University of Texas at Austin.

———. "Togetherness." *Aerospace Safety* 16.12 (1960): 6–8.

———. *V.* New York: Lippincott, 1963.

Seed, David. *The Fictional Labyrinths of Thomas Pynchon*. Iowa City: University of Iowa Press, 1988.

Slade, Joseph W. *Thomas Pynchon*. New York: Peter Lang, 1990.

Stephen Michael Tomaske Memorial Collection of Thomas Pynchon. Huntington Library, San Marino, California.

Stimpson, Catharine R. "Pre-Apocalyptic Atavism: Thomas Pynchon's Early Fiction." *Mindful Pleasures: Essays on Thomas Pynchon*. Ed. George Levine and David Leverenz. Boston: Little, Brown, 1976. 31–47.

"Homer Is My Role Model"
Father-Schlemihls, Sentimental Families, and Pynchon's Affinities with *The Simpsons*

JEFFREY SEVERS

> Sorry, guys. Homer is my role model and I can't speak ill of him.
> —THOMAS PYNCHON, annotating his edits to a *Simpsons* script

As every Pynchon obsessive knows, while photographs and video of the man remain scarce, Pynchon's voice has been, relatively speaking, all over the mass media in the early twenty-first century. He provided the voice-over to the "book trailer" for *Inherent Vice* in 2008, and we knew the gravelly voice was his mainly because of his two 2004 cameos on *The Simpsons*, TV's longest-running scripted series, now nearly six hundred episodes into its run. The writer lent his voice to the episodes "Diatribe of a Mad Housewife" (wearing a bag over his head, he reviewed Marge's novel and offered passersby a chance to get their picture taken "with a reclusive author") and "All's Fair in Oven War" (again with the bag on his head, he judged Marge's cooking as "V-licious!"). My epigraph—from Twitter images shared by the writer of the latter episode, Matt Selman—arises in the margins of a script as Pynchon's justification of inserting some super-corny jokes (regarding, for example, "The Frying of Latke 49") while crossing out lines about Homer being "such a fat-ass" (@MattSelman). In this inside peek, Pynchon expresses an attachment not just to the show's general vision but to the bumbling Homer in particular, his "role model."

In this chapter, I argue that this line is much more than an off-the-cuff quip. Pynchon's work, especially in *Vineland* and after, converges with *The Simpsons* (which began its run in late 1989, just weeks before *Vineland*'s publication) on several key points, particularly regarding masculinity, family, and sentimentalism. I suggest too that in *Bleeding Edge*—his first novel set in a time when *The Simpsons* is on the air—he not only makes explicit allusions to the show but slyly refers to central characters in naming the large, boorish father Horst (a nod to *H*omer) and the long-suffering, morally minded mother Maxine (a tribute to *Marge*), parents to two outspoken children, Ziggy and

Otis, who at times echo Bart and Lisa. There is a passing reference to "Marge Simpson hair" (322), and Pynchon even invents a *Simpsons* episode titled "*D.O.H.*," after Homer's catchphrase (316). But it is Horst Loeffler in particular, a sometimes troublingly violent father, who has Homer as his direct "role model." Like Homer, Horst is distinguished by his TV watching and appetite: in his first scene in the 2001 plot, raiding the fridge and displaying "a dowser's gift specific to Ben & Jerry's ice cream," he "brings out a semicrystallized quart of Chunky Monkey" and, with "an oversize spoon in each hand, [...] digs in," the "extra spoon" being for "mooshing it up" (92). Diners, steaks, and takeout menus are other areas of his expertise. Horst, a financial expert whose name literally means "man from the forest," is a smarter, somewhat more refined Homer, the donut, sandwich, and beer aficionado who stands in the kitchen with a tub of ice cream and says, "Marge, where's that ... metal dealy ... you use to dig food?" ("Bart's Friend Falls in Love").

Why does Pynchon pay tribute? Aside from largely sharing Pynchon's sense of humor, the cartoon has an ethos that matches up well with his post-*Vineland* output, particularly in balancing aggressive satire with family-centered sentimentalism. As Joanna Freer argues, "from *Vineland* onwards the basic tenor of [Pynchon's] writing is sentimental," and this later Pynchon "comes to view the family as a social ideal and even as a last bastion of *communitas* in self-interested times" (144). *The Simpsons* and the post-*Vineland* Pynchon follow similar paths in portraying family roles, I argue: their stumbling, outlandish schlemihls are faced (whether twenty minutes into a madcap episode or twenty-five years into a career) with growing up (some) and taking on parental and social responsibility. Here, after first defining the postmodern stylistic traits Pynchon's fiction and the cartoon share, I trace the maturation and chastening of Pynchon's schlemihl figure through *Vineland*'s Zoyd Wheeler before turning to the resemblance of Homer to both Zoyd and Horst, pointing out along the way the resistance of both Pynchon's families and *The Simpsons* to the simplifying, right-wing discourse of "family values" in the early 1990s. I also analyze female characters (such as Maxine and March Kelleher) in *Simpsons* terms while suggesting why Simpsonian masculinity, especially in its contradictory qualities, does certain ideological work for Pynchon's cartoon/human hybrids. Ultimately I contend that Pynchon's long-term identification with Homer and his clan helps illuminate a mode of familial and patriarchal recuperation at work in the author's novels—a mixing of satire of traditional family roles with the safe reinscription of those same roles. On the evidence of *Vineland, Mason & Dixon, Against the Day*, and *Bleeding Edge*, it seems undeniable that, as Kathryn Hume argues, family is to Pynchon, in an otherwise grim world, "a forgiving and supportive and flexible network," "a support system that avoids control" (Hume 9, 10). But viewing *The Simpsons* and Pynchon together helps make family and the home not signs of the novelist's capitulation to a certain suspect solace but complex sites all their own, zones featuring a mixture of irony, cynicism, sentimentality, and patriarchal assertion and with a particular relevance to the post-9/11 political situation and cultural response that *Bleeding Edge* probes.

To begin, Pynchon's works and *The Simpsons* clearly have much in common stylistically. Utterly digressive and farcical plotting, relentless parody, shallow (yet still sharp) characterization, zany reference making, the removal of all barriers between high and low cultures, merciless satires of mainstream stances, a self-consciousness about mediation and simulation, a core set of leftist humanist values, and low puns with high magic—in all these respects, Pynchon's novels and the TV show offer the example par excellence of postmodern techniques for their respective media. Regularly playing irony to the hilt, both writer and show relentlessly filter their portrayals through generic conventions. Interpreting the subversive effects of its rampant intertextuality, Jonathan Gray argues that *The Simpsons* constantly exploits "genre literacy" (30–33) in its audience, and Brian McHale characterizes Pynchon's work as an act, particularly intense in *Against the Day*, of "genre poaching" ("Genre as History"). From allusions to *Rear Window* when Bart is bedbound with a broken leg in "Bart of Darkness" to the glory that is a musical version of *The Planet of the Apes* in "A Fish Called Selma" (to cite merely two of countless examples), rare is the *Simpsons* plot that does not in some way mimic and mock the moves of a classic film, TV show, or entire lowbrow genre. Pynchon's genre parodies (such as the "cute meet" of Jessica and Roger in *Gravity's Rainbow* [39] or the turn-of-the-century boys' adventure books spoofed in *Against the Day*) are more often evocative of entire genres rather than specific works, and Pynchon's genre allusions require much more historical digging (or recourse to a reader's guide). But they are, as McHale comprehensively demonstrates, the currency of Pynchon's fiction and his way of accessing historical reality from *Gravity's Rainbow* forward.

Pop cultural references do not exhaust the common ground. As Simon Singh demonstrates in *The Simpsons and Their Mathematical Secrets*, among the show's writers have been many with graduate-level backgrounds in higher math and science (Ken Keeler has a PhD in applied mathematics and worked at Bell Laboratories, and David X. Cohen has an MS in computer science, for example), and there are dozens of episodes littered with rather esoteric puns, mathematical paradoxes, and jokes about things like the digits of pi ("mmm, pie," as Homer would say) (Singh). As is well known, Pynchon—former engineering physics major, technical writer for Boeing, and one-time aspiring mathematics grad student—is heavily invested in math and science and their metaphorical potential. Groening's follow-up to *The Simpsons*, *Futurama*, debuted in 1999 and, with its time-travel plot and oddball ensemble of robots, aliens, and crackpot scientists, resembles *Against the Day* in a few ways—a sign not of any direct influence but of a mutual high regard for *Star Trek*, time travel, and other science fiction references.

Pynchon's body of work and *The Simpsons* share some basic political aims as well. As Chris Turner notes in *Planet Simpson*, "Several of the show's creators are on record—repeatedly—as saying that the main goal of *The Simpsons*, beyond making its fans laugh, is to inculcate them with a strong distrust of authority" (10)—primary Pynchonian goals as well. And perhaps there are Pynchon/*Simpsons* affinities too, in their respective receptions as they have aged, after early, magnificently jolting peaks of social critique: there is a popular perception that Pynchon's work has been in decline since *Gravity's Rainbow*, a view often supported by the claim that a turn toward the refuge of family indicates Pynchon has gone "soft" or lost his edgy anger. It is also an established narrative among (certain) fans that, since what Turner calls its "Golden Age" of "early 1992 to mid-1997," *The Simpsons* has lost much of its political mojo too, as well as its cultural centrality (4).

In terms of gender, there is a clear point of intersection on the Venn diagram of male characters in Pynchon and *The Simpsons*: schlemihls. This cosmic fool of fortune, derived from Jewish literature, is Pynchon's explicit term for Benny Profane in *V.* ("a schlemihl and human yo-yo" [1]), the implied one for Tyrone Slothrop in *Gravity's Rainbow*, and an oft-cited reference point in critical work. The schlemihl is a kind of cousin to the preterite, the cousin who leavens the misery of human suffering with pratfalls. David Buchbinder, reviewing twentieth- and twenty-first-century masculinities, names Homer as a prime example of a schlemihl, alongside film characters portrayed by Charlie Chaplin, Ben Stiller, and Jon Heder (better known as Napoleon Dynamite) (161). Homer's incompetence with objects is occasion for many a set piece, and his lax approach to safety at the Springfield Nuclear Power Plant is an endless source of (often apocalyptic) humor. His trademark phrase, "D'oh!," is a verbal accompaniment to accident, to an animate creature running "afoul of the inanimate" (*V.* 308). From Lardass Levine (of "The Small Rain") forward, Pynchon's schlemihls are usually pudgy too, a nod to the waistline-expanding pull of personal entropy and the power of craven appetites. Buchbinder calls the schlemihl in contemporary culture "an inadequately or incompetently masculine male," "a man who seems constitutionally incapable of being masculine according to the current norms of the culture" (161). Here, Homer is a more classic schlemihl, for there is generally little or no menace in the schlemihl's masculinity: passivity, incompetence, and a lack of control are his trademarks. Pynchon's schlemihls, by contrast, do have a terrifying tendency to turn toward aggression and fascism—Slothrop's sex scenes with Greta and Bianca in the Zone are one example—but this mainly points to the greater depths of psychological insight Pynchon can achieve in his compendia of comic lightness, dark excess, and meditations on moral agency, features I probe in greater detail in my reading of *Horst*.

It is with *Vineland* that the connections between cartoon and novelistic schlemihls first begin to take on a more richly conflicted texture. Let me project a world: Pynchon, ready to rejoin the literary world when *Vineland*, his first new novel in seventeen years, is published in January 1990, tunes in right at the beginning of *The Simpsons*' run, on December 17, 1989, the night the first full-length episode was aired (over the course of the preceding two years, Groening had provided short segments for *The Tracey Ullman Show*). What does Pynchon see? Regardless of when exactly he became a fan of the show (which was an early hit for Fox, a new network), it is difficult to imagine Pynchon not noticing some uncanny convergences with his latest novel. *Vineland* marked Pynchon's turn toward television as a major vehicle for the parodic impulse that he had explored through spy fiction in *V.* and through cinema in *Gravity's Rainbow*, and *The Simpsons* depends heavily on references to (mostly live) TV shows, down to the parody of the sitcom family that is inherent to the show's structure. As McHale writes in summary, *Vineland*'s characters are "preoccupied with conforming their lives to TV models" and speak often in TV's "idioms" (*Constructing* 118–19).

Pynchon's turn in *Vineland* toward more generally stable domestic scenes and parenting issues—those staples of sitcom life—also marks an affinity with *The Simpsons*. Zoyd Wheeler is in several senses a Pynchonian schlemihl: in the opening chapter he has a run-in with an inanimate window (if in scripted fashion), and Pynchon links him with the contingencies of the wheel of fortune through both his surname and a reference to the game show (12–13). Yet Zoyd is no Profane or Slothrop: while the latter two man-children ricochet around their respective novels as sexual adventurers engaging in relationships devoid of intimacy, Zoyd faces many advanced emotional problems and responsibilities. Through Zoyd Pynchon begins asking the question, What happens when the schlemihl grows up and becomes a parent? Gone are the distant, betraying figures of Sidney Stencil and Broderick Slothrop, who influence their sons' minds from afar but have no real presence. Ascendant is a newly intimate take on intergenerational linkages. Gone too is the sordid psychosexual dynamic of Franz Pökler in relation to Ilse. Zoyd is beset not just by paranoia and battles with a police state but the exigencies of single parenthood. In many senses he is both mother and father to Prairie; his appearance in drag in the opening reads as a gag, fulfillment of his attempt to appear "insane-looking enough for the mental-health folks," but also as a comment on the positive feminizing Pynchon's schlemihl has undergone (4).[1] Zoyd's is a world of teenage-daughter sarcasm, fatherly tenderness, and "always [. . .]

his love for Prairie, burning like a night-light, always nearby, cool and low, but all night long" (42).

An insight of Frenesi into adulthood applies even more readily to Zoyd, who cares for Prairie when her mother takes off: Frenesi has moved "further into adulthood perilous and real, into the secret that life is soldiering, that soldiering includes death, that those soldiered for, not yet and often never in on the secret, are always, at every age, children" (216). Unraveling the question of Prairie's parenthood, a Darth Vader–like Vond asserts to Prairie near the end that he, "[n]ot Wheeler," is "[y]our real Dad" (376), but whatever the truth of this assertion, readers recognize that Vond's paternity claims wither in the context of Zoyd's ardent adult soldiering for Prairie. Vond's Vader-like claims are functionally part of his imperialist program of infantilizing governance and surveillance, his exploitation of the "deep . . . need" of former flower children "only to stay children forever, safe inside some extended national Family" (376, 269).

Reducing the complex U.S. populace to a "national Family" of impressionable children was a moralizing effort of right-wing politicians throughout the 1980s and early 1990s, both captured and anticipated by *Vineland* and reaching a high (or low?) point in Vice President Dan Quayle's infamous May 19, 1992, remarks about the scandalizing of "family values" wrought by the depiction of single motherhood on TV's *Murphy Brown*. Quayle's speech and *Murphy Brown* go down in history for that phrase, "family values," but throughout the 1992 campaign President George H. W. Bush had taken many other shots in this ideological war by invoking *The Simpsons*. At the Republican National Convention in August 1992 he called on a line from his stump speech once again, stating his resolve "to strengthen the American family, to make American families a lot more like the Waltons and a lot less like the Simpsons" (1371). The line attests to the barbed prominence of the cartoon in the early 1990s media environment but also embodies a thorough misreading of it in terms of underlying sentimentality. Matthew A. Henry responds to the "family values" critique of *The Simpsons* by calling its definition of the concept "much more authentic" than that of the right-wing critics: on the show, "'family values' most often means mutual respect and deep compassion for the other members of the family unit," a resolve on the part of Marge and Homer "to remain together and work through their differences" (44). Brattiness, bad parenting, and mockery of familial, marital, and communal happiness may suffuse a *Simpsons* episode, but by its end the family does often emit a bit of a Waltons glow. Slightly more distanced and critical, Paul A. Cantor, writing in 1999, summarizes the show's overall pattern: "For all its slapstick nature and its mocking of certain aspects of family life, *The Simpsons* [. . .] ends up celebrating the nuclear family as an institution" (735–36). Freer suggests that family is a vehicle for *communitas* in Pynchon's work, and Cantor sees the family politics of *The Simpsons* extending outward to a civic vision of Springfield, the American everytown: "The show celebrates genuine community [...]. By recreating this older sense of community, the show manages to generate a kind of warmth out of its postmodern coolness" (745).

Pynchon readers will see a parallel with his own late-career retreat into the warmth of family reunions and limited communities after early work redolent with "postmodern coolness" (a phrase that echoes the distanced affect in the line often invoked as a credo of the early Pynchon, "Keep cool but care" [*V.* 394]). With *The Simpsons*, the combination of attempts to *épater les bourgeois* and reinforce "family values" is based not in a midcareer shift so much as a drive to push the envelope and then fall back on the mores of traditional resolution within each frenetically paced episode. Homer's boorishness and other masculinist transgressions, for instance, almost always come with an expected safety valve. In "'We're All Pigs': Representations of Masculinity in *The Simpsons*," Karma Waltonen argues that Homer begins many episodes "embod[ying] all that is bad about patriarchy and masculinity" (or, for Pynchonians, all that is Seaman Pig Bodine) but comes closer, by the end of the episodes, to being "the early-twenty-first-century liberal, sensitive man" (par. 1).

Consider the tensions in the first episode in which Pynchon appeared, "Diatribe of a Mad Housewife." In the first few minutes Homer, having crashed his car, buys an ambulance and goes into business as its driver without consulting Marge. When she wants time off from child care to work on the novel Pynchon will later endorse, Homer responds, "Slow down, Picasso! You were gonna start a novel without informing me?" The novel, *The Harpooned Heart*, scandalizes Springfield with its portrayal of Marge's longings for Ned Flanders beneath the guise of her protagonist's preference for "Cyrus Manley" over the "brute" (i.e., Homer) she has married. Upon publication, Homer is revealed to the town as a "cuckolded boob" who, when he kills Manley in the book, triumphantly announces he is now "free to be selfish, drunk, emotionally distant, [and] sexually ungenerous." But in a typically unlikely resolution, rather than attack Flanders in real life, Homer learns from him to be a more sensitive husband, getting, he says, the "wake-up call I needed." Homer and Marge end the episode with their marital bond restored. However, in accordance with laws of sitcom seriality (heightened by the cartoon framework), this restoration does not last the week; as Waltonen notes, by the start of every new episode Homer returns "to his beginnings," lessons "unlearned" (par. 1).

By contrast, Pynchon, as a novelist, offers resolutions that leave families and marriages in a reintegrated state. To address the full implications of that movement toward familial recuperation and its relation to the politics of American responses to 9/11, let me now turn my attention fully to *Bleeding Edge*. Pynchon's central families have often been marked by nomadism, disintegration, and other destabilizing forces, some impossible to overcome in realistic terms: Frenesi and Prairie are thoroughly alienated from one another for many years in *Vineland*; Mason longs for his dead wife throughout *Mason & Dixon*; and the Traverses of *Against the Day*, true to their name, tramp independently around the globe after the death of their father. Only in *Bleeding Edge* does a family sit long enough to have its (largely comedic) portrait done—and for the situations of situation comedy to develop.

While the novel's direct allusions to *The Simpsons* may seem on the surface just attempts to flesh out its attention to turn-of-the-millennium child culture, which includes allusions to video games and Beanie Babies, the book to some degree understands itself through its affinity with *The Simpsons*. Ziggy and Otis, Maxine's sons (wise beyond their years and sassy, but perhaps not to Bart's and Lisa's levels), play a graphically violent video game with their friend Fiona involving the massacre of "yup[s]" that evokes the gratuitous violence of *The Simpsons*' cartoon within a cartoon, *The Itchy and Scratchy Show* (34). On another occasion, "Otis, Ziggy, and Fiona settle in in front of Homer Simpson, playing an accountant of all things, in a film noir, or possibly jaune, called '*D.O.H*'"—a play on the 1950 classic of the genre, *D.O.A.*, which focuses on an accountant and notary (316). No such *Simpsons* episode exists, and here we see Pynchon, as in my epigraph, rewriting the show to make it even more to his liking and bend it to his purposes. Maxine will play the role of accountant in the text's own version of *D.O.A.* and of film noir, but a film "jaune"—a reference to the yellow bodies ubiquitous in *The Simpsons*—also captures some of Pynchon's tendency toward mixing the wacky, brightly colored, and cartoonish with the dark grittiness and mostly humorless preoccupation with corruption and sick societies in the film genre. While cartoon and comics references are nothing new in the Pynchonverse, in *Bleeding Edge*, where the primary alternate world depends on computer animation and pixelated avatars for finding the right angles at which to depart from received reality, connections to cartoons take on a new importance.

In the Horst/Homer overlaps and divergences, though, lie the novel's most intense and intriguing grappling with the cartoon's influence. Horst's appetites and aggressions are more than just setups for gags and Pynchon's usual food humor; Horst is offensive, insensitive, and even violent. "Fuckin Horst" says to Maxine, "you're Jewish right?" when telling his then-girlfriend about Jewish fraudsters, adding with a hint of anti-Semitism, "Thought you might have a rapport" (24). Horst is not a Major Marvy or Doctor Hilarius, perhaps, but his sharing a name with Nazi martyr Horst Wessel, in combination with these traits, suggests some Nazi tendencies among average American males, a longtime Pynchon assertion. Later, more shockingly, Maxine writes off an incident in which Horst "started choking" her in the midst of an argument, relaxing his grip only when he is distracted by televised football and beer retrieval (215). Maxine's tolerance of such abuse is an awkward narrative ploy to set up her attraction to Windust and make it plausible by confirming her weakness for fascists, as Pynchon did with Frenesi and Vond in *Vineland*. There, TV's cop shows—specifically *CHiPs*, to which Frenesi enjoys masturbating (83)—are, Pynchon implies, the gateway through which a real-life adoration of fascists enters: with *CHiPs* playing, screen and screen door merge for Frenesi, and "there outside on the landing, through the screen, broken up into little dots like pixels of a video image, [. . .] was this large, handsome U.S. Marshall" in uniform (84).

When *Bleeding Edge* revisits this troubling topos, TV's Homer is, strangely, a key mediating and mollifying figure in the chain of violent masculinities and woman-blaming moments. About thirty pages before Horst's strangling is recounted, Maxine parses a similar event in terms of *Simpsons* characters: her "fascination" with Latrell Sprewell, a pro basketball player for the Knicks who famously choked his coach, is based, she thinks, "on the principle that Homer strangling Bart we expect, but when Bart strangles Homer . . ." (181). Pynchon seems to have a particular affection for this feature of Homer's parenting, which is more often criminal by way of its negligence than its direct abusiveness. *Against the Day*, the 2006 novel that followed his *Simpsons* appearances, makes one of its many anachronistic references when Lindsay Noseworth blurts a Homer-like "Why you insufferable little—" during one of his apparently "constant attempts to strangle" the insouciant young (and Bart-like?) Darby Suckling (409). With the Chums of Chance, who are impervious to aging and mortality, the violence is more properly cartoonish than it is disturbing. Made a part of Maxine's reckoning with her marriage, though, Homer's choking becomes a moment when Pynchon's parodic impulse to attenuate the human clashes with not just feminist reading practices but the expectations of nuanced psychological realism that much else in Maxine's portrayal creates.

Focused on Homer as complex "role model," I have largely left Marge out of the discussion, but *Bleeding Edge* is the Pynchon novel that devotes the greatest number of pages to the vicissitudes of mothering. There are really two mothers to consider, both with Ma(r)—names that seem intentionally evocative of Marge, the definition of a long-suffering wife and mother. While Frenesi in *Vineland* is largely a failure as a parent to Prairie, Maxine is dynamic on all fronts, functioning as the novel's moral center in her quest to expose Ice, Windust, and the 9/11 plot and in her protection of her family. Marge Simpson, too, often ends up enforcing moral duties and reintegrating the family unit when they take it off the rails or ignore her insight. The longtime activist March Kelleher, divorced mother of Tallis and mother-in-law to Gabriel Ice, is even more of a righteous moral crusader, introduced as one ready to spray Easy-Off oven cleaner in the face of corrupt landlords (55) and the most viscerally left wing of the characters. March relates a parable about an old street woman and the waste of the world that illuminates much in the book's ethical stance, and she is hugely invested in protecting her grandson Kennedy. March is a kind of DL to Maxine's Frenesi, an older DL with deep ties to family. Pynchon also grants to March what sound like many of his own opinions about New York and U.S. life, as when she calls out the "fucking fascists who call the shots" for keeping "everything ugly and brain-dead" (56–57).

There is no strong match here, admittedly: March is too aggressive to be a Marge, Maxine has too much depth, and the political conflicts of *Bleeding Edge* are far more realistic and intractable than those of Springfield. But the most important element of this constellation of *Simpsons* associations is the recuperative role played by a reductive and compensatory family sentimentalism in *Bleeding Edge*, made visible if we take a step back and take in the broad outlines of strategically deployed irony and sentimentality in a traumatized culture. In the last third of the book, in the wake of 9/11, the reserves of sentiment the novel has built up begin to function for their creator, giving him a local family underplot to support the larger story of New York's and the U.S.'s recovery. Such plotting has become de rigeur in a large swath of 9/11 literature: Don DeLillo's *Falling Man*, for instance, features Keith Neudecker instinctively returning to his estranged wife after surviving the attack on the towers. Jonathan Safran Foer's *Extremely Loud and Incredibly Close* centers on a nine-year-old boy mourning his father's death in the towers and simultaneously exonerating him from suspected infidelity. Elizabeth Anker, surveying the compromised men of DeLillo's, Foer's, and many other novels of 9/11, argues that the genre in U.S. literature has proven reactionary, reflecting a "longing to return to a bygone era of American omnipotence wherein white, heteronormative, patrician masculinity was still sacrosanct" (468). Anker argues that these narratives explore "the fractured American self-image" after 9/11 "through the insecurities of white, upper-middle-class manhood" (468).

Bleeding Edge, while told from the perspective of a woman, invests in some of these same regressive patterns, forming its subliminal response to 9/11 by seeking to resecure a nuclear family with the children's biological father at its head, the bygone structure on which the novel lavishes attention. For instance, in a relatively gratuitous subplot designed to heighten the emotional stakes of the combination of Maxine's role as detective and parent, young Ziggy is targeted after 9/11, only to be saved by his krav maga teacher. The novel is obviously bookended by parallel scenes of parenting and, in the end, parental helplessness, as Maxine's sons head to school on their own, down the elevator (a technology meant to symbolically restore the fallen towers and the many victims who could not descend). "The only question it's come down to is, where will Ziggy and Otis be protected from harm?" Maxine ruminates, offering a think-of-the-children ideology that seems out of sync with Pynchon's usual complexities on the subject of identifying and saving the innocent (412).

The reader of *Bleeding Edge* knows 9/11 is on its way for the first three hundred plus pages, and in this light, some of Pynchon's moves register as an attempt to offer a kind of affective defense of the nation before the attacks come. A month before 9/11 is due to arrive, as Horst and his sons go on a trip to visit his parents, the reader is thus primed with a nostalgic portrait of the interior of the country and of solid family structures (more of Anker's "bygone era"). Here, as Horst the trader moves from exchange to exchange on "a tour down memory lane" in Chicago, Pynchon soaks the prose in a strangely sentimental vision of his financial career magically transforming the abstractions of the commodity trading floor into involvement in the material world, strains of "America the Beautiful" and its amber waves of grain seemingly swelling in the background as Horst goes from "Eurodollar activity" to American products:

> For a while he shifted to Treasuries, but soon, as if answering some call from deep in the tidy iterations of Midwest DNA, he had found his way into the agricultural pits, and next thing he knew, he was out in deep American countryside, inhaling the aroma from handfuls of wheat, scrutinizing soybeans for purple seed stain, walking through fields of spring barley squeezing kernels and inspecting glumes and peduncles, talking to farmers and weather oracles and insurances adjusters—or, as he put it to himself, rediscovering his roots. (289)

Here the man of the forest expresses a wistfulness for the land and seems to block out the transnational complications that will envelop the United States (and its economy) in a few weeks, when the symbolic center of American financialization and capital is attacked. This farmland elegy takes on an especially political cast if we connect it to an earlier scene of Horst the trader with his sons in his office at a portentously swaying World Trade Center. Love of native landscape combines with love of multigenerational family "roots" here, with light again serving as a key symbol of familial ardor: "The Loeffler grandfolks, all through their visit, were over the moon, the specifically Iowa moon, which from the front porch was bigger than any moon the boys had ever seen," and a better spectacle than "what they might've been missing on the tube" (290). Such passages serve some of the same purposes as passages describing the Traverse family reunion in *Vineland*, where fulsome quotations from Emerson, communal meals, and family reintegration are the implied antidote to what Pynchon calls the "prefascist twilight" in which the United States lingers (371). Thirty pages after the Loeffler males' trip, the attacks draw them and other families back together: at school, with Horst along, "Maxine notices other sets of parents, some who haven't spoken for years, showing up together to escort their children" (321).

Such sentimental writing in *Bleeding Edge* needs to be seen as a counterbalance to the book's explicit defense of an opposing mode within U.S. culture: irony, that technique that thoroughly links Pynchon's work in general to *The Simpsons*. Addressing a cultural debate of late 2001, *Bleeding Edge* makes a strong rhetorical case for the survival of irony post-9/11, voiced through Heidi the cultural studies scholar. An article she is writing proposes that

> irony, assumed to be a key element of gay humor and popular through the nineties, has now become another collateral casualty of 11 September because it somehow did not keep the tragedy from happening. "As if somehow irony," [Heidi] recaps for Maxine, "as practiced by a giggling mincing fifth column, actually brought on the events of 11 September, by keeping the country insufficiently serious—weakening its grip on 'reality.' So all kinds of make-believe—forget the delusional state the country's in already—must suffer as well. Everything has to be literal now." (335)

Heidi identifies this anti-irony trend with reality TV that supposedly "free[s] [viewers] from ... fictions" and "made-up lives," and Maxine chimes in that her kids' English teacher "has announced that there shall be no more fictional reading assignments" (335). The mention of English class makes it especially clear that this is a defense of the fiercely "nonliteral," deeply ironic *Bleeding Edge*, DeepArcher, and similar narratives, but it is also a defense of ironic, far-from-literal cartoons, like *The Simpsons*, which (along with its heirs, such as *South Park*) was routinely invoked as an emblem of the culture of irony that supposedly came to an end on 9/11.

Roger Rosenblatt was the first to say irony was dead, in *Time* on September 24, 2001, and indeed, Heidi's speech seems to be drawn directly from Rosenblatt's much-discussed (and much-maligned) op-ed. Pynchon may even have grounded Heidi's argument in gay studies to reply to the homophobic undertow of Rosenblatt's essay. Heidi's "giggling mincing fifth column" recasts Rosenblatt's ponderous mentions of "chattering classes" who, "with a giggle and a smirk," claim that "nothing is real—apart from prancing around in an air of vain stupidity" (79). In response Rosenblatt intones, "The planes that plowed into the World Trade Center and the Pentagon were real. The flames, smoke, sirens—real. The chalky landscape, the silence of the streets—all real" (79).

Heidi's scornful remaking of the Rosenblatt thesis as a call for exclusively "literal" art is one of many moments when Pynchon's novel benefits from the greater calm of retrospect on events it narrates in present tense. As the initial post-9/11 weeks of shell shock recede further into history, Rosenblatt's essay looks more foolish: irony did not fall with the Twin Towers, nor should it have. As David Cowart writes regarding Rosenblatt and *Bleeding Edge*'s trenchant response, after 9/11 the subversive power of "irony becomes all the more indispensable, the last thing thoughtful people ought to relinquish" (par. 47). At the same time, the operative binarism that *Bleeding Edge* lampoons here—irony versus the real—obscures the role played by another element, sentimentality, in highbrow and lowbrow culture that might seem wholly invested in ironic unreality. By underscoring the ironic/realistic binarism Rosenblatt posed in the immediate aftermath of 9/11, Pynchon's response effectively misconstrues the more complex balancing act that *Bleeding Edge*, shows like *The Simpsons*, and many other cultural artifacts have pulled off, both before and after 9/11: a blend of the ironic and the sentiments that irony so often mocks and undermines. Sentimentality is not defended or analyzed in *Bleeding Edge* or *The Simpsons*; it is, rather, occasionally enacted, used as a necessary ballast—and thus granted all the more power to draw readers and viewers toward its conclusions. Irony did not die with 9/11, but neither did sentimentalism, nor irony leavened with sentimentalism. Both modes, Pynchon and his favorite cartoon characters show, are necessary to a sophisticated and affectively effective response to geopolitical trials.

In conclusion, Pynchon has for a while now been traveling along a line that intersects with *The Simpsons*' own at a number of points, and in his latest novel he finally gets a chance to both allude to the Springfieldites and self-consciously draw on some of the cartoon's characterizations of men, women, and family. With hindsight and the archive, the Pynchon/*Simpsons* intertwining might be seen as the culmination of a decades-long arc in the writer's ambition to connect TV and his novels as vehicles of familial parody, though now with a more progressive vision of masculinity and a greater degree of sentimentality in tow. As Luc Herman and John Krafft show elsewhere in this volume, based on their study of the *V.* typescript, Pynchon cut from his first novel a satire of a family sitcom typical of 1950s TV that, if published, would have complicated the book's gender politics. Herman and Krafft argue that the sitcom's male characters (which include an "ambitious but ultimately clueless white-collar father") "neither quite figure out what it means to *be* a man nor manage to do whatever it would be to *act* like a man" (180). In the twenty-first century, after several more decades of sitcom families, it is still hard to figure out what it means to be (or even act like) a man—and even more so, what a man ought to be. Pynchon seems to have modified his view of the father and male role model over the years such that he now looks quite a bit like Homer Simpson—given to excess and folly, taking existence as a joke on himself, ultimately doing no real harm, and in the end, there as an overweight bulwark for his family to lean on.

NOTES

1. James Berger reads Zoyd's gender ambiguity this way: "Zoyd is a father with the qualities of a mother, a father without the phallus [...]. He is not quite a void—some

figure for feminine absence entirely outside the symbolic order; he is [...] a Zoyd: passive but capable" (par. 21). In a reading of *V.* Mark Hawthorne sees much earlier evidence of Pynchon "feminiz[ing]" a schlemihl, Benny, whose behavior, he argues, is constructed "to contrast the socially and psychoanalytically defined male gender identity of the 1950s" (75–76).

WORKS CITED

"All's Fair in Oven War." *The Simpsons: The Sixteenth Season.* Written by Matt Selman. Dir. Mark Kirkland. 20th Century Fox Home Entertainment, 2013.

Anker, Elizabeth. "Allegories of Falling and the 9/11 Novel." *American Literary History* 23.3 (2011): 463–82.

"Bart of Darkness." *The Simpsons: The Complete Sixth Season.* Written by Dan McGrath. Dir. Jim Reardon. 20th Century Fox Home Entertainment, 2012.

"Bart's Friend Falls in Love." *The Simpsons: The Complete Third Season.* Written by Jay Kogen and Wallace Wolodarsky. Dir. Jim Reardon. 20th Century Fox Home Entertainment, 2012.

Berger, James. "Cultural Trauma and the 'Timeless Burst': Pynchon's Revision of Nostalgia in *Vineland*." *Postmodern Culture* 5.3 (1995). DOI: 10.1353/pmc.1995.0020.

Buchbinder, David. *Studying Men and Masculinities.* London: Routledge, 2013.

Bush, H. W. George. "Remarks at the Bush-Quayle Welcoming Rally at the Republican National Convention in Houston, Texas, August 17, 1992." *Public Papers of the Presidents of the United States: George Bush, 1992–93.* Vol. 2. Washington, D.C.: Government Printing Office, 1993. 1371.

Cantor, Paul A. "*The Simpsons*: Atomistic Politics and the Nuclear Family." *Political Theory* 27.6 (1999): 734–49.

Cowart, David. "'Down on the Barroom Floor of History': Pynchon's *Bleeding Edge*." *Postmodern Culture* 24.1 (2013): DOI: 10.1353/pmc.2013.0060.

"Diatribe of a Mad Housewife." *The Simpsons: The Fifteenth Season.* Written by Robin J. Stein. Dir. Mark Kirkland. 20th Century Fox Home Entertainment, 2012.

"A Fish Called Selma." *The Simpsons: The Complete Seventh Season.* Written by Jack Barth. Dir. Mark Kirkland. 20th Century Fox Home Entertainment, 2012.

Freer, Joanna. *Thomas Pynchon and American Counterculture.* New York: Cambridge University Press, 2014.

Gray, Jonathan. *Watching with The Simpsons: Television, Parody, and Intertextuality.* New York: Routledge, 2006.

Hawthorne, Mark. "A 'Hermaphroditic Sort of Deity': Sexuality, Gender, and Gender Blending in Thomas Pynchon's *V.*" *Studies in the Novel* 29.1 (1997): 74–93.

Henry, A. Matthew. *The Simpsons, Satire, and American Culture.* London: Palgrave Macmillan, 2012.

Hume, Kathryn. "Attenuated Realities: Pynchon's Trajectory From *V.* to *Inherent Vice*." *Orbit: A Journal of American Literature* 2.1 (2013). DOA: 10.7766/orbit.v2.1.50.

@MattSelman. "The fax sent to us by Thomas Pynchon with his jokes written on the script page." *Twitter.* 28 Aug. 2014, 1:01 p.m. twitter.com/mattselman/status/505082780561051649.

McHale, Brian. *Constructing Postmodernism.* London: Routledge, 1992.

———. "Genre as History: Pynchon's Genre-Poaching." *Pynchon's* Against the Day: *Corrupted Pilgrim's Guide.* Ed. Jeffrey Severs and Christopher Leise. Newark: University of Delaware Press, 2011. 15–28.

Pynchon, Thomas. *Gravity's Rainbow*. New York: Penguin, 1973.
———. *V.* 1963. New York: Harper Perennial, 2005.
———. *Vineland*. New York: Penguin Books, 1990.
Rosenblatt, Roger. "The Age of Irony Comes to an End." *Time*, 24 Sept. 2001: 79.
Singh, Simon. *The Simpsons and Their Mathematical Secrets*. London: Bloomsbury, 2013.
Turner, Chris. *Planet Simpson: How a Cartoon Masterpiece Documented an Era and Defined a Generation*. Toronto: Vintage Canada, 2008.
Waltonen, Karma. "'We're All Pigs': Representations of Masculinity in *The Simpsons*." *The Simpsons Archive*, 16 Sept. 2001, www.simpsonsarchive.com/other/papers/kw.paper.html. Accessed 16. Nov. 2017.

Conservatism as Radicalism
Family and Antifeminism in *Vineland*

CATHERINE FLAY

This chapter argues that the central political concern of *Vineland* (1990) is understanding the function of capitalism and exploring options for opposition to it. Although gender is, therefore, not the central focus of the novel, the relationship between different ways of performing gendered identity and capitalism is a crucial part of Pynchon's exploration of why the counterculture failed in its overall revolutionary intent, how the status quo reasserted itself in the neoliberal context of the 1980s and 1990s, and what methods of resistance might be viable. Challenging norms and expectations associated with masculinity, for example, contributes to an anticapitalist stance, as Pynchon valorizes the refocusing of male attention from work and the value of money to family and the value of love. Conversely, however, female sexual and social liberation is presented as leading to damaging duplicity in the character of Frenesi, who justifies and rationalizes her betrayals of Weed, Zoyd, and her revolutionary lineage, as well as her abandonment of her daughter, Prairie, by appealing to ideas of radical individual freedom and female emancipation from roles such as wife and mother. In *Vineland*, Pynchon levels heavy critique at strands of countercultural feminism that promote sexual and social liberation. Although he arguably celebrates traditional female roles and qualities while criticizing macho masculinity—amounting to an embrace of one model of femininity—his representation of a female genetic propensity toward sexual masochism across *Vineland* and *Against the Day* (2006) seems to go beyond a critique of one particular school of feminist thought, suggesting a general distrust of women's ability to support radical political change.

In previous considerations of gender in *Vineland*, Molly Hite has foregrounded the character of DL Chastain as a feminist figure, Joanna Freer has built on Hite's work, analyzing the Kunoichi Sisterhood as a potential site for feminism in the novel, and Madeline Ostrander has explored Frenesi's role as a "locus" for ideology. This chapter, however, focuses in particular on the characters of Zoyd and Frenesi, considering how Pynchon's representation of the family as a counter to capitalism facilitates the diversification of masculinity but limits the kinds of female behavior that can be considered either moral or radical.

In *Vineland*, Pynchon considers the trajectory from the postwar countercultural era to the neoliberal 1980s and 1990s, and the novel documents convergences between counterculture and capitalism as well as depicting the co-optation of the former by the latter. Pynchon problematizes a countercultural characterization of power as rationalistic and considers the implications for postwar countercultural stances of capitalism's reliance on values such as transgression, youth, novelty, and change. In the postcountercultural era, the very pleasure principle that Molly Hite argues Pynchon champions in *Gravity's Rainbow* (1973) to counter the death drive of Western society ("Fun Actually") now supports power and can no longer supply the foundation for radical opposition. The centrality of capitalism to *Vineland*'s assessment of power and a cultural mainstream echoes the concerns of prominent academic cultural theorists also publishing in the 1990s such as Zygmunt Bauman, Luc Boltanski and Eve Chiapello, Thomas Frank, and David Harvey, all of whom highlight the importance of fluidity, transgression, creativity, novelty, and change to contemporary power. *Vineland* emerged alongside prominent social theories that sought to make capitalism once again central to critiques of society, culture, and power. The novel depicts capitalism not only as functioning on the basis of values associated with counterculture and other radical movements but also as being capable of functioning on the basis of any values that do not contravene the generation of profit; all individuals and actions are valued or disregarded according to their ability to generate profit. Against this vision stands one in which a moral and radical way of life rests on the intrinsic value of individuals or actions. In *Vineland* this amounts to a valorization of love, of familial duty, and less compromising ways of making a living. Interrogating not only particular capitalist values in post-Fordist society but the nature of value itself within a capitalist framework, Pynchon delineates a moral, intrinsic value system as the only sound opposition to the extrinsic value system of capitalism that converts everything into equations of profit and loss. Pynchon's moral and political opposition in *Vineland* correlates with dominant strands of virtue ethics (particularly the work of Alasdair MacIntyre), a school of thought that secured its position in the modern philosophical canon during the 1990s.[1]

In the consumer market there is an apparent countersubversive intent in the generation of products to meet popular, radical tastes. Zoyd and Mucho Maas perceive reactionary intentions behind mass production and marketing of rock and roll; for Zoyd, there is a "They" operating with intent behind the production of popular music culture. He laments, "They just let us forget. Give us too much to process, fill up every minute, keep us distracted." For him, television is, and rock and roll is becoming, "just another way to claim our attention" (314). The proliferation of countercultural commodities represented in *Vineland* is corroborated by factual accounts of the period such as Kirkpatrick Sale's recollection that "an economy continually in search of artificial stimulants immediately made [the young] into a 'youth market,' accountable for no less than $40–45 billion by 1970" (20). Not only did this market "supply the young," he argues, but "it eventually defined the group, economically and socially, establishing a consciousness in society at large (and particularly among the young) of their separateness" (20).

Behind these shifts in the market toward catering to countercultural appetites, however, Zoyd perceives an intention to distract and ultimately to undermine subversive intent, the effect of which is to convert the movement into an image rather than an actuality, rendering it a revolution in style rather than substance. For critics such as Neil Brooks, the commercialization of counterculture is the result of cynical co-optation, a thesis that upholds a binary distinction between counterculture and capitalism. He argues, for example, that "Rock and Roll represents a form of popular culture which had been able to present truly oppositional social values" (181) but that, in *Vineland*'s 1984, has become a superficial image of, rather than metonym for, social revolution. He corroborates Zoyd and Mucho Maas, who worry that "the green free America of their childhoods" is "turning into" something unrecognizable (314).

The very inclusion of Maas, however, a character first introduced in *The Crying of Lot 49* (1966), compromises the idea that a pure counterculture has been co-opted. In reprising Maas, Pynchon displays a similar imperative to Boltanski and Chiapello when they describe their desire to understand "why many of the 'class of '68' felt so at ease in the emerging new society that they made themselves its spokesmen and egged on the transformation" (xxxvi). Like such critics of 1980s and 1990s capitalism and its social realities, Pynchon seeks to understand the complicity of the counterculture in the generation of his contemporary sociopolitical situation. The 1966 Maas was already connecting the togetherness of LSD experience with mass consumerism, hearing a multitude of voices repeating advertising slogans while on his acid trips (109). Maas's reappearance in *Vineland* recalls *Lot 49*'s analysis of the manufacturing of teenage dreams on radio stations like the one at which Maas worked and of the liminality between capitalist mainstream and counterculture of not only products such as drugs but a variety of nonmaterial goods and services relating to image and lifestyle (see Sale 11). Maas's comeback prefigures Frank's 1990s analysis that depicts the parallel revolutions of the counterculture in society and within business itself. Frank describes new economic social organization as predicated on liberation and transgression, on the appreciation of constant novelty and variety (19): "During the 1950s and 1960s, management thinkers went through their own version of the mass society critique, first deploring the demise of entrepreneurship under the stultifying regime of technocratic efficiency (*The Organization Man*), then embracing all manner of individualism-promoting, bureaucracy-smashing, and antihierarchical schemes (*The Human Side of Enterprise, Up the Organization*)" (20).

Frank lists business publications and examples from advertising of the period to argue not only that businesses adopted the images of countercultural rebellion and overlaid them on the same conformist system but also that a new form of capitalism emerged as a revolution within business that identified with the values of liberation from the old, with youth, change, and the new. Through figures such as Maas who work in a post-Fordist service economy of radio stations, advertising, and health care/well-being, *Vineland* implies that the counterculture challenged Fordist social organization but not capitalism itself, augmenting the generation of a new model of economic-social organization without challenging the underlying principle of society's organization around capitalist principles.

Deborah Madsen considers *Gravity's Rainbow*'s waning popularity among students as a phenomenon of the profound sociopolitical effects of developments in economic organization between the 1970s and the 1990s: "In the seventies, what was called at the time Pynchon's paranoid vision of global conspiracy mounted by the military-industrial complex against the interests of the individual was very compelling" (144). But by the 1990s, Madsen suggests, this paranoid vision has become "so real as to be passé" and "inauthentic" (144). She argues that "recent developments in management theory and public-sector initiatives like Al Gore's National Performance Review [...] indicate a trend toward decentralization, worker empowerment and diversification of 'organized anarchy' in late capitalism," evincing a postindustrial capitalist context perhaps foreshadowed by, but markedly different from that of the novel (144).

Vineland presents capitalism as the structuring force of society, and changes in its form between the countercultural era and the 1990s amount to changes in the nature of power that requires a reconsideration of the qualities needed to formulate potentially successful opposition. As Madsen observes, the characterization of capitalism in *Gravity's Rainbow* is no longer accurate, and *Vineland* represents a recognition of the necessity for socially radical opposition to reconsider its values and activities in response to socioeconomic shifts that reveal a correlation between characteristics of counterculture and capitalism. In part, then, the novel corroborates the identification of a shift from Fordism to post-Fordism. Erik Swyngedouw, for example, has associated Fordism with "mass consumption of consumer durables," "modernism," and "socialization," and post-Fordism with "individualized consumption": "'yuppie'—culture," "postmodernism," and "individualization" (qtd. in Harvey 178–79). Similarly, Scott Lash and John Urry have noted a movement from "organized" to "disorganized" capitalism between the postwar period and the 1990s (qtd. in Harvey 174). *Vineland* recognizes that the ascendancy of this new form of capitalism has popularized countercultural values such as individuality as opposed to conformity and freedom from rigid social expectations without challenging fundamental social inequalities. This new form of capitalism ascended in the postcountercultural decades, marked, as Harvey puts it, "by a direct confrontation with the rigidities of Fordism" (147). No longer industry-centric, this new form is sustained by services and immaterial commodities like the hundred-dollar mantra that *Vineland*'s Van Meter owns (11). It is no longer the industrial production of material goods that is of value but the production of images; the Bodhi Dharma Pizza Temple where pizza cut into the shapes of mandalas offers a unique selling point and the "Hip Trip" pinball machine that employs psychedelic countercultural imagery exemplify the primacy of image in the marketplace (49, 314). Madsen notes this development, corroborating Lash and Urry's distinction between Fordist, modern, "organized" capitalism and post-Fordist, postmodern, "disorganized" capitalism. One example that she cites from management guru Tom Peters is that "the prominent group California Raisins earned more in 1989 from personal appearances, the sale of T-shirts and from other forms of merchandising than farmers earned from raisins" (150).

Shopping malls such as the Noir Centre in *Vineland* make manifest the profitability of image rather than material goods in the form of the movie-themed names of shops and the visual effects of the center that bear no relation to the products on offer and even less to the economic system they serve: "Noir Centre here had an upscale mineral-water boutique called Bubble Indemnity, plus The Lounge Good Buy patio furniture outlet, The Mall Tease Flacon which sold perfume and cosmetics, and a New York–style deli, The Lady 'n' the Lox" (326). The connection between noir film and the products for sale is entirely based on wordplay rather than content. Such marketing is symptomatic of the revolution in business that Frank depicts as mimicking and intimately related to the revolutionary intent of the countercultural movement, revolving around the genesis of market segmentation, advertising based not on the qualities of the product for sale but instead on the images used to sell the product (*VL* 24). Pynchon explicitly references the "marketing philosophy of the mid-1980s" when Prairie is offered a "designer seltzer" by a robot. The product epitomizes the bifurcation between style and substance in the novel's economy: "[T]here was the stylish seltzer stone-cold in its YSL-logo container in the essentially Reagan-era fashion colors of gold and silver" (193).

Despite the ascendancy of a form of capitalism that popularized countercultural images, liquidated social rigidity, transgressed norms and taboos, and elevated the value of creativity and individuality as opposed to functionality and homogeneity, the broad social revolutionary aims of the counterculture have not been achieved. Pynchon takes up the fact that capitalism, albeit in an altered form, has continued to underpin sociopolitical reality, exploring the limits this places on the depth of change that can be achieved. The valuing of capital above all else has meant that counterculture can succeed insofar as it doesn't contravene profit but that it cannot alter the foundational values of society without challenging the economic system and its powerful social and cultural effects. Here Harvey is illuminating, arguing that the first tenet of capitalism across its different forms is that it must "achieve the expansion of output and a growth in real values, no matter what the social, political, geopolitical or ecological consequences" (180). It is this devaluation of all values except that of profit within a capitalist system that Pynchon sees as undermining the potential for radical sociopolitical improvement within any form of capitalist social organization. While the counterculture was largely anti-Fordist, Pynchon explores the necessity of anticapitalism for radical sociopolitical change. Peter Singer, discussing the normalization of the supremacy of economic value evidenced by, among other things, a lack of strong public outcry at politicians claiming undue expenses and state legislators accepting bribes in the early 1990s, recalls representative Bobby Raymond's words: "There is not an issue in this world that I give a (expletive) about. My favorite line is, 'What's in it for me?'" (qtd. in Singer 129–30). While *Vineland* explores the values that counterculture and specifically post-Fordist capitalism have in common, it also characterizes capitalism as entailing a "cash nexus," representing it as amoral and capable of adopting different and even opposing causes in its zeal to maximize profit.

When Hector meets Zoyd to discuss Frenesi, Zoyd half-jokes, "I really need to hear some advice right now about how I should be bringin' up my own kid, we know already how much all you Reaganite folks care about the family unit, just from how much you're always in fuckin' around with it" (31). The narrative of the disruption of Zoyd, Frenesi, and Prairie's family by direct federal action and also by Brock's manipulation of Frenesi—through which he pushes her to embrace individualistic, neoliberal models of identity—microcosmically reflects the ways in which the emerging neoliberal "Reaganite" culture "fuck[ed] around" with family and the human values it fosters. In *Vineland*, Pynchon presents ways of being engaged, invested, and dedicated to an occupation undertaken without the motivation of remuneration, presenting familial roles as providing a model of the individual embedded in community as opposed to the individual making and remaking himself or herself as a commodity as well as a worker in the public sphere of the neoliberal era.

Here Pynchon intersects with 1990s virtue ethics and MacIntyre's concept of pursuit of "practices" as distinct from the roles, both social and professional, that capitalist society offers, particularly in the post-Fordist era. MacIntyre argues, "In many pre-modern, traditional societies it is through his or her membership in a variety of social groups that the individual identifies himself or herself and is identified by others" (33). Importantly, he uses the familial roles of "brother, cousin and grandson"—which do not "belong to human beings accidentally" but are essentially a dominant concept of "the real me"—to illustrate his point (33). "[T]he peculiarly modern self, the emotivist self, in acquiring sovereignty in its own realm," he adds, "lost its traditional boundaries provided by a social identity and a view of human life as ordered to a given end" (34). MacIntyre's thinking illuminates Pynchon's attempt to recuperate an alternative model of self to replace that of the free, self-made individual. In opposition to the amoral individualism supportive of the kind of capitalism described in *Vineland*, Pynchon valorizes the family and love not tied to concern for financial or personal profit. The Traverse-Becker family, for example, represents a strong sense of collective identity and acceptance of inherited sociopolitical roles. Sasha thinks of each generation as like a monument to its ancestors, as she recalls her mother saying that "[a]ll we can do about it now is just stay. Just piss on through. Be here to remind everybody— any time they see a Traverse, or a Becker for that matter, they'll remember that one tree, and who did it, and why. Hell of a lot better 'n a statue in the park" (76).

MacIntyre denaturalizes and traces the history of the belief that individuals are role players rather than defined by birth and inheritance, arguing that this popular belief amounts to a self-fulfilling prophecy that shapes sociopolitical reality. In *Vineland*, Pynchon demonstrates how the market facilitates the popularization of this model of the individual; Mucho Maas, for example, constantly transforms himself in line with the dominant industries and marketable fashions of the moment. Although satirized, Maas is not denigrated for his mutability. By contrast, Frenesi's changeability is presented as disloyalty, climaxing in the abandonment of her child, which is depicted as unnatural due to its precipitation by a fear of being limited to a pregnant and postnatal physiognomy. Pynchon's critique of post-Fordist capitalism is astute, but the different treatment of these characters arguably reveals that his perspective on the issue involves different implications for men and women, if not outright gender bias.

For Macintyre, the modern and contemporary model of the self as created and constantly changeable (which has become ubiquitous) is antithetical to morality because it licenses and demands the alteration of behavior depending on what is advantageous or expected in different situations. Morality, he argues, requires staying faithful to beliefs and ways of being, in doing the right thing in any situation despite the consequences. In opposition to the amoral role-playing of work and social life in the fluid age of individualism, MacIntyre suggests a means of recuperating integrity, of reattaching and recommitting the individual to an occupation and way of life. "Practices," on his view, are antithetical to roles that are performed for the pursuit of goals external to them; a practice is undertaken for its own sake, "piss[ing] on through," as Sasha puts it, despite a lack of success. MacIntyre describes, for example, a child who would cheat at chess if she simply wished to be seen to be good at chess and to gain a reward but who would not if she saw chess as a practice and wished to genuinely gain skill at it (196). MacIntyre's conceptualization illuminates Pynchon's valorization of family roles undertaken with love in *Vineland*. The human value of loved family members is an intrinsic value that cannot be bought and that provides a moral affront to the amoral value system of capitalism: a commitment to roles such as mother or father denies that the individual is free to make and remodel themselves, insisting that some things are still "sacred." In his presentation of the family Pynchon implicitly highlights the key failure of the "radicalism" of neoliberal subjectivity's challenge to Fordist-era alienation; it preserves capitalism itself even as it alters its form, and the supremacy of profit under capitalism necessarily subducts the human values that underpin the radically new society toward which Pynchon writes.

The implications of the mode of radicalism elaborated by Pynchon in recognition of the necessity to revise countercultural tactics, however, carry uneven consequences for male and female characters. Although the theorists of capitalism and culture cited in this chapter assume a gender-neutral concept of the individual, *Vineland* explores how the turn toward neoliberalism affects men and women. Against the social fluidity that Pynchon sees supporting the status quo in *Vineland*, the novel retreats into the private sphere to disentangle potentially radical groups from capitalist society and valorizes the family and traditional roles in contrast with the social liquidity reaching a climax in the post-Fordist period of the novel's setting and publication. While *Vineland* depicts a capitalist economy that can operate alongside any value structure that does not hinder the accumulation of profit (an extrinsic value system), it also delineates a private community context in which a different moral value system (an inherent/intrinsic value system) is at work. Employment becomes a problematic node between the public and private in the novel and an act that embodies extrinsic value. The comparison between the means through which Zoyd and Frenesi get paid by the state stages the concern about how to attain money to live on without compromising integrity. David Thoreen argues that "[t]he only true revolutionary, the only really dangerous insurgent, in the consumption economy is the non-participant" and suggests that Zoyd is such a nonparticipant ("The Economy" 60). While

Thoreen locates Zoyd's countercapitalism in his ability to make a living from piecemeal employment (his dependence on the state notwithstanding), a case can be made that Zoyd's real achievement is in exchanging a yearly performance of instability for a "mental-disability" welfare payment: he plays the system in such a way that he can preserve his authentic self (however problematic a concept this is) the rest of the time. Having completed the yearly task, he is able to peel off the persona who has "earned" a paycheck from the state: "Zoyd had begun removing the large and colorful dress [...]. He was wearing ancient surfer baggies underneath, and a dilapidated Hussong's T-shirt" (14). Even though Zoyd is still complicit in the system, through him Pynchon provides a model for social engagement that is less morally compromising than other jobs presented. The reinscription of conscious alienation as a counter to capitalist power in this example is a central way in which Pynchon moves beyond a countercultural position in the novel. Pierre Dardot and Christian Laval describe the breakdown of alienation between the subject and his job and the implication of the subject in his or her work as characteristic of neoliberal society. Like Pynchon, they recognize that the conceptualization of power as rationalistic and embodied in the organization man is now obsolete: "We are no longer dealing with old disciplines intended to train bodies and shape minds through compulsion to render them more submissive [...]. It is a question of governing beings all of whose subjectivity must be involved in the activity they are required to perform" (260). For them, the employee is now viewed "as an active subject who must participate fully, commit himself utterly, and engage completely in his professional activity" (260).

By preserving his alienation from his means of gaining an income, Zoyd avoids becoming a neoliberal subject, thereby retaining a sense of himself as an end rather than as synonymous with his function as means to money in a capitalist working environment. In comparison, Frenesi appears as the archetypal neoliberal subject according to Dardot and Laval's definition. The rendering useful of her sexuality robs Frenesi of this private, personal and intrinsically valuable aspect of her life or rather allows her to exchange her very self for the extrinsic value of pay. Brock Vond appears precisely as "the Other who speaks softly within the self" when he convinces Frenesi to abandon her baby, and his sexual appeal means that following her own desire equates to obeying the Other (Dardot and Laval 260). The concept of earning money is critiqued, and Zoyd's reliance on a disability benefit is validated as a means of preserving oneself from regular and frequent engagement in any practice for extrinsic financial gains. Ultimately, while Zoyd's cross-dressing is comic, Frenesi's assumption of rights to freedom and public life previously monopolized by men is threatening and rigorously critiqued, reflecting the diversification of models of masculinity that the novel offers but also the novel's constriction of acceptable female behavior.

For male characters, the private sphere, family roles, and love model ways of living that are valuably distinct from traditional ideals of masculinity. In his care for Prairie, for example, Zoyd epitomizes a sight described in *Inherent Vice* (2009) as shocking to members of the "straight world," who are confused to see that "the male one is carrying the baby" (209). Zoyd challenges the model of *homo economicus* through his accession to *homo familiaris* in Frenesi's absence, and this challenge of normative masculinity embodies the challenge Zoyd's parenting poses to the privileging of capitalist value. In his "devotional routine" of changing Prairie's diaper, Zoyd experiences a shift of priorities in his recognition of the ultimate intrinsic value of his daughter for which there can be no substitute and to which nothing compares (296). Later, when a young Prairie falls ill and asks him, "Dad? Am I ever gonna get bett-or?" Zoyd "had his belated moment of welcome to the planet Earth, in which he knew, dismayingly, that he would, would have to, do anything to keep this dear small life from harm" (321). While he does want to be seen to be a good father—he "made sure his ex-mother-in-law noticed he was wiping in the right direction" as he changed Prairie's diaper—fatherhood is more than a performance conducted to reap an external reward; this is also the moment that he recognizes how meaningful even the most banal and perhaps unpleasant aspects of fatherhood are for him (296). In Pynchon's version of radicalism, male characters are able to embrace the diversification of gendered behavior championed by the counterculture, but Frenesi is critiqued for her interpretation of sexual and social liberation.

Zoyd is contrasted with other male characters whose destruction of private lives and familial communities matches their seeking to reinforce normative masculinity and to uphold the social and cultural status quo. While Zoyd cares for Prairie as a single parent, for example, Brock has his "own baby," the "Political Re-Education Program" (PREP); that Brock loves and nurtures an aggressive arm of politicized policing encapsulates his machismo, his "feminine" and caring qualities being directed toward violent ends (268). Pynchon describes Brock as offering a perverted version of family to members of "the sixties left," perceiving in them "the deep—if he'd allowed himself to feel it, the sometimes touching—need only to stay children forever, safe inside some extended national Family" and offering an alternative to the sense of belonging they found in political activism (269). His intent to use these "children in need of discipline," however, suggests a relationship that is opposite to the kind of relationship that Zoyd discovers with Prairie in his becoming conscious of her unique individual worth to him (269). While Brock plans to conduct "some reconditioning" on his "children" (269), Zoyd gives up any individualistic agenda that is not compatible with protecting his child, fusing his identity with that of "parent."

As Madeline Ostrander notes, Brock is "the most masculine figure of the novel" (128). She highlights his assertion of a patriarchal ideology that understands himself and his male adversaries as the only real social actors, with Frenesi as a mere "medium" to be used (128). Pynchon represents the proximity to homosexuality that such love and respect for men and disregard for women might entail when Brock reminds Frenesi, "Remember last time, when I told you not to bathe, hm? because I knew you'd be seeing him that night, knew he'd go down on you—didn't he? ate your pussy, hm? of course I know, because he told me. You were coming in his face and he was tasting me all the time" (213–14). Brock, however, denies Frenesi's claim that the reason he feels violent toward Weed is "because you can't love each other" (214) and remains on the normative side of the homosocial/homosexual divide. Brock's comments, however, highlight the degree to which his understanding of social action negates female importance; in this novel, as Hite notes, even sex between a man and woman is really a power relationship between two men ("Feminist Theory"). In such a description of the manipulative quality of individualistic social relations, Pynchon presents a peculiarly masculine means of upholding the capitalism-based status quo that undermines the individual worth of each person and the type of community that is fostered by recognizing such worth. Recognizing the human worth of women is a necessary aspect of Pynchon's anticapitalism and prohuman politics in *Vineland*, and in this respect converges with feminist principles.

As Joanna Freer argues, "particular men are found guilty of smaller-scale brutality as the novel offers support for feminist critiques of the vulnerability of women and girls to male relatives in the contemporary familial power hierarchy" (147). Freer discusses the representation of Moody Chastain, for example, the abusive husband of DL's mother whose abusive personality is rooted in a machismo that encompasses, as Freer notes, "driving fast" and "discharging firearms inappropriately" (148). She discusses the Kunoichi Sisterhood's Sister Rochelle's condemnation of masculinity as to blame for large-scale historical brutality and raises the possibility that "the novel's general attitude to men as historical actors" might coincide with this radical (and essentialist) feminist perspective (147). Zoyd's movement away from normative masculinity, however, offers a means for men to become positive social actors, and the novel's diversification of models of male identity is fused with Pynchon's politics.

Although the novel's men are often depicted as being culpable, however, women's capacity for effecting radical change is limited in the novel. Arguing that Pynchon questions the efficacy of the Kunoichi Sisterhood, Freer references Germaine Greer's analysis of Judith Brown's perspective on separatist feminism: "Brown 'did not see that an all-female commune is in no way different from the medieval convents where women who revolted against their social and biological roles could find intellectual and moral fulfilment, from which they exerted no pressure on the status quo at all'" (148). As Freer points out, the Kunoichi Sisters' building was once a nunnery and Freer concludes that "Pynchon's distrust of feminist separatism [...] is thus confirmed in *Vineland*" and that "Pynchon's political distaste for separatism reflects his repeated affirmation of the value of community" (148). In particular, in *Vineland*, Pynchon's representation of anticapitalist community modeled on the interpersonal love and human value within a family intersects problematically not only with female-only separatist enclaves such as the Kunoichi Sisterhood but also with female social and sexual liberation that sees female characters entering into public life. Frenesi's individualism, for example, her will to define herself rather than be defined by her sex and her physical as well as social role as mother and her employment by the state support the sociopolitical ethos that the novel rejects in ways that are not peculiar to Frenesi as an individual character but more generally applicable to women as a group.

Frenesi abandons Prairie, for example, owing to Brock's manipulation of the countercultural/feminist movement's individualism and its antitraditional sentiment. As David Thoreen notes, Brock plays on the perceived limitation that the definition of motherhood places on the individuality of female identity and encourages Frenesi in her depression ("In Which" [56–57]): "Brock came to visit, and strangely to comfort, in the half-lit hallways of the night, leaning darkly in above her like any of the sleek raptors that decorate fascist architecture. Whispering, 'This is just how they want you, an animal, a bitch, with swollen udders lying in the dirt, blank-faced, surrendered, reduced to this meat, these smells...'" (287).

In Frenesi's case Pynchon rebrands the countercultural feminist agenda of social liquidation and its valorization of the individual as opposed to the rigid social role as disloyal promiscuity that is useful to the state. In part, Frenesi's betrayal represents another instance of convergence between counterculture and the status quo; Frenesi was not manipulated by Vond because she did not share countercultural values of openness and freedom but because of the way she interpreted those values. When she begins allowing Vond to see her footage, for example, "[s]he told herself she was making movies for everybody, to be shown free anywhere there might be a reflective enough surface" (209). It is particularly this feminist embodiment of countercultural desire for personal freedom and for individuality that Pynchon's representation of Frenesi explores and critiques for its support of the status quo. Vond is able to seduce Frenesi, for example, because she believes it is acceptable to have multiple sexual relationships, a belief in line with an embrace of liberated female sexuality. Frenesi describes the reabsorption of female promiscuity, which had been transgressive and countercultural in itself, under state control in her work for the government. She explains to Flash, "Once they find out you're willing to betray somebody you've been to bed with, once you get that specialist's code attached to you, don't have to be glamour beefs like high treason anymore, they can use you the same way for anything, on any scale, all the way down to simple mopery, anytime they want to get some local judge tends to think with his dick, it's your phone that rings around dinner time, and there goes the frozen lasagne" (70–71). Interrupting her familial duties of preparing the frozen lasagne, the state in fact requires the kind of transgression of social roles that the counterculture had believed would threaten state stability. Rather than asserting his conservative ideology through traditional values such as the family or defined gender roles, Vond encourages social fragmentation and, in particular, female liberation against a sense of duty toward fulfilling roles within a family. While MacIntyre's virtue ethics assumes a general, ungendered subject, theorists of virtue such as Martha Nussbaum and Iris Murdoch have considered "goodness" in relation to gender. Murdoch, for example, notes that "[g]oodness appears to be both rare and hard to picture. It is perhaps most convincingly met with in simple people—inarticulate, unselfish mothers of large families" (51–52). Although Pynchon gives Sasha, a mother and grandmother figure whom the novel casts in a positive light, strong political convictions as well as articulacy, his celebration of the family and parental love is as problematic as Murdoch's definition of "goodness." That self-sacrifice for the sake of a loved child testifies to "goodness" is a standard that holds true for both male and female characters in the novel, but it has different implications for both when considered in the context of the history of gendered social expectations and ideals.

While, as Hite notes, DL Chastain is celebrated for her political activity, her feminist social and sexual emancipation is set against a backdrop of domestic abuse and lack of care. Pynchon sets limits on the toleration of feminism within his anticapitalist ethic and aesthetic; when female individualism comes at the cost of a loving family or relationship it is heavily critiqued. Furthermore, that Pynchon presents a situation in which female sexual and social liberation amounts to the destruction of the family that maps onto undermining countercapitalist sociopolitical radicalism arguably overemphasizes the role of that brand of feminism in limiting the radical impact of counterculture.

Frenesi's transgressive, individualistic, free, and arguably immoral behavior exemplifies the convergence between counterculture and capitalism that Pynchon is concerned with in the novel and constitutes a critical representation of the way in which some women embraced the "anything goes" characteristic of market values to escape domestic expectations. Pynchon's critical representation of Frenesi's sexuality, however, particularly when we read *Vineland* in the context of Pynchon's oeuvre, goes beyond illuminating convergences between counterculture and capitalism and casts doubt on female trustworthiness and the ability of women to support any radical sociopolitical movement. In *Against the Day* (2006) an ancestor of Frenesi, Lake Traverse, asserts her right to choose her own husband rather than be guided by her family, marrying her father's murderer and subsequently engaging in a masochistic ménage à trois with him and his partner in crime (297–98, 302). The inheritance of masochistic sexual desire through Traverse family women depicted in both *Against the Day* and *Vineland* suggests a female genetic propensity toward it that represents a generalized fear of female sexual liberation; in Pynchon's novels women are presented as inherently attracted to power and their own sexual as well as social subjection. Women's liberation, thus delineated, is not only a false achievement for women (as women paradoxically assert their freedom by choosing subjection) but also undermines wider agendas for radical social change by supporting the status quo. Noticing an early fetish for uniformed men in her daughter, for example, Sasha Traverse concludes she must have genetically passed this trait on because she has the same fetish: "Since her very first Rose Parade up till the present she'd felt in herself a fatality, a helpless turn toward images of authority" (83). It was "as if some Cosmic Fascist had spliced in a DNA sequence requiring this form of seduction and initiation into the dark joys of social control" (83). Despite distancing himself from Sasha's perspective by foregrounding the comically unlikely idea of a "Cosmic Fascist," Pynchon's representation of Lake as a sexual masochist in *Against the Day* entertains the notion of female genetic inheritance of the trait. In *Inherent Vice*, too, wherein Pynchon again turns to the era of the waning of counterculture, a majority of the female characters share this propensity to sexual masochism, suggesting that the genetic characteristic might affect all women rather than simply all one family's women.[2] Again Pynchon criticizes women as being unfaithful to counterculture, paying negative attention to a peculiarly female way of selling out. The relatively generalized mistrust of women implied by female characters' representation as innately desirous of sexual masochism and the policing of female sexuality that Pynchon's radicalism demands in *Vineland* problematically sacrifices feminist notions of progress in the process of modeling sociopolitical change.

The critique of the paradoxically conservative implications of the status quo's social fluidity in *Vineland* is embodied in Pynchon's criticism of "loose" or free female sexuality leading to masochism and infidelity; Frenesi's betrayal of Weed and Zoyd stands for the counterculture's betrayal of radicalism both through selling out and through its similarities with capitalism. A woman and—through the theme of genetic and essentialist female masochism—women as a category take a large share of figurative blame for the movement's failure and are neither comic nor endearing, as many of the male figures are; the moral implications of Maas's drug selling, for example, are less rigorously critiqued than Frenesi's choice of sexual partner and abandonment of her family. Although there is a problematic mutual constitution between feminist movements emerging from the postwar period and capitalism, Pynchon's unequal treatment of female and male characters' betrayal of counterculture appears to belie a gender-biased attitude. Pynchon's use of the family as a model for a community based on notions of worth and value other than those on which capitalist society is founded valorizes nonnormative masculine behavior. Indeed, what redeems men from being essentially culpable as a group of historical actors is that they move away from macho masculinity and enter into caring roles in the family and in community structures based on human value and love. Conversely, where monogamy and/or a loving family is the context, women are criticized for straying from their domestic role as partner/wife and mother, and female social and sexual liberation is commended only so far as it doesn't impinge upon this alternative community structure.

NOTES

1. See Hursthouse for a discussion of virtue ethics' professional history.
2. The stewardii (as Pynchon calls them), Lourdes and Motella, for example, are fatally attracted, drawn "out of some helpless fatality," to the company of male "lowlifes" (*IV* 71). As Doc observes Clancy Charlock "deep in conversation with two motorcyclists of a sort mothers tend not to approve of," he is told that she has "always been into two at a time" (148–49). Trillium recalls for Doc her first encounter with Puck Beaverton: "Before Trillium knew what was happening she found herself in the back seat of a stolen '62 Bonneville parked in a cul-de-sac off Sunset, being seen to California Department of Correction style" (223). Later she is driven by "humiliating heat" to seek him out for sex, disempowered by her desire for him, which "would seize hold of her," "envelop her," and leave her unable to think (223). Penny, too, is fascinated by the masochism of female members of the Manson cult. She tells Doc, "The only part [of the trial] I enjoy anymore is hearing how all these hippie chicks did everything Manson told them to do" (280).

WORKS CITED

Boltanski, Luc, and Eve Chiapello. *The New Spirit of Capitalism*. Trans. Gregory Elliott. London: Verso, 2005.
Brooks, Neil. "Perplexing Utopia: Modern and Postmodern Alienation in *Vineland*." *Pynchon Notes* 40–41 (1997): 180–96.
Dardot, Pierre, and Christian Laval. *The New Way of the World: On Neo-Liberal Society*. Trans. Gregory Elliott. London: Verso, 2013.
Frank, Thomas. *The Conquest of Cool: Business Culture, Counterculture, and the Rise of Hip Consumerism*. Chicago: University of Chicago Press, 1998.
Freer, Joanna. *Thomas Pynchon and American Counterculture*. New York: Cambridge University Press, 2014.
Harvey, David. *The Condition of Postmodernity: An Enquiry into the Origins of Cultural Change*. Cambridge: Blackwell, 1990.
Hite, Molly. "Feminist Theory and the Politics of *Vineland*." *The* Vineland *Papers: Critical Takes on Pynchon's Novel*. Ed. Geoffrey Green, Donald J. Greiner, and Larry McCaffery. Normal: Dalkey Archive Press, 1994. 135–54.

———. "'Fun Actually Was Becoming Quite Subversive': Herbert Marcuse, the Yippies, and the Value System of *Gravity's Rainbow*." *Contemporary Literature* 51.4 (2010): 677–702.

Hursthouse, Rosalind. *On Virtue Ethics*. Oxford: Oxford University Press, 1999.

MacIntyre, Alasdair. *After Virtue: A Study in Moral Theory*. Notre Dame: University of Notre Dame Press, 1984.

Madsen, Deborah. "The Business of Living: *Gravity's Rainbow*, Evolution, and the Advancement of Capitalism." *Pynchon Notes* 40–41 (1997): 144–58.

Murdoch, Iris. *The Sovereignty of Good*. New York: Routledge, 1970.

Nussbaum, Martha. *Love's Knowledge*. Oxford: Oxford University Press, 1990.

Ostrander, Madeline. "Awakening to the Physical World: Ideological Collapse and Ecofeminist Resistance in *Vineland*." *Thomas Pynchon: Reading from the Margins*. Ed. Niran Abbas. Cranbury, N.J.: Associated University Press, 2003. 122–35.

Pynchon, Thomas. *Against the Day*. London: Vintage, 2007.

———. *Inherent Vice*. London: Vintage, 2010.

———. *Vineland*. London: Vintage, 2000.

Sale, Kirkpatrick. *SDS*. New York: Vintage, 1974.

Singer, Peter. *How Are We to Live? Ethics in an Age of Self-Interest*. New York: Prometheus Books, 1995.

Thoreen, David. "The Economy of Consumption: The Entropy of Leisure in Pynchon's *Vineland*." *Pynchon Notes* 30 (1992): 52–61.

———. "In which 'Acts Have Consequences': Ideas of Moral Order in the Qualified Postmodernism of Pynchon's Recent Fiction." *American Postmodernity: Essays on the Recent Fiction of Thomas Pynchon*. Ed. Ian D. Copestake. New York: Peter Lang, 2003. 49–70.

Choice or Life?
Deliberations on Motherhood in Late-Period Pynchon

INGER H. DALSGAARD

> Your mama is the most important person in your life. The only one who can get those potatoes mashed exactly the way you need 'em to be. Only one who understood when you started hangin with people she couldn't stand. (*BE* 466)

Motherhood issues are present throughout Thomas Pynchon's work—spanning the early discussion of abortion in *V.* at one end and the maternal credentials of Pynchon's latest heroine, single mother Maxine Tarnow, at the other. But although motherhood and how it defines women have been central elements in feminist theory and criticism during the time Pynchon has been writing, such concerns have rarely been discussed in relation to his work.[1] This gives the deceptive impression that the question of whether motherhood is a biological right or an institution of oppression—a question feminists have grappled with for decades—is not a significant one for Pynchon.

In fact this question *is* a concern, and one to which his answer seems to have changed. Having children, in Pynchon's later fiction, is not framed in terms of choice, as it is in his earlier work, and the family value of parenting is also increasingly sentimentalized. Such depictions might seem retrograde compared to second-wave feminist ideologies. Yet they reflect the liberal identity politics and choice ideology of a newer generation of feminists. This places Pynchon's writing in a contemporary feminist field between judgmental conservative values and a judgment-free ideal of multivalency. This essay explores how specific Pynchon characters respond to complex questions about the value of maternal life and choices.

Pynchon's "late-period" fiction is a term used in this essay as a chronological and thematic marker to refer both to his most recent novels and to the number of female characters who become pregnant in them. To chart this development I start, after reflecting on the dearth of feminist Pynchon readings, by presenting three specific characters, Leni Pökler from *Gravity's*

Rainbow, Frenesi Gates from *Vineland* and Lake Traverse from *Against the Day*. These are characters who share traits, including their experience of a conflict between sexual and maternal feelings, which raise questions about how feminism and Pynchon's writing have apparently failed to connect over the central issue of motherhood.

In the next section I highlight parallels between feminism and Pynchon on the maternal and outline the advent of identity political "choice feminism" and how new maternalism in recent decades risks idealizing family life at the expense of women's liberation. Submissive female sexuality, as presented in Pynchon's recent novels, can be construed as perversely empowering to the extent that the characters choose to be submissive, while the privilege of giving life, I argue, ties mothers in these novels to new maternalist expectations of also providing a certain type of happy family for their babies. Leni and Frenesi fail to mother their daughters, and Lake is a different test case for the unhappy family formation of the nonmaternal woman. Finally, Maxine Tarnow, who stays imbedded in her family in *Bleeding Edge*, seems to be a redeemed version of those female characters who struggle to free themselves from family ties. Maxine's professional, sexual, and maternal credentials thus comment on identity politics and on Pynchon's valuation of connections and communication within families.

The final section points to the biological necessity implied in Pynchon's increasing focus on the sanctity of life, expressed in the lack either of real choice concerning conception given to female characters or acceptable alternatives to somewhat conservative models of appropriate mothering. Late-period Pynchon texts celebrate life in the clichéd form of radiant pregnancies and bouncing babies in ways feminist criticism would argue tie women to a closed, capitalist system by creating expectations that they are responsible for the happiness of families and the success of their children and, by extension, the welfare of a wider society.

Pynchon and Feminism

When *Vineland* was published in 1990 Terry Caesar was optimistic about the "reassessment of the whole of Pynchon from feminist perspectives that may follow," since of all the movements "experienced by his audience since 1973" feminism was the most decisive ("'Take'" 189, 188). But assessments, let alone reassessments, of how his texts "treat female characters and relevant issues like motherhood, gender, and sexuality" (Freer 127) have been scant until very recently. Marjorie Kaufman's "Brünnhilde and the Chemists: Women in *Gravity's Rainbow*" from 1976 remained singular in the field for a very long time. Reasons for this dearth could be either that Kaufman exhausted the topic with respect to early Pynchon, that Pynchon's texts were of no interest to feminist readers because his female characters appeared marginalized and were demeaned beyond redemption, or, finally, that feminists were busy fighting battles in "real life" far more urgent than scrutinizing an author who was in the process of being inducted by other academics into the canon of literary postmodernism in the late twentieth century anyway.

If one thing is clear in academia it is that topics are rarely if ever exhausted and, if anything, that idea is invalidated by this volume itself. The suggestion that Pynchon's female characters are unsalvageable is more convincing: Pynchon's early fiction is admittedly marred by sexual immaturity according to himself (*SL* 6, 10), by casual misogyny according to criticism (e.g., Fitzpatrick 106), and, to date, by anachronistically helpless females according to a recent reviewer who found it hard to credit that a female character in the twenty-first century would realistically get into the sexual predicaments Maxine Tarnow does in *Bleeding Edge* (Traynor). Few outright feminist figures or women making overt feminist statements in his oeuvre spring to mind, but three, who also share complicated, painful, and conflict-filled experiences of motherhood as well as of sexuality, do. One is Leni Pökler, whose reaction to the phrase "male supremacy," bandied about at political meetings (*GR* 155), is to fight her own weakness for masculine domination at a personal and intimate level, hardening herself to strengthen her daughter (*GR* 156, 219). Another is Frenesi Gates, who can choose to collaborate with Vond, to whom she is sexually attracted, or "pussy out" (*VL* 241). This makes her reflect on the linguistic dimension of patriarchal power, where a gun/penis is more than a physical tool of control, meaning that men "had it so simple" (*VL* 241) while women are stuck with complicated choices such as hers between capitulating to her sexual desire for Vond and heeding her family attachment to her infant daughter, husband, and mother. Finally, a minor character, Tace Boilster, encourages Lake Kindred, née Traverse (who is caught between romantic clichés and illicit desire), to rewrite the script by freeing herself from conventional expectations that her destiny is to be a mother and wife. When Lake finally fights her abusive husband, Tace only regrets that her response was insufficient: "What's wrong with fatal? Only reason it wasn't is you girlied out with that tin shovel" (*AtD* 487). Weak, girly pussies—women like Leni, Frenesi, and Lake not only fight from a position of sexual weakness, if they fight oppression at all, but also make unpopular personal choices in life. These include rejecting modern "soft" men and willing fathers—Peter Sachsa, Zoyd Wheeler, and Doc Willis Turnstone—who represent one kind of feminist vision for equality of the sexes. Sexual patriarchal domination is almost genetically programmed into these women, which implies that their lack of redeeming features is not a result of choices they have made as much as a biological "fact of life." If motherhood is a redeeming feature, it is noticeable that Leni, Frenesi, and Lake prove themselves politically unwilling or emotionally and biologically unable to live up to traditional ideals of uncomplicated motherhood.

Chicks, bimbos, and cuties, susceptible to sexual exploitation and the leering (male) gaze of other characters and readers, seem still to outnumber strong and admirable female characters in Pynchon's fiction to a greater degree than is justifiable given the temporal setting of his historical novels (Cook 1147). This is disheartening indeed if one expects his agenda to be that of a late 1960s feminist literary critic. But the gratuitous nature of the excessive sexual domination of female characters in his later work would take some fancy critical footwork to explain away and has led critics like Mattessich, Cook, Severs, and Freer to doubt to varying degrees whether or not Pynchon has ultimately moved beyond his early sexism. Two exonerating reinterpretations are possible: one is that the apparent misogyny is part of a complex postmodern writer's arsenal for exposing our own flawed assumptions and expectations, and another is that it is part of a political writer's coded way of illustrating the inequality and institutional oppression of women. Those two interpretations would be in keeping respectively with the expanding "Pyndustry" of the 1970s and 1980s that embraced literary readings in tune with linguistic and poststructuralist theories gaining popularity in literature departments at the time and, in recent decades, culturally contextualizing readings and interdisciplinary approaches. A deal of work is required of both these approaches to redeem Pynchon as a writer with feminist credentials, since there is so far little direct evidence of this beyond his knowledge of specific feminist texts that is suggested by glancing allusions (Hite 136) and his awareness of, but limited engagement with, brands of political feminism in general (Freer 140).

This brings me to the third explanation for the dearth in feminist readings of Pynchon's work: that feminists were too busy with real life to bother with a writer who was not contributing significantly to the struggle to resituate women, be it in social power structures or literature, in spite of his critique of oppressive systems in other respects. "Feminism" itself is not a movement with uniform goals and opinions, however useful that would be to analysis and political action, though it has been criticized for representing oppressive thought systems. Monolithic feminisms (white, middle class, and Western), however, have been challenged from within, forcing the movement to fragment or diversify to stay alive and relevant. If feminism in all its permutations avoids solidifying into a "they," it becomes a counterforce resisting the deathly stasis of the systemic, resonating with readings of early Pynchon. Pynchon criticism, which has grown almost exponentially in the same period in which modern feminism developed, is not exactly homogenous itself in terms of method or conclusions, but many of the recurring concerns identified in his fiction—power, control, oppression, and resistance (sexual, political, ethnic, etc.)—at least parallel feminist agendas.

Motherhood has been a significant subject of feminist debate and functions as a lens through which the "interests of male dominance, capitalism, religious power, homophobia, and racism" can be made visible as they define expectations of "good mothering" (Kinser 2). "Mother knowledge," on the other hand, has also been used to posit a maternal authority allowing women to comment on politics, community, peace, and the environment (Kinser 2). It is possible that Pynchon likewise hijacks "motherhood" to make broader structural rather than specific feminist points about power or politics. It is also possible that just as there have been revisions to feminism, Pynchon has revised his view of the value of motherhood and the role of women as mothers in family structures, allying it with a new maternalism that claims to be able to empower women who choose a maternal lifestyle without denying them individuality and liberty. Motherhood may not be a (battle)field Pynchon or many of his critics overtly contend with, but the mothers and nonmothers in his texts invite readers to engage with some form of feminism, whatever his intentions.

Motherhood, Family, and Feminism

"Mother" may have started out as an uncomplicated biological and then a social definition applied to a woman who has given birth or who raises a child, but her nature and identity have been further theorized by psychoanalysis as the constituter of subjects and by social scientists as a "constructed" identity and socializer of daughters into historically defined institutional roles, theorizations that threaten to reduce the mother to a "function" (Baraitser 16). A mother figure who is used in this way to investigate structural issues easily becomes a flat stereotype. Kaplan has argued that Pynchon adds the allegorical mother, another flat type, to the "unconscious mother" and "the institutionally positioned mother" (6). An early example is Oedipa Maas—a nonmother misidentified by Grace Bortz as a fellow mother due to her "harassed style" (104)—in *The Crying of Lot 49*. Oedipa is both childless and parentless. She is not inscribed in a biological family system but instead in a political one: she feels "motherly" (65) toward a character like Genghis Cohen, who wears a Barry Goldwater sweatshirt, and was herself "mothered" by Republican politicians "Secretaries James and Foster and Senator Joseph" as a youth (71).

Pynchon himself cautioned against starting from a "theme, symbol or other abstract unifying agent" (*SL* 12) in the writing process, but his depictions of mother-daughter hostility read plausibly as allegorical or emblematic and resemble a generational allegory to which feminism has also been subject. Mothers like Leni Pökler, Sasha Gates, Mayva Traverse, and March Kelleher, who are part of hardline political communities and who in several cases are willing to leave their men (whether for their own or their children's sakes), end up distancing themselves from their daughters physically and emotionally. Their daughters, Ilse, Frenesi, Lake, and Tallis, surrender themselves to dominant men. Setting personal preferences for and attraction to certain men above independence, or even letting their survival depend on men, they fail to live up to their mothers' ideals in ways that may seem intentionally rebellious. Pynchon has acknowledged that *Vineland* contains a plot reversal where "the parents are progressive and the kids are fascists," an idea his undergraduate tutor suggested to him thirty years before.[2] The repetition of this figure in Pynchon and mostly as a mother-daughter conflict seems almost programmatic and parallels the way in which different waves or generations of feminists are sometimes cast either as politically correct mothers disappointed in politically unengaged younger women or as daughters who see older feminists as maternal establishment figures against whom they must rebel.[3]

The period of the 1970s and 1980s, between the publication of *Gravity's Rainbow* and *Vineland*, saw a number of feminist thinkers argue that motherhood restricted women psychologically and socially and even led some early feminists to view children coldly and unsympathetically, according to Bernice Lott (Freer 142–43). Leni's programmatic and distancing attitude to how Ilse is raised can be seen as selfish in this context, though her wish to raise her daughter to be better able to resist patriarchal domination may be read as well intentioned, even if it is as likely to fail as the strategies Mayva, Sasha, and March employ in raising their daughters. Whether motherhood was oppressive or "one of the most important women's rights" continued to divide feminists in the 1980s (Gimenez 287; Thurer 290), while feminists in the 1990s identified growing pressure (political in origin, supported by government-produced statistics, and successfully transmitted by the media) placed on women to live up to ideal images, emblematized by the "family values" platform introduced during the Reagan years, or risk the social and personal ruin resulting from barrenness (Faludi 21–65). Women without children were suspected of promiscuity and selfishness—two behaviors Lake has to contend with in herself—and "grim feminists" were vilified and seen as setting unreal standards for "living women, down in the world" (*VL* 83) according to Frenesi, who indulges in submissive sexual fantasies but who also feels guilty because she does not have "proper" maternal feelings for her newborn.

If second-wave feminists were seen as antifamily, then logically anyone profamily would be antifeminist. Pynchon's novels reflect such a logic, moving from depicting motherhood as a symbol that has been co-opted by totalitarian regimes and conservative forces to idealizing mothers and families. Pynchon's first work after the "decisive change" of feminism, *Vineland*, is dedicated to his mother and father and inaugurates a series of novels that retrench around the family unit, an ideal that is recouped in happy endings in which families are reunited or reconstituted. In *Vineland* Sasha, Frenesi, and Prairie are brought back together. In *Mason & Dixon* both protagonists start new families, and Mason repairs emotional relations with his father and sons. In *Against the Day* several couples have children in the final sections including Stray and Frank and Yashmeen and Reef, and all the Chums of Chance get heaven-sent spouses and likewise have children. In *Inherent Vice* Doc's grandest gesture reunites the fragmented Harlingen family, and in *Bleeding Edge* 9/11 helps bring Maxine back together with her ex-husband.

A deceptively minor character, Lake Traverse, from another late period text, *Against the Day*, puts the term "choice feminist," the idea that all there is to being a feminist is making individualistic choices, in relief.[4] Her trajectory seems a negation of more successful mother characters and could be a test case for the sexual and procreational repercussions of being antifamily in a Pynchon fiction. Her ménage à trois submission with Sloat Fresno and Deuce Kindred mirrors that of Cyprian, Yashmeen, and Frank but fails to produce a happy ending or a baby. Lake's sexuality makes her a victim in the eyes of second-wave feminists, and while choice feminists might read her as empowered in her embrace of masochism, it brings her no personal rewards beyond the sexual, and there is a suspicion, in her own mind at least, that her lack of maternal bliss marks her as a failed as well as a fallen woman. If Lake embraces her sexuality but fails as a mother she exposes a paradox in the twenty-first-century movement from prescriptive to descriptive feminism, which validates the choices women make, including the choice to work and the choice to embrace "the stereotypical role of female/mother/caregiver" (Belkin qtd. in Kirkpatrick 241). Being barren is not a lifestyle choice, but it has biological finality, so pregnancy remains a genre cliché in a postmodern end to Lake's narrative arc (*AtD* 1057).

As a biologically failed mother, Lake serves as a comment on the late twentieth-century "new momism," which "draws from and repudiates feminism" by insisting that women "have choices, that they are active agents in control of their own destiny" but ties them inevitably to a "highly romanticized yet demanding view of motherhood" (Douglas and Michaels 5), since working women are now saddled with the demands of "intensive mothering" and the notion that working full time at home as well as outside the home is by choice, a choice that women make because they care for and love their families, not out of financial necessity (Hays 152–3). If Leni can be read as an anachronistic radical feminist, Frenesi as a sexual traitor to the women's liberation movement, and Lake as an (unsuccessful) choice feminist before her time, the question that remains is whether Maxine Tarnow, an almost contemporary female character, is an oppressed "new mom" or a liberated postfeminist.

Maxine is a working single mother, with a "history of safe choices" (353), who lives up to predictable cultural expectations of her as a mother throughout *Bleeding Edge*. Single motherhood may not be a choice but nor does it ruin her life. She does not struggle to make ends meet or to have her children cared for while she works odd hours. She even looks after children of less-together parents at short notice. If you don't know how she does it, the answer seems to be child support, grandparents, and maternal resourcefulness. She is subject to expectations, often her own expectations, subvocalized by the narrator: the novel is bookended by her getting her two children to school, while her concern about whether their video games are too bloody or their diet varied enough draws repeated attention to the self-conscious evaluation of her as a mother—one who has to learn to be successfully left by her growing children (Baraitser 5). Like so many other leading female characters in Pynchon, she has parents who represent the political left while she finds herself attracted sexually to the uniformed males of a repressive system on the other side (*BE* 421). In keeping with maternalist care feminism, Maxine's moral strength and ability to heal people around her comes from that female "weakness." Unlike the parenting Leni's, Frenesi's, and Lake's mothers offer, Ernie Tarnow's self-reflecting efforts at fathering enable him to recognize that there is compassion behind his daughter's fascination with Windust and reason to trust the values she can pass on to her own sons (421–22). Maxine's life at the dawn of the twenty-first century also embraces conservative "family values" including Horst Loeffler's commodities-based interpretation of domestic bliss (25, 363), but although she is flawed she is not as fallen as are Lake, Leni, or Frenesi, nor as cut off from connections and communication with her family. The question is whether she is nonetheless subject to judgmental readings of her choices that, where men are concerned, seem less than free.

The ratio of Maxine's direct speech to indirect suggests a running interior commentary on her performance, but whether this is her own or a narrative judgment is not always clear. This is no more evident than in the scene where she, somewhat inexplicably, fails to resist Nicholas Windust when he orders her to present herself for sex. The text reads "Shouldn't she be saying, 'You know what, fuck yourself, you'll have more fun,' and walking out? No, instead, instant docility—she slides to her knees" (258). It is unclear if the question is her own "junior prom" reflex (259), a narratorial injunction, or an expression of the reasonable doubt readers would have, given how unappealing the man is and given how the location and the circumstances for the tryst are described. Are we invited to condemn Maxine for "being used like buttons on a game controller" (258) or approve of her for seeking pleasure regardless of her, Windust's, or our normative expectations for women and mothers? We get a lot of Maxine's interior dialogue in Pynchon's narrative, but the question of her agency and whether she even reflects on it herself afterward is left uncertain. The text acknowledges, snidely I think, that "in some circles it is held to be something of a big deal . . ."—"it" being whether in her mind "it's him moving or if she's doing it herself" (258). It would be a big deal in recent feminist debate, where agency—to choose to be a bad girl or be free to say no to men—is central to understanding and supporting women's lives.

Maxine returns to the decorum of marriage, where the narrator simultaneously veils and idealizes marital sex. Windust, and many other *Bleeding Edge* characters, benefit instead from her mothering impulses. Families are brought back together, and she uncovers Windust's better self for redemption. However, Lake, who also sees "just a boy that's lost" in Deuce Kindred and subjects herself to him sexually, cannot love her "enemy into some kind of redeemin grace for the both" of them according to her feminist conscience in the form of Tace (*AtD* 482–83). One obvious distinction between Maxine and Lake, which could explain these different outcomes, is that Maxine is maternal and Lake is nonmaternal. In making her biologically unable to mother, it is as if Pynchon also deprives Lake of the redeeming power of motherly feeling. Not coincidentally, we see in Lake's life experiences, as both a nonmother and sexual deviant, the double fulfillment of the expectation that to become a mother "proves, first, that you are a 'real' woman, and second, that you are a decent, worthy one" (Douglas and Michaels 5). Lake is not scripted as "a long-suffering movie heroine" who finds "herself pregnant at last" (*AtD* 1057), and Pynchon's description of Lake's unsympathetic choices where family loyalty is concerned, insofar as her attraction to Deuce Kindred is a betrayal of her own kin, contributes to the idea that his texts are increasingly pronatalist and prolife in the sense that the needs of small children come before those of their mothers. Good women have children, and children deserve good mothers. The implication is that Lake is a bad woman and would be a bad mother, and she and Deuce come to believe infertility is the price she pays for her being a bad daughter to boot (486). This raises the question of whether good women and good families have become connected as if by biological necessity in late Pynchon texts, especially as the question of choice in women's lives is barely applicable to conception in late-period Pynchon.

Choice or Life?

Pynchon's first three novels were written before *Roe v. Wade* originally established abortion rights and are the only ones that reference abortion or that offer an apparently neutral treatment of the childlessness of a main female character. The questions raised in *V.* when Esther Harvitz's wish for an abortion is discussed concern her choice and autonomy, which are confronted with positions on fetal rights, financial difficulties in obtaining an illegal abortion, and her community's deliberating whether to condemn, defend, or ultimately fund her choice. Abortion is promoted by the Empty Ones for the Hereros in *Gravity's Rainbow*, not as an individual choice but as a joint act of revolution, since tribal death is a "simple choice" that denies their colonizers the power to benefit from their subjugation (316–18). Pregnancies in Pynchon's fiction may be accidental, but with these exceptions they are not terminated. Instead, we have, on the one hand, political mothers (Leni Pökler in *Gravity's Rainbow* and Frenesi Gates in *Vineland*) who seek what could instead be called a "postpartum termination" of the bond with their daughters in ways that dramatize both identity and feminist politics, and, on the other hand, political fathers (Webb, Reef, and other struggling miners in *Against the Day*) who cause mothers to choose between sticking with them or with their children, as political struggles and personal affiliations clash.

It seems clear that motherhood in Pynchon is increasingly about family constructions inside which the choices and autonomies (political and personal) available to female characters are negotiated. Pynchon's women increasingly are clearly situated within existing family structures instead of being outside such structures deciding "freely" whether to opt in by "starting a family." Only one child in *Against the Day* is "accidental" (Stray has Jesse out of wedlock and is pressured to a degree by her community to marry). While the Kindreds are infertile, Yashmeen and Reef's child, Ljubica, is conceived as if by assisted fertilization and nurtured initially by a surrogate parent (882, 891, 950). Both children end up in extended but heteronormative family constellations (1076) reminiscent of the late family reunion in *Vineland*. Various male characters in Pynchon's first three novels, specifically Fausto Maijstral in *V.*, Otto Gnahb in *Gravity's Rainbow*, and Metzger in *The Crying of Lot 49*, characterize mothers as generically or specifically suspect and predatory. In Pynchon's later novels, rather than being controlling monsters, mothers are more likely to fail "gently" by losing control of and failing to communicate with their daughters, leading to greater or lesser degrees of estrangement as is the case with Sasha, Frenesi, and Prairie in *Vineland*, Mayva and Lake and Erlys and Dally in *Against the Day*, and March and Tallis in *Bleeding Edge*. In other words, in late-period Pynchon, children are no longer disruptive "accidents" but neither are they sources of power to women who conspire to perpetuate Maijstral's purported "fictional mystery about motherhood" (*V.* 321–22). Rather, if girls, they are sources of personal pain and guilt, and the relationship with their mothers is defined by miscommunication. Pynchon's first novels raised the emasculating specter of "controlling women"; his latest conjure up the structures which continue controlling women to this day.

Pynchon's latest novels were written during a period in which individual states began encroaching on access to free choice. Increasingly, the Supreme

Court upholds the rights of life against the woman's right to choose not to reproduce (Mazec 428–29). In mainstream feminism, reproduction has increasingly become a question of whether childlessness by choice is an acceptable redirection of attention toward self or career or even a stand against dominant ideologies ascribing value to children, mothering, and family (Gimenez). Oedipa's childlessness is not belabored, unlike her political mothering instincts, but Lake Traverse's lack of children is significant, especially in comparison to the more sympathetic characters of *Against the Day*, who have "babies [who] crawled and stumbled, dropped, picked up and threw things down again" or whose abodes "teem with children of all ages and sizes who run up and down [...], whooping and hollering" (482, 1084). Children, for Pynchon, are "life incarnate," combining fecundity and vivacity. But having children is not a choice characters seem to make very actively. Bringing new life into the world is just something that happens—except for Lake, who both struggles to conceive and to accurately determine for whose sake she needs a baby. Lake's case focuses on the right to become a mother as a feminist issue rather than the political right to freely choose not to on which white second-wave feminists had insisted (Hayden 279). In a time of decreasing fertility in industrialized Western countries, ecofeminists have taken issue with "constructions of fertility and infertility as natural or deviant within a social framework that stigmatizes the nonmaternal woman" (Marafiote 182). On the one hand, not having children is an increasingly difficult choice, not only in political and practical terms as family planning is vilified but also ideologically as the cult of new momism and intensive mothering grows.[5] On the other hand, low fertility due to environmental and lifestyle factors (from the effects of hormone pollutants to the older age of first-time mothers who tend to be well-educated career women) only gives more power to the cult of the "priceless child" and provides fodder for the adaptive preference for wanting one in rational market societies that have benefited economically from having women in the workforce but that also needs them to be productive economically and maternally so that this system can be perpetuated (Hays 152–54). The intimate, biomechanical, and emotional aspects of mothering have been fully integrated with capitalist systems, adaptive preferences for mothering being supported implicitly and explicitly forming a Pynchonean closed-system plot where women are integrated beyond being a "civil-service category" working for "Them" (*GR* 219). Ironically, Pynchon's late writing contributes to this attempt at integration by sanctifying motherhood and not highlighting acceptable alternatives.

Births logically perpetuate a system that controls possibilities and dictates behavior to women at all levels. Nonetheless, even Pynchon seems to glorify the aura of pregnancy, whether it be Stray's "composed and dreamy" state (*AtD* 201), Petunia Leeway's "radiance" (*IV* 361), or even Brooke's "glow"

(*BE* 425), although it is arguable that he is just drawing on lazy clichés, trying to be tongue-in-cheek in using such clichés, or simply reflecting a romantic view of procreation that is still viable in a postfeminist era. Brock Vond's indifferent or scornful "[s]o you've reproduced" (*VL* 294) is obviously not the (re)mark of a sympathetic character. I would argue that Frenesi's rejection of motherhood adds an unsympathetic dimension to her character. However exonerating brain-chemical explanations of postpartum depression should be to informed readers, a mother who fails to live up to expectations of motherly, unconditional love and instead expresses "hatred for the tiny life" (*VL* 287) is pitted unfairly against the complete helplessness and innocence of a newborn. Frenesi's rejection of the characteristics of normative motherhood aligns her with Leni, whose refusal to be (called) a "Mama" (*GR* 220) may be ideologically motivated but reads as defective empathy for a child's needs. Leni fails to live up to the standards of care, or illusions thereof, expected of productive mothers in Nazi Germany and of mothers in the Western world today, which subjects working mothers to both the "ethos of a rationalized market society" *and* "the ideology of intensive mothering" (Hays 152). However, her act of resistance against an oppressive system seems cruel and perverse because it is achieved seemingly at the expense of the vulnerable members of the family into which Ilse's birth tied her. Psychoanalysis tells us, after all, that a mother is not an agent who can freely choose when to sever ties with her child postpartum. She is expected, if successful, to simply "be there to be left" (Furman 15), as Maxine finally is.

In *Gravity's Rainbow*, Leni expresses the feminist idea that birth can literally trap individual women in powerful systems of control at multiple levels. In Pynchon's next novel, that oppressive dimension of procreation transcends a gendered experience to become allegorical of a general human condition. Both Brock Vond and postpartum-depressed Frenesi express the fear that birthing leads to death (a system of control) and that obtaining freedom is about believing in immortality and escaping the cycle of life and the earthly bondage births perpetuate (*VL* 277, 287, 289, 314). I have argued elsewhere that Pynchon's first three novels show that life itself is an inherently degenerative system and that a certain deterministic hopelessness leaves few if any other ways out short of Herero-style sui-genocide. Later novels still show his leaning toward biological determinism, asserting a sexual predilection in women toward the (symbols) of male supremacy and giving few examples of sympathetic women who chose freedom from the systemic by electing not to marry or have children.

Pynchon's increasing faith in the value of family and the parent-child bond has been noted (Freer 146). Out of necessity children may be left with sisters and grandmothers (as Jesse and Prairie are) for longer periods of time, but leaving a child outright is a postpartum termination—a severing of the mother-child bond but by the mother's choice and prematurely to the child's desire to detach—and Pynchon's texts encourage us to sympathize with the child over the mother in such situations. Nonmaternal women are not just women who have refused or failed to become mothers but women who fail at mothering. There are several nonmaternal candidates in addition to Leni, whose unforgiving brand of mothering makes her "one of the least attractive characters in the novel"—"unlovable, unpitiable, cold" (Kaufman 220), and Frenesi, whose habit of "repeatedly ankling every situation that it should have been her responsibility to keep with and set straight" (*VL* 58) makes her parenting choices "essentially the wrong ones" (Freer 143). Abortion is no longer part of Pynchon's narrative, but a child's right to (family) life is increasingly asserted, if not at conception then certainly at parturition: in Pynchon's 1966 novel, children roam the nighttime streets free of maternal oversight, and a childless Oedipa loses husband, lover, and plot at the end. In 1990, Pynchon has Prairie, whose mother fails to protect her, only just manage to deny Brock Vond a sexual and paternal role in her life. Twenty-three years later Pynchon's conscientious mother, Maxine, recovers the lost boy capable of good deeds in Windust to the point of resurrecting his one family connection, Xiomara, the wife who had tried to save him earlier (*BE* 426–27, 443). The most maternal of Pynchon's female detectives also gets the closest to closure and fixes the most families; she reestablishes Windust's family, she patches up relations with both her ex-husband and sister, and she brings March Kelleher, Tallis, and Kennedy Ice back together. One senses that for Pynchon, the issue is not a child's right to life (at conception or later) but his or her right to family. Freer makes the point that Pynchon's increasing sentimentality elevates family to the status of "last bastion of *communitas* in self-interested times" (144), an idea epitomized in *Bleeding Edge*, when newly reunited Horst and Maxine include in their reestablished nuclear family unit (and apartment) some of the "real-estate casualties" of September 11, 2001 (332). Maxine, like Mary Mason and Meg Bland in *Mason & Dixon* or Tace Boilster or Stray Briggs in *Against the Day*, represents a mater familias, a brand of well-meaning and inclusive woman who builds, rebuilds, or extends her family with "bonus children" great and small. In Maxine's case, her maternal instinct attaches itself to her abusive lover, Nicholas Windust, in whom she sees a lost boy to be saved. If Pynchon's message is that you owe your baby a family, at whatever price, at least Tace and Lake question that message (*AtD* 485–86).

Accommodating Motherhood

On the merits of *Gravity's Rainbow*, in which issues of oppression and control are clear, critics have found Pynchon to be a politically and analytically astute writer. Therefore, if he does not present the institution of motherhood, with all its expectations, constraints, and challenges, including childlessness, as a continuing political battleground in that same vein but instead as an uncomplicated personal identity issue, then part of his fan base might be justifiably disappointed. It would be tempting to echo Greil Marcus, who famously asked "What is this shit?" (16) when Bob Dylan found family and later religion and produced albums like *Self Portrait* (1970), which fans and critics hoped was satire or iconoclasm but feared was premature dotage. Pynchon's apparently genuine appreciation of family and the "safe" construction of motherhood in his old age need not be accommodated as the perennially juvenile or senile chauvinism of a man born in the 1930s. His conversion to "family man" is in keeping with views on mothers and family values embraced in versions of feminism emerging during the latest decades of his writing career. As the united social front aspirations of feminism have seemed to give way to individual identity politics, twenty-first-century readers confronting the confusion of post-second-wave and postfeminism might even accommodate the changing position—from motherhood being a politicized choice to being a life(style)—seeing it as endorsing acceptable individual variations in an equal (but different) world and make similar allowances for those Pynchon characters at odds with their motherhood roles.[6]

Ultimately, whatever he seems to say about maternal and nonmaternal women, the beauty of Pynchon's texts is that they and their changing cultural and historical contexts produce new insights through reader-tendentious rather than author-intentional readings. Whatever his point of view or ours, Pynchon's texts can, like Bob Dylan's songs, "serve as metaphors, enriching our lives, giving us random insight into the myths we carry and the present we live, intensifying what we've known and leading us toward what we never looked for, while at the same time enforcing an emotional strength upon those perceptions" (Marcus 19). Whether Pynchon writes weak female characters as a feminist critique of patriarchal structures or from a determinist or misogynist position, reading them allows us to reflect on how women are viewed and presented in our culture and whether "Badgirl shit pays off " (*AtD* 268).

NOTES

1. Only a handful of articles or chapters, by Kaufman, Caesar ("Motherhood "), Hayles, and Freer, have significantly addressed motherhood in Pynchon over the past four decades.

2. *Vineland* title page inscription by Pynchon to Walter Slatoff (Hite 140, 150n).

3. See Stevenson, Everingham, and Robinson.

4. Choice feminism, introduced in 2005 by Linda Hirshman, assumes that gender equality has been achieved and that accepting women's individual identities and ensuing choices validates and empowers them.

5. See Douglas and Michaels and Hays.

6. A criticism of both third-wave and choice feminism is that their inclusiveness dilutes the brand of feminism and renders concerted social action impossible (Snyder-Hall 260).

WORKS CITED

Baraitser, Lisa. *Maternal Encounters: The Ethics of Interruption.* New York: Routledge, 2009.
Caesar, Terry P. "'Take Me Anyplace You Want': Pynchon's Literary Career as a Maternal Construct in *Vineland*." *Novel: A Forum on Fiction* 25.2 (1992): 181–99.
———. "Motherhood and Postmodernism." *American Literary History* 7.1 (1995): 120–40.
Cook, Simon. "Manson Chicks and Microskirted Cuties: Pornification in Thomas Pynchon's *Inherent Vice*." *Textual Practice* 29.6 (2015): 1143–64.
Dalsgaard, Inger H. "The Linking Feature: Degenerative Systems in Pynchon and Spengler" *Pynchon Notes* 44–45 (1999): 97–116.
Douglas, Susan J., and Meredith W. Michaels. *The Mommy Myth: The Idealization of Motherhood and How It Has Undermined All Women.* New York: Free Press, 2004.
Faludi, Susan. *Backlash: The Undeclared War on Women.* London: Chatto and Windus, 1992.
Fitzpatrick, Kathleen. "The Clockwork Eye: Technology, Woman, and the Decay of the Modern in Thomas Pynchon's *V.*" *Thomas Pynchon: Reading from the Margins.* Ed. Niran Abbas. Madison: Fairleigh-Dickinson University Press, 2003. 91–107.
Freer, Joanna. *Thomas Pynchon and American Counterculture.* New York: Cambridge University Press, 2014.
Furman, Erna. "Mothers Have to Be There to Be Left." *Psychoanalytic Study of the Child* 37.1 (1982): 15–28.
Gimenez, Martha E. "Feminism, Pronatalism, and Motherhood." *Mothering: Essays in Feminist Theory.* Ed. Joyce Trebilcot. Totowa: Rowman and Allanheld, 1984. 287–314.
Hayden, Sara. "Purposefully Childless Good Women." Hayden and Hallstein 269–90.
Hayden, Sara, and D. Lynn O'Brien Hallstein, eds. *Contemplating Maternity in an Era of Choice: Exploration into Discourses of Reproduction.* Lanham: Lexington Books, 2010.
Hayles, N. Katherine. "'Who Was Saved?' Families, Snitches, and Recuperation in Pynchon's *Vineland*." *Critique: Studies in Contemporary Fiction* 32.2 (1990): 77–91.
Hays, Sharon. *The Cultural Contradictions of Motherhood.* New Haven: Yale University Press, 1996.
Hite, Molly. "Feminist Theory and the Politics of *Vineland*." *The Vineland Papers: Critical Takes on Pynchon's Novel.* Ed. Geoffrey Green, Donald J. Greiner, and Larry McCaffrey. Normal: Dalkey Archive Press, 1994. 135–53.
Kaplan, E. Ann. *Motherhood and Representation: The Mother in Popular Culture and Melodrama.* London: Routledge, 1992.
Kaufman, Marjorie. "Brünnhilde and the Chemists: Women in *Gravity's Rainbow*." *Mindful Pleasures: Essays on Thomas Pynchon.* Ed. George Levine and David Leverenz. Boston: Little, Brown, 1976. 197–227.
Kinser, Amber E. *Motherhood and Feminism.* Berkeley: Seal Press, 2010.
Kirkpatrick, Jennet. "Selling Out? Solidarity and Choice in the American Feminist Movement." *Perspectives on Politics* 8.1 (2010): 241–45.

Marafiote, Tracy. "The In/Fertile, Un/Natural Body: Ecofeminism, Dis/Embodiment, Technology, and (the Loss of) Choice." Hayden and Hallstein 181–200.

Marcus, Greil. "Self Portrait No. 25." Rev. of *Self Portrait*, by Bob Dylan. *Rolling Stone* 23 Jul. 1970: 16–19.

Mattessich, Stefan. "Imperium, Misogyny, and Postmodern Parody in Thomas Pynchon's *V.*" *ELH* 65.2 (1998): 503–21.

Mazec, Robert P. *The Mid-Atlantic Region*. Westport: Greenwood Press, 2004.

Pynchon, Thomas. *Against the Day*. London: Jonathan Cape, 2006.

——. *Bleeding Edge*. London: Jonathan Cape, 2013.

——. *The Crying of Lot 49*. London: Vintage, 2000.

——. *Gravity's Rainbow*. London: Picador, 1975.

——. *Slow Learner*. London: Picador, 1985.

——. *Vineland*. London: Minerva, 1991.

Severs, Jeffrey. "'The abstractions she was instructed to embody': Women, Capitalism, and Artistic Representation in *Against the Day*." *Pynchon's* Against the Day: *A Corrupted Pilgrim's Guide*. Ed. Jeffrey Severs and Christopher Leise. Newark: University of Delaware Press, 2011. 215–38.

Snyder-Hall, R. Claire. "Third-Wave Feminism and the Defense of 'Choice.'" *Perspectives on Politics* 8.1 (2010): 255–61.

Stevenson, Deborah, Christine Everingham, and Penelope Robinson. "Choices and Life Changes: Feminism and the Politics of Generational Change." *Social Politics* 18.1 (2011): 125–45.

Thurer, Shari L. *The Myths of Motherhood: How Culture Reinvents the Good Mother*. Boston: Houghton Mifflin, 1994.

Traynor, Desmond. "Part Detective Story Part Paean to New York City." Rev. of Thomas Pynchon, *Bleeding Edge*. *Irish Independent* 2 Dec. 2013, www.independent.ie/entertainment/books/part-detective-story-part-paean-to-new-york-city-29796570.html. Accessed 16 Nov. 2017.

Contributors

JENNIFER BACKMAN is an associate professor of English at Palomar College in Southern California. She received a PhD in contemporary literature from Purdue University and a master's degree in the humanities from the University of Chicago.

SIMON DE BOURCIER is the author of *Pynchon and Relativity: Narrative Time in Thomas Pynchon's Later Novels* (2012), as well as articles on Thomas Pynchon, David Foster Wallace, and Neal Stephenson and entries in *The Literary Encyclopedia* and the *Dictionary of Nineteenth-Century Journalism in Great Britain and Ireland*. He has degrees from the University of Cambridge, Anglia Ruskin University, and the University of East Anglia. He is one of the editors of *Orbit*.

ALI CHETWYND is an assistant professor and the chair of the English Department at the American University of Iraq, Sulaimani. He works on the constructive argumentative capacities of antimimetic fiction usually taken to be intrinsically antirational. His work on Thomas Pynchon, William Gaddis, Ben Jonson, and postwar fiction has appeared in *College Literature*, *English Studies*, *Orbit*, *Textual Practice*, *Twentieth Century Literature*, and other venues.

SIMON COOK teaches journalism, creative writing, and contemporary literature at Utrecht University in the Netherlands. He is conducting research for a PhD on the impact of sexualized societies and pornification on literary fiction since 1970.

INGER H. DALSGAARD is an associate professor in American studies at Aarhus University. She has published extensively on Thomas Pynchon, is a coeditor (with Luc Herman and Brian McHale) of the *Cambridge Companion to Thomas Pynchon* (2012) and is the editor of *Thomas Pynchon in Context* (forthcoming).

CATHERINE FLAY is a tutor at Birkbeck College, University of London, and course convenor of the Reading 21st-Century Fictions module. Her previous research has focused on neoliberalism and contemporary radicalism in fiction, and her current work explores the centrality of pornography in contemporary Western culture, interrogating sites of its inclusion in literature and mainstream cinema and considering its empowering as well as oppressive effects on both men and women.

MARIE FRANCO is a doctoral candidate in English at the Ohio State University. Her dissertation examines the relation among explicit representations of sex in American postmodern fiction, queer erotica, and post–World War II sexual subcultures.

JOANNA FREER is a lecturer in American literature at the University of Exeter. She is the author of *Thomas Pynchon and American Counterculture* (2014) and currently an editor of the journal *Orbit*.

DOUG HAYNES is a senior lecturer in American literature and visual culture and head of American studies at the University of Sussex, UK. His research interests are in the dialogue between modern American literature and visual culture and critical theory. In particular, he works on notions of the affective and economic, broadly conceived, ranging from telepathy to security to transnationalism. He has a special interest in Thomas Pynchon and is a guest editor of a 2018 special issue of *Textual Practice* with Joanna Freer. He has recently coedited (with Tara Stubbs) *Navigating the Transnational in Modern American Literature and Culture* (2017), which includes his essay on telepathy and terror in the work of Don DeLillo and painter Gerhard Richter.

LUC HERMAN teaches American literature and narrative theory at the University of Antwerp. He has coedited (with Inger Dalsgaard and Brian McHale) the *Cambridge Companion to Thomas Pynchon* (2012), coauthored (with Steven Weisenburger) *Gravity's Rainbow, Domination, and Freedom* (2013), and (with John Krafft) a series of essays on the typescript of *V.* His work for journals has appeared in, among others, *Poetics Today, Narrative, Style, Contemporary Literature, Critique, English Studies*, and *Texas Studies in Literature and Language*.

MOLLY HITE is an Emerita Professor of English at Cornell University, specializing in twentieth-century experimental fiction. She has written about Thomas Pynchon's novels throughout her career. Her most recent book is titled *Woolf's Ambiguities: Tonal Modernism, Narrative Strategy, Feminist Precursors*.

KOSTAS KALTSAS is a PhD candidate in creative writing at the University of Southampton and Bath Spa University, funded by the Arts and Humanities Research Council's South, West and Wales Doctoral Training Partnership. He also works as a freelance translator and is currently translating *Infinite Jest* into Greek.

CHRISTOPHER KOCELA is an associate professor of English at Georgia State University, where he teaches contemporary U.S. literature, theory, and popular culture. His current research focuses on intersections between Eastern thought (particularly Buddhism) and the depiction of racial and gender difference in American fiction after World War II.

JOHN M. KRAFFT, professor emeritus of English at Miami University, was a founder and editor of the journal *Pynchon Notes*, which was published from 1979 to 2009. Recently he has collaborated with Luc Herman (University of Antwerp) on a series of essays analyzing the evolution of Pynchon's *V.* from typescript to published novel.

GEORGIOS MARAGOS is an independent scholar from Athens, Greece. He did his PhD at Panteion University, Athens, on networks of information in Thomas Pynchon's novels and stories. His work has appeared in *Orbit*, as well as two collections: *Against the Grain: Reading Pynchon's Counternarratives* (edited By Sascha Pöhlmann) and *Thomas Pynchon and the (De)vices of Global (Post)modernity* (edited by Zofia Kolbuszewska).

ANGUS MCFADZEAN studied literature at Glasgow and Edinburgh universities and received a DPhil in the novels of James Joyce at Wadham College, University of Oxford. His thesis is a genetic and narratological study reading Joyce's concept of epiphany as part of a compositional strategy in which epiphanies are organized into sequential narratives through a theme of transgression. His research interests include the interaction of narrative, genre, and history across post-1945 cinema and literature. He currently lectures on fantastic literature of the nineteenth century in the Oxford Department of Continuing Education.

RICHARD MOSS is a tutor at Durham University. He recently completed a PhD thesis entitled "Towards a Preterite Theology: Resistance and Spirituality in the Novels of Thomas Pynchon." His current research interests include theology in Thomas Pynchon's work, as well as the religious components of mid-twentieth-century Californian literature.

JEFFREY SEVERS is an associate professor of English at the University of British Columbia. He is coeditor (with Christopher Leise) of *Pynchon's* Against the Day: *A Corrupted Pilgrim's Guide* (2011) and the author of *David Foster Wallace's Balancing Books: Fictions of Value* (2017). He has published articles on Pynchon and other writers in *Twentieth-Century Literature, Pynchon Notes, Critique, Modern Fiction Studies*, and edited collections.

Index

Abbas, Niran, xix, xx
abortion, 225, 233–34, 237
abuse: child, xxvi, 75, 145–61; domestic, 54, 201, 221; sexual, ix, 114, 117, 137; slave, 165
Acker, Kathy, xii
Against the Day, xiv, xvi, xxi, xxiii, xxvi, xxviiin3, 73, 209; child abuse and, 151–52, 155–58, 159; family and, 195–97, 201, 202; Melanie resurrected in, 85–86; motherhood and, 222, 226, 231, 234, 235, 237; women conduits and, 125–28, 133, 135–36, 139, 140–41, 142n10, 145; women's liberation and, 222
agency, xxiv, xxviii, 5, 22, 27, 90, 106n9, 139; external, 115; moral, 198; sexual, 92, 119, 138; women's, xviii, 20, 112, 114, 117–19, 131, 151, 153, 233
Allen, Mary, xvii–xviii, xx, xxixn15, 190
anarchism, 42, 49, 130, 131, 135, 212; sado-anarchism, 88–91, 103–5, 106n6; sexual, 79
Anderson, Paul Thomas, ix, x, 109, 119

Backman, Jennifer, xxiv
Barth, John, xi, xvii, xviiin7
Bataille, Georges, 74, 75, 83
BDSM, 126, 132, 135, 136, 141, 142n9
Bellow, Saul, xi, 3
Bergh, Patricia, xix, 61
Berressem, Hanjo, 84, 174n13
Bérubé, Michael, xxii, 77–80, 88, 95, 126, 142n12
Bianca, 73, 77, 86, 129, 146–48, 157, 159, 160n1; conception of, 142; as seductive, 150; with Slothrop, 79, 132–33, 152, 153–54, 155, 197
binary, 90, 206; gender, 90, 98, 174, 180; master-slave, 162–76, 174n2; sex, 89, 90, 94, 180; thought, 52
Bleeding Edge: family and, 194, 195, 196, 200–206; gender roles and, 19–35, 36–41, 43–50; motherhood and, 226, 227, 231–33, 234, 237; sexualized children and, 158–59; mentioned, xiv, xvi, xxiv, xxvii, xxviiin3, 6, 142n7, 145, 146
Blicero. *See* Weissman
Bodine, Pig, 10, 97, 121n1, 200; attempted rape of Paola, 186
Borgesius, Katje, xvi, 5, 129, 133, 136; pornography and, 115–19, 121n3, 141; S/M and, 12, 88, 89, 92–95, 98, 102, 104
Breu, Christopher, xxiv, 20–25, 31, 32, 33n3
Butler, Judith, 75, 106n14, 174n1

censorship, 126, 139, 145, 148, 155
Chapman, Wes, xix, xxviiin8, 81
Chastain, DL, xviii, xix, xxv, 5, 54–64, 127–28, 130, 134, 142n6, 203; as feminist figure, 209, 219, 221; role reversal and, 53
Chetwynd, Ali, xxviiin5, 54
Chirpingdon-Groin, Ruperta, 125, 135, 136, 137, 139, 141, 142n10
Chums of Chance, 140, 145, 152, 156, 158, 159, 202, 231
Colette, xiii
conservatism, 11, 44, 209–24; Pynchon's sexual, 180

245

Cook, Simon, xvi, xxv, xxvi, 23, 111, 113–15, 120, 228
counterculture, 22, 34n5, 125, 127, 130, 141, 209–23; Buddhism and, 53, 63; free love and, xiv; 1960s, xxi, 55, 129
Cowart, David, 42, 47, 61, 81, 141n3, 205
cross-dressing, 98, 154, 217
Crying of Lot 49, The: childless Oedipa, 229; conservatism and, 211; gender roles and, 36–51; mentioned, xvi, xx, xxiv, xxviiin3, xxixn16, 15n4, 70, 73, 151

Dalsgaard, Inger H., xvii
Davidson, Cathy, xxixn16, 40, 48
de Beauvoir, Simone, 85
de Bourcier, Simon, xxvi
DeepArcher, 41–43, 49n1, 205
Deleuze, Gilles, xxv, 70, 71
DeLillo, Don, xi, 203
disempowerment: female, 98, 167, 223; male, xxvi
domination, xxii, 97–98, 103–5, 131–32, 136, 162–63, 188, 190, 227–30
Ducornet, Rikki, xii
Dworkin, Andrea, xiv, 75, 118

empowerment, xi; female, 54, 63, 64, 139, 226, 229, 231, 238n4; worker, 212
"Entropy," 191n8
Erdmann, Margherita (Greta), 5, 93, 119, 129, 132, 133, 138–39, 141, 147; BDSM and, 89–90, 101; making Alpdrücken, 74, 139; with Slothrop, xxviiin3, 136, 197
essentialism, xiv, 219, 222; Pynchon's, xi, xxiii, xxvii; queer theory's rejection of, 105n4

family, xxvii, 4, 30, 127, 155, 162, 166; bonds, xvi; conservative structure of, 70, 209–24; different models of, xxiv; motherhood and, 225–40; as normative structure, xviii, xxvi, 94, 102; nuclear, xiv, 43–45; as represented in sitcoms, 179–93; sentimental, 194–208; sexuality and, 84; S/M and, 103, 110; mentioned, xxiii, xxv
fatherhood, 37, 43, 218
femininity, xxiv, 5, 27, 72, 85, 98, 163, 165, 207n1, 218; associated with objecthood or slavery, x, xviii, xix, 166, 167, 170, 171, 174; in males, 102, 157, 172, 217; mythological, 179; passive, 8, 61, 94; traditional/conventional, xvi, xxiii, 36, 37, 39, 40, 49, 133, 209; V. and, 7
feminism, 4–6, 52–64, 225–39; antifeminism, 209–24; antiporn, 117, 127; feminist criticism and theory, xvii, xviii, 28, 128, 219; feminist movement, 3, 14n3, 220; second wave, xiv, 75, 148, 190; third wave, xv
femme fatale, 21–30, 34n6
fetishism, xi, xxi, 63, 82, 84, 91, 119, 128, 131–37, 139, 141, 222; fetishistic desire, 78–80; fetishized body, xiv, 63, 81, 83, 99, 101, 106n12, 126, 148
Fitzpatrick, Kathleen, xxviiin2, 174n13, 180, 227
Flay, Catherine, xxvii
Foucault, Michel, 75–79, 81, 82, 84–85, 89, 90, 94, 96, 99, 103–5, 174n1
Fowles, John, xiii, xxixn11
Franco, Marie, xxii, xxv, 110, 113
Freer, Joanna: on Pynchon and family/community, 44–45, 195, 199, 220, 236–37; on Pynchon and feminism, xxi, 52, 54, 209, 219–20, 226, 228, 237, 238n1; on Pynchon and sexism, xvi, xxviiin9, 73–74, 113, 115, 119, 151, 158, 180, 228
Freud, Sigmund, 7, 76, 78, 80, 82, 86n2, 129, 149, 155
Friedan, Betty, xiv

Gaddis, William, xi
Gass, William, xiii
Gates, Frenesi, xxv, 5, 50n4, 139, 203, 216; as absent mother, xviii, 199, 201, 202, 209–10, 214, 215, 226, 228, 230, 231, 232, 234, 236–37; Buddhism and, 54–57, 59, 60–64; conservatism and, 217–22; as subservient to male power, xix, 127–28, 130, 134, 227, 231
gaze, 6, 63, 147; male, xvi, 28, 63, 113, 129, 153, 170, 184, 228
gender politics, xii, xxvii, 6, 40, 43, 52, 55, 206
gender roles, xviii, xix, xxiii, xxiv, 19–65, 102, 190; blending of, 180; traditional, 221
Gottfried, 12; Blicero and, 88–89, 97–103, 106n13
Graves, Robert, 7, 179, 187, 188, 191n12
Gravity's Rainbow: child abuse and, 145, 146–48, 149–54; conservatism and, 210, 212; family and, 196, 197, 198; female conduits

and, 125–29, 132–33, 135, 137, 139, 141n2, 142n10; motherhood and, 225–26, 230, 234, 236, 237; pornography and, 77–80, 81, 83, 84, 109–17, 119; S/M and, 88–108; mentioned, xiv, xvi, xix, xx, xxi, xxv, xxvi, xxviiin3, 5, 12, 73,
Greer, Germaine, xiv, 219

Halfcourt, Yashmeen, xxviiin3, 129, 155, 231, 234; assertive, 136, 140; incest and, 155–56
Hawthorne, Mark D., xix, xxi, 180, 190, 207n1
Hayles, N. Katherine, xviii, 5, 238n1
Haynes, Doug, xviii, xxv, 22
Hepworth, Shasta Fey, ix–xi, 24–26, 30, 34nn6–7; compared to Katje, 118, 121n3; seduction and, 117; sexual fantasies and, 21–23, 113–16, 119, 141n1
Hereros, xx, 12, 110, 236; abortion and, 234
Herman, Luc, xxi, xxvi, 13, 72, 79, 88, 104, 109, 128, 132, 141n2, 206
heteronormativity, xxvi, 55, 76, 97, 99, 114, 117, 129, 162, 168–70, 203, 234; heteronormative fantasies, 109; heteronormative society, 91, 98; heteronormative values, 56
Hite, Molly, xvi, xviii, 210; on DL Chastain, 209, 221; on male communication through women's bodies, xix, 127, 219; on Pynchon's familiarity with feminist texts, 54, 228
homosexuality. *See under* sexuality
Hutcheon, Linda, xviii

identity, 19, 24, 31, 148, 159, 214, 215; authorial, xxii; biological, xi, xxixn16, 229; disidentification, 90, 91, 97–99; female, 9, 46; gender, xxvi, 3, 53–56, 163–64, 168, 173, 207n1, 209; karmic, 60, 61; male, 180, 218–20; marginalized, xxiii; othered, xx; performed, 169–74; personal, 30, 238; sexual, 83, 85, 94, 111, 179, 184; mentioned, xvii, 69
identity politics, 186, 225, 226, 234, 238
incest, 69, 72, 79, 83, 145, 148–49, 151, 154–55, 155–58
Inherent Vice (film), ix–xi; porn and, 109
Inherent Vice (novel): noir and, 19–35; pornography and, 109–21; mentioned, xvi, xxiv, xxv, 73, 125, 133, 134, 141n1, 194, 218, 222, 231
intertextuality, xxvi, 196
"Is It O.K. to Be a Luddite?" 69, 71

James, Henry, xiii
Jardine, Alice, xvii–xviii, xx

Kaltsas, Kostas, xxiv
Kelleher, March, 32, 41, 158; as activist, 31, 33, 44–45; as mother, 43, 195, 202–3, 230, 234, 237
Kim, Sue J., xx, xxii
Kocela, Christopher, xxi, xxiv
Kolbuszewska, Zofia, 146, 157
Krafft, John M., xxvi, 13, 160n1, 206
Kunoichi sisterhood, 53, 55, 57–58, 62, 121n4, 209, 219–20

Lacan, Jacques, Bérubé's use of, 77, 95
Lakewood, Cyprian, 231; as queer spy, 139; with Yashmeen and Reef, 136, 140
law, 26, 30, 74, 139, 141; illegality, 134, 234; lawlessness, 103, 129; as natural or constructed, 12, 54, 71; obscenity, xxi, 72
Lawson, Jessica, xxii, 133, 151
lesbianism, xxi, 55, 64, 72, 83, 169–70
LGBT rights movement, xiv
l'Heuremaudit, Mélanie, 151; death of, 156; as fetish, xiv, 73, 81–85
liberation, 93, 156, 212; gay, 126; pornography, 110, 111, 112, 115; sexual, xxvii, 120, 209, 218, 220, 221, 223; social, xxvii, 209, 218, 220, 221, 223; women's, 119, 126, 149, 220, 221, 222, 223, 226, 231
libertinism, 82–83; sexual, xiv, 84
Lolita (Nabokov), 72, 73, 76, 82, 86, 131, 145, 149–50, 151–54, 155, 159
love, xxii, 13, 77–80, 89, 166–69, 209, 210, 215, 216, 220, 223, 236; altruistic, 44; familial, xxiii, 198, 204, 218; free, xiv, 23, 120; homosexual, 131, 219; parental, 46, 48, 221
"Low-lands," 73, 84

Maas, Oedipa, xxiv, xxviiin3, 5, 15, 36–51, 73, 229, 235, 237; as passive, xvi, xxixn16
Macleod, Scott, 20, 54n5
Maijstral, Paola, 5, 10, 11, 15n9, 154, 186, 190
Mailer, Norman, xi, xii, xiii, 7–8, 11, 14, 85
male gaze, xvi, 28, 63, 113, 129, 153, 170, 184, 228
Manson, Charles, 23, 111, 120, 223n2
Maragos, Georgios, 42, 54

INDEX 247

marriage, xiii, 11, 165, 169, 200, 202, 233; arranged, 57; slavery and, 166; traditional, 30, 76

masculinity, xxixn11, 7, 14n1, 97, 113, 184, 186, 195, 197, 200; associated with power, x, 163, 165–68, 170–72; black, 93; conservatism and, 209–10, 217–19, 223; hard-boiled, xxiv, 19–35; hypermasculinity, 98, 101, 102, 106n12; pornography and, 78, 140; Pynchon's idea of, xvii, xviii, xix, 121n3, 206; values and, 72; violent, 202; mentioned, 194

masochism, ix, 88, 92–94, 97, 102, 115, 134, 139, 209, 231; associated with women, x, 222, 223n2

Mason & Dixon, xvi, xxvi, xxviiin3, 73, 145, 151, 153, 162–76, 195, 201, 231, 237

masturbation, 81, 99, 118, 125, 130, 136, 139, 202; interrupted, 62; lonely, 112; as spectacle, 135

Mattessich, Stefan, 80, 81, 163, 228

Maxwell, Marilyn, xx–xxi, 139

McClure, John, 55, 110

McFadzean, Angus, xxvi

McHale, Brian, xxv, 90, 92–97, 101, 105n5, 127, 139, 174n1, 174n12, 196, 198

Mendoza, Fina, 181; rape of, xxviiin3, 11–12

Millett, Kate, xiv

misogyny, xviii; in midcentury culture, 3, 6, 8, 11, 14, 98; as noir trope, 23, 26; in pornography, 134; Pynchon's alleged, xi, xiii, xxiii, xxiv, xxviiin6, xxviiin9, 21, 81, 88, 179, 180, 189, 190, 227, 228, 238

Mondaugen, Kurt, 12, 70

Morgan, Robin, xiv, 75

"Mortality and Mercy in Vienna," 6

Moss, Richard, xxv

motherhood, xxvii, 48–49, 79, 199, 220, 225–40

Murdoch, Iris, 221

Nabokov, Vladimir, xxvi, 85, 145, 149; *Lolita* and, 151–54, 155

narrative structure, xxii, 92, 125

objectification, 27, 54, 84, 112, 116, 127, 131, 138, 139, 188

Olster, Stacey, xviii, 63

onanism. *See* masturbation

orgasm, x, xxviiin3, 115, 117–18, 137; mutual, 117; self-induced, 80, 112

Owlglass, Rachel, 5, 9, 15n9, 189

pastiche, 19, 33n1, 112, 126

patriarchy, 126, 131, 163–65, 168–74, 191n2, 195, 196, 238; patriarchal culture, 64, 73; patriarchal domination, 227, 230; patriarchal gender roles, 61, 94, 105n2; patriarchal hierarchy, 53, 58, 74–75, 129; patriarchal ideology, 219; patriarchal power, 227; mentioned, xiii, xviii, 181, 200

pedophilia, 73, 80, 113, 128, 132, 140, 145–61

performativity, 74, 75, 82

perversion, 76, 78–79, 96, 139, 218, 226; of archetypes, 188; as harm 88, 236; of the natural 105, 129

perversity, 8, 69, 110, 129–30, 132, 134; "polymorphous", xxi–xxii, 126, 128

Phoenix, Joaquin, ix

Playboy magazine, xiv, 70, 72, 73, 85

pleasure, x, xxiii, 74–79, 89, 94–97, 117, 179, 210, 232; audience's, 12, 63, 110, 115, 148; mindless, 129; queer, 91, 102–5

Pointsman, Ned, 96, 106n7, 137, 138, 146, 158; as predator, 151; against Pudding, 92–95, 119

Pökler, Ilse, 73; as Leni's daughter, 230, 236; as object of desire, 78–79, 84, 86, 154–55, 159, 198

Pökler, Leni, 5, 79, 129, 154; as a feminist, 230–32; as mother, 225–28, 234, 236, 237

pornography, ix, xiv, xv, xvi, xxii, xxv, xxvi, 63, 150; Pynchon as pornographer, x, xxiii, xxvii, xxviii, xxviiin2, 69–87, 109–22, 125–44; S/M and, 88–90, 95, 104, 105; mentioned, 153, 157, 158, 159

postmodernism, xvii–xviii, xxii, xxixn17, 92, 95, 104, 121n1, 195–96; as literary canon, xi–xii, 227; "Otherness Postmodernism," xx; queer theory and, 89–90, 105n4, 113

preterite, xxiii, 24, 41, 52, 55, 110, 113, 127, 197

privilege, 189; interrogation of, 24, 90, 98; male, xviii; white, 13

Profane, Benny, 8–12, 191n7, 191n9, 192nn13–15, 197, 206n1; Alligator Patrol and, 11, 181, 186; Rachel Owlglass and, 189–90; mentioned, 182, 198

prostitution. *See* sex work

Pudding, Ernest, 88–90, 101, 104, 105n1; coprophagia and, 92–97, 133; ritual with Katje, 119, 120, 136
Pynchon studies (as field), 4, 88, 90, 228; treatment of sex and gender, xvii–xxii

queer, 84, 88–108, 139; pornographies, 113, 115; practice, 110; sex, xxv, 82; theory, 83

radicalism, 173, 209–24
rape, xv, xx, xxviiin3, 11–14, 142n13, 157, 189; as concept in Pynchon, xxi, 139; encouraged by pornography, 74, 77; sexualized, 75; torture and, 88; mentioned, xiv, 69, 81, 117, 119, 186
Rideout, Dally, xvi, xxiii, 130, 135, 234
Rilke, Rainer Maria, xiii
Roth, Philip, xi, xiii, xvii, xxixn10, 3
Russ, Joanna, xii

Sade, Marquis de, xxv, 74, 82, 101
sadism, 26, 100, 102, 106n13, 139, 183; appeal of, 32; as means of control, xi, 94, 97, 169; masculinity and, x; patriarchy and, 126; mentioned, 57, 82, 132
sadomasochism, xxv, 12, 74, 77, 88–108, 110, 120, 131–37; power and, 126; mentioned, 128, 140, 156
Schaub, Thomas, 42, 174n1
schlemihl, xxvii, 9, 10, 12, 189, 195, 197–98, 207n1
Sears, Julie Christine, 88, 126, 132, 141n2, 174n6, 174n8
"Secret Integration, The," 50n5
Sedgwick, Eve Kosofsky, 60, 127, 140
Severs, Jeffrey, xvi, xxi, xxiii, xxvii, 74, 81, 135, 228
sex slavery, 59, 119
sex trade, 59, 63
sex work, xxiv, xxviiin3, 10, 52–65, 76, 130, 135, 152, 164, 167, 189
sex writing, xxi, xxii, xxiii, xxv, 69–122
sexism, xxviiin9, 3, 6, 158, 228; in *V.*, 180, 183, 189
sexology, 74, 82–85, 105, 230
sexual revolution, xiv, 111, 112, 114, 120, 126
sexuality, xi, xv, xxv, 4–5, 126, 127, 133, 135, 217; bisexuality, 132; changing attitudes toward, xxv, 105n4; children and, 84, 85, 148, 154–55, 158; deviant, 132; exploitation and, 22, 115, 119; female, 220–22, 226–27, 231; Hollywood and, 139, 148; homosexuality, 6, 82, 83, 88, 90, 101, 106n8, 132, 139, 154, 168, 219; as means of control and power, 22, 90–97, 99, 103–4, 127, 220–22, 226–27; noir genre and, 22, 26; normative and nonnormative, 111, 163, 167–70, 173, 174; in pornography, 74–79, 115, 119; queer, 89; religion and, 53, 119; transgressive, xxv, 90–97, 109–11, 220–22
Slothrop, Tyrone, xvi, xix, 126, 139, 140, 141n5, 197, 198; with Bianca, 79, 132, 147, 148, 150–54, 155, 160n1; fate of, 96–97; with Geli, 146; with Greta, xxviiin3, 133, 136; with Katje, 115–17, 119, 129; mentioned, 77, 93, 120
Slow Learner, 73, 191n8; introduction, xiii, 72
S/M. *See* sadomasochism
"Small Rain, The," 72, 76, 191n8, 197
Sontag, Susan, xxv, 71, 74, 82, 90, 142n8
Sportello, Doc, ix–x, xxiv, 141n1, 223n2; as detective, 19–35; as voyeur, 112–20, 121n2
Stein, Gertrude, xiii
Steinem, Gloria, xiv
Stencil, Herbert, 179, 180, 184, 187–90, 192nn12–13
Stencil, Sidney, 14, 81, 83, 198
Stimpson, Catharine R., xxi, 48, 50n5, 119, 154, 180
Stockton, Sharon, xxi
submissiveness, x, 22, 30, 88, 92, 125, 130–31, 138–39, 217, 226, 230–31
Sukenick, Ronald, xii
Swanlake, Jessica, 5, 129, 146

Tarnow, Maxine, xvi, xxiv, xxviii, 36–51, 142, 158–59, 195; as detective, 19–35; as feminist, xxix; as mother and/or wife, 194, 201–5, 225, 226, 227, 231–33, 236, 237
Temple, Shirley, 86, 145, 146–50, 155, 158, 159
textuality, xvii, xxii
Thanatz, Miklos, 129, 141n5; sadomasochism and, 88, 89, 91, 103, 110, 112, 120
Thomas, Samuel, 86, 121
transgression, xxv, 97, 105, 125, 140, 173; anxiety about, 168, 220; as commercial imperative, 132, 135, 210; of cultural gender codes, 59, 74, 85, 214, 220–21; literary-formal, xii, xiv; oedipal, 78; valorized, xxi, 89

Traverse, Lake, 135, 139, 141n3; attracted to power, 222; motherhood and, 226, 227–28, 230–33, 234, 235, 237; objectified, 127, 131, 137, 140, 141
Tripping, Geli, 73, 119, 129, 146
Tristero, 38, 39, 41–43, 46, 47, 48, 49nn1–2, 129, 151
Trystero. *See* Tristero
typescript, of *V.*, xxvi, 179–93, 206

"Under the Rose", 187, 190n1
Updike, John, xi, xvii, xxixn10, 126

V. (character), xxiv, 10, 14, 83, 179, 180, 184, 187, 191n12; dismantling of, 12; as hybrid, 174n13, 188, 190, 192n13
V. (novel): early Pynchon on gender and, 3–16; family and, 197, 198, 200, 206, 207n1; motherhood and, 225, 233, 234; pornography and, 69, 70, 81–86; typescript of, 179–93; mentioned, xiv, xvi, xxiv, xxv, xxviiin9, 121n1,
Varo, Remedios, 46–47
Vineland: Buddhism and, 52–65; family and, 194, 195, 198–99, 201, 202, 204, 209–24, 226, 230, 231, 234, 238n2; female conduits and, 125, 127, 130, 133, 134, 139, 140, 141n3; as feminist book, 4–6; pornography and, 121n4; mentioned: xvi, xvii, xviii, xix, xx, xxiv, xxvi, xviiin3, 44, 50n4, 73

violence, ix, xvii; representational, xxvi; against transgender people, xv; against women, xv, xxi
voyeurism, x; as fantasy, 112, 114; as practice, 128, 136

Wallace, David Foster, xi, 140
WASTE, 38, 48, 49n1
Waterston, Katherine, ix
Waugh, Patricia, xviii, xxi
Weisenburger, Steven, xxi, 72, 79, 88, 104, 106n11, 109, 128, 132, 141n2
Weissman, 12, 73, 88–90, 105, 105n1, 106n11, 106n13, 115, 121n3, 129; in drag, 134; with Gottfried, 97–102; with Katje, 94, 116
Wheeler, Prairie, 14n2, 58, 127, 213, 214, 236; relationship with Frenesi, 60, 61, 141n3, 201, 202, 209, 220, 231, 234, 237; relationship with Zoyd, 198, 199, 218
Wheeler, Zoyd, xix, 60, 139, 195, 198–99, 206n1, 209–11, 214, 216–19, 222, 227
Whole Sick Crew, 6, 10
Windust, Nicholas, 40, 202, 232, 233, 237; death, 41; as male version of femme fatale, 28–30; sex with Maxine, xxviiin3, 142n7, 159
Winsome, Mafia, 8, 9–10, 11
Wolfley, Lawrence, 91, 137
Wolfmann, Mickey, ix, 22, 116, 118–19, 121n3
Wren, Victoria, 7, 82

www.ingramcontent.com/pod-product-compliance
Lightning Source LLC
Chambersburg PA
CBHW010719300426
44115CB00020B/2960